RAJ *to* SWARAJ

A Textbook on
Colonialism and Nationalism
in India

RAJ to SWARAJ

A Textbook on
Colonialism and Nationalism
in India

Ram Chandra Pradhan

Published by
PRABHAT PRAKASHAN PVT. LTD.
4/19 Asaf Ali Road,
New Delhi-110 002 (INDIA)
e-mail: prabhatbooks@gmail.com

ISBN 978-93-5266-430-6
RAJ TO SWARAJ
by Ram Chandra Pradhan

Edition
2025

Price
₹ 600.00 (Rupees Six Hundred only)

Printed at
Narula Printers, Delhi

To
My Guru-like Dr Ramashray Roy,
an eminent scholar and an outstanding human being
and
many generations of my students
whose love has sustained me through
vicissitudes of life.

Lord Buddha
The Ideal Teacher

'At one time, "the Exalted one" was staying at Kosambi in the Sinsapa grove. And the Exalted one took a few Sinsapa leaves in his hand and said to his disciples: what think ye, my disciples, whether are more, these few Sinsapa leaves, which I have gathered in my hand, or the other leaves yonder in the Sinsapa grove?'

'The few leaves, sire, which the Exalted one holds in his hand are not many, but many more are those leaves yonder in the Sinsapa grove.'

'So also, my disciples, is that much more, which I have learned and have not told you, than that which I have told you.'

Dr Hermann Oldenberg
Buddha: His Life, His Doctrine, His Order
p. 204

Contents

Part III: The Minor Streams of the Indian National Movement

Part IV: Armed Rebellion and the Indian National Movement

Part V: Towards Independence and Partition

Preface

In the art of history writing, only that scholar deserves all praise who is free from all personal likes and dislikes. His vidya alone, transcends the limitations of time and space.

KALHAN *RAJATARANGANI*: 1:7

During my long years of teaching courses on 'Colonialism and Nationalism in India', my students and I, felt the need for a concise and authentic textbook. Such a felt-need had many reasons. First, it is a major and compulsory paper being taught both at the undergraduate and postgraduate levels at Delhi University, as well in some other universities. Second, the themes and contents of this paper require an interdisciplinary approach with some sound foundation in several branches of social sciences, viz., history, sociology, anthropology, economics, political science and even psychology. Frankly speaking, this is a tall order even for the teachers, not to talk of the students. I have often wondered whether this is the reason why this paper is in dire need of an authentic textbook while others have enjoyed a plethora of them. Indeed, there are many books on 'modern Indian history'. But they are too heavy on historical facts and somewhat lighter on the processes of political developments. Besides, some of these books appear to have fallen between two stools of research and textbook writing. All these considerations have in fact prompted me to write this book.

I have kept a number of objectives before me in penning this book. First, it should be comprehensive enough to cover the syllabi and the related issues in their entirety. Second, it should be comprehensible to the students – who should be able to easily grasp the fundamentals along with the whole gamut of issues involved. Third, it should be easily readable. In fact, in a subject like this which is full of factual details, the greatest challenge a writer faces is how to maintain the flow and readability of the narrative without compromising on the quantum of facts and interpretations. Bearing the problem in mind, I have taken the following steps to find a way out:

(a) An attempt has been made to keep the book's language simple and lucid while keeping the intricate nuances of the subject intact. In fact, I have always longed for a linguistic style which combines in itself mathematical precision, musical flow, felicity and sculptural picturisation.
(b) I have also tried to strike a right balance between factual presentation and interpretative and evaluative formulations.
(c) It has also been my endeavour to recreate the feelings, emotions, guts and grit with which our forebears fought for the independence of our motherland.

I sincerely hope that the younger generation would get a feel of the subject and derive inspiration from the environment of selfless service and limitless sacrifice, which marked the different phases of our freedom struggle. However, I am instantaneously reminded of the haunting words of Lao Tzu: 'In the world every one knows enough to pursue what he does not know, but no one knows enough to pursue what he already knows.'

Let me add a word about my basic approach to the subject. So far as its ideological framework is concerned, I am fully conversant with the major schools of thought relating to modern Indian history: the imperialist, the nationalist, the Marxist, the semi Marxist and even the subaltern. I have my own views about them but I have not written this book as a protagonist of any of these schools. I am firmly of the opinion that any kind of doctrinaire approach goes totally against the ethical norms of textbook writing. In fact, textbook-writing dharma demands an integrated and inclusive approach, so that the students get a comprehensive feel of the subject and also of the issues involved in their entirety. I am also aware that a textbook writer's job is not just to prepare a catalogue of facts, figures, arguments and counter-arguments. In fact, the textbook writer has to be, what the *Bhagvad Gita* calls, a *sakshi*, a detached witness, so that he or she is not carried away by the passionate waves of arguments and counter-arguments of any particular school. The textbook writer should be firmly rooted in the subject matter and be well-equipped with a *sakshi-bhav*, so that he or she can easily see through the smokescreen created by the passionate argumentation and counter-argumentation of the rival schools. I further believe that only with this kind of intellectual equipment would a scholar be able to dive deep into the core of the subject and come out with a detached and quintessential presentation. I have used this approach in my studies on the *Bhagvad Gita* and characterised it as *samanvaya yoga.* I am persuaded to adopt the same approach in this study also.

So far as the arrangement of the material is concerned I have made it thematic rather than chronological. It makes the book more precise and comprehensible. To enhance its readability, the main text of each topic has been intertwined with its historical context in such a way that each chapter can be read independently, without going back to the previous one for its contextual understanding. As such, the book is divided into five parts. Part I deals with the British conquest of India and its consequences for the different aspects of life of our people. Part II deals with the mainstream of the national movement. Part III deals with the sectional and minor streams of the national movement. The armed revolutionary movements are the subject matter of Part IV which also has a section on the INA led by Subhas Chandra Bose and the RIN rebellion. All constitutional plans and negotiations, from the Cripps Mission to the Mountbatten Plan, constitute Part V of the book. I hope the present arrangement will add to its readability.

In the preparation of this book, I owe my intellectual debt to many scholars, freedom fighters and a large number of my friends. Shri Devendra Swarup, a man of vast learning and profound human sympathy, not only lent books but also offered 'tea and sympathy' when I needed them most. Another friend of mine would like to remain anonymous on account of his official position. I am also indebted to a number of authors whose works I have used in the preparation of this study. Admittedly, to all of them I owe more than I can acknowledge here. But some of them need to be mentioned by name. All scholars working in this subject area are greatly benefited by the works of two eminent historians – Dr Tara Chand and Dr R C Majumdar who produced multi-volume works on freedom movements. Their works, now though dated, are rich in terms of documentation and their own interpretations. Besides, I have also widely consulted the works of the next generation historians, viz., Prof. Bipan Chandra, Prof. Sumit Sarkar, Shri B R Nanda and a host of others. All of them have integrated in their works the material made available by the new researches. I have greatly benefited from all these works and would like to acknowledge it with a deep sense of gratitude. Besides, I have also consulted topic-specific works done by other scholars which are acknowledged in the bibliographical presentation at the end of the book.

I would also like to thank the librarians and the staff of the following libraries: Delhi University Library; Sapru House Library; Sinha Library, Patna, and a host of other Libraries. I would like to record my indebtedness to all members of Nehru Memorial Museum and Library, New Delhi, who helped me in many ways including permitting me to use photographs and illustrations. To my surprise, I find that there is a vast variation in spelling the names of leaders, freedom fighters, officials and places. I have solved this problem by following the spelling pattern of the *Dictionary of National Biography*, edited by Shri S P Sen, Director, Institute of Historical Studies, Kolkata. I also owe a lot to the Khatri family, the proprietor of Om Laser Printers and P K Mishra for taking a lot of care and interest in the preparation of the manuscript. I would also like to record my appreciation for many other friends who helped me in various ways, including Pastor V Thomas who often reads out the passages from the Holy Bible when my 'soul is on ice'. I would be failing in my duty if I do not acknowledge my indebtedness to my publishers, Macmillan India Ltd. for their professional support.

I must say that my students have contributed to this study more than I can acknowledge here. In the course of my long years of teaching, I recall with a lot of fondness, all the scintillating dialogues and penetrating questions they raised that have greatly contributed to the cogency, coherence and clarity of my ideas. Kumar Rahul, one of my old students who now teaches in Ramjas College, Delhi University, went through the entire manuscript with care and sensitivity and suggested many stylistic improvements. Only now do I realise what the Talmud recorded eons ago: 'Much Torah have I learned from my teachers, more from my colleagues, but, from my students most of all.'

In a book like this, despite our best efforts, some errors of fact and interpretation are quite likely to have crept in. I would like readers to help me in identifying them. However, for the present, I alone should be held responsible for any fault with regard to facts or interpretations.

New Delhi
October 2007

R C Pradhan

PART I

The British Challenge and the Indian Response

Let us only make common cause with her (Indian) people; let them feel that we are there to give more than we receive; that their interest are not traversed and frustrated by selfish aims of ours; that, if we are defending ourselves upon the line of the Hindu Kush, it is them and their interest that we are defending even more and far more than our own. Unless we can produce conviction in the mind of India, in vain shall we lavish our thought and our resources upon a merely material defence.

WILLIAM E GLADSTONE

Therefore, it is incumbent on all to give up the hope of the continuation of the British sway, side with me . . . in promoting the common good, and thus attain their ends, otherwise if this golden opportunity slips away, they will have to repent their folly.

BAHADUR SHAH ZAFAR

1 The Story of the British Conquest of India

The trader's scale turned overnight into the ruler's sceptre.

RABINDRANATH TAGORE

The gradual occupation of India by the British in the course of the eighteenth and nineteenth centuries was more than a mere amazing and even bizarre act in the arena of world history. That England, a tiny country both in terms of population and territorial size, could occupy and master a big country like India, with such an ancient culture, is a fact which cannot be taken as just an unexpected accident in human history. Obviously, it raises questions of a fundamental nature regarding the actual strengths and weaknesses of both the parties involved in the process. Thus, our study will have to delve into the deeper processes and recesses of history, and as such it has to go beyond a merely descriptive and chronological account of how India was gradually enslaved by the British. Primarily, one has to tackle two fundamental questions. One, why could not India either at the central level or even at the level of regional powers – all of which were much bigger than England – successfully resist the British aggressive attempts? In other words, what was wrong with our polity or economy which prevented us from successfully thwarting all British attempts at the occupation of India? On the side of England we have also to confront a fundamental question: how could a company (the East India Company) of profit-seeking merchants equipped with a weighing scale in its hands, turn itself into a power-weighing and power-wielding spectre? With a view to go into the nitty-gritty of these questions, we propose to delineate and analyse the actual conditions as well as the motive force of their history that led to the British occupation of India. To do that, we have to go back to the middle of the eighteenth century when the initial steps towards British occupation of India were being taken. We could begin our study with a peep into the decline of the Mughal Empire, resulting in the emergence of regional powers in India, which virtually took over the bulk of the Indian territory leaving the Mughals only with a symbolic presence.

There is virtually a near unanimity among the scholars of Indian history about the sharp decline in the glory, inner vitality and visible might of the Mughals after the death of Aurangzeb in 1707. A number of historical facts are cited in support of such a formulation. One, the Marathas who had earlier resisted and fought against Aurangzeb's aggressive moves, succeeded in plundering the area around Delhi in 1738. But what really exposed the soft underbelly of the Mughal Empire was Nadir Shah's sack of Delhi during 1738-39, which gave a mortal blow to the glory and prestige of the Mughal Empire. It soon emboldened and encouraged the Afghan ruler Ahmad Shah Abdali (also known as Durrani), who not only took over Punjab but also sacked Delhi during 1756-57. He even defeated the Marathas at the battlefield of Panipat in 1761, which gave a big blow to their ambition of inheriting and wearing the imperial mantle of the Mughals. In brief, it was clear by the middle of the eighteenth century that something had already eaten into the vitals of the Mughals and their empire. However, there is no unanimity among the historians about the nature of the debilitating disease afflicting the Mughal body politic. Three groups of scholars have differently accounted for the decline of the Mughal Empire. Historians like Jadunath Sarkar have underscored the faulty policies of Aurangzeb, including his prolonged fight for supremacy in the Deccan region. That war virtually drained the Mughal imperial army – the mainstay of the empire. This, coupled with his anti-Hindu policy and the personal failings of his successors and the nobles of the court, led to the decline and the final demise of the Mughal Empire. The second group, comprising Marxist scholars led by Satish Chandra and Irfan Habib, have laid their hands on the weaknesses and infirmities of the institutional and economic set-up of the Mughal imperial system. In their view, the Mughal's system of jagirdari and iniquitous agrarian system were the chief villains of the piece. A third group of scholars underline the fact that it was not the economic crisis but the loosening of the Mughal central authority that encouraged overambitious zamindars, often backed by the peasants of their own caste, to assert their local authority, which finally resulted in the emergence of a number of regional powers. A detailed examination of all these formulations is beyond the scope of this book.

Perhaps it was the cumulative impact of all these causes, which might account for the decline of the Mughal Empire. It is sufficient here to say that by the middle of the eighteenth century the central striking power of the Mughals had considerably weakened, leading to the emergence of a number of regional powers. An understanding of the dynamics of these regional powers is also needed, as it was from them that the British gradually took over the entire country. Besides, the British also faced, fought and eliminated three rival European powers, namely, Portugal, Holland and France from the field of Indian trade. It was by gradually subduing both regional Indian states as well as her European rivals that England took over the entire Indian territory and became its ruling power. We would now briefly describe the landmarks of the process through which the British occupied the Indian territory and became its ruling power. But let us first have a look at the major regional Indian states that the British had to face subsequently.

Major Regional States of the Eighteenth Century

In the wake of the decline of the Mughal central authority, a number of Indian regional states emerged. It is relevant to note here that states like Hyderabad, Bengal and Awadh were earlier an integral part of the Mughal Empire. But subsequently they emerged as autonomous states acting mostly on their own, though they also kept a semblance of allegiance with the Mughal central authority. Hyderabad was reorganised as a state by Nizam-ul-Mulk who had earlier been a wazir at the Mughal court at Delhi. He was made a subedar of the Deccan in 1724, and by the time he died, in 1748, he had succeeded in establishing Hyderabad as an independent state, though he never formally severed its umbilical ties with the Delhi throne.

Bengal was another regional power that emerged on the ruins of the Mughal Empire. Murshid Quli Khan was appointed as the Governor of Bengal by the Mughal emperor in 1717. Soon he, for all practical purposes, became his own master, though he continued to send a tribute to the Mughal court. He died in 1727 and was succeeded by Suja-ud-din who, in turn, was succeeded by Alivardi Khan, an army commander, in 1739. Alivardi Khan made Bengal virtually an independent power, as he stopped paying tribute to Delhi and made all official appointments on his own. After his death in 1756, he was succeeded by his grandson Siraj-ud-daula who fought and lost the

Battle of Plassey with the British, which virtually laid the foundation of the British Empire in India.

Awadh also belongs to the same category of successor states of the Mughals, along with Hyderabad and Bengal. Saadat Khan became the Mughal Governor of Awadh in 1722. He successfully subdued the local zamindars who had earlier refused to pay land revenue. He made Safdar Jung as the deputy governor and even appointed him as diwan and made this office totally free from Delhi's control. Safdar Jung succeeded him during 1740 and took Awadh further on the road to autonomy. After his death in 1754, his son Shuja-ud-daula became the Governor of Awadh. Shuja aligned himself with Ahmad Shah Abdali at the Battle of Panipat, against the Marathas, and maintained his autonomous status. This was challenged only in 1764 when he, along with the Mughal Emperor and the Bengal Nawab, lost the Battle of Buxar.

The Marathas, Sikhs, Jats and Afghans primarily constituted the rebel groups who subsequently succeeded in emerging as powerful regional powers. The Maratha Kingdom was initially set up by Shivaji in 1674, who had started his political career as a rebel against the Mughals. But it was Balaji Vishwanath who, as the all-powerful Peshwa, built up the basic structure of the Maratha state power. On his death in 1720, he was succeeded by Baji Rao who further strengthened and expanded the Maratha territory by taking over Malwa and Gujarat. In 1737, the Maratha army invaded Delhi and even held the Emperor captive for some time. When Baji Rao died in 1740, he had vastly expanded the Maratha Empire. In 1740, his son Balaji Baji Rao succeeded him, who is also known as Nana Saheb. When Shahuji, the Maratha king died in 1749, Nana Saheb consolidated his position further and virtually became the supreme authority in Maratha affairs. In fact, in the course of its historical development, the Maratha state-structure underwent a political and administrative metamorphosis which, though apparently leading to its physical–spatial expansion, came to contain within itself the seeds of its destruction. The centralised state-structure solely headed by Shivaji was gradually turned into a multi-polar military confederacy with its in-built system of mutual jealousies and rivalries. Besides, it ultimately turned into a system of nominal monarchy with the Maratha king at Satara, while real power came to be exercised by the Peshwas with their *gaddi* at Pune. This metamorphosis of the Maratha state contributed a great deal to its decline and ultimate demise.

Maratha glory reached its peak when they even forced Alivardi Khan of Bengal to cede Orissa to them. The Marathas also remained in constant struggle with the Nizam of Hyderabad. In the Mughal durbar also, the Marathas started playing a big role and during 1752-53 the Mughal Emperor came under their protection. One fundamental weakness of Maratha rule, however, was that they were more interested in exacting *chaudh* and *sardeshmukhi* from the area they overran rather than in establishing a permanent administrative set-up. But it was the Maratha defeat at the Third Battle of Panipat in January 1761 at the hands of the Afghan ruler, Ahmad Shah Abdali, which gave a big blow to the Maratha ambition of wearing the imperial mantle of the Mughal Empire. Nana Saheb died soon. Subsequently, a succession war broke out, which provided an opportunity to the British in 1772 to intervene, and then onwards Maratha power declined leading finally to its eclipse.

The Sikhs were another group of people who built up a powerful state in Punjab in the eighteenth century. Earlier, Guru Nanak Dev had founded the Sikh Panth as a part of the Bhakti Movement. But soon the Sikhs acquired the reputation of a fighting servant of God rather than a suffering servant. Guru Arjun Dev was executed by the Mughal Emperor, Jahangir. The situation became worse when the ninth guru of the Sikhs, Guru Teg Bahadur, was executed by Aurangzeb in 1675 in Delhi. As a sequel, his son, Guru Govind Singh, who established the Khalsa Panth in 1699, turned the Sikhs into a warlike militant group. He soon tried to build up an autonomous state located at Anandpur, but was ousted from there by the combined forces of the Mughals and chieftains of Himachal. The death of Aurangzeb (in 1707) changed the situation, but the Guru was murdered in October 1708. However, his chief follower, Banda Bahadur, continued the rebellion till his execution in March 1716. The Sikh rebellion did not wane and by 1761 they came to control a vast territory in Punjab. But there was no well-organised central Sikh authority till the gap was filled by Ranjit Singh who built up a powerful state by the first decade of the nineteenth century. He died in 1839. Soon Punjab was caught in royal family feuds, as well as the power struggle among Sikh chiefs, which helped the British to takeover the Sikh state by 1849 after the second Anglo–Sikh War.

In the east of Punjab, a small kingdom of Rohilkhand was founded by Ali Muhammad Khan, an Afghan chief. And yet another kingdom, established by another Afghan chief, Ahmad Khan Bangash, emerged around Farukhabad. These kingdoms were small in size and the only thing notable about them was that at the time of the Third Battle of Panipat they aligned themselves with Ahmad Shah Abdali. In the south-west of Delhi a number of Rajput principalities had also come up. Generally, they did not face much of a problem with the Mughals except in the case of the Mewar Kingdom. But when the Mughal Empire weakened, the Rajput chiefs gradually asserted their independence.

The Jats, who were primarily located in and around the Delhi-Mathura region, also succeeded in establishing a Jat kingdom at Bharatpur in Rajasthan. The Jats had a long history of rebellion against the Mughals since the days of Jahangir, but it was the Jat chieftain Suraj Mal, who consolidated the Jat kingdom at Bharatpur during the middle of the eighteenth century. At one stage, his kingdom spread from Ganga in the east to Agra in the west and from Delhi in the north to the Chambal in the south. However, after the death of Suraj Mal in 1763, the Jat kingdom lost much of its sheen.

That leaves us with south India wherein Mysore emerged as a powerful state during the eighteenth century, under the Wodeyar dynasty. But a radical change took place in 1761 when Haider Ali, an officer of the Mysore army, took over the political power. He soon launched a programme of modernisation of his army with French assistance. Haider Ali expanded his kingdom by taking over Malabar and Calicut in 1766. Soon Mysore emerged as a powerful regional power in south India under the dynamic leadership of Haider Ali and his son Tipu Sultan. Travancore was also another state which had an independent status even during the heyday of the Mughal Empire. It reached its full glory in 1729 under the headship of King Martanda Varma. He modernised his army and introduced a state monopoly in trade that led to a considerable increase in state resources. Travancore survived the Mysorean invasion of 1766 and was known for its progress, displayed in the field of irrigation, transport and communication. It had an equally good reputation in the field of art and culture. However, in 1800, Travancore, ultimately, succumbed to the British pressure as it agreed to the presence of the British Resident.

We have briefly delineated the state of affairs in India during the eighteenth century, along with the condition of major Indian regional political players. For a better understanding of the process of the British occupation of India, we have to go through a brief history of the East India Company's encounter both with European rival powers as well as with the Indian regional powers. The whole process is so chronologically intertwined that it becomes a difficult task to untangle them and make a neat presentation. To unravel this, a brief history of the Company's encounter and its ultimate victory over both its European rival powers and with the regional Indian states would be presented here separately. This would provide a clear picture of the entire process of the British occupation of India. But let us first look at its encounter with the European powers.

The East India Company and Its European Rivals

As we know, the East India Company was set up by a Charter with a privilege to carry on trade in the area east of the Cape of Good Hope. It was a shareholders company to be governed by 20 elected members who constituted its Court. In the initial years, it concentrated on its trade with the Spice Islands. But very soon it came to discover that some of the Indian products, primarily textiles, could be used as barter for the South-East Asian spices – making its entire business exceptionally profitable. But it also realised that in this venture it faced a major challenge from three European powers, namely, Portugal, Holland and France, as they were also competing with the British for the control of the Indian trade.

It is also relevant to note that the Portuguese were the first European power to enter into the arena of Indian trade after the opening of the Atlantic route. Vasco da Gama of Portugal had reached Calicut, on the Malabar Coast, in 1498, after discovering a new sea route through the Atlantic to India. Prior to that, Indian trade in the west was dominated by the Arabs on account of their control over the land route as well as the Mediterranean sea route. The Portuguese were the first to open their factories in India and dominated the Indian trade throughout the sixteenth century.

But the Portuguese suffered their first defeat at the hands of the British in 1611 near Surat. The British inflicted another defeat on the Portuguese in 1620 and they were finally expelled by the Mughals from Hugli in Bengal in 1633. The Portuguese hold on India further declined when, in 1634, they entered into an agreement with the British for a good commercial relationship. This was followed by two other treaties between these two powers in 1654 and 1661 respectively, which not only guaranteed the British right to the eastern trade but also bound both powers to act jointly against the Dutch in India. Consequently, except Goa and Diu, the Portuguese virtually lost their interest in the Indian trade. The Dutch were another power who had opened a number of factories in India in the middle of the seventeenth century. The Dutch East India Company was set up in 1602. What was more, a warlike situation developed when a large fleet of Dutch ships reached Swally, near Surat, forcing the British to suspend their trade at Surat. However, by 1667 they reached an agreement by which the Dutch agreed not to interfere with the English settlement in India as a *quid pro quo* of the British surrender of all claims of trade in Indonesia. Gradually, the Dutch lost more ground when their naval expedition to Hugli failed in 1675. Their position further weakened, and by 1695 the Dutch were finally expelled from India by the British.

The third power that competed with the British was France. Though it was a latecomer to India, it did put up a stiff competition and even fought with the British for the control of the Indian trade. In 1668, the first French factory was opened at Surat. Subsequently, Chandernagore near Calcutta was built up by them during 1690–92. The French position in this part of the world was further strengthened when they occupied Mauritius in 1721, and soon they also acquired some foothold on the Malabar coast. By the 1740s the British and the French emerged as the main rival powers in India. The British conflict with the French is known as the Carnatic Wars which covered a period of twenty years from 1744 to 1764. The First Carnatic War had its genesis in the Austrian succession-war in Europe, with its overspill in India as the British and French were on opposite sides in that war. The British took the initiative and seized some French ships on the east coast of India, which prompted the French to attack and capture Madras with support from their naval force located in Mauritius. In a clever move, the British sought the help of the Nawab of Arcot who sent troops to Madras but his forces were badly defeated by the French forces. This provided a new sense of confidence to the French officials led by Dupleix. When the hostilities ceased in Europe by 1748, there was an agreement between the two powers by which the French got back all their possessions in North America and they, in turn, returned all British possessions in India. The Second Carnatic War started on the issues of succession both at Hyderabad and Arcot in which the French and the British were supporting the opposite groups. In 1750, the French obtained several concessions from the new subedar of the Deccan at Hyderabad, including Dupleix being appointed Governor of all Deccan dominions to the south of the Krishna river. In return, he stationed a strong French military contingent at the Deccan court under the French General Bussy. But Robert Clive sent a strong contingent to Arcot and in the process the French General got captured and was beheaded. Subsequently, Chanda Sahib, the Nawab of Arcot, was also murdered. Thus, the Second Carnatic War was ultimately lost by the French and the prestige of the British soon skyrocketed. This led to the recall of Dupleix – the main architect of French policy in India. He was replaced by a pliant French Governor, Godeheu, who suspended the French action and chose to negotiate with the British.

The French and the British forces had their final round of armed engagement, which came to be known as the Third Carnatic War. In the backdrop of the war was the outbreak of the Seven-Year War (1756–63) among European powers and their colonies in Europe. In 1756, the British captured Chandernagore, a French town near Calcutta and Siraj-ud-daula had a tiff with the British as he gave shelter to the French. That led to a Nawab–British confrontation during 1756-57. In south India, a confrontation between these two powers could not take place as the British forces had been committed to Bengal and the French reinforcement could not arrive there before 1758. On their arrival, French forces launched an offensive which resulted in the capture of a large chunk of territory under the British, including the port at Vishakhapatnam. Meanwhile, the British reinforcement from Bengal also reached Madras. But due to internal problems of the French Army, including lack of coordination between the land and naval forces, the French could not take full advantage of their initial gains. And finally on 16 January 1761, the French surrendered Pondicherry, followed by the surrender of their possessions on the Malabar Coast. Earlier, French forces had been defeated at Wandiwash on 22 January 1760. At the end of the Seven-year's war in Europe the treaty of the Peace of Paris restored the French possessions in India to them. However, the French East India Company was formally wound up in 1769. In a way that marked the end of the French attempt to take over the Indian trade from the British hand. Thus the British succeeded in eliminating all three major European rivals from India which left a free field for them alone.

The British Occupation of India: Its Encounter and Victory Over the Regional States

We have already delineated the state of Indian affairs, including the decline of the Mughal Empire and the emergence of a number of regional states. Now, let us turn to the British face-off with the Indian states. Our story covers a period of one hundred years starting with the British victory at the Battle of Plassey (1757) and ends with the final annexation of Awadh by the British Empire in 1856, followed by the 1857 rebellion and the Crown's takeover (1858) of the Indian Empire. In the process, the British encountered and subdued the Marathas, Tipu Sultan of Mysore and the Sikhs – all major political players of the period.

The British Occupation of Bengal and Awadh

It would be relevant here to highlight how the British acquired a foothold in India which ultimately enabled them to enter and subdue all its rivals, both Europeans and Indians in due course. After coming to India, towards the beginning of the seventeenth century, the East India Company concentrated on business for many years by continuously trying to be on the right side of the Mughal authorities. Sir Thomas Roe was the first resident English envoy to be received at Jahangir's Court in 1617. However, after opening a factory at Surat in 1613 they sought its fortification in 1625, but the Mughal authorities refused to give permission. A golden opportunity came to the Company in 1639 when it succeeded in obtaining Madras on lease from a local king who was promised 50 per cent of the customs revenue. It was a very good bargain for the Company as they got an opportunity to fortify the area as well as a right to mint their own coins. Soon they built up the Fort St. George at Madras. This was followed by the fortification of Bombay Port which was transferred to the Company by the British king in 1661. The British king had received it as a dowry from the Portuguese king. British factories had also been opened in eastern India, including Hugli in Bengal. In a clever move to build up a centralised authority, the Company officials put all its other establishments under the control of Fort St. George at Madras. Another milestone was reached by the Company when it got permission from the Mughals to do customs-free business. However, during the 1680s Aurangzeb seized British factories at a number of places but soon the Company got them back after making a lump sum payment. Thereafter, there was no looking back for the Company.

In 1698, it obtained the zamindari right to collect revenue from three villages of Sutanuti, Govindapur and Kolikata in Bengal. In 1700, all Bengal factories were put under the control of Fort William at Calcutta. Another major development occurred in 1717 when the new Mughal Emperor Farrukhsiyar gave the company permission to use its coins throughout the Mughal territory along with the freedom to do customs-free business. Thus by the middle of the eighteenth century, the East India Company was more than a mere trading company. With factories at the important corners of the country and control over the ports of Bombay, Madras and Calcutta, and with an army at its disposal, it had become a dominant power. With the introduction of a large number of army personnel during the Anglo–French conflict in India, the Company was confident regarding its own strength.

Bengal was the first state where the Company's newly acquired strength was tested vis-à-vis the Indian states. The period from 1757 to 1764 virtually brought about a radical change in the fate of Bengal as well as that of the Company. Here the Company enjoyed customs-free business which became the real bone of contention between the Company and the local Nawab. In 1756, Siraj-ud-daula succeeded Alivardi Khan who had virtually made Bengal independent. Siraj had developed serious grievances against the Company which was acting a little too independently. The Company's officials were not only misusing their right to customs-free business but they were also indulging in the fortification of its factories without the Nawab's permission. Siraj attacked Fort William, which precipitated the crisis as it brought into the open the conflict between the Company and the Nawab. This led to the Battle of Plassey where the Company's forces defeated the Nawab's army.

The Battle of Plassey marked a turning point in the fate of India as well as that of the Company: the British occupation of India had started with a big bang. What actually led to the defeat of the Nawab's forces had been debated since the day it occurred. Perhaps two things proved decisive. Robert Clive's strong contingent from Madras and the betrayal of the Nawab's officials including Mir Jafar. Siraj was killed and Mir Jafar succeeded him on Bengal's throne. The Company wanted its pound of flesh and made undue financial demands on him which he was unable to meet. Ultimately, he succumbed to the pressure and was forced to step down. Mir Kasim, his own son-in-law, succeeded him in September 1760. He began to act in an independent manner and shifted his capital from Murshidabad to Monghyr and also reorganised his army and the bureaucracy. Soon he fell from the grace of the Company as he protested against the misuse of the Dastak (customs-free business) by the Company's officials, which was resulting in a huge revenue loss for the Nawab. When the Company tried to pressurise him, he refused. In the process he was replaced by Mir Jafar with the open support of the Company and some courtiers and financial magnates of Bengal. He sought the support of the Mughal Emperor, Shah Alam, as well as the Nawab Shuja-ud-daula of Awadh. This led to the battle royal at Buxar where the Company's forces again became victorious. This virtually sealed the fate of India and was a real turning point on the road to the British occupation of India. Mir Jafar was made the Nawab with the open support of the Company. But the real power remained vested in the hands of Robert Clive, the Governor of Bengal. And the Nawab for all practical purposes became the titular head. In 1765, Robert Clive entered into an agreement with the Mughal emperor and got the *diwani* right of Bengal, Bihar and Orissa for the Company in lieu of a lump sum payment to the Mughal Emperor. Thus the Company came to have the real control of the financial administration of Sube-Bengal. The real significance of the Company's victory at Plassey and Buxar followed by its *diwani* right was that it became the real ruler of the Sube-Bengal reducing the status of the Nawab to a mere puppet in its hand.

With Bengal under its thumb, the Company set its eyes on the Sube-Awadh. By the treaty of August 1765, a war indemnity of Rs 50,00,000 was imposed on Awadh and the Mughal Emperor Shah Alam got some area around Allahabad as a part of the bargain. Shuja-ud-daula, the Nawab of Awadh, tried to regain his position by reorganising his army, but the Company tightened its noose around his neck by forcing him, in 1773, to make a monthly payment of Rs 2,10,000 to each brigade of the Company stationed in Awadh or Allahabad areas. The Awadh Nawab fell in the debt-trap of the Company. That enabled the Company to directly interfere in the affairs of Awadh. Soon the Company got hold of a sizeable part of Awadh's territory around Banaras, earlier held by Chait Singh. Subsequently, the Company forced the Awadh Nawab into an agreement excluding the Mughal Emperor from all future Anglo–Awadh transactions and posting a British Resident at the Nawab's court. The Awadh Nawab did get some respite when his debt to the Company was reduced by Rs 50 lakh in view of his strong protest. But with the death of Asaf-ud-daula in 1797, the new Nawab, Saadat Ali agreed to pay an enhanced sum of Rs 76 lakh. But when, in subsequent years he expressed his inability to pay such huge sum, he was forced in 1801 to cede a large chunk of his territory, comprising Rohilkhand, Gorakhpur and Doab to the Company. This gave a mortal blow to Awadh's glory and might. This state of affairs continued till Awadh was finally annexed by the East India Company in 1856.

Annexation of Punjab

After the defeat of the Marathas at the hand of Ahmad Shah Abdali the Sikhs took advantage and established their own states, known as 12 misls. Subsequently, Ranjit Singh subdued them and built-up a big and powerful empire which extended not only from the Sutlej to the Indus but also to trans-Indus regions like Dera Ismail Khan and Dera Ghazi Khan. However, the British were keeping a watch over Punjab's affairs and in 1809 they entered into a treaty with Ranjit Singh – known as the Amritsar Treaty. Accordingly, Ranjit Singh had to forgo his claim over the trans-Sutlej areas. However, much of the problem existed between the Sikhs and the British till 1839. But after the death of Ranjit Singh in 1839, there was a succession feud which provided an opportunity for the British to interfere in Sikh affairs. This resulted in the first Anglo–Sikh War in 1845 which resulted in the Lahore Treaty, which reduced the status of Punjab to a British dependency. This was followed by the Second Anglo–Sikh War in 1849 which finally ended in the annexation of Punjab to the British colonial empire. Thus from 1757 (Battle of Plassey) to 1856 (final annexation of Awadh) the entire eastern and northern India came to be occupied by the British.

The British Occupation of the South and Western India

In southern and western India the main challenge to the British trade and territorial ambition came from two major state systems – Mysore, and the Marathas. In subsequent sections, we would have a bird's eye view of the processes through which the British subdued these regions and finally occupied them.

After the disintegration of the Vijayanagar Empire the state of Mysore was built up as an autonomous state by the Wodeyar dynasty. Soon, Haider Ali, one of the military officers of the Mysore army captured power after overthrowing the Wodeyar dynasty of Mysore and the boundary of Mysore state extended from the Krishna River in the north to the Malabar Coast in the west. As we have seen earlier,

Haider Ali and his son Tipu Sultan tried to build up a very powerful, militarised and centralised state with an ambition to control entire south India. Thus the East India Company perceived a threat from Mysore State and decided to tackle and subdue it.

There were four wars that took place between the British and Mysore State between 1767 and 1799, when Mysore was finally taken over by the British. It has to be remembered that three major powers existed in the region, viz., Hyderabad, Mysore and the Marathas; all of which were struggling to establish their political and territorial supremacy. The British had their own political game and, more often than not, they took advantage of the rivalries of the regional states among themselves. The First Anglo–Mysore War took place during 1767–69, when Haider Ali, with the support of the Marathas and the Nizam of Hyderabad attacked the British near Madras and forced them to sign an alliance treaty with Mysore. The treaty provided that they would support each other in case of a third party attack. The Second Anglo–Mysore War broke out in 1781 when the British succeeded in subduing Haider Ali by neutralising the Marathas and the Nizam. Haider Ali died in 1782 and was succeeded by his son Tipu Sultan. Tipu Sultan continued the war and forced the British to sign the Treaty of Mangalore which gave him a temporary respite. When Lord Cornwallis became the Governor-General he managed to bring the Marathas and the Nizam on his side. Meanwhile the Third Anglo–Mysore War started when Tipu Sultan attacked Travancore State which was allied to the British. The war continued from 1790 to 1792 in which Tipu ultimately surrendered half of his territory to the British. But he remained defiant and the British forces had a final showdown with him in 1799, which resulted in his defeat and his death. Tipu's dominions were divided between the Nizam and the British. The British restored the Wodeyar dynasty, but Mysore lost its independence and became a British dependency.

Anglo–Maratha War

The Marathas had suffered a great setback when they were decisively beaten by Ahmad Shah Abdali at the Battle of Panipat in 1761. But the British, after consolidating their position in Bengal and Awadh, were looking for an opportunity to settle a score with them. The opportunity came when Raghunath Rao sought British help for becoming the Peshwa, as he was facing opposition from the Council of Regency headed by Nana Phadnavis. That led to the First Anglo–

Maratha War (1775–82), which resulted in the Treaty of Salbai in 1782, by which Madhav Rao Narayan was recognised as the real Peshwa. The other consequences of the Treaty of Salbai were that the British acquired control of Salsette and Bassein and also established a foothold in the internal conflicts of Indian states. This peace treaty with the Marathas helped the British to concentrate on Mysore and other states, as the lull continued for 20 years on the Marathas' front. Meanwhile the Marathas were gripped by internal dissension and local Maratha chiefs tried to expand their areas as much as possible, which obviously weakened the central Maratha authority. However, they refused the British offer of subsidiary alliance with them. This was followed by Holkar's victory over the Peshwa's forces in the year 1800 which prompted the Peshwa Baji Rao II to accept the British offer of subsidiary alliance in 1802 by signing the Treaty of Bassein. According to this treaty, the Peshwa had to pay a huge sum as subsidy. Besides, he agreed not to enter into any alliance with any other power without British consent. However, the Treaty of Bassein was rejected by the Maratha chiefs which led to the second Anglo–Maratha War (1803-05). Consequently, the treaties of subordination were imposed on a number of tributaries of the Marathas. Besides, most of the territories controlled by Sindhia, including Delhi and Agra, were taken over by the British. Moreover, the British acquired the right to be the final arbiter in any disputes among the Maratha houses. The third Anglo–Maratha War erupted when Peshwa Baji Rao tried to unite all Maratha chiefs against the British during 1718-19. The Marathas were badly beaten, which resulted in abolition of the office of the Peshwa and his dominions were taken over by the British. Thus, the Maratha dream of inheriting the Mughal imperial mantle was finally dashed to the ground.

The defeat of the Marathas opened the road for establishing the Company's paramountcy over the Rajputana region. Some of these Rajput states like Ajmer, Udaipur and Jodhpur, were under the Maratha's sway earlier. In the wake of the Maratha's defeat, bigger states like Udaipur, Jodhpur, Ajmer and Jaipur, were forced to accept British paramountcy through individual treaties with them in 1918. Subsequently, similar treaties were imposed on smaller Rajputana states like Kota, Bundi, Bikaner, Jaisalmer, Banswara, Dungarpur Pratapgarh, Karauli and others.

Soon, the British turned their attention to the Himalayan region. They were engaged in several battles with Nepal, which had emerged as a powerful state. That ultimately led to the Treaty of Sugauli by which the British got control of the Terai region as well as areas of Kumaon and Garhwal. Besides, the Gorkhas had to withdraw from Sikkim. And they also agreed to keep a British resident at Kathmandu. All this led to further consolidation of the British power in India.

British Policy towards Frontier Regions

No study of the British occupation of India would be complete without referring to the frontier policy of the British. Basically, there were two major frontier regions – the north-west and the north-east. In the north-west, Sikhs were the major power and the annexation of Punjab in 1849 had cleared the road for pursuing a forward frontier policy in the region. In fact, the British had always been concerned over the developments in the north-western region as they were apprehensive about the Russian desire to advance in Central Asia. When Russia and France signed a treaty in 1819, the British concern reached an alarming stage. They responded by occupying Kutch in 1819 and subsequently forced a number of unequal treaties on the Amirs of Sindh. They, also played their clever policy of 'divide and rule' between the Sikh rulers and the Amirs of Sindh and Afganistan. All this led to the First Anglo–Afghan War (1839–41), which went against the British. Partly to compensate for their loss of face and partly to build up an inner rampart against Russia, the English were prompted to make unabashed use of fraud and force and succeeded in occupying Sindh in 1843. The annexation of Sindh brought universal condemnation for the British but it hardly deterred them: they continued to take an acute interest in the region. Their Russo-phobia reached a feverish pitch after the Crimean War (1854–56). Consequently, in 1876, the British occupied Quetta and Baluchistan. Soon they went in for the Second Anglo–Afghan War and got Abdur Rahman installed on the Afghan throne. However, the region continued to remain turbulent in view of the tribal raids and uprisings and the British continued to pursue a forward policy. Ultimately it was in 1893 that an agreement was signed resulting in the demarcation of the northern-western frontier of India, which came to be known as the Durand Line, named after the chief negotiator, Sir Henry Durand. However, the region continued to be volatile and subsequently Chitral (1895) and Tirah (1897) were taken over after military expeditions. Subsequently Lord Curzon constituted the entire region as a new province called North-Western Frontier Province (NWFP) in 1901.

The situation in the northern-eastern region was equally turbulent. Burma had emerged there as a powerful state during the eighteenth century. The British fought three wars with Burma: the first one during 1824–26, the second in 1852 and the third one in 1885. As a result of the first Burmese–British War, the King of Burma was forced to cede Assam and Nagaland as well as Arakan and Tenasserim, followed by annexation of Cachar in 1830. In the second Indo–Burmese War, Rangoon was captured and Pegu was annexed. In the third war, upper Burma was added to the British Empire. It was only after the Act of 1935 that Burma was separated from the British Indian Empire.

All these successes emboldened the British officials to seek further expansion and annexations. Subsequently, using the 'Doctrine of Lapse' a number of Indian states like Satara (1848), Sambalpur and Baghat (1850), Udaipur (1852), Nagpur (1853), Jhansi (1854) and Berar (1853) were annexed. Thus by 1857, a large part of India, both in terms of population and territory had come under the direct control of the British. The rest of Indian territory and population were left under the control of the Indian princes who themselves were under the indirect control of the British under the policy of Paramountcy.

This is the brief history of the British occupation of India. We have seen that the eighteenth century in India was marked by the decline of the central authority of the Mughals. But fortunately it did not lead to a total power vacuum in the country as the political space vacated by the Mughals was gradually occupied by a number of regional powers. One of these regional powers, the Marathas, even made a serious bid to inherit and wear the imperial mantle of the Mughals. The Sikhs in the north and Tipu Sultan in the south at some stage became equally powerful. Besides, historians have also dug up enough data to support the thesis that the regionalisation of Indian political power did not destroy the economic and social fabric of the country. In fact, before the British occupation, India was doing pretty well on the economic front. Why all this could not help our people to successfully resist the British takeover is an issue, which has been a subject of debate among our historians for a long time.

A number of practical explanations have also been advanced by our scholars for the inability of our people to face up to the British challenge. One, the regional powers in India were constantly at loggerheads with each other, always trying to occupy as much territory as possible by overstepping on each-other's toes. It resulted in frittering away of their energy and resources. More than that, such a cut-throat competition among the regional powers provided the British with an opportunity to play one region against the other, and subdue them one by one, instead of facing the collective might of all Indian states. Mysore–Maratha rivalry is an illustrative case. Besides, these regional powers were also weakened by court rivalries and intrigues. Mir Jafar's treacherous role in the Battle of Plassey is a case in point. The second reason for the failure of the Indian states was their incapacity to mobilise enough resources to match and surpass the Company. The financial magnates of India found the British Company more creditworthy and trustworthy than the Indian princes. Besides, the Company used ruthless methods to force the local states and nawabs to extend larger and larger amount of subsidies, which greatly facilitated British operations in India. The resource crunch on the part of the Indian princes resulted in irregular payments to their army which often created demoralisation and dissensions among them. Perhaps, the technological superiority of the British also played a role, as it succeeded in neutralising the numerical superiority of the Indian army. A large number of British troops in India were inducted during the Anglo–French War, which also helped the British in consolidating their position in India.

However, in respect of the British occupation of India, one of the central theoretical questions is: what was the primary strength, which enabled the British to occupy India so easily? Scholars have tried to find its direct correlation with the unprecedented ascendance of the Western World in the course of the last few centuries, prior to the British occupation of India. One theoretical explanation is that in the wake of the Renaissance followed by the Reformation and the Enlightenment, the European mind was freed from the shackles of superstitious belief. That made human 'reason' as the powerful and final arbiter in all human affairs, pushing claims of 'revelation' in the background. That led to the secularisation of society which, in turn, promoted a deep spirit of enquiry, innovation and inquisitiveness. As a result, the old ideas and instrumentalities, viz., compass, gunpowder, printing press, charcoal, saltpetre, navigational aids, borrowed from the older civilisations, were put to better and more effective use for long sea voyages as well as in forging new weapons. Their innovative use helped their mariners to reach places as distant as South and North America in the West, and China and India in the East. In sharp contrast to that, the East, for various reasons, including those being old civilisations, lacked such an adventurous, innovative and outgoing spirit. Perhaps that settled the scale in the favour of the British.

A related question is, why of all the rival powers who were struggling for colonial possessions, England alone could forge ahead. The explanation is not far to seek. In the European subcontinent, Germany and the Italian States were still divided, and France suffered from the excesses of revolutionary ferment. Holland did not possess much natural resources and Spain and Portugal were still being dominated by priests and soldiers. And they also lacked a sufficient number of innovative middle classes. England had a sufficient store of coal and iron ore and a surging, innovative middle class and also superior naval force. All that was lacking was an adequate supply of capital which came from the plunder of India. That worked as a launching pad both for the initiation of the industrial revolution as well as for colonial possessions. Thus it is not all surprising that England surged ahead of all its European rivals and occupied India in a period of less than a hundred years.

To sum up, the seed of decline of the Mughal Empire could be traced to Aurangzeb's religious bigotry and his overambitious

> *Their prey is lodged in England; and the cries of India are given to sea and winds . . . In India, all the vices operate by which sudden fortune is acquired; in England are often displayed, by the same persons, the virtues which dispense hereditary wealth. Arrived in England, the destroyers of the nobility and gentry of a whole kingdom will find the best company in this nation, at a board of elegance and hospitality. Here the manufacturer and the husbandman will bless the just and punctual hand, that in India has torn the cloth from the loom, or wrested the scanty portion of rice and salt from the peasants of Bengal, or wrung from him the very opium in which he forgot his oppressions and his oppressor . . . Our Indian government is in its best state a grievance.*
>
> —EDMUND BURKE, "SPEECH ON MR. FOX'S EAST INDIA BILL," 1783

expansionist venture into the Deccan – a policy which not only alienated a large chunk of the Indian populace but also led to the overstretching of the imperial resources. However, what hastened the process of its decline and ultimate demise, was the fact that his successors, one after another, turned out to be political weaklings. It is true that in the wake of the decline of the Mughal Empire, a number of regional powers did emerge with a fair chance to occupy the political space vacated by the Mughals. Unfortunately that hope was soon belied as they crumbled under the weight of British political machination as well as their superior military might. What added to their failure were their mutual recriminations and rivalries. The elimination of the rival European powers had been made possible partly due to the British superiority in naval power and partly due to its capacity to influence and manipulate the contours of the European power politics. Admittedly, the new intellectual revolution which had galvanised Western Europe during those days also facilitated the British game in the foreign land. It had unshackled the human mind and helped to build up a string of new secular institutions. Besides, it had widened the arena of individual's freedom and even initiated a new discourse on religious affairs. All this created a new mindset which prompted the British to set out for a foreign 'kill'. All this helped the British in occupying the bulk of the Indian territory in a remarkably short span of time and at the minimum cost in terms of men and materials.

With this brief story of the British occupation of India, we would take up a study of its impact on Indian society in the subsequent chapters.

> *India was never conquered by the English sword – not by military valour, but by a subtle and cunning diplomacy. To have used force . . . would have roused the warring chiefs to a sense of mutual danger, and united them against the common enemy. Lulled by professions of a purely commercial interest, the native chieftains vied with one another in extending opportunities of trade to the British in return for military service rendered by these armed merchants in subduing local rivals. Too late they found that the mailed fist which encompassed the ruin of their enemies was turned with equal effectiveness against themselves.*
>
> LALA LAJPAT RAI

INDIA
in 1561
English Miles
0
300
600
Akbar's Dominions
K. = Kingdom
PERSIA
KABUL
Kabul
Ghazni
PROV.
Kandahar
Peshawar
KASHMIR
Srinagar
PANJAB
Sialkot
Lahore
HIMALAYAN STATES
Multan
Panipat
Delhi
TRIBES
RAJASTHAN
Agra
Ajmer
Sihwan
SIND
Chitor
Gwalior
Benares
HIMALAYAN STATES
RAJAS
AFGHAN
BENGAL
Patna
Prayag
MALWA
Ujjain
Patan
KACHH
GUJARAT
Ahmadabad
Cambay
Diu
Dacca
Chittagong
GONDWANA
ORISSA
Surat
KHANDESH
BERAR
Daman
Bassein
Bombay
Chaul
AHMAD-
NAGAR
GOLKONDA
K.
BIDAR
Bidar
VARIOUS RAJAS
Puri
ARABIAN
SEA
BAY OF
BENGAL
Bijapur
BIJAPUR
K.
Goa
Masulipatam
Honawar
VIJAYANAGAR
EMPIRE
Nellore
Mangalore
Pulicat
Andaman Is.
Lacadive Is.
Calicut
Tanjore
Negapatam
Cochin
Quilon
CEYLON
Maldive Is.

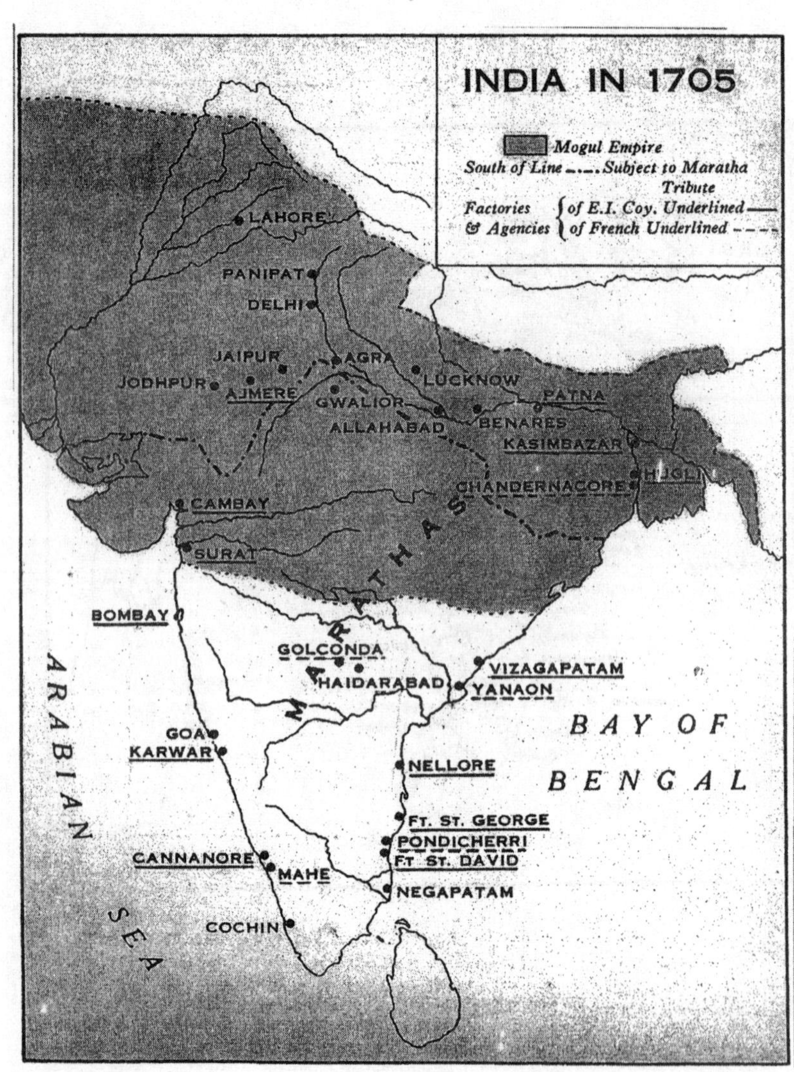
INDIA IN 1705
Mogul Empire
South of Line — . — . Subject to Maratha Tribute
Factories & Agencies { of E.I. Coy. Underlined ——
of French Underlined - - - -
LAHORE
PANIPAT
DELHI
JAIPUR
AGRA
JODHPUR
AJMERE
LUCKNOW
GWALIOR
PATNA
ALLAHABAD
BENARES
KASIMBAZAR
HUGLI
CHANDERNAGORE
CAMBAY
SURAT
MARATHAS
BOMBAY
GOLCONDA
HAIDARABAD
VIZAGAPATAM
YANAON
ARABIAN SEA
BAY OF BENGAL
GOA
KARWAR
NELLORE
FT. ST. GEORGE
PONDICHERRI
FT. ST. DAVID
CANNANORE
MAHE
NEGAPATAM
COCHIN

INDIA
in 1795
British Territory
British Protected States
Mahrattas
Scale of Miles
0 50 100 200 300 400
AFGHANS
Kabul
Peshawar
Kandahar
Lahore
Multan
Indus R.
Jhilam R.
Chenab R.
Ravi R.
Sutlej R.
Panipat
Delhi
Ramnagar
ROHILKAND
Bareilly
NEPAL
OUDH
Lucknow
Cawnpore
Kara
Agra
Gwalior
Salbai
Allahabad
Benares
Patna
BEHAR
Plassy
Chandarnagar
Calcutta
BENGAL
Balasore
Cuttack
Cooch Behar
RAJPUTS
Jodhpur
Hyderabad
Luni R.
MAHRATTA
Ahmadabad
Bhopal
Indore
Baroda
Junagarh
Broach
Somnath
Surat
Diu
Asirgarh
Nagpur
CONFEDERACY
Bassein
Salsette I.
Bombay
Aurangabad
Wargaon
Poona
Kardla
Bankot
Purandhar
NIZAM'S
Hyderabad
DOMINIONS
Ellore
Bijapur
Masulipatam
BAY OF BENGAL
Karnul
Goa
Cuddapah
MYSORE
Mangalore
Bangalore
Madras
Seringapatam
Cannanore
Mysore
Mahe
Calicut
Pondicherry
Tanjore
Cochin
Madura
ARABIAN SEA
WAXTYPE
GEORGE PHILIP & SON, LTD.

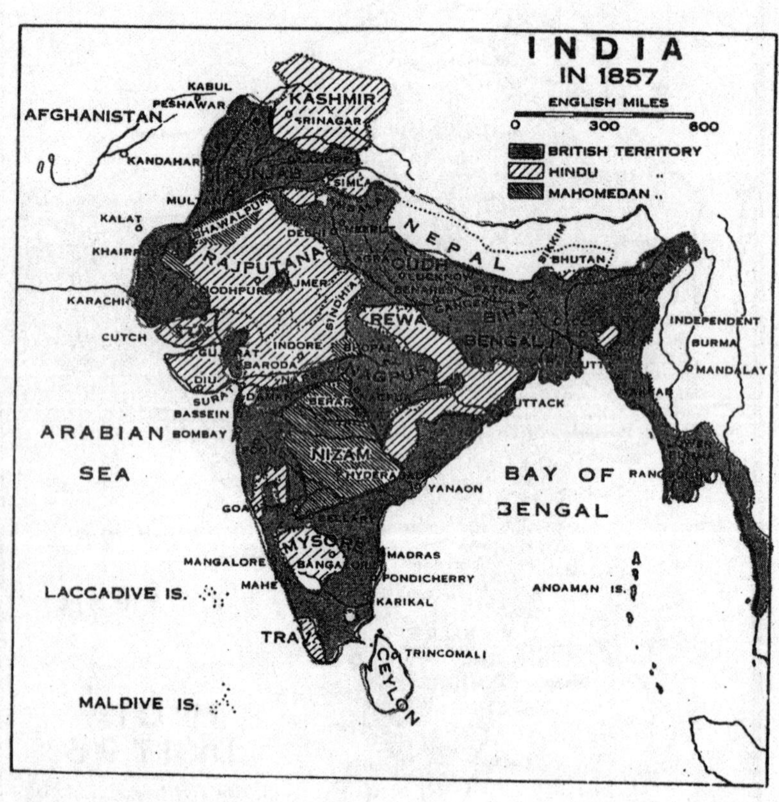

INDIA
IN 1857
ENGLISH MILES
0
300
600
BRITISH TERRITORY
HINDU
MAHOMEDAN
KABUL
PESHAWAR
AFGHANISTAN
KASHMIR
SRINAGAR
KANDAHAR
PUNJAB
SIMLA
KALAT
DELHI
NEPAL
SIKKIM
BHUTAN
RAJPUTANA
AGRA
OUDH
LUCKNOW
PATNA
KARACHI
CUTCH
SINDHIA
REWA
BENGAL
INDEPENDENT
BURMA
MANDALAY
INDORE
BHOPAL
BARODA
DIU
SURAT
BASSEIN
BERAR
CUTTACK
ARABIAN
SEA
BOMBAY
NIZAM
YANAON
BAY OF
BENGAL
GOA
MYSORE
MADRAS
MANGALORE
BANGALORE
PONDICHERRY
MAHE
LACCADIVE IS.
ANDAMAN IS.
KARIKAL
TRINCOMALI
CEYLON
MALDIVE IS.

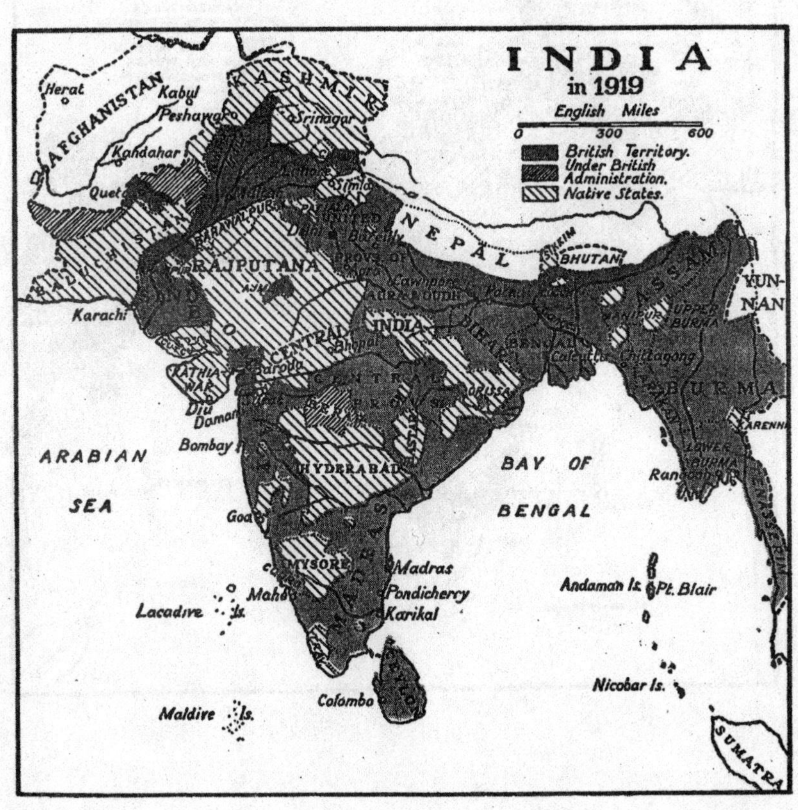
INDIA
in 1919
English Miles
0 300 600
British Territory.
Under British Administration.
Native States.
AFGHANISTAN
Herat
Kabul
Peshawar
Kandahar
KASHMIR
Srinagar
Lahore
Simla
NEPAL
BHUTAN
ASSAM
YUN-NAN
RAJPUTANA
SINDE
Karachi
Delhi
Bareilly
Cawnpore
OUDH
BIHAR
BENGAL
Calcutta
Chittagong
UPPER BURMA
BURMA
MANIPUR
CENTRAL INDIA
Bhopal
Baroda
KATHIAWAR
Diu
Daman
Bombay
CENTRAL PROVINCES
ORISSA
HYDERABAD
ARABIAN SEA
BAY OF BENGAL
Goa
MYSORE
Madras
Pondicherry
Karikal
Mahe
Lacadive Is.
MADRAS
Colombo
Maldive Is.
Andaman Is.
Pt. Blair
Nicobar Is.
Rangoon
LOWER BURMA
KARENNI
SUMATRA

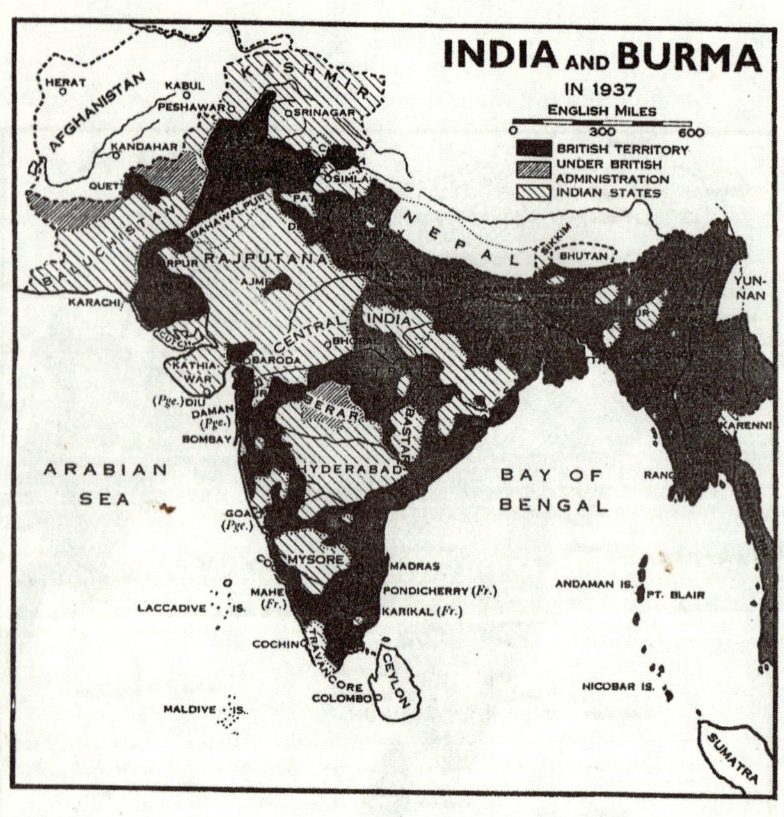
INDIA AND BURMA
IN 1937
ENGLISH MILES
0 300 600
BRITISH TERRITORY
UNDER BRITISH ADMINISTRATION
INDIAN STATES
HERAT
AFGHANISTAN
KABUL
PESHAWAR
KANDAHAR
KASHMIR
SRINAGAR
SIMLA
BAHAWALPUR
BALUCHISTAN
RAJPUTANA
NEPAL
SIKKIM
BHUTAN
YUN-NAN
KARACHI
CUTCH
CENTRAL INDIA
BARODA
KATHIA-WAR
(Pge.) DIU
DAMAN (Pge.)
BOMBAY
BERAR
BASTAR
HYDERABAD
KARENNI
ARABIAN SEA
BAY OF BENGAL
GOA (Pge.)
MYSORE
MADRAS
MAHE (Fr.)
PONDICHERRY (Fr.)
KARIKAL (Fr.)
LACCADIVE IS.
ANDAMAN IS.
PT. BLAIR
COCHIN
TRAVANCORE
CEYLON
COLOMBO
NICOBAR IS.
MALDIVE IS.
SUMATRA

2 Impact of British Rule on Indian Agriculture

> *The poverty of the Indian population at the present day is unparalleled in any civilized country; the famines which have desolated India within the last quarter of nineteenth century are unexampled in their extent and intensity in the history of ancient or modern times. . . . A population equal to half of that of England has been perished in India within a period which men and women, still in middle ages, can remember.*
>
> RAMESH C DUTT

We have already seen how the British colonial rule spread its network of political and economic tentacles throughout the length and breadth of India. To that end, it had adopted a strategy of outmaneuvering and outforcing its major European rivals as well as the native regional powers. As we know, the East India Company had come as a trading company and hence it initially concentrated on buying Indian goods cheap and selling them dear in the European market. In the process, the Company made good money as the margin of the profit was pretty high. But there was a problem: since England did not have enough exportable goods for the Indian market, it had to bring bullion to pay for the Indian goods. In this process, a large amount of British gold and silver had to be brought to India.

The Company got a golden opportunity when it managed to get the *diwani* rights of Bengal, Orissa and Bihar in 1765 in the wake of its victories at the battlefields of both Plassey (1757) and Buxar (1764). One major positive result for the Company from its newly acquired *diwani* rights was that it could buy Indian goods by paying from the accumulated fund from its land revenue exactions. In other words, the Company easily received sufficient funds for buying Indian goods without bringing the bullion from England. What was more, the earnings from Indian goods sold in the European market went straightway to the treasury of the Company located at London and was never ploughed back to India. Thus the quantum of land revenue collection became very crucial and critical to the trading capacity of the Company. Therefore, it became imperative for the Company officials to exact the maximum amount of land revenue from the Indian tenants, even by resorting to force and fraud. Such a callous and inhuman policy had its disastrous impact on Indian agriculture.

In this section we would concentrate on examining the various land revenue systems introduced by the British and their implications for the Indian peasantry. Commercialisation of agriculture in India, which led to the change of its cropping pattern, is another issue which we would take up for our study. But before going into the details of these issues, let us present a brief and succinct account of the state of rural life and the agrarian system prevalent in pre-British India.

Indian Rural Society in the Pre-British Days

There is a near unanimity among scholars about the salient features of rural India in the pre-British days. Briefly stated, they are:

1. First, self-sufficiency and interdependence were the hallmarks of rural life in India. Such a system ensured every one's contributions as well as shares in the economic life of the village, putting it permanently on an even keel. It further proved to be a real bulwark against any major change or disruption of rural life on account of any political change. Thus it not only marginalised the role of the state but also ensured stability and continuity of its socio-economic-cultural life.
2. A unique land ownership pattern was the second feature of our village life. Generally, the land ownership was vested either in king or in community or in the peasant proprietors. But the traditional Indian system did not fall within any of these categories. Here the peasant families did enjoy hereditary rights to cultivate the land from generation to generation but they were mostly using their own family labour for cultivation. Besides they did not have the right to buy and sell land and hence they could not be categorised as the peasant proprietors.
3. Third, according to the traditional land revenue system, Hindu kings could only collect one-sixth of the produce from the peasant cultivators. But the kings could not dispossess or change the hereditary rights of the cultivators. The Mughals made some

changes in the land revenue collection system, including payment in cash and collection through intermediaries. But even they did not have the right to dispossess the actual cultivators, so long as they were willing to pay the rent. And that is why kings, over the ages, tried to have control over the village and not inside it.

4. Fourth, on account of the caste system there was a real interdependence among the various groups of the village. Apart from the cultivating families, there were other groups, viz., carpenters, blacksmiths, potters, barbers, oilmen, cobblers, scavengers, washermen and weavers, who mostly worked as service-providers. Brahmins took care of the ritual and religious ceremonies of the village. Thus an army of village artisans took care of every need of the village population. In lieu of their services, they were either allotted a piece of village land for cultivation or were given a fixed measure of grains at the time of harvest. By and large, these artisans got raw materials for their produce in and around their village. The rest of their needs were met at the weekly local markets. Thus a kind of village-autarchy did prevail in traditional India which is why major political changes at the national level hardly created any ripples in the village life.

There is an extensive debate among scholars about the overall pattern of the village life in the pre-British era. On the one hand, B R Ambedkar and a number of Marxist scholars believe that the entire traditional life was based on a subtle and shrewd system of exploitation of the depressed classes by the dominant upper castes. On the other hand, Mahatma Gandhi and a number of other scholars are of the opinion that the entire village system was marked by complimentarity and harmony, and not by exploitations and exactions. In our view, it is difficult to say at this stage with so much historical distortions and accretions in between, whether the village life was so idyllic or exploitative, as pointed out by some of the scholars. In our times, all that one can say is that the system would not have survived for millenniums had it been that unjust and exploitative. Despite differences of opinion among scholars, there is almost a general agreement on the quintessential characteristics of the Indian agrarian system: that there was no landed aristocracy in India with the kind of proprietary right which the European manors enjoyed. Nor was slavery and serfdom an integral part of our agrarian system, as was prevalent in Europe. Besides, there was no system of private ownership of land, not even peasant proprietorship, as it was the village which virtually remained a unit of revenue assessment.

Indian Agriculture under the British Rule

The introduction of a new land revenue system and the subsequent commercialisation of Indian agriculture brought about far-reaching changes in the nature and structure of Indian agriculture. Let us discuss how these changes came into effect.

New Land Revenue System

The British introduced three different systems of land revenue fixation and collection, which came to be known as: (a) Zamindari, (b) Ryotwari and (c) Mahalwari. Before going into their details, let us get an overview of the expectations they had from the new land revenue system. We have already seen that soon after the Company got the *diwani* right (in 1765) its primary aim had been to collect as much land revenue as was humanly possible. With its newly acquired authority, the Company unscrupulously extracted the maximum land revenue from peasants, so much so that Bengal suffered an unprecedented famine during 1769–70, which virtually wiped out one-third of its population. Alarmed by this, they experimented with a new system of revenue which was called, 'farming'. The quintessence of the new system was that the job of the revenue collection was given to the highest bidders. The new system only accelerated the pace and process of the ruination of the peasantry. What perhaps prompted the Company officials to look for another system of revenue collection was the fact that ruination of agriculture had also adversely affected Company's trade as some of the export items, like silk and cotton were intimately linked with agriculture. This search led to the introduction of yet another new system of land revenue collection which came to be known as zamindari or Bengal Permanent Settlement under Lord Cornwallis. There were two major components of the new system: (a) the quantum of land revenue would be fixed once and for all; and that (b) the job and responsibility for its collection would be given to zamindars. The major rationale behind permanent fixation of the quantum of land revenue was that it would rid the system of its corruption and would also eliminate its uncertain and fluid character. It was further argued that the permanent settlement would encourage zamindars to make investment for the improvement of land, as the increased income would entirely remain with them on account of the fixed nature of the land revenue to be paid to the Company. But the Company was the net gainer in the entire process, as the revenue was to be fixed on the point of absolute maximum. How the new system helped the Company could be illustrated by a simple fact: the quantum of land revenue doubled between 1765 and 1793 – a period less than thirty years. The other question as to who should be given the job of revenue collection was decided by Lord Cornwallis in favour of the zamindars. The rationale behind the zamindari system was that it would be much easier to get the revenue collected through a small number of zamindars, rather than collecting it directly from thousands of cultivators. Perhaps, the real calculation was that zamindars would also provide a strong social support base for the Company–Government. The quintessence of the zamindari system was that the zamindars were given private property right in land: they could own, sell, purchase and mortgage it and their successors could also inherit it. The only limitation was that in case of non-payment of the fixed rent, a zamindar was bound to lose his zamindari. Thus for the first time private property right in land had been introduced in India.

It did not take long for the pernicious consequences of the zamindari system to come to light. Peasants, of course, were its worst victims. They were soon reduced to the status of tenants and subtenants as they could be dispossessed of their lands at a zamindar's whim or fancy. The high quantum of rent virtually broke their back, reducing them to a state of penury and poverty. What was more, they had hardly any avenue even to ventilate their grievances, what to talk of their being redressed. It was only during the later part of the nineteenth century that peasant occupancy rights were recognised by new tenancy legislations. Though the zamindars enjoyed their newly acquired prosperity, a number of them did lose their zamindari as and when they failed to pay their rent in time. Interestingly, the Company officials also had their own grouse against the permanent settlement system: they found in it a stumbling block to increase the revenue at their sweet will. It is for this reason, perhaps, that the permanent settlement system could cover not more than 20 per cent area of British India – prevailing only in Bengal, Bihar, Orissa and north Madras areas. It was this desire to enhance the quantum of revenue collection, which prompted the Company to look for another system which came to be known as Ryotwari.

Ryotwari System

Ryotwari system of land revenue collection was first introduced in Madras by its Governor Thomas Munro. In this system the land revenue was to be collected directly from the cultivators instead of being collected through intermediaries as under the zamindari system. But the new system did not establish peasant proprietorship as they were to pay the rent directly to the government, which was supposed to be the owner of the land. The apparent rationale behind the introduction of Ryotwari system was that it was better suited to the Indian tradition where the cultivators had enjoyed certain rights since time immemorial. Perhaps the real reason behind the introduction of the new system was the Company–Government's need for enhanced revenue on account of its continuous engagement in war with its rivals. It was also argued that though the Company would be getting more revenue, the peasants would be paying less, as intermediaries would be eliminated from the system. Ideally the Ryotwari system was supposed to be based on fixation of the rent for each Ryot and each field. A Ryot was to be given a choice to accept or reject the offer made by the government for a particular piece of land. However, in actual practice it did not happen as the quantum of rent was fixed arbitrarily by the Company officials and both force and fraud were used to extract maximum rent from the cultivators. The system had become obnoxious and repressive, which was brought out by the Report of the Madras Torture Commission in 1855. Subsequently, the Ryotwari system was also introduced in the Bombay Province, where too it encountered similar problems.

Mahalwari System

Mahalwari system was another system of land revenue collection, which was primarily introduced in north-west provinces and subsequently in Punjab and some parts of the central provinces. In these areas, initially an attempt was made to collect the land revenue through the Talukdars of these areas, but it failed primarily on account of excessive rent demand from the Company–Government. This prompted the British to shift their attention to local zamindars (landowners) who were actual cultivators and the village community. In Mahalwari system, the entire village or Mahal was taken as a unit, and thus rent was fixed for the entire Mahal, though every cultivator had a joint responsibility for payment of the rent. Generally, the rent was collected through the village pradhan or any other cultivator of high standing in the village. Mahalwari system was also supposed to be based on detailed field survey to assess the potential of the produce as a basis for the fixation of the rent. But in actual practice, such detailed field surveys were never conducted and the rent so fixed remained too high. Soon the entire system virtually broke down under the weight of high rent. Subsequently, an attempt was made to retrieve the system by the Regulation of 1833 which did bring some relief to these cultivators. But on the whole, Mahalwari system also ruined the cultivators giving a field day for moneylenders.

It can be fairly concluded that all the three new land revenue systems, ultimately, resulted in fixation of high rent and harsh ways of its collection. Besides, what further aggravated the miserable conditions of the Indian peasantry was a system of cash payment of rent and that too during the harvest time when the prices of the agricultural produce were always low.

Commercialisation of Indian Agriculture and Its Consequences

Commercialisation of agriculture was another major change brought about by the British rule. New crops and other agro-based products were being produced for the market and not only for local consumption. It is true that some kind of commercialisation of agriculture was already prevalent even in the pre-British days, particularly after the Mughals had introduced the system of cash-payment for land revenue. But the British brought about a major change both in quantitative as well as qualitative terms. In other words, the new system differed from the old one in that now the Company–Government started forcing Indian peasants to produce agro-based exportable goods. Initially, it attempted to force the Indian peasants to produce those agro-based goods, that were in great demand in the European markets. The process was further intensified once the industrial revolution began to gather momentum in England. This led to a new strategy on the part of the British to concentrate on the export of those Indian agricultural goods, which would work as the raw materials for the British industries. Such a strategy also solved their problem of the adverse balance of payments in respect of China. There was a good market in China for Indian agro-products like cotton, ivory and opium, and their export to China would mitigate the problem of balance of payment arising out of the import of Chinese tea by the Company. Thus in view of the demand for Indian agro-products, both in China and in the European market, the British concentrated on the acquisition of products such as indigo, cotton, raw-silk, opium, pepper, etc. Different strategies were adopted to induce production of these exportable goods by Indian peasantry, which ranged from binding the producers by advancing a paltry sum to open use of force and fraud. In the process, the Company did not hesitate to treat the workers in tea-gardens of Assam as virtual slaves.

The question that is often asked is why the commercialisation of Indian agriculture did not help peasants as it did elsewhere in a similar situation. The reasons are not far to seek. First, small peasant families who were predominantly engaged in the production of these goods were not doing it by choice but under compulsion. Second, they were not free to market their goods on competitive prices. They had to supply these goods to the Company under the threat of force. Hence by producing these goods, they did not get enriched, instead they were impoverished. What was more, the earnings of these exports went to the Company's account in London, and they were never ploughed back to India. Nor could India import British goods on those accounts. Hence the export of these goods led to the impoverishment of India and not to its enrichment.

It is true that in subsequent years a number of steps were taken by the British to improve the state of affairs in the field of Indian agriculture. This included new irrigational facilities by new canal systems particularly in Punjab, western UP and some parts of Madras. Besides, the new tenancy laws of 1859 and 1885 did give some relief and protection to the impoverished tenants. But all these measures proved too inadequate to tackle the problem actually faced by the Indian cultivators. Even where some positive results came out of these measures; they were confined to some areas like Punjab, western UP and parts of Madras. And there too, it was only a small group of privileged few who actually benefited from it.

Taking a synoptic view, certain other consequences of the British intrusion in the Indian agrarian system could also be traced out. Some of these long-term consequences were: rural indebtedness, fragmentation of landholdings and emergence of certain new classes in respect of rural India, viz., moneylenders, landless labour and absentee landlords in the form of zamindars. In sum, it was the British intrusion in the field of Indian agriculture which led to the total disruption of the millennium-old village systems, destroying its social as well as its economic fabric.

Finally, so far as the overall balance sheet of the impact of the British rule on Indian agriculture is concerned, there are two diametrically opposite views on it. Some of the Marxist historians like A R Desai and R P Dutt are of the opinion that with all its limitations, the British rule played a positive and progressive role in respect of the rural life of India, as it elevated it to the status of national agriculture and linked it up with the national and even world market. On the other hand, a number of nationalist leaders, including Mahatma Gandhi, held the British rule squarely responsible for total ruination of the rural life of India, leading to the mass pauperisation of the peasantry.

In our view, if foreign slavery would have been that liberating force in human history, it would not have been such a hated system inviting fierce human anger and defiance. It is not for nothing that in the social history of man thousands have laid down their lives in the process of resisting it. Slavery is nothing but a direct and frontal attack on the dignity of man. Hence, it is a total travesty of truth to say that slavery could ever become a tool of human liberation and social progress.

> *Millions of peasants in India are struggling to live on half an acre. Their existence is a constant struggle with starvation, ending too often in defeat. Their difficulty is not to live human lives, . . . but to live at all, and not to die.*
>
> W S Lily

3 Impact of British Rule on Indian Industries

The bones of the cotton weavers are bleaching the plains of India.

LORD BENTINCK

We have already seen how Indian agriculture was ruined under the British rule on account of excessive exactions of land revenue and by its forced commercialisation. Equally pernicious and destructive was the impact of the colonial rule on Indian handicraft industries, which were the mainstay of the Indian economy during the pre-British days. In the subsequent sections we propose to analyse the basic strategy adopted by the colonial administration for the destruction of Indian handicraft industries and the consequences thereof on the Indian economy. Before delving into details, it would be expedient to make a synoptic presentation on the nature and structure of the Indian handicraft system prevalent in pre-British days.

The Nature of Indian Handicraft Industries in the Pre-colonial Era

We have seen earlier that one of the chief characteristics of Indian village economic life was its self-sufficient and autarchic nature. An average Indian village not only produced enough food and clothes but also took care of its other material needs, primarily through village artisans, viz., cobbler, potter, oilman, blacksmith, carpenter and silver-smith. The socio-religious ceremonial needs were taken care of by the village brahmin and barber. Drawn primarily from environment-friendly local resources, these goods were produced and consumed locally. These artisans were supported by the village on the basis of a *Jajmani* system and not on a commercial basis. In brief, self-sufficiency and interdependence were the hallmarks of a traditional Indian village.

In the urban areas, the nature and structure of handicraft industries were slightly different. Here goods were being produced on a commercial basis, both for local as well as the world markets. For instance, the Indian textile industry had no rivals in the world. Besides, India enjoyed a high reputation in metal work, stone-work, dyeing, pottery and leather work. What was more, some of these high-quality items were being produced for the elite section of the society: kings, nawabs, and high officials both civilian and non-civilian. These urban handicrafts had their market all over the world. Thus, these urban industries were taking care of the needs of every section of the society, from the commoner to the king. And these urban artisans ranged from bangle-markers to weapon-forgers. However, Indian villages were generally not within the orbit of these urban industries, as their needs were being met by the village-artisans. Besides, a part of urban goods was being produced only for the elite section of the society and for export to other countries. All these factors contributed to a limited market being made available to artisans. Consequently, they faced problems both in the process of capital formation as well as in the field of technological innovations.

British Rule and Indian Handicrafts

We have earlier noted that the East India Company was set up around A.D. 1600 with an exclusive trading right in the east. Initially, textile was one of the major items which the British East India Company traded with India. The Company had to compete with other European companies particularly the Portuguese, Dutch and French for the control of Indian trade market. Besides, it had to struggle to keep itself on the right side of the Indian rulers, including the Mughal Emperor. Despite these challenges, even in the initial stages, the Company did a flourishing business in India, as Indian goods were in great demand in European markets and the profit margin was quite high. For India too, it was not a bad bargain as its textile industries got a boost on account of expanding demands. Moreover, since England did not have many goods to be exported to India, the Company had to bring British bullion (gold and silver) to pay for the goods bought from the Indian market. At that stage, a mutually beneficial commercial relationship existed between India and the Company.

However, in subsequent years, two major developments occurred, which changed the entire relationship. The gradual elimination of other

European companies from the Indian region by the British East India Company indeed facilitated its monopolistic control over the Indian market. By the middle of the eighteenth century, the East India Company had successfully accomplished this task. A second and more decisive event, which virtually changed the fates of both India and the Company, was the latter's victory at Plassey (1757) followed by its victory at Buxar (1764) and the grant of *diwani* right to it in 1765. These momentous events entirely changed the relationship between India and the Company. Rabindranath Tagore captured the entire scenario in his poetic words when he said that the 'weighing scales in the merchant's hands changed into the imperial sceptre'. One can add that the Company continued to hold the weighing scale in one hand but had got a sword in the other, to back up its freedom to turn and twist it the way it liked to do. In other words, a fundamental change was brought about even in respect of the Company's commercial dealings in India – as they did not have to be governed by the market forces alone on account of newly acquired political power.

The period between 1757 and 1947 had been divided by the Marxist scholars like R P Dutt and others into three phases (based on the Leninist's theorisation pattern): the phase of commercial capitalism 1600–1800); the phase of industrial capitalism (1800–60); and the phase of finance capitalism (1860 onwards). During all these phases different strategies were adopted by the British which impacted the Indian industries. It would be expedient for us to dissect and analyse the British colonial policy during these three stages and see how they impacted the Indian industries.

Commercial Capitalist Phase: The First Phase (1600–1800)

The hallmark of this phase of the East India Company's trade with India was that it wanted to maximise its margins of profit by buying goods in the Indian market at the cheapest possible rates and selling them at the highest possible rates in the European market. Before the victory at Plassey, it had to compete with other European companies in the Indian market and also had to deal with Indian rulers. On the whole, its trading patterns were being governed by the market forces. Besides, it had to bring British bullion to India to pay for the Indian goods. In the post-1765 period it, however, managed to overcome all these restrictions. Through the *diwani* rights (the collection of the land revenue) of Bengal, Bihar and Orissa, it evolved and perfected a system of land revenue collection by maximum exactions and extortions from the hapless Indian peasants. A second major revenue source for the Company–Government came from taxes on internal trade items like shops, looms, sheep, cattle, and sundry professions. The third source of income for the Company was seizure of wealth from native rulers, merchants and bankers. The cumulative impact of all these mobilised resources was that the Company was able to solve one of its fundamental problems: how to pay for the purchase of Indian goods without bringing bullion from England. Now, it started paying for them from the surplus of land revenue collections. Not only that, its surplus revenue was subsequently used to wage war and acquire more territory, leading to the further enhancement of its financial strength. The Company–Government experimented and perfected ruthless and rapacious methods for maximum exactions and extortions from the Indian people. These measures can be listed as follows:

(i) Maximum exactions from the Indian peasantry in the form of land revenue collection either directly or through intermediaries.
(ii) Blatant use of force and fraud to force the Indian producers to sell their goods at the minimum price. At times, the forcibly fixed price was less than 35 per cent of the market price. To make the system more ruthless, the Company soon got rid of Indian merchants who used to work as middlemen between the Company and the producers. And it replaced them by a system of *gomastas* who followed a no-holds barred policy to force the producers to sell their goods to the Company at unremunerative prices. One of the techniques used was to 'bulldoze' the producers to take some advances on behalf of the Company. And once they fell in the advance-trap they could never get out of it. For instance, according to a regulation of 1789, any producer failing to deliver goods in time to the Company would have to pay a penalty of 35 per cent on his advances.
(iii) The Company officials engaged in private business using their position to engage in private extortions.
(iv) Loot and extortions from the Indian princes, bankers and merchants.
(v) The profits derived from the exports of goods.

All these measures started telling upon the health of Indian handicrafts. Forcible imposition and compulsory fixation of prices on the handicrafts producers started making the whole business unremunerative and many of them started closing their shops. Thus the process of de-industrialisation had set in. In fact, at this stage, the Company–Government was hardly concerned with the problems of the Indian people as its primary concern remained maximum revenue generation from trading. Another point, which deserves special mention here, is that the proceeds from the Company trading in Indian goods were directly deposited in the Company's account in London and were never brought back to India, either in monetary or material terms. They were treated as a kind of tribute from India, which became a major constituent of primary capital accumulation in England. This, in turn, contributed significantly to the emergence of industrial revolution in England. Thus a direct linkage was established between Indian impoverishment and British enrichment.

Industrial Capitalism: The Second Phase (1800–1860)

Around the close of the eighteenth century, England started emerging as an industrial country having crossed the threshold of the industrial revolution. What really brought about the industrial revolution in England is beyond the scope of this book. However, there is no denying the fact that the plunder of India certainly was a contributory cause to it. Be as it may, the important point is that once the industrial revolution gathered momentum in England, it had big implications for the Indian handicraft industries. Indian handicrafts, including textiles, were still popular in England and other European markets, and export from India was still a profitable business. But England had a greater need for a captive market for its industrial goods. India, in view of its vast size, population and the Company–Government's control over it, made a tantalising proposition. But the destruction of the Indian handicraft industry was a pre-condition for turning her into a captive market for British industrial goods. Hence, a more concerted and concentrated strategy was evolved to achieve that objective. The ending of the monopolistic trading right of the Company was another pre-condition to open up the Indian market for the British goods. This created a lobby of 'free traders' in England who demanded an immediate end of the monopoly of the East India Company over Indian trade. This resulted in the Charter Act 1813, which abolished the Company's monopoly over Indian trade. The Indian market was further opened by the Charter Act of 1833. Thus India was turned into a free zone for the flow of the British industrial goods. However, the real challenge was to destroy the Indian handicraft industries, which alone could turn her into a captive market for British industrial goods and a supplier of raw materials for the British industries. A sixfold strategy was adopted to achieve these twin objectives.

(i) Manipulation of export and import duty with a view to making Indian goods more expensive in the British markets and the British industrial goods less expensive in the Indian markets.
(ii) Maximisation of land revenue collection by adopting various methods and stratagems so that enough funds could be generated for buying goods from the Indian markets.
(iii) Commercialisation of Indian agriculture so as to turn India into a supplier of raw materials for British Industries.
(iv) Opening of the Indian hinterland by developing means of transportation, making it possible for the British goods to reach out to the remotest corner of the country.
(v) Spread the network of the British administrative machinery even to the remotest area and new legal and judicial system, so as to ensure the safety of trade routes as well as to make secure the British financial-commercial interests. The entire structure of the legal system, including Indian Penal Code (IPC) and Criminal Procedure Code (CrPC), was raised during this phase.
(vi) Promote the English medium-based western education so as to generate enough low-paid manpower to lower rungs of the administrative machinery at the minimum cost. It was not accidental that the Macaulay system of education was introduced during the phase.

All these measures soon yielded their desired results. The cumulative impact of the new strategy was the total destruction of the entire structure of Indian handicrafts, making it possible for the British goods to reach each and every corner of the country. As a result, India soon became a supplier of raw materials for the British industries. India went through a process of what historians have called 'de-industrialisation', which was primarily responsible for mass pauperisation and impoverishment of our people. Even one illustration could prove the point: from 1814 to 1835 the export of the British cotton clothes to India increased by 51 times, whereas that of India to England decreased by 13 times. Cotton Mills of Lancashire were built up on the ruins of Dacca, Murshidabad and Surat and some of these cities went through the process of de-urbanisation as well.

Finance Capitalism: The Third Phase (1860–1947)

In the later part of the nineteenth century, capitalism matured in England and also in some other European countries like Germany, France, Belgium and Holland. This led to a cut-throat competition among European powers, which ultimately resulted in the First World War. Meanwhile, capital accumulation had taken place in England and they were looking for new investment opportunities. With India under their thumb, there was no better place where the British capital could be invested. Besides, India was also endowed with abundant raw materials along with the availability of cheap labour. Moreover, the system of rapid transportation including railway had opened up the Indian hinterland. Hence around 1860, British capital started getting invested in India. The main areas of British investments were railways, irrigation projects, banking and insurance. British investment grew rapidly and by 1914, the total investment came to the tune of 500 million British pounds.

However, there were a number of problems in this phase of finance capitalism in India. In the first place, there was no genuine desire to lay down a sound base with strong infrastructure for rapid industrialisation of India. The idea behind the British investment was to strengthen its stranglehold on Indian people and also to maximise their profits. It was not driven by a genuine desire to put India on the right track of industrialisation. For instance, financial institutions like banks never supported genuine Indian entrepreneurs in a big way. Second, no attempt was made to encourage Indian entrepreneurs to work for the rapid industrialisation of India. For example, till 1924, no attempt was made to give protection to the Indian industries. Besides, there was no attempt to develop heavy industries, which alone could have worked as the motive force of industrialisation. Other factors responsible for the limited, retarded and lopsided growth of Indian industries were lack of well-trained technical hands and lack of purchasing power of our peasantry, which constituted the bulk of our population. Third, the bulk of the British capital invested in India was essentially raised from Indian plunder, which was shown as 'public debt'. Besides, India had to pay for so many expenses from which it derived no benefits. Perhaps the drain of wealth from India to England was much more than the British investment in India.

Indeed, the early nationalist leaders were genuinely aghast at the excessive exploitative nature of the British rule in India, resulting in the mass pauperisation of our people. It was on that account that one of the early nationalist leaders, Dadabhai Naoroji, propounded his oft-quoted 'Drain Theory' which underlined the process of the British enrichment at the cost of the Indian people. The quintessence of his 'Drain Theory' was that Indian wealth was being drained out to England on account of 'home-charges', high salaries and allowances of the British employees in India, and a huge amount of profit on the British capital investment being taken away to England.

Thus, the British colonial rule, adopting different strategies at different stages of its rule, consistently destroyed the traditional base of Indian handicrafts both in urban and rural areas. In the process India went through a phase of rapid de-industrialisation which broke the economic back of the Indian people – reducing them to a state of penury and poverty. Even when an attempt was made to start certain industries in India, it was more out of a profit-motive rather a genuine desire for creating a sound industrial base in India. This could be proved by the simple fact that no attempts were made to develop heavy industry by the British entrepreneurs. Nor were the Indian entrepreneurs encouraged in these directions. Therefore, it was not surprising that on the eve of its independence, India continued to be an industrially backward country despite century-old British rule.

A corollary issue, emerging out of the discussion about the impact of the British on the industrial structure of India, relates to the Marxist theory of growth of capitalist production and its progeny, imperialism. For a long time, the Marxists have been offering their own explanations for the decline of the Indian handicrafts industries, rise of capitalist production and imperialism. Karl Marx put forward a basic formulation that in its initial stages, capitalist system had played a progressive role. He wrote: 'The cheapness of articles produced by machines and the improved means of transport and communications furnish the weapons for conquering foreign markets.' Similarly, Lenin also said that imperialism was the highest stage of capitalism. He further tried to establish a direct correlation of monopoly capitalism with imperialism and militarism. He also called it a stage of finance capitalism. Indian Marxists have been repeating these Marxian formulations ad nauseam without subjecting them to critical evaluation in the context of India. They have also been asserting that with all its limitations, the British rule played a progressive role as it introduced a higher system of production in India. In brief, this has been the position of Marxist scholars like A R Desai, R P Dutt and others.

However, a section of Indian scholars have always rejected the

Marxist thesis of capitalism and imperialism. Even the early nationalists who never outrightly rejected the British rule, were of the opinion that plunder of India played a crucial role in the coming of the industrial revolution in England. Dadabhai Naoroji was perhaps the first to propound the 'Drain theory' through which he conclusively proved that it was the transfer of the plundered wealth of India which triggered the industrial revolution in England. But, he was not the only one to propound this theory. A number of other scholars like Cunningham, William Digby and Brooks Adams have been equally enthusiastic supporters of this line of thinking. Adams, in fact, tried to establish a chronological correlation between the British occupation of India and the coming of the industrial revolution in England. He wrote:

'Plassey was fought in 1757 and perhaps nothing has ever equaled the rapidity of change which followed. In 1770 the fighting-shuttle appeared, and coal began to replace wood in smelting. In 1764 Hargreaves invented the spinning-jenny, in 1779 Crompton contrived the mule, in 1768 Watt matured a steam engine, the most perfect of all vents of centralising energy.... In themselves, inventions are passive, waiting for the sufficient store of force to have accumulated to set them working. That force must always take the shape of money, and not hoarded, but in motion'. Arguing further in the same vein Adams concluded: 'Before the influx of the Indian treasure and the expansion of the credit which followed; no force sufficient for the purpose existed, and had Watt lived fifty years earlier, he and his inventions must have perished together'.

Back home in India, the socialist leader Rammanohar Lohia has also faulted the Marxist–Leninist theory of capitalism and imperialism on several counts. He particularly challenged their validity in the Indian context. Lohia in his paper on 'Economics after Marx' took up the Marxist theory of capitalism for a critical evaluation. Lohia asserts that Marxist–Leninist theory on capitalist production and its overspill, imperialism, does not have intellectual legs to stand on. According to Lohia, if we take the Indian context, the emergence and growth of industrial revolution and capitalist production occurred in the following manner:

(i) The British came for trading purposes.
(ii) On account of certain weaknesses of the Indian political set-up they succeeded in occupying India through political intrigues and superior military force.

(iii) They unabashedly indulged in the plunder of India and transferred the wealth of India to England, including gold and silver.
(iv) It was this plundered wealth of India which provided the basic capital which spurred the industrial revolution and capitalist production in England.

On the basis of this historical sequence, Lohia concluded that capitalism and imperialism grew together and reinforced each other. Thus, he challenged Marx's assertion that capitalism ever played any progressive role in respect of colonial labour. He writes: 'There is no greater collapse of human intelligence than when an Indian or any other colonial repeats parrot-like the Marxist formula that capitalism had at one time been progressive, but has now ceased to be so. Capitalism has at no time been progressive to the colonial masses, it has increasingly wasted their economic and spiritual welfare' (Lohia: Economics after Marx).

In brief, the British rule had a disastrous impact on the entire industrial structure of India. During the entire period of the British rule, there was a total dichotomy between the economic interests of the British and those of the Indian people. Initially, the British interest lay in buying Indian goods at the minimum price and selling them with the maximum margins of profit in the European markets. In the process, the British had hardly any compunction in using both force and fraud to achieve their basic objective. Subsequently, with the coming of the industrial revolution in England, they doggedly pursued their policy of turning India into a captive market for their finished goods and also as a supplier of raw materials needed for their factories. At a still later stage of their rule, the British found it more profitable to make capital investment in India so that it could be wedded to cheap labour and raw materials, which were easily available in India. Thus the maximisation of their margin of profit and pocketing the bulk of the economic surplus extracted from the Indian people remained a common and constant refrain of the British colonial policy. If in the process, some stray industrialisation took place in India that was an unintended fringe benefit for the Indian people. In any case, that was hardly an adequate compensation for the process of de-industrialisation which India went through under the British rule. As one of the early nationalist leaders, G Subramaniya Aiyer put it: 'Millions of workmen who pursued hereditary occupations, who called into exercise their intelligence and imagination, and who therefore, led a life of decent means and self-respect, have been reduced to a condition of abject poverty having become agriculture labourers or day-labourers in towns.'

It is clear that the Industrial Revolution, the foundation on which England's economic prosperity was built-up, was made possible only by the influx of Indian treasure, and that but for this capital, not loaned but taken, and bearing no interest, the ascendancy of the steam engine and mechanical appliances for mass production, might have remained unutilised.

LALA LAJPAT RAI

4 Impact of British Rule on the Socio-Cultural Life of India

The British connections had made India more helpless than she ever was before, politically and economically.

MAHATMA GANDHI

We have already examined the impact of the British rule on the economic life of India and its disastrous consequences. In this chapter an attempt would be made to evaluate the impact of the British colonial rule on the socio-politico-cultural aspects of our life.

Western Education and the Indian Society

Education was one of the areas in which the British rule made a tremendous impact – changing its contours beyond recognition. In the pre-British days, school education was quite widespread, as revealed by Dharampal's study (*The Beautiful Tree*) on the Tamil Nadu School system. The regional language was the medium of instruction at the school level. There were also centres of higher learning where the medium of instruction was either Persian or Sanskrit. Initially the British did not interfere in the traditional system of education. In fact, being inspired by the Orientalists like Willam Jones and others, they preferred promoting oriental languages. A number of institutions like Calcutta Madarsa (1781), Banaras Sanskrit College (1791) and Asiatic Society of Bengal (1781) were opened with British initiative and support. Those were the days of the Orientalists who favoured oriental learning for a better understanding of the Indian people. But there was another group of British scholars who favoured introduction of Western scientific education with English as the medium of instruction. Thomas B.

Macaulay was one such scholar who passionately believed in the usefulness of the introduction of English education. The Indian elite was also divided on this issue. While Raja Rammohun Roy favoured the introduction of Western education, others were opposed to it. In this connection it is relevant to note that it was the Charter Act of 1813, which for the first time recognised the responsibility of the British in the promotion of education in India. Consequently, a sum of rupees one lakh was set apart for this purpose. Subsequently, a general committee on public instruction was set up in 1823. Finally, in 1835, a new system of education was introduced, which subsequently came to be known as the Macaulay System of Education. This was followed by Wood's Dispatch of 1854, which laid down the basic contours of educational policy in India that led to opening of universities at Bombay, Madras and Calcutta, as well as the creation of a new department of Public Instruction in all provinces. It also favoured opening of vernacular schools. This was followed by the setting up of the Hunter Committee which favoured private initiative in the field of education. Lord Curzon set up the Indian University Commission in 1902, and on its recommendation passed the Indian University Act of 1904, which led to a big controversy as it opened the floodgate of governmental interference in university education.

Taking a synoptic view of the role of the British in the field of education, two diametrically opposite views appeared about its impact on the educational and cultural life of our people. On the one hand, many people believed that it opened a window to Western scientific knowledge and its democratic value system. Besides, it resulted in the emergence of a new elite which played a crucial role in our educational and cultural life. Interestingly, it was these new elite which challenged the British rule and ultimately led the country to its independence. On the other hand, a number of leading countrymen like Tagore, Karve, Swami Shraddhanand and Gandhiji were very critical of the new educational system. They pointed out that the basic purpose behind its introduction was to create a group of people who would be Anglophiles, providing a big support base for the British. All these leaders tried to evolve alternative systems of education which, unfortunately, could not assume a mass character.

Taking an overview of the entire educational system introduced by the British, one can safely conclude that it suffered from a number of infirmities. They could be summed up as follows: it neither attempted to universalise primary education nor did it lay proper stress on technical education. Besides, no serious attempts were made to spread education among women and other deprived sections of the Indian society. In a word, the lopsided development of education under the British rule created a number of problems, including widespread inequality in our social system.

The British and the New Polity in India

The British rule also made decisive and lasting impact on the evolution of the nature and structure of the Indian polity. In fact, the British impact in this area was so lasting that it even left its imprint on our constitution, which came into being in the post-independence era. In this section we would be primarily concerned with the evolution of colonial state structure and its impact on the other aspects of our social life.

Soon after the Company Raj came into being in the wake of its victory at Plassey and Buxar, it was realised by the British political establishment that the Company could not be permanently allowed to have a free hand and hence its domain in India had to be brought within the ambit of the British crown. Subsequently, a parliamentary committee was set up in 1772 to look into the matter in its entirety, which ultimately resulted in the Regulation Act of 1773. This Act introduced some government control mechanism over the Company's possessions in India, as the Company had to keep the Government informed about all civil and military developments in India. Another change that was introduced under the new Regulation Act was the status of the Governor of Bengal: he was made Governor-General and governors of two other presidencies, Madras and Bombay, were put under his control. The Governor-General was to be assisted by a Council comprising four members. Besides, the Act also provided for the establishment of the Supreme Court in Calcutta. The passage of Pitt's India Act of 1784 further strengthened the governmental control over the Company in respect of its possession in India. To that end, the Company's Board of Control was reconstituted which was to comprise 6 members, including two ministers of the Government. The newly constituted Board of Control was to guide both the Company's Court of Directors as well as the Government of India. Thus under the new dispensation, the Governor-General was forbidden to take any vital decision on the issue related to war and peace, without the Board of Control being taken into confidence.

The Charter of the East India Company was renewed for another 20 years in 1793. The Charter Act of 1793 provided for the introduction of a new system of written laws which virtually laid the foundation of the rule of law as the law courts were given authority to interpret the laws. The Charter Act of 1813 ended the Company's monopoly of Indian trade, though it was allowed to keep the Indian possessions for another 20 years. The Charter Act of 1833 ended the trading rights of the Company in its entirety as Indian trade was opened for everybody. Besides, the new Charter Act further strengthened the position of the Board of Control vis-à-vis the Company, as its President was made a minister for Indian affairs. The Act provided for the codification of laws and a Law Commission was soon set up. On the recommendation of the Law Commission, such pieces of legislation as the Indian Penal Code and Code of Criminal and Civil laws were soon enacted. Through these Acts everybody became equal in the eyes of law. The Charter Act of 1853 further strengthened the hands of the Government as the Company was allowed to retain its Indian possessions till the Parliament made some alternative arrangements. Besides, the Executive Council of the Governor-General was to consist of 12 members, out of which 6 were to be the legislative members. But the 1857 rebellion changed the entire scenario as through a new Act of 1858 the Government of India came directly under the Crown. The Act instituted the new office of the Secretary of State for India. The Secretary of State was made a member of the British cabinet. This was followed by the Indian Council Acts of 1861 and 1892, which provided for the Indians being associated with the legislative process of the country in a very limited way. The Act of 1909 provided for very limited election and as such, it failed to satisfy the Indian people. The process of election was further strengthened under the Act of 1919, which introduced a new system of dyarchy at the provincial level. This resulted in the limited responsible government at the provincial level. The Act of 1935 did provide for a fully responsible government at the provincial level but it was also hedged by the Governor's impressive powers.

Looking back, it becomes clear that the British Government was not willing to transfer power in the hands of Indians. And whatever little measures of democratisation it took; it was under compulsions of circumstances and not out of a genuine desire for introduction of a responsible government in India.

New Administrative Set-up Under the British Rule

As we have seen, from Lord Cornwallis onward, a strong section of the British establishment believed that the Indian society could be improved only by raising a strong legal, judicial and administrative set-up. The British Utilitarians and the Evangelists gave a big hand to this line of thinking. But behind all the façades for the improvement of the Indian society lay a strong desire for the perpetuation of the British rule in India, with its primary emphasis on the maintenance of law and order. To that end, the British raised three main institutions: the civil services, the police and army, and used them as bulwark for the perpetuation of their rule.

So far as the management of the civil personnel was concerned, till 1833 the court of directors of the East India Company enjoyed full freedom in their selections and appointments. But under the Charter Act of 1833, the civil services came directly under the Board of Control that introduced a system of limited competition which was further strengthened by the Charter Act of 1853. After the Crown takeover of the Indian administration in 1858, an independent Civil Service Commission came into being. But an Indian could not enter it as the examinations were being held only in England. It was only in 1892 that the structure of the civil service was reformed and it came to be called Indian Civil Service (ICS). Theoretically, Indians could compete in the ICS examination, but in practical terms, till 1922 their number remained marginal. It was the Act of 1919 that provided for a separate recruitment examination to be held in India, which greatly enhanced their number in the subsequent years. The members of the Indian Civil Service virtually ran the entire administrative set-up. And it came to be described as a 'steel-frame'. In fact, civil administration became the mainstay of the British rule in India.

Civil administration was heavily backed by the police and army who were ever ready to serve the interests of the colonial administration. It was Lord Cornwallis who created the police set-up of the Company Raj. Earlier, zamindars had enjoyed the policing power. Lord Cornwallis put an end to it. At the grass roots level, the *thana* (police station) was created, which was manned by a daroga. Initially the *thana* was under the control of the District Judge. But in subsequent years, the office of Superintendent of Police at the district level was created, who became the head of all *thanas* falling in that district. Finally, the police set-up at the district level was brought under the control of the District Collector. Apart from maintaining law and order, the police became the main instrument for the suppression of nationalist protest movements as well as for armed insurrections. The army was another pillar of the British rule in India. Though at the level of sepoys, it was primarily manned by the Indians, but at the level of officers it was the British domain. And it was the resentment of the British-Indian at the sepoys' level that greatly contributed to the rebellion of 1857. The Indian army played a crucial role in the British conquest of India. Later on, the army and police were frequently used by the British to suppress the national movement. However, towards the end of the British Rule, there was widespread disaffection and discontent too in the Indian sections of both the army and the police, which weakened the British resolve to hold on to India.

In brief, the entire focus of the colonial administration was on the maintenance of law and order. A dichotomy always existed between the people and the administrative set-up. Perhaps, that was the reason why Indian administration could never become people-friendly and development oriented.

British Rule and Indian Social Structure

So far as the social policy of the colonial rule was concerned, initially it adopted an attitude of non-interference in the societal affairs. Such a policy was based on the Orientalist's perception of the Indian problems. But there was another school of thought comprising Evangelists and the Utilitarians who favoured strong and radical measures on the part of the administration to get rid of certain decadent and obnoxious aspects of Indian social life. Consequently, a number of steps started being taken in the light of the new perception of the problem. The first major step was banning of female infanticide in 1802. It hardly evoked any strong protest from the Indian public. The practice of *sati* was much more complex as it was more widely prevalent than female infanticide. The first major step in this regard was taken in 1813, when the Government decided to fix 16 years as the minimum age for becoming *sati*. Another condition was that her child should not be of less than three years of age at the time of her becoming *sati*. Meanwhile, Raja Rammohun Roy led a campaign against the *sati* practice, which ultimately led to its being banned by the Government in 1829. Another abhorrent system prevalent during those days was that of slavery which was also abolished in 1845. The

Government, despite initial hesitation, did act to remove some of the abhorrent social practices in India. The British rule affected the Indian social system in another way also. The new economic policy followed by the British colonial administration had an unsettling impact on the Indian social structure. The economic policy resulted in the emergence of certain new classes in the Indian society. These new classes primarily comprised landless labour, moneylenders, zamindars, peasant proprietors, urban proletariat, capitalists and above all, a new middle classes. Thus the traditional social structure was certainly undermined by the process of urbanisation and industrialisation coupled with a new legal and judicial system.

In retrospect, the overall impact of the British rule on Indian society was a mixed bag. It did play a role in breaking off the fabric of the traditional Indian society which, unfortunately, created more problems than it solved. The social system, created by the British rule, despite its theoretical egalitarian character, became more exploitative as it created greater inequalities and infirmities. For instance, by completely smashing the traditional system of production, both in the rural and urban areas without laying a well developed system of alternative industrialisation, it created a new class of landless labour which continues to plague the rural life of India even today and might turn out to be the most destabilising factor of its social life. Similarly, by creating a new institution of private property in land, it created a new class of exploiters – zamindars. However, the creation of new middle classes which spearheaded the freedom struggle was one of the positive impacts of the British rule on the Indian social system. But, a hiatus was created between the classes and the masses on account of the former colonial character.

British Rule: A Balance Sheet

A final word is required on presenting a balance sheet of the British rule in terms of its impact on the various aspects of our national life. As noted earlier, there are two diametrically opposite views on the nature of the impact of the British rule: (a) it brought nothing but misery and suffering in its trail for our people; and (b) that despite its apparent weaknesses it was a positive development for our countrymen. Even the Marxist scholars like A R Desai and others have been taking the stand that despite its debilitating impact on the people of India, on balance, the British rule played a positive and progressive role.

Three major contributions of the British rule are generally recognised by many students of Indian history. First, they played a crucial role in creating a new united India. They point out that in the course of its history, India was never united and it never came under one single authority as it did during the British rule. In this connection, it is pointed out that even after partition, the bulk of India remained intact and it covered a much larger area (being brought under one single authority) than it had done during any time in its history. The second contribution of the British rule is that it led to the establishment of a legal system that was marked by the basic principles of the rule of law and equality before the law. Besides, it founded a judicial system that had the potential of being independent. In a word, very sound basic rules of governance were laid down during the British rule, which had stood in good stead even after independence. Thus the basic legal and political structure which the British laid down in the course of their rule in India had all the potential to survive even in post-independence India. It is a different matter that the British in their eagerness to hold on to the empire did not themselves observe the rule of law. It is also being pointed out that the very structure of our constitutional framework bears the imprint of the colonial political structure, which the British raised in the course of their rule in India. The third aspect of the British rule, which has stood the test of time, is the new system of English education which was introduced by the British. Today, if we are on the verge of emerging as a knowledge power in the world, a part of the credit goes to the Macaulay System of Education. Besides, by introducing the new educational system, the British succeeded in producing the 'grave-diggers' of their empire. It was the new elite emerging out of the new educational system, which raised the first banner of revolt against the British. Not only that, they successfully led the national movement till the independence of India in 1947. However, there is no denying the fact that the British evolved and adopted the new educational system as a part of their larger strategy of political and cultural domination.

What about the debit side of the balance sheet? It goes without saying that the British rule brought untold and unprecedented misery for our people in its trail. Famine visited the country regularly, resulting in the death of millions of our countrymen. What is more, the evidence is so overwhelming that even the British had not been able to counter it by producing any creditable facts and arguments. Not only that, serious attempts were made to keep India industrially backward so as to make it a producer of raw material for the British industries and a captive market for their industrial goods. If we simply compare 60 years of our post-independence period with the Company's two century-long rule, the contrast becomes too marked to be lost sight of. Further, it proves not only British complacence but complicity in keeping India industrially backward during the entire period of colonial rule. Finally, what about the partition of India? Even if one accepts that we, as a people, are to blame ourselves, primarily, for our own internal bickering, leading to the partition of the country, the British, however, cannot completely absolve themselves of this gigantic tragedy in which millions of people were uprooted, half a million were killed and thousands of women were raped and murdered.

A final word with Marxist writers like A R Desai, R P Dutta and others who assert that despite its disastrous impact on the Indian economy, the British rule in India laid a foundation for a progressive India, taking her from the feudal to the capitalist stage. The underlying idea behind this Marxist formulation is that the British successfully took India from a backward feudal stage to modern bourgeois society, which is supposed to be a stage ahead. In our view, if slavery and alien rule had played a liberating role in human history, thousands who laid down their lives in the course of our national struggle could have died in vain. The banality of such formulation is only matched by its stupidity. Besides, the worst of all, the British tried to impose cultural hegemony on our people. Thanks to Ramakrishna Paramhansa, Ramana Maharshi, Aurobindo, Dayanand, Vivekananda and last but not the least, Gandhiji, who stood against it and turned the tide of cultural domination, eventually the British could not succeed in this nefarious game. If judged on the negative and positive basis, nothing in the world can be condemned and cursed, as one can always find some positive side in everything. That might be good philosophy but indeed not good politics.

> *I shall only say that such a scene of an anarchy, confusion, bribery, corruption and extortion was never seen or heard of, in any country but Bengal; nor such and so many fortunes were acquired in so unjust and rapacious a manner.*
>
> LORD CLIVE

5 Indian Responses to the British Challenge

Every nation secures precisely as good a government as it merits.

A O HUME

As discussed earlier, the British occupation was the greatest political challenge ever faced by India in the course of her long history. In fact, this was an entirely new and unprecedented challenge and for a while our people could not grasp its full implications. But once they gathered their guts and wits they picked up the gauntlet in three different ways: (a) armed resistance including the 1857 rebellion, (b) social-religious reformation; and (c) new nationalism. In this chapter, we will take up all three expressions of Indian responses to the British challenge for a brief and concise analysis.

The Armed Resistance till the 1857 Rebellion

We have already discussed how Indian peasants and artisans became the worst victims of the British occupation of India. While other sections of society might have their own compensation and consolation, rural India could not see the light even at the end of the dark tunnel in which they had found themselves under the British rule. The fate of some of the dispossessed zamindars was no better. Hence, they did not hesitate to join hands with their less-privileged countrymen. It is not surprising that during the eighteenth and nineteenth centuries, the Indian countryside was marked by a number of peasant's rebellions. Perhaps the first major rebellion was led by Raja Chait Singh of Banaras during 1778-81, which was followed by the revolt of the deposed Awadh Nawab Vizier Ali in 1799. The local zamindars of Awadh continued this tradition of revolt during the early part of the nineteenth century. Similar revolts were led by Bundela chieftains in 1842. But the tradition of rebellion was not confined only to the northern part of the country. In south India, Poligars (local chieftains) launched their rebellion in the beginning of the nineteenth century. Down south, Malabar was also affected by similar uprisings during 1796–1805. However, the British succeeded in suppressing all these uprisings by strong-arm tactics. Indian peasants were also not free from such a rebellious trend. Thus, one of the earliest spontaneous revolts occurred in Rangpur in North Bengal in 1783, on the issue of excessive land revenue exactions on the part of the East India Company. A similar peasant rebellion at Nagar in Mysore state also occurred during 1830–31. At places, religious sensibility also played a role in these rebellions as in the case of the Sanyasi-rebellion and Fakir-rebellion in Bengal during 1763–1800 and also the Wahhabi movement. At a number of places including East Bengal and Malabar Coast (the latter being inhabited mostly by the Moplahs) the Muslim peasantry also revolted. Not only that, even the tribal people revolted on account of the loss of autonomy and governmental interference in the forest and it's produce – once a private domain of the tribal people. Some of the important tribal uprisings were the Bhils insurrection (1819), Kols uprisings of 1830–31, the Santhals-rebellion of 1855–56 and the Munda rebellion (1899–1900). In all these rebellions, excessive exploitation and interference by the Company in the private domains of the people were the main issues. However, all these rebellions were put down with heavy-handed measures by the British.

The Rebellion of 1857

The rebellion of 1857, which V D Savarkar described as India's First War of Independence was the biggest armed rebellion against the Company Raj in terms of its territorial spread and the number of people involved in it.

Briefly stated, it started on 29 March 1857, when Mangal Pandey, a sepoy of the Bengal Army, shot dead his British officer. He was protesting against the introduction of new Enfield Rifles which were allegedly greased by cow and pig fat. The fact that cartridges had to be bitten off before loading gave credence to their suspicion. Hindu and Muslim sepoys of the Bengal Army thought that the Company was out to despoil their religion. The rumour had travelled to a large number of army cantonments spread over different places under Bengal Presidency. The daring act of Mangal Pandey and his subsequent execution had its repercussion: on 10 May 1857, a much bigger rebellion started at Meerut. They killed their British officers and freed their colleagues who had been earlier imprisoned on account of their refusal to use the new cartridges. On 11 May 1857, they marched to Delhi and both persuaded and pressurised Bahadur Shah Zafar, the last Mughal Emperor, to accept the leadership of the rebellion. He was proclaimed as the emperor of Hindustan on that very day. Soon the rebellion spread covering north and central India, and a part of Bengal. However, south India was not touched by the rebellion. A large number of sepoys stationed at Banaras, Allahabad, Bareilly, Jhansi, Danapur and Jagdishpur soon joined the rebellion. At certain places, particularly in the Awadh area, local chieftains and zamindars, persuaded by the sepoys assumed the leadership as they had their own grievances against the Company Raj. Begum Hazrat Mahal of Lucknow, Nana Saheb of Bithoor, Khan Bahadur of Bareilly, Kunwar Singh of Jagdishpur, and Rani Lakshmi Bai of Jhansi soon started leading the rebellion from the front. They had joined the rebellion partly out of their own resentment against the Company Raj and partly under the pressure and persuasion of the sepoys.

Soon the civilian population also joined the rebellion. For a while it seemed that the days of the Company Raj were numbered. But there was swift and strong mobilisation by the British. By 20 September 1857, the British forces supported by Gorkhas and forces from Punjab succeeded in capturing Delhi. Bahadur Shah Zafar's children were captured and killed and he himself was deported to Burma. But that did not mark the end of the rebellion: it continued in other centres like Kanpur, Banaras, Allahabad and a host of other places. In all these places, it had assumed a form of civil rebellion in which people belonging to all sections of the society participated. By the middle of 1858, the rebellion virtually collapsed. Kunwar Singh died in May 1858, the Rani of Jhansi died fighting in June 1858, Nana Saheb fled to Nepal, and Tantia Tope was captured and executed in April 1859 after being betrayed by a local zamindar. Thus by the beginning of 1859 the rebellion was crushed by the British, in which they followed no holds-barred policy.

A number of questions have been raised regarding this rebellion. First, what led to the eruption of such a massive rebellion? The British on their part tried to explain it as a sepoy mutiny, primarily on account of their resentment against the introduction of the new cartridge. But this was an attempt to cover up the seamy side of their colonial rule. Because it does not explain the involvement of masses in the rebellion, which calls for a deeper probe. Historians have found a number of reasons behind the rebellion. They could be summed up as follows:

The Bengal Army was dominated by the upper castes drawn mostly from the Awadh region. They were conscious of their religious and caste sensibilities. Initially, the Company respected their religious sensibility but subsequently it tried to organise the Army on more professional lines. The sepoys perceived it as an attempt on the part of the Company Raj to promote conversion to Christianity. Added to that were the grievances of the local zamindars, nawabs and local chieftains. They had lost everything, including their status, on account of the growing, greedy acquisitiveness of the Company Raj. What was more, peasants and artisans had been ruined by the Company Raj. And armymen, mostly coming from these families, were greatly affected by its excesses and exactions. Besides, Dalhousie's Doctrine of Lapse, which refused to accept the adopted sons as the heirs of the Princely States, had played the real mischief. A large number of states, viz., Sambalpur, Baghat, Udaipur and Jhansi had been annexed on that count. The bulk of the leadership of the rebellion came from the erstwhile rulers of these annexed states. Perhaps, Muslims looked at it as an opportunity for the restoration of their past glory including the restoration of the Mughal Raj. In brief, large sections of Indian society had been licking their wounds and when the rebellion broke out they simply grabbed it as an opportunity. But despite the participation of large sections of the Indian populace, many historians, including R C Majumdar, have refused to accept it as a national rebellion. Their main argument was that it did not present any concrete national alternative and was mostly confined to north and central India. But V D Savarkar insisted that it was nothing less than India's First War of Independence.

Another question that has been asked and often debated is: why did the rebellion collapse?. The reasons are not far to seek. A superior army with greater discipline and better weaponry did not find it difficult to crush the rebellion, more so when they followed a no holds-barred policy in letting loose their entire repressive machinery. Perhaps the disunity among our people also helped the British. A section of the Indians, including the elite of Bengal and Punjab, refused to support the rebellion. A number of Princely States stood by the British. South India remained aloof. Had there been a simultaneous spread of the rebellion all over the country, the British might have been forced to spread their forces thinly and might have failed to suppress it.

Lack of coordination among the leaders of the rebellion also helped the British.

What about its long-term impact? The most concrete fall-out of the rebellion was the end of the Company Raj. The crown took over the reign of India on 2 August 1858. Second, the new administration took a right turn in an attempt to placate the influential sections of the Indian society – the princes and other feudal elements. The reformist agenda slowed down as the new dispensation became more aware of the sensibility of the Indian people. For the people of India the old, traditional elite had lost the game and they had to look for a new leadership from the newly educated classes. Perhaps they could see a ray of new hope and light at the end of the dark tunnel. And, as the subsequent development would show, their hopes were not belied as the newly emerged middle classes were soon to pick up the gauntlet. However, in the wake of the 1857 rebellion, a change of fundamental nature was carried out in respect of the recruitment policy and organising principles of the armed forces. As the people including the army from the Hindi heartland were in the forefront of the struggle, a new recruitment policy for the armed forces was adopted. The new policy shifted the catchment area for the recruitment of soldiers from the Hindi heartland to Punjab and its adjoining areas. A new concept of martial races covering Sikhs, Jats, Rajputs, Dogras and Gurkhas from Nepal was introduced and they were recruited on a mass scale. People from eastern India were virtually left out. A more fundamental change took place in respect of the structure and organisation of the army. The army units started being organised on a caste and regional basis. The idea was to make them conscious of their primordial identities, so that they could never unite and stand under one banner. This was an attempt to rule out any united opposition to the British from the side of the armed forces. It is entirely a different thing that towards the end of the British rule (1946–47), there did emerge a distinct possibility of an army rebellion in the wake of the INA trial and Royal Indian Navy (RIN) Revolt. Perhaps, that was one of the factors which made the British retreat.

Socio-Religious Reforms Movements

A second expression of the Indian response to the British challenge came in the form of the socio-religious reform movements which virtually spread over the major part of the nineteenth century. The leaders of these movements were fully aware of the nature of the twin challenges they were confronted with: the cultural challenge of the West and the challenge to reform the decadent aspects of the Indian society. The western challenge consisted primarily of the work of the Christian missionaries working with an evangelistic spirit for religious conversion. Besides, an attempt was also being made by them to permanently inflict a sense of cultural inferiority among our people. All this was being done to underline the civilising mission of the West. But that was only one aspect of the challenge before the leaders of these movements. They were equally aware of the decadent nature of Indian social conditions manifested in various forms, viz., degrading conditions of women, shudras and other 'low-caste' people, polygamy, polytheism, idolatry, child marriage, widow-burning and female infanticide. They had evolved a two-pronged strategy to meet these twin challenges. Most of them went back to ancient Indian scriptures and tried to argue that prevailing social evils are not in consonance with the original moorings and teachings of the ancient scriptures. Hence, they did not enjoy religious sanction or sanctity. Simultaneously, they tried to meet the challenge of the West by rediscovering the modernity inherent in the Indian tradition. Hence, their message was that our people need not suffer from any sense of cultural inferiority on that count. In fact, they could take pride in our cultural tradition. Besides, they also underlined universalism as a part of our cultural tradition. In fact, universalism was deeply rooted in the all-inclusive nature of our cultural heritage. Apart from universalism they also underlined the symbiotic relationship between faith and reason. In other words, they denied that reason and revelation are mutually exclusive in the case of Indian culture.

Looked at from this perspective, the works of Brahmo Samaj, Arya Samaj, Prarthana Samaj, Theosophical Society and Ramakrishna Mission are not as divergent as they appear on their face value. They might differ on nuances or on the points of laying stress on a particular aspect of cultural heritage; but essentially there was a unity of purpose among all these movements. They were fighting on both fronts and were trying to take the bull of twin challenges by its two horns. They could not have done otherwise in the kind of situation they found themselves. They could not have gone along with all those who were entrapped in the glamour of the rising West. At the same time they could not have turned a blind eye to all the dirt and distortion that had accumulated as a part of Indian heritage. In the name of modernity, they could not fix themselves in the cultural embrace of the West, nor could they take a revivalist road in the name of Indian heritage, which is why even Raja Rammohun Roy and his Brahmo Samaj were not willing to go along entirely with the West, though they did favour Western education and scientific knowledge. Rammohun Roy launched a relentless campaign against social evils prevalent in our society and did not relent from the campaign till the *sati* system was banned by the government in 1829. But he also challenged the Christian Missionaries' claim of superiority of Christianity. He was a great admirer of the Vedantic texts. On the other hand, Swami Dayanand was a strong critic of the entire Semitic religious tradition and, in fact, was ever convinced about the superiority of the Vedas as a repository of all knowledge. He was also a relentless fighter against Brahminic orthodoxy and worked for the complete emancipation of women, shudras and other low-caste sections of the Indian society. Despite his clarion call of 'back to the Vedas', he was no revivalist. Perhaps he contributed more than any other leader towards the modernisation of Indian tradition. He underlined the importance of Swaraj, Swadeshi and Swabhasa. If we look at the working of the reformist groups like Paramhans Mandali, Manav Dharma or Prarthana Samaj in western India, all of them were also working in the same direction. But they differed from their Bengal cousins (Brahmo Samaj) in one respect; unlike the former, the social reformers of Maharashtra did not want to break with the past. In fact, they wanted to work as insiders and not as outsiders.

It is true that these socio-religious reform movements could not build up the kind of mass movement they might have liked to do. But at a critical moment of our history they did help our people to meet the twin challenge of the cultural onslaught of the West, and while playing a crucial role in the modernisation of own tradition. They underlined the role of education in bringing about social changes and pleaded for universalisation of education. They specifically laid emphasis on women's education. They also underlined the contribution of human rationality in social affairs.

But above all, they did create a strong current of nationalist feelings among the Indian people. It is worth noting that Vivekananda, one of the disciples of Ramakrishna Paramhansa put vedantic knowledge on the world map and made Ramakrishna Mission a major instrument of the social and cultural regeneration of India. Swami Dayanand and his Arya Samaj laid a strong foundation of Indian nationalism. In subsequent years, Arya Samaj played a crucial role in the freedom struggle of India. Swami Shraddhanand became a real pillar of Indian nationalism. Second, in the wake of the failure of the great rebellion of 1857, the morale of the Indian people was low and credit goes to these cultural movements which infused a new sense of confidence among our people without which nationalism could not have grown in our country. Third, they did lay a path for the Indian people to walk in pursuit of their socio-cultural salvation. In brief, they created the right environment in which the seeds of nationalism could sprout.

Emergence of Indian Nationalism: The Historical Backdrop

Apart from these two responses, i.e. armed rebellion and socio-cultural reformism, the third response came in the form of Indian nationalism. It underlined the greater unity of the Indian people and provided a new forum for the ventilation of their grievances. This process, ultimately, culminated in the formation of the Indian National Congress (INC) in 1885. However, that momentous event was preceded by a number of other developments. And it is to them that we focus our attention in this section. These background developments leading to the formation of the Indian National Congress could be put into two categories: distant causes and proximate or precipitating causes. We can even study the distant causes under the following sub-categories:

1. Rise of Modern Intelligentsia

As we have seen earlier, the traditional elite comprising nawabs, talukdars and zamindars backed up by peasants and other sections of the society, had tried and failed in their attempt to oust the British from the Indian soil during the 1857 rebellion. Thereafter, they went into disarray: some of them compromised and worked as collaborators with the British, others were destroyed and still others were left to fend for themselves. Thus a vacuum was created at the traditional elite level, which was filled up by the newly educated elite, thrown up by the Macaulay System of Education. These new elites were well-versed in discourses on democracy, rule of law, liberty and equality among men, which was emerging as the reigning ideology of the West. Above all, they were becoming victims of discrimination even at their own personal levels. Moreover, being the product of a new educational system based on English medium instruction, they had developed a pan-India character which enabled them to formulate and articulate the new themes of discourses at an all-India level. All this provided them with a new opportunity to plan an all-India organisation with more pronounced political and economic programmes. It is not surprising at all that they actually founded the Indian National Congress (INC) in 1885.

2. Deteriorating Economic Conditions

The deteriorating economic condition of people which had assumed gigantic form in the last quarter of the nineteenth century created a psychological base for the emergence of the Indian nationalism. In the process of their mass pauperisation, the people came to identify the British colonial rule as the chief villain of the piece. What gave greater credibility to their general perception was the solid intellectual work undertaken by the early nationalists like Dadabhai Naoroji, M G Ranade, R C Dutt and others, who dug out facts and figures to prove beyond any reasonable doubt, that the British rule was definitely contributing to the mass impoverishment of our people. Of particular interest was the Drain Theory which came to be associated with Dadabhai Naoroji. The quintessence of this theory was that the Indian wealth was being drained out to Britain in various ways, viz., salaries and pensions of the British civil and military officials, payment of interest on the loan taken by the Government of India, ploughing back of the profit proceeds to Britain arising from British capital investment in India, and home charges (expenses) on the Indian Government establishment in England. They even identified the actual channel through which the drain of Indian wealth to Britain was taking place: it took the form of an excess of Indian exports over its imports for which India received nothing in economic and material terms. Naoroji even calculated that this drain of Indian wealth amounted to one-third of its total savings. Thus, Naoroji succeeded in establishing a direct correlation between British colonial rule and mass poverty in India. It is true that Naoroji and others did not push their findings to their logical conclusions as they did not demand the end of the British rule. But by focusing on the ugly face of the British rule they greatly contributed to the emergence of Indian nationalism.

3. Contributions of Social-Religious Reform Movements

No discussion on the causes leading to the emergence of Indian nationalism would be complete, without taking into account the contributions of socio-religious movements in this regard. It is true that they became ardent critics of the decadent aspects of the Indian social system, viz., caste system, idolatry, polygamy, child-marriage, widow-burning (*sati*), etc. But at the same time they underlined the significance of some of the key components of ancient Indian heritage, viz., its universalism, rationalism and monotheism, etc. Thus they were working to bring about renaissance, reformation and enlightenment in India at one go. This created a new sense of self-confidence among our people and released a tremendous source of energy. They charted a new path for our people and impressed upon them that some of the key concepts of modern times, like equality, nationalism and universalism are not alien to our real cultural heritage. All these greatly contributed to the emergence of new nationalism in the country.

4. Role of Earlier Political Associations

The formation of the Indian National Congress was preceded by the emergence of a number of secular political organisations which prepared the soil in which the Congress could be planted subsequently. Bengal was the first place where such organisations came first. Bengal British India Society, was founded in 1843 which had been preceded by the Landholders Society of 1837. In 1851, both these organisations merged, and thus came into being the British Indian Association. This was followed by the Madras Native Association and the Bombay Association, both of which came into being in 1852. All these organisations were raising secular issues like excessive land revenue and other related issues. They had a narrow social base and their work was marked by great caution and circumspection, but as pioneers their role could not be minimised. Dadabhai Naoroji organised one such organisation in London in 1860 which was called the East Indian Association. This was followed by the foundation of the Indian Association by Surendranath Banerjea in 1876. The other presidencies soon followed suit. Poona Sarvajanik Sabha organised by Ranade and others and Satya Shodhak Samaj founded by Jyotiba Phule also played a critical role in this regard. Thus came into being a number of associations in other places, viz., Bombay Presidency Association, Madras Mahajan Sabha, Allahabad People's Association and Indian Association of Lahore. All these associations raised issues concerning the people and actually prepared the congenial background for the formation of the Indian National Congress in 1885.

5. Role of the Indian Press and Literature

The protests against the unjust and exploitative nature of the British rule did not end with the failure of the 1857 rebellion. Some of the leading lights of the rebellion of 1857 like Kunwar Singh and Rani Lakshmi Bai were soon turned into icons and a number of patriotic songs were composed praising their heroic deeds. Patriotic songs and dramas started being circulated through fairs and melas and this kept the lamp of nationalism burning. The vèrnacular press also played a leading role in raising the political consciousness of the people. *Bharat Mitra* (Hindi) and *Jam-e-Jahan Numa* (Urdu) are worth mentioning in this regard. The English Press did not lag behind either. *Amrita Bazar Patrika* and *Som Prakash* from Calcutta, *Indu Prakash* and *Native Opinion* from Bombay, and *the Hindu* from Madras played a leading role in building up nationalistic feelings in the country. Litterateurs also lent a helping hand to that venture. Dinabandhu Mitra, the writer of a drama 'Neel Darpan' vividly described the atrocities committed on the indigo growers. Perhaps more than any other writer of his time, Bankim Chandra Chattopadhyaya played a critical role in building up the nationalistic feelings in the country. His song *Bande Mataram* which he later on incorporated in his historic novel *Anandmath* depicted the daring acts of Sanyasi revolts. *Bande Mataram* soon became the battle cry of Indian nationalism. In the Hindi region, Bhartendu Harishchandra played a similar role in arousing and sustaining patriotic feelings among the people of the Hindi heartland.

Proximate or Precipitating Causes for the Emergence of Indian Nationalism

Apart from these distant causes, there were a number of precipitating causes which also contributed to the emergence of Indian nationalism. The most important was Lord Lytton's (the Viceroy of India from 1876–80) new anti-India policy. In the four years of his rule he imposed two draconian acts – Vernacular Press Act (1878) and Arms Act (1877). The Press Act tried to censure, control and dominate the Vernacular Press which had emerged as the strongest medium for the ventilation of the people's grievances. Through the Arms Act he sought to disarm the people of India once for all and, thus, rule out any future possibility of armed resistance to the British. Not only that, he removed import duty on cotton clothes for facilitating greater entry of British textile goods into the Indian market. The lowering of age from 21 to 19 as the maximum age for Indian candidates of ICS examination further alienated the educated Indian middle class: it was seen as an attempt on the part of the Government to prevent Indians from the ICS competition.

All this infuriated the Indian middle classes and a plethora of protest movements were launched in which the Indian Association led by Surendranath Banerjea played a crucial role. Lord Ripon who had

VANDE MATARAM

HAIL to thee, Mother! Thy proud sons greet thee,
Fair as the moon and clear as the sun;
Terrible fair as a bannered army;
Patient and strong till the day be won;
Calling thy sons to the high endeavour;
Sealing them true to the task begun.

Others will fight with hatred and slaying,
Wade to a kingdom through blood outpoured.
We will conquer with God's own armour;
We will slay with the Spirit's sword;
Vanquish by Love that can meekly suffer;
Die and arise in the name of the Lord.

Prophet souls that have watched for the dawning,—
Patient hope in your sleepless eyes,—
Cry and exult! for the flags of morning
Flame on the face of the eastern skies!
Welcome the end of your night's long travail!
See your sun in his strength arise!

India, my India! Mother beloved!
Shatter the chains of thy thraldom past!
Ransom thy captives and raise thy fallen!
Fold to thy bosom thy sons outcast!
Rise in the might of thine ancient splendour!
Shout for thy great Release at last!

J. C. W.

replaced Lord Lytton in 1880, virtually stirred up a hornet's nest when he sought an amendment in the Criminal Procedure Act, so as to empower the Indian Judges of *muffasil* towns to try the European accused involved in criminal cases without jury. He introduced a Bill to that effect which came to be known as Ilbert's Bill. This infuriated the Anglo-Indian community and they rose virtually in rebellion. The Government was forced to withdraw the Bill in the face of a powerful protest from the Anglo-Indian community. This was an eye-opening experience for the Indian political elite: they were now convinced more than ever that a properly organised protest movement could force the Government to make a retreat on any important issue. The Ilbert Bill controversy gave a new urgency for floating an all-India organisation. At the behest of the Indian Association, a national conference was held in Calcutta from 28 to 31 December 1883, which was largely attended, drawing people from all quarters of the country. This experience further encouraged our leaders to call another conference, which ultimately resulted in the foundation of the Indian National Congress in December 1885.

To sum up, India responded to the British challenge in several ways including armed rebellion. But ultimately she opted for a new national movement that led our people to their independence in 1947. In the next chapter we would examining how the first step on the long road to independence was taken in the form of the foundation of the Indian National Congress in 1885.

> *As the Bible says, 'unto everyone that shall be given'. We must be strong in everyway. . . . So long as they (the British) look down upon us they can not fraternise with us. If we stand at their doors with palms over-stretched, we shall only be turned away, again and again.*
>
> RABINDRANATH TAGORE

Part II

The Mainstream of the Indian National Movement

This poverty is the greatest danger both to us and the rulers. In what shapes and varieties or forms the disease of poverty may attack the body politic, and bring out and aggregate other evils, it is difficult to tell or foresee, but that there is danger of 'most serious order', nobody can deny.

Dadabhai Naoroji

We are not armed and there is no necessity for arms either. We have a stronger weapon, a political weapon, in boycott.

Lokmanya Bal Gangadhar Tilak

Non-violence in its dynamic condition means conscious suffering. It does not mean meek submission to the will of the evil doer, but it means the pitting of one's whole soul against the will of the tyrant. Working under this law of our being, it is possible for a single individual to defy the whole might of an unjust empire, to save his honour, his religion, his soul and lay the foundation for the empire's fall or its regeneration.

Mahatma Gandhi

6 Founding of the Indian National Congress

We can't blame them for the attitude they adopted as pioneers of Indian political reform any more than we can blame the brick and mortar that is buried six feet deep in the foundation and plinth of a modern edifice. They had made possible the superstructure . . . of colonial self Government, Home Rule within the Empire, Swaraj and on the top of all, complete independence. . . . If today our course is plain and our goal is obvious, we owe it all to our forebears who did the spade work and cleared the forest.

P SITTARAMAYYA

For several reasons the birth of Indian National Congress towards the end of December 1885 was a historic event in the life of our national movement. In the first place, it was the first major all-India political organisation, committed to pursue common and general political objectives on the national scale. Second, it marked a significant shift in the social base of the political elite: instead of the old aristocratic landed elite comprising zamindars, talukdars and nawabs, the new elite was located in the English-educated, upwardly mobile middle classes. What was more, the new elite was well-versed in the political debates and discourses on democracy, liberty, equality and fraternity – the discourses that were raging all over Europe. Third, it was a natural culmination of the process of socio-politico-cultural initiatives at local and regional levels. And, as such, it was capable of subsuming and even transcending their potentialities and possibilities.

A close look at the list of the founding fathers of the Indian National Congress gives us a comprehensive view of the social and cultural base of the new organisation. Prominent among them were the intellectuals from the three Presidencies of Bengal, Bombay and Madras. From Bengal came W C Bonnerjee, Manmohan Ghosh, Lalmohan Ghosh, and Narendranath Sen, and from Bombay,

Pherozeshah Mehta, Dadabhai Naoroji, Badruddin Tyabji, and K T Telang, while from Madras, G Subramaniya Aiyer, Anand Charlu, S Subramaniya Iyer, and others.

W C Bonnerjee Pherozeshah Mehta

It would be relevant to note that some of the founding fathers were no greenhorn social workers, rather they had already spent considerable time and energy in the cause of the people of their respective areas. Not only that, they had even raised the issues, which concerned the entire country. For example, Dadabhai Naoroji, well-known as a propounder of the 'Drain Theory', was among the first few Indians to have castigated the British for their 'un-British Rule', holding them squarely responsible for the mass poverty of the Indian people. His book *Poverty and Un-British Rule is India* remains till date a classic in the economic history of India. He went to London in 1851, lived there for 25 years, propounded his 'Drain Theory' in 1867, and inspired a generation of Indian leaders like, Pherozeshah Mehta, Badruddin Tyabji, W C Bonnerjee, Manmohan Ghosh, Lalmohan Ghosh and a host of others. Similarly, S Subramaniya Iyer was active in the Mahajan Sabha of Madras while M G Ranade in the Prarthana Samaj of Bombay. In a word, there were a number of concerned intellectuals active in the different parts of the country. What was missing was a uniting link, an inspiring spark, and an honest heart-linker. And that bill was ably fitted by A O Hume, a retired member of the Indian Civil Service. Since A O Hume played the role of a catalyst in the formation of the Indian National Congress, it would be relevant to look at his detailed profile. A man of British descent, Hume had joined the Indian Civil Service in 1851 and retired in 1882. While working in India, he was well acquainted with the problems of India and was in personal contact with a large number of its emerging leaders. He was also a witness to the 1857 rebellion and as such, was convinced about the need for opening a new channel of communication between the British and the Indian people in general and with the Indian leaders in particular. After his retirement in 1882, he had greater freedom and better opportunities to give a concrete shape to his ideas. It is in this perspective that his letter of March 1883, which he addressed to the graduates of Calcutta University, should be viewed. In that letter he called upon them to 'realise the eternal truth, whether in the case of individuals or nations, self-sacrifice and unselfishness are the only unfailing guides to freedom and happiness'. He further opined that if even fifty men could be not found 'with sufficient power of sacrifice' and willing to devote the rest of their lives to the cause, 'then there was no hope for India'.

Hume not only wrote that letter but pursued his ideas with vigour and resolute determination. He also further consolidated his network of personal contacts. In December 1884, Hume went to Bombay to bid farewell to Lord Ripon, the outgoing Viceroy of India and stayed there for three months and impressed upon the leaders of Bombay about the need for a political action. He also discussed with them the details of the political programmes. Subsequently, it was decided that during Christmas holidays in 1885, a national conference would be held. Initially, it was to be known as 'Indian National Union'. Since *Poona Sarvajanik Sabha* offered to host the conference, Poona was the venue chosen for the first conference. The circular, which was issued in March 1885 for the conference, made it clear that the delegates to the conference, to be held at Poona from December 25 to 31, would comprise leading politicians from Bengal, Bombay and Madras Presidencies. The conference was supposed to serve a twofold purpose: to promote personal intimacy and relationship among the invited leaders; and to decide about the political programmes for the subsequent years. On account of the outbreak of cholera in Poona, the venue was shifted to Bombay, and the historic first conference was held on 28 December 1885, in Gokaldas Tejpal Sanskrit College, Bombay. It was attended by 72 delegates. Prominent among those who attended the conference as delegates were: A O Hume (from Simla), Dadabhai Naoroji, K T Telang, Pherozeshah Mehta, D E Wacha, B M Malabari, N G Chandavarkar (from Bombay), W S Apte and G G Agarkar (from Poona), W C Bonnerjee, Narendranath Sen (from Calcutta), Ganga Prasad Varma (from Lucknow), P R Naidu, G Subramaniya Aiyer, M Viraraghavachariar (from Madras), P Kesav Pillai (from Anantpur) and a host of others. W C Bonnerjee presided over the meeting which listed the following major objectives of the Congress:

(i) Promoting personal relationship among the leaders of the country by eradicating all kinds of prejudices – personal, social or racial – leading to consolidation of national unity.
(ii) To lay down the future course of political action.

It is also relevant to note that the president made it clear that the Congress was not going to be 'the nest of conspirators and disloyalists' rather it primarily aimed at representing their well-considered views to the authorities. A perusal of the resolutions passed by the conference makes it clear that they pleaded for the base of the government to be widened by increasing the number of Indians in the legislative councils and raising the age of candidates for the ICS exam, and simultaneously holding of the ICS examination in India and England. They further called upon the government to reduce the military expenditure. Thus the thrust of their demand was appointments of Indians to higher posts in civil services and providing greater say of Indians in the legislative councils.

A number of issues and controversies have been raised about the genesis of the conference. The most significant controversy is about the actual role and motive of A O Hume in the process of the formation of the Indian National Congress. Earlier, it was believed that A O Hume took this initiative for convening the Congress at the behest of the British authorities, particularly at the behest of Lord Dufferin, the Viceroy of India. It was further believed that Hume, prompted by Lord Dufferin, wanted Congress to be used as a 'safety valve', a peaceful and constitutional outlet for the discontent among the educated Indians. And, thus the aim was to thwart any threat to the British rule. With the opening of the Dufferin papers, the myth of 'safety valve' and conspiracy theory has been exploded. As per Bipan Chandra, there is not even a shred of evidence in his papers to prove the earlier apprehension. Besides, a survey of the general political scene of the period would reveal that there was a very strongly felt-need for an all-India political organisation to meet the rising hopes and aspirations of the middle classes of India. Thus, the formation of the Indian National Congress was a culmination of a long process of political work rather than a result of whims and fancies of any individual or group of individuals. It did mark a distinct phase in the emergence and growth of Indian nationhood.

A second related question is: why did the Indian leadership of the Congress accept the pivotal role of A O Hume in the entire process of the formation of the Congress? To understand this question, we may recall the exact nature of the then-prevailing political scene in the country and hostility and suspicion on the part of the colonial administration against any voice of protest and dissent. Perhaps the events of the 1857 rebellion and the subsequent uprisings of the people like Indigo riots of Bengal in 1859, tribal revolts in Chhota Nagpur and a host of other anti-British events had made them very suspicious about any Indian groupings. Thus, the close association of A O Hume in the initial stages gave a certain legitimacy and protection to the Indian members of the Congress, which was badly needed to protect the Congress saplings from the inclement weather of the British hostility. Hume provided that much sought-after cover – a fact which was underlined by Gopal Krishna Gokhale when he said: 'No Indian could have started the Indian National Congress. . . . If the founder of the Congress would not have been a great Englishman and distinguished official such was the distrust of political agitation in those days that the authority would have at once found some way or the other of suppressing the movement'.

Another question that has been raised by some scholars and historians is about the representative character of the delegates who attended the first Congress in Bombay in December 1885. Their representative character has been challenged both on the counts of regional and class imbalance. It is argued that among the provinces Bombay, Calcutta and Madras had the lion's share of the delegates. Thus, out of 72 delegates 21 came from Madras, 4 from Bengal, 37 from Bombay, 7 from North Western Province and Awadh and 3 from Punjab. Thus it is argued that there was no balanced regional representation in the first Congress and, hence, it could not claim to represent the different regions of the country. Similarly, it is also argued that despite its claim to the contrary, viz., Congress being the representative organisation of all Indians irrespective of caste, creed, profession, trade and occupations, the fact remained that there was a great disparity in the social and class composition of the delegates. Among the classes, the middle class was heavily represented, among the professionals, lawyers were in an overwhelming number (as 39 out of 72 delegates were from the legal profession). Among the castes, the brahmins were overrepresented. The two classes conspicuous by their absence were landed aristocracy and the common masses. Once again, we have to recall and understand the social conditions of the country during that time. Admittedly, this was a gathering of the newly emerged English-educated middle classes. Hence, they were bound to be present in large numbers. Besides, all over the world the first political stirrings come from the middle class and other classes join the movement at a later stage. A close study of all communist revolutions will also bear a testimony to this social rule. So there is nothing surprising if the common masses did not join the party in the first instance. So far as participation of the landed aristocracy, zamindars and nawabs was concerned, they had been decisively beaten during the 1857 rebellion and, hence, their conscious absence was quite understandable.

Another question has been asked about the nature of the demands put forward by the first Congress. The first Congress altogether adopted nine resolutions on different subjects. In brief, the Congress demanded Indian association and participation in composition and functions of the central and provincial legislative councils; holding of the Indian Civil Service examination simultaneously in Britain and India; and raising of qualifying age of candidates for the ICS examination, which had been earlier reduced from 21 to 19. Besides, it demanded a reduced expenditure on the army, condemnation of annexation of Burma, abolition of Indian Council for Secretary of State and making him (Secretary of State) responsible to the British parliament.

Three points need to be noted in respect of the disparity in regional representation of the Congress. In the first place, it is relevant to note that the conference of Indian National Association was being held in Calcutta during the same period (December 1885) when the first Congress was meeting in Bombay. Hence, even Surendranath Banerjea could not attend the Congress and that explains the small representation from Calcutta in the first Congress. Second, Congress was aware of the need for eliminating the regional disparity, which is why two decisions were taken at the very inception of the Congress. It was decided that the Congress session would be held annually in different parts of the country, and the President would be from the region in which the conference was being held.

It has been further argued that in terms of communal representation also, there was an imbalance, as only two Muslim delegates attended the conference. Here a number of points need to be emphasised. In the first place, it is to be remembered that Sir Syed Ahmad Khan, the founder of the Aligarh School, was opposed to the Muslim participation in the Congress and had even given a call for a boycott of the Congress. Despite this, the number of Muslim representation increased at least in the first few sessions of the Congress. Second, it has to be remembered that Congress was so much concerned about this problem that in 1888 it was decided that no resolution would be passed if it was objected to by an overwhelming majority of the delegates of any community. Third, it has to be remembered that the number of the English-educated elite among the Muslim community was much less than Hindus and other communities, as Muslim elite primarily came from the Persian-educated landed aristocracy. Hence their representation was found to be much, much, less than the Hindus even in terms of their population. So far the question of non-representation of the non-elite groups of the Indian society is concerned, it was on account of non-inclusion of that section in the English education system rather than any deliberate attempt on the parts of organisers. In sum, the Congress was demanding a share in the governance for the Indians which should not only serve the interests of elite classes but might serve those of the entire Indian people. Thus, it would not be correct to say that they were only concerned about their own class interests and were totally oblivious of those of the masses.

To sum up, the birth of the Indian National Congress in December 1885 marked a new and decisive phase in the history of Indian nationalism. The new organisation provided a broad national platform for (a) discussing the burning problems of the country and its people, (b) formulating befitting policy and programmes, (c) articulating concrete demands and (d) for taking up a plan of action to further the cause. Once these demands were put in well-reasoned documents, a serious attempt was made to create favourable public opinion around them so that both the colonial administration as well as the British could be persuaded, and if possible could be pressurised, to concede these demands. What was more, it was highly creditable to the Congress that from the very inception it got itself committed to work for the national unity and a new awakening among our people transcending the great divides of caste, creed, region and religion. Thus the 72 delegates who gathered in Bombay in December 1885 were real pathbreakers, the real sappers and miners of the struggle for independence. They sowed the seeds of a new national unity and awakening which amply flourished, subsequently, under the towering and inspiring leadership of Mahatma Gandhi. They took the first step of a long journey, ultimately leading the country to independence on 15 August 1947. The fact that their pace was slow and marching movements were halting, does not take away anything from their role as the pathfinders for our national struggle. Writing in 1905 in the context of the partition of Bengal, Dadabhai Naoroji underlined the real worth of the work of the early nationalists when he said:

> The very discontent and impatience it (Congress) has evoked against itself as slow and non-progressive among the rising generation are among its best results or fruits. The real task is to evolve the required revolution whether it could be peaceful or violent, the character of the revolution will depend upon the wisdom or unwisdom of the British Government and action of the British people.

These were really prophetic words coming from one of the early prophets of Indian nationalism.

Sons of Ind, why sit ye idle
Wait ye for some Deva's aid
Buckle to, be up and doing
Nations by themselves are made.

UNKNOWN POET

7 The Moderates and the Indian Freedom Struggle

Let us not forget that we are at a stage of the country's progress when our achievements are bound to be small and our disappointments frequent and trying. . . . It will, no doubt, be given to our countrymen of future generations to serve India by their success; we of the present generations would have to serve her mainly by our failures.

GOPAL KRISHNA GOKHALE

In the preceding chapter, we have traced out the formation of the Indian National Congress (in 1885) as well as the major contours of its policies and programmes at the time of its inception. It is relevant to note that the slow and diffident response of our people to the stupendous challenge, arising out of the British stranglehold on our national life, virtually set the parameters of political actions on the part of the Congress. There is almost unanimity among the scholars of our freedom struggle to call the first twenty years of the Congress (1885–1905) as the phase of the Moderates. One reason for the first generation of the Congress leadership to be called Moderates was to differentiate them from the other two streams of our national struggle, viz., the Extremists and the revolutionaries, who dominated the next stage of our national movement. Another reason for their being called Moderates was that they were inspired by the British liberal tradition known for its moderate political stance. The fact that they were modest in presenting their political demands as well as in means and methods of pursuing them was yet another reason for their being called the Moderates.

As noted earlier, in the initial years the Congress was dominated by the middle class leadership and that too, coming primarily from three presidencies, viz., Bengal, Bombay and Madras, which is why the Congress remained a middle class organisation in its initial stages. It is worth-mentioning that the old aristocracy was too skeptical about the new leadership, in fact too scared of the British wrath to join hands with the new organisation. Similarly, the masses were too repressed to lend their shoulders to the new movement. And, therefore, the role of the Moderates in the freedom struggle would have to be appraised keeping in mind all these constraints.

The Moderates: The Basic Approach

The ideological foundation of the Indian National Congress under the leadership of the Moderates was primarily inspired by the British liberal tradition, comprising lofty ideas of liberty, justice, democracy, rule of law, impartiality of state, and a close association of the people with their governance. Moreover, they had firm faith in the British sense of equity, justice and fairplay. In fact, they even went to the extent of believing in the providential nature of the British rule in India. This was so much blended in their psyche that Dadabhai Naoroji, one of the leading lights of the early Congress, went to the extent of saying that it would be a sad day, nay, the day of disaster, if the British were to quit India, which is why they never challenged the continuation of the British rule in India. But what appalled them was the 'un-British Rule' of the British in India: their colonial administration was totally at variance with their political philosophy and precepts. However, here again they took it more as an aberration rather than the natural corollary of the British rule in India. And for these acts of aberration, they viewed the colonial bureaucracy as the chief villain of the piece. It was from this basic understanding of the British rule that they reached the conclusion that if the un-British character of the colonial administration was properly exposed through well-reasoned arguments, well-collected and collated facts and figures, the British could be persuaded to follow a new policy, more beneficial to the people of India. Furthermore, they were convinced that the iniquities and injustices of colonial rule could be corrected, if properly formulated and well-articulated demands were put forward before the enlightened British public opinion. Hence, they seriously engaged themselves in exposing the iniquitous nature of the colonial administration and, in making serious attempt to get it corrected through well-informed debates. However, they were not totally unamenable to the changing contours of the Indian political scene. This could be illustrated by the fact that in the wake of the partition of Bengal, they also started talking of 'swaraj' and 'dominion status' for India. They even went to the extent of supporting the resolution on boycott and 'swadeshi' at the Calcutta session in 1906. But all this was more under the compulsion of circumstances rather than out of genuine conviction. That could be proved by their role in the Congress split of 1907, better known as the Surat-split which made the Extremist leadership walk out of the Congress – leaving the Moderates to pursue their policy of 'political mendicancy'. The essential nature of their demands for Indians were based on the premise that the Congress was a body of loyalists and not that of 'conspirators'. Hence, they were of the opinion that their association and participation in the administrative and legislative works would certainly enhance the quality of both administration and legislation. It was this rock-bottom of their faith which informed all their demands, ranging from the repeal of unjust laws to the greater participation of Indians, both in administration and legislative processes.

The Moderates: Their Policies and Programmes

It is in this perspective that we would examine the Moderates' policies and programmes in different areas. We can discuss these under three categories:

Administrative Demands

The Moderates' demands in the administrative field arose from their basic understanding that for all the ills and iniquities of the colonial rule, the bureaucracy was the chief villain of the piece. This was so because Indians were not given an opportunity to work in the higher echelons of the administration and they were primarily confined to the lower levels. For instance, there were two problems concerning the ICS examination: (a) the examinations were being held exclusively in England, which proved too expensive and inconvenient to Indians; and (b) the maximum age of qualifying the examination was as low as 19 years, making it very difficult for Indian aspirants to compete. Further, the Moderates were also convinced that to make the British administration more responsive to the hopes and aspirations of the Indian people, better service conditions at its lower levels and greater number of entries at the higher level were required. They further underscored the point that the bureaucrats of British descent were a great burden to the Indian exchequer on account of their high salaries and allowances. This along with the 'home charges', the British expenses on the Indian administration, was proving to be a liability on the Indian exchequer. In view of these facts, they put forward the following major demands in the administrative field:

(i) They pleaded for the Indianisation of the colonial administration. To that end, they demanded holding of the examination for the ICS in India and England simultaneously.
(ii) They also demanded better salaries for the employees of the lower grade, which was primarily manned by the people of Indian origin.
(iii) Better promotional avenues for Indian employees.
(iv) Raising the upper qualifying age limit for the ICS exam.

Economic Demands

As noted earlier, the Moderates' critique of British imperialism remains, till today, as one of their most seminal contributions. Some of the Moderates, namely, Dadabhai Naoroji, G Subramaniya Aiyer and R C Dutt produced well-documented studies to conclusively prove that the British rule was primarily responsible for the total ruination of the Indian handicrafts industries as well as Indian agriculture, resulting in the mass pauperisation of the Indian people. Through their studies, they further demonstrated that India went through a phase of 'de-industrialisation' under the British rule. In fact, India was gradually turned into an industrial-goods importing and raw-material exporting country. They also underlined the fact that the Indian economy remained attached to the apron-strings of British economy, and in the process it became not only subordinate but also subservient to the British economic interests. What was more, India has been unabashedly turned into a hunting ground for profit-seeking foreign investors, particularly in the arena of plantations, railways and other industries. They also presented a critique and opposed the British policy of 'free-trade' which was resulting in the strangulation of the nascent Indian industries by encouraging import of British industrial goods. One of the stalwarts of the Moderate school, Dadabhai Naoroji, propounded his much-publicised 'Drain Theory' which, in substance, argued that Indian wealth was being drained out to England on account of 'home-charges', ploughing back the profit of the British investment in India, as well as on account of high salaries and allowances of the bureaucrats of British descent working in India. As a remedial measure, the demand of tariff-protection for Indian industries was raised. They even went to the extent of demanding state-assistance for Indian industries. To sum up, it could rightly be asserted that so far as the economic critique of the British rule was concerned, the Moderates did not mince words. And, in fact, they made bold, categorical and well-reasoned formulations exposing the dark faces of British imperialism. And in the process, they trashed the British claim of the benevolent nature of their rule. Thus the Moderates conveyed a powerful message: there was a direct correlation between the British rule and mass poverty in India, which, in turn, resulted in mass disaffection among the Indian people. And it was the mass discontent which, subsequently resulted in radical demands like swadeshi and swaraj, culminating in purna swaraj. For a better understanding of the Moderate's work in the economic field, let us put their economic demands in more concrete forms. Among other things they demanded:

(i) Cessation of 'free trade' policy and tariff-protection for the Indian industries
(ii) State assistance for the nascent Indian industries
(iii) Drastic reduction of land revenue
(iv) Immediate cessation of the drain of wealth from India to England
(v) Cessation of the exploitation of the workers of the plantation industries
(vi) Permanent land revenue and reduction of water-cess
(vii) Appropriate changes in the forest law to make it people-friendly
(viii) Abolition of the excise-duty on cotton manufactured goods
(ix) Reduction of salt tax
(x) Raising the tax incidence on intoxicants except for those being used for medical purposes.

Political Demands

Admittedly, the Moderates adopted a very cautious and modest approach to their political demands. As mentioned earlier, they looked at the British rule as a boon in disguise and even went to the extent of acclaiming its providential nature. It may be noted that the Indian Councils Act of 1861 had provided for the inclusion of a few non-official members in the council to be nominated by the government. These non-official members, more often than not, toed the official line. The Congress demanded amendments to the original Act in the very first session in 1885 and went on reiterating and somewhat expanding its demands on this score. The Congress pleaded for: (a) widening of the powers of the Councils both at the provincial and Central levels; (b) the right of members to discuss all administrative matters including the budget; (c) election of the non-official members, instead of being nominated, and similar Councils be constituted in NWP, Awadh (UP) and Punjab. The Congress further demanded that a standing committee of the House of Commons should be set up to receive and consider the formal protests from the majority of the council members against any bureaucratic actions. Subsequently, in 1886, the Congress demanded that 50 per cent of the Council's members should come through election. The members to the local councils were to be elected by municipalities, local boards, chambers of commerce and universities. And the members to the Supreme Council were to be elected by the local councils.

It was on persistent demands of the Congress that the Indian Council Act of 1892 was passed, which partially conceded these demands on some counts. It conceded the right of interpolation for the members of the Council, though the concomitant demand for their right to preface their question with a brief explanation was not conceded. Thus, the Act of 1892 did not really provide for election of the representatives to the Legislative Councils in the real sense of the term. Similarly, the Act did concede the members' right to discuss the budget but they were not given the right to vote on the budget. Subsequently, the Congress under the leadership of the Moderates further raised its demand: they wanted elected members to have majority positions in the Councils. Besides, they also pleaded that these members must be given control over the Indian purse reminding the British of the slogan raised during the American War of Independence, 'no taxation without representation'. However nothing much came out of these demands. But they persisted, and by the beginning of the first decade of the twentieth century they further raised their political demands to the level of self-government, based on the pattern of self-governing colonies of Canada and Australia. The demand was raised to a still higher level when, in the Calcutta Congress (1906) they went to the extent of demanding 'swaraj'. The same session further demanded adequate representation of Indians in the Council of Secretary of State and in the Executive Councils of the government of Madras and Bombay and also greater autonomy for the local self-government bodies, freeing them from excessive official control. Thus, without challenging the very basis of the British rule, the Moderates went on raising their political demands keeping them in tune with the changing times.

The Moderates and the Issue of Civil Liberty

As noted earlier, the Moderates, being inspired by the British liberal tradition, were bound to be deeply concerned about the issues affecting civil liberties of the people. Besides, being representatives of the Indian middle classes, they were directly affected by any governmental act curtailing civil liberties. The freedom of press and expression became one of the cardinal principles of their belief system. Even before the formation of the Congress in 1885, some of them had successfully opposed the Vernacular Press Act of 1878, which tried to curb and control the press. Not only that, whenever the government tried to curb the freedom of the press, the Moderates lodged strong protests. For example, when Tilak was tried and awarded 18-months rigorous imprisonment for his writings in his paper *Kesari* and *Maratha*, all nationalists including the Moderates unitedly rose to the occasion to protest against it and held protest rallies all over the country. The Moderates were in the forefront of the protest even though they had their own differences with Tilak. Similarly, they demanded the separation of judicial powers from the executive power, which was vitiating the entire process of delivery of justice in the country. The problem was that at the district level, the collector was both the judicial and executive head, which marred fairplay of the judicial system. To protect and promote the civil liberties of the people, the Moderates also demanded the extension of the jury system as an integral part of the judicial system. Similarly, they pleaded for the abolition of the Arms Act (1877) which curbed the right of Indians to bear arms. Some of the other demands put forward by the Moderates to widen and strengthen the arena of the people's liberties were: (a) abolishing of the system of *begar* (forced labour) and Rasad (forced contribution of supplies) and repealing of the Sedition Act of 1898 and Criminal Procedure Code Amendment Act of 1898, and repealing of Official Secrets Act of 1904. In fact, whenever there was any threat to the civil liberties, the Moderates raised their voice: they demanded repealing of Criminal Law Amendment Act of 1908, as well as the Indian Press Act of 1910.

The Congress also raised a number of other miscellaneous demands. The Congress, from time to time, passed a number of demands in the field of education, local self-government, and foreign affairs. It is clear from the preceding discussion that the Moderates did not hesitate in raising any issue affecting the lives of our people. In the perspective of our radical times, these demands, it is true, appear more moderate than radical. However, there is little doubt that they were quite progressive if we take into account their constraining context.

The Moderates: Their Methods and Instruments

Finding suitable means and methods of political action is almost a stupendous and challenging task for any political group, particularly for the first generation of leadership. Hence, the Moderates being the first generation of freedom fighters, were also confronted with this problem. Therefore, they engaged themselves in creating a favourable public opinion both in India and England to persuade and pressurise the colonial administration to concede their major demands. To that end, they preferred prayerful petitioning, publicity and public meeting. One of the major means for their public works was organising and addressing public meetings in which they delivered well-informed and well-reasoned speeches to politically educate the people about the nature of the problems and solutions thereof. They used these meetings for passing resolutions which contained an analysis of the problem and suggested remedial measures. A second, and perhaps more effective, means they adopted was making use of the press for publicising their demands. They were in the forefront of the fight for freedom of the press. In this connection it is also relevant to note that some of the early nationalists leaders edited newspapers and magazines and used them effectively to propagate their views. For example, Surendranath Banerjea edited *Bangalee*, Subramaniya Aiyer edited *Hindu*, Gokhale, *Sudhara* and Naoroji edited *The Voice of India*. All of them used these papers to highlight the burning problems of their times. Another means used by them for putting forward their demands was submission of well-drafted memoranda and memorials to the government. And even the cold and indifferent attitude of the government could not deter and discourage them. Commenting on the real significance of their memoranda, Justice Ranade said 'these memorials are nominally addressed to the government, in reality, they are addressed to the people so that they learn how to think in this matter'. He further observed, 'This work must be done for many years without expecting any other result because the politics of this kind is altogether new in this land'.

In fact, the Moderates had so much faith in the efficacy of publicity that they even tried to beard the British lion in its own den. They set up a British committee of the Indian National Congress in England in 1889 and subsequently floated a journal called *India* to mobilise the British public opinion about the Indian conditions. Not only that, Naoroji became a member of the British Parliament to further their cause from inside the House.

Another method used by the early nationalists was their work in the Supreme Council, which provided them with an opportunity to expose the unjust nature of the British rule. Even though they were not happy with the new Council Act of 1892, that did not prevent them from using it to the fullest extent. Some of the prominent Moderates like Surendranath Banerjea, C Shankaran Nair, Gopal Krishna Gokhale, Pherozeshah Mehta made significant contribution to the proceedings of the Council. They exposed the misdeeds of the colonial administration through their well-reasoned speeches in the Council. Pherozeshah Mehta did not hesitate to take up cudgels on behalf of the local bodies when the amendment to the Police Act of 1861, seeking enhancement of police powers over local bodies, came before the Council. Subsequently, Gokhale took his place and his speeches in the Council were the epitome of eloquence, elegance and oratory, so much so that even his opponents started admiring him and treating him as the 'leader of the opposition'. Gokhale's speeches in the Council, opposing the University Act of 1904 and the partition of Bengal (1905), became memorable both for his passionate oratory and persuasive skills.

Gopal Krishna Gokhale

The Moderates and Their Critics

The Moderates were subjected to severe criticisms by militant nationalists. They have also been critiqued by the historians and other scholars. It would be expedient for us to recall some of these critical comments for making a real appraisal of their contributions to the national cause. The real touchstone for testing their worth is what was the British response to their demands and to what extent the people responded to their public education campaign.

Let us have a look at the major criticisms the Moderates have been subjected to over a long period of time. In the first place, their works and achievements have been trashed; their pusillanimous style of working has been ridiculed and they have been even accused of being hand in glove with the British. Besides, their instrumentality of work is said to have no cutting edge. While reviewing their work Lala Lajpat Rai, one of the leading lights of the militant school, made a caustic comment when he said: 'after more than twenty years of more or less futile agitation for concessions and redresses of grievances they have received stones in place of bread'. Thus their overall work and achievements have been trashed by their contemporary militant nationalists.

A second line of attack on the Moderate policy has been on the means they chose to employ to achieve their objectives. As they primarily believed in prayerful petition to the British, they were accused of being 'political mendicants' by their more extremist colleagues. Distinguishing the methods of Moderates and the Extremists, Tilak rightly observed 'the old party (the Moderates) believes in appealing to the British, and we (the Extremists) do not'.

A third criticism against the Moderates has been that there was a contradiction in their perception and practice. Their understanding of the role of the British in the ruination of the Indian national economy, resulting in the mass poverty of our people, logically called for a more radical set of political demands and more militant forms of action. But they dithered on this count and their actions did not match with their words. It is further argued that even when they started talking in terms of 'self-government' and swaraj with dominion status', it was more under the pressure of the Extremist's politics rather than on their own convictions. Besides, they continued to confine themselves within the four walls of constitutionalism so far their agitational plan was concerned. Thus they did not pursue the more radical line of action, which logically flowed from their analysis of the British rule.

A fourth point of criticism against them is about their failure to create a mass movement. This has been basically attributed to their middle class background which created a hiatus between them and the common masses. Similarly, it is said that they failed to keep the national movement united: both Extremists and the Muslim leadership could not be integrated in the national movement under the leadership of the Moderates. In fact, they cooperated with the British in making the Act of 1909 which provided for a separate electorate for the Muslims. They not only failed to oppose it, but Gokhale, the tallest among them, even supported it in his own way.

Lastly, it has been further argued that even the British, to whom, the Moderate leadership always looked up to, had a sceptical, nay hostile attitude to their work. For instance, Viceroy Dufferin, who was a witness to the birth of the Congress, expressed his apprehension that in course of time the Congress might put forward demands, which would be impossible to grant. Besides another Viceroy, Lord Curzon, even went to the extent of vowing to work for the peaceful demise of the Congress. Not only that, the British used the Moderate leadership to further the ends of their policy of 'divide and rule'. They played the Moderates against the Extremists and the Muslim minority against the Hindu majority. And, there is no denying the fact that the Moderates willingly or unwillingly became the playmates of the British in their policy of 'divide and rule'. As such, the British response to the Moderates always remained a mixed bag – its policy swinging from trivial but tantalising reforms to terrorising repression. And, in all this the Moderates remained a willing partner of the British.

In the defence of the Moderates, it could be fairly argued that despite all their weaknesses, they did play a vital role in getting some constitutional reforms done which heralded a new era of democratisation of Indian politics. For instance, it was because of their persistent effort that the Indian Council Act of 1861 was amended in 1892, paving the way for somewhat greater association of the Indians with administrative and legislative works. This was followed by the Acts of 1909, 1919, and 1935, leading to further democratisation of Indian politics. The Moderates did play some role in the making of all those Acts. Not only that, it was on their initiative that some of the Indians got high positions of responsibilities like High Court Judges, memberships of Executive Councils, etc., which they held with great dignity and ability. The Moderate leadership could legitimately claim credit for the gradual transfer of power to the people of India.

However, for making a more dispassionate appraisal of their contributions to the national movement, a better understanding of all the practical constraints and limiting political circumstances in which they were pursuing their objectives is called for. The bitter memories of the First War of Independence (1857), in which the Indian people had been beaten decisively, were still fresh in the minds of the people. Besides, the British imperialism was on its ascending height with all its repressive wherewithal at its disposal. And, the morale of our people was low and their suffering and fear were immense. All this must have weighed heavily on the minds of the Moderate leadership. Perhaps that partially explains their hesitant, halting political action and even 'political mendicancy'. Being the pathfinders, nay, the sappers and miners of the national movement, they had to walk very cautiously and carefully.

But with all their limitations, they undeniably did make some seminal contributions to the national movement. In the first place, they laid the foundation of the national movement upon which its entire edifice was built up by the leaders of subsequent generations. Second, in the form of the Indian National Congress, they created an all-India organisation transcending caste, creed, region and religion, which ultimately became the main instrument and vehicle of our freedom struggle. Third, they in fact ignited and fomented people's discontent against the British rule which came to be identified as the first cause of popular revolt. Indeed, they themselves could not turn this latent mass disaffection into mighty and concrete agitational politics. However, they did succeed in sending powerful messages underlining the basic contradiction between the interests of the British and those of the Indian people, which ultimately snowballed into a mighty stream of national struggle. Besides, they also laid down the basic ideological planks of our national life: unity of India, modern progressive and secular state, modernisation of national economy, firm faith in the rule of the law and liberty of citizens and shared life for our people, cutting across the barrier of caste, creed, colour, region and religion. By any standard, this was no small achievement on the part of the Moderates.

There are (among the European officials) who think that unless an Indian speaks to them with bated breath and whispering humilities, he is seditious.

Gopal Krishna Gokhale

8 Partition of Bengal and the Swadeshi Movement

The tremendous upheaval of popular feelings, which has taken place in Bengal in consequence of the partition, will constitute a landmark in the history of national progress.

GOPAL KRISHNA GOKHALE

Partition (Bengal) grievance will be the edifice for the regeneration of India.

BAL GANGADHAR TILAK

The Partition of Bengal (1905) and its twin the Swadeshi Movement (1906–8) marked a decisive phase in the history of our freedom struggle. It not only revolutionised the political life of Bengal, but also led to the emergence of Extremist politics and violent revolutionary movements in India. It also helped in forging new and powerful instruments of national struggle, viz., boycott, Swadeshi, passive resistance, national education and even armed resistance. Moreover, it sowed the seeds of mass movements and militant protests, which flourished and fructified under the dynamic leadership of Mahatma Gandhi in subsequent years.

To begin with, let us try to understand the background of the partition of Bengal. In this connection, a brief discussion on the role of Sir Syed Ahmad Khan is relevant. He began his career as a moderniser of the Muslim community. To that end, he not only tried to interpret the Koran to the changing spirit of his times but also founded the Mohammedan Anglo-Oriental College at Aligarh in 1875, with a view to spread modern education among the Muslim community. He tried to tackle the problem of educational backwardness among the Muslims, who had been left behind the Hindus on account of their cultural resistance to modern education. Therefore whatever new jobs were coming, the Muslim community found it difficult to get its due share.

Initially, he was a supporter of Hindu-Muslim unity and even called India as the 'motherland'. What changed his perspective was the emergence of the Indian National Congress in 1885, which started with its demand for Indianisation of government service and greater association of Indians in the governance of the country. This frightened leaders like Sir Syed Ahmad Khan who feared further marginalisation of the Muslim community. Added to this, the Congress, from its very inception looked at India as a nation based on universal citizenship. But Sir Syed Ahmad Khan looked at India as a 'federation of *Quoms*' (ethnic community) based on common descent. Not only that, he believed that Muslims should enjoy greater share in power as they belonged to the erstwhile ruling community. He not only did not attend the foundation conference of the Indian National Congress in 1885, but also called upon the Muslims to keep away from it. He used the Mohammedan Educational Conference from 1886 onward to spread his ideas as well as to consolidate the Muslim community. The British bureaucracy was also getting scared of the rising tide of Indian nationalism represented by the Congress. As such, the Congress started being taken as the chief villain of the piece both by the British and by some sections of Muslim leadership, led by Sir Syed Ahmad Khan. Perhaps Theodore Beck, the Principal of the Aligarh School, played a crucial role in bringing Sir Syed Ahmad Khan closer to the British bureaucracy. It is relevant to mention here that with all his limitations, Khan never allowed ulemas and mullahs to play the centrestage role in his movement. But after his death, the younger leadership of the Aligarh School, particularly Muhammad Ali and Shaukat Ali came under the influence of a well-known Ulema Maulana Abdul Bari. That, started the process of Islamisation of Muslim politics. It is this paradigm shift in the thinking of the Muslim leadership which laid the foundation of Muslim communal politics in India.

The British found a groundswell of Islamic sentiments which could be used as a counterveiling force to checkmate the rising tide of the Indian National Congress. Perhaps, the personal predilection of Lord Curzon, the Viceroy of India (1898–1905), also played an exceptionally crucial role in designing and executing the partition of Bengal. Lord Curzon was a known anti-Indian hand and also a hard-headed imperialist. During his Viceroyalty, he initiated a number of draconian measures to curb and control the freedom of the people and their institutions. The Calcutta Corporation Act (1899), the Official Secrets Act (1902) and Indian University Act (1904) were some of his notorious measures. But the worst was still to come: he partitioned Bengal in 1905, which turned out to be the last straw on the people's patience.

Bengal was indeed a big province in terms of population, which comprised almost 78 million – constituting a quarter of the population of British India. Thus it was rightly considered to be administratively unwieldy and even unmanageable. It was on account of its unwieldy size that the division of Bengal Presidency was being considered, since the days of the Orissa famine of 1866. It is also relevant to note that since 1874, when Assam was separated from Bengal, many proposals were mooted to include some areas from Bengal to Assam. But nothing came out of such ideas. Lord Curzon mooted the idea of the partition of Bengal in 1903 and put forward a concrete proposal. Immediately Bengal rose in opposition and even the Moderate leadership of the Congress disfavoured the idea. There were widespread protests and measures like petitions, public meetings, and memoranda were being used against the idea of partition. All this fell on the deaf ears of the British, as it yielded no concrete results. Thus the partition of Bengal in its final form was announced on 19 July 1905. A new province of the East Bengal and Assam was to be carved out in which the Muslims had a population of 18 million, out of a total population of 31 million. Obviously, this would be a Muslim majority province. The remaining part would be known as the province of Bengal with a total population of 54 million, out of which 9 million would be Muslims. But here again there was a catch. In this province also, the Bengali-speaking population would be outnumbered by the Hindi-speaking and Oriya-speaking population put together.

Thus, it was quite clear that the real purpose of the partition was to thwart the rising tide of nationalism among the Bengali-speaking Hindu *bhadralok*, which was in the forefront of the national movement. This is further proved by the fact that if the administrative manageability and efficiency would have been the real purpose behind the idea of the partition of Bengal, the government would have simply accepted the alternative proposal of dividing Bengal on a linguistic basis and not on a religious basis. Simply taking away Hindi-, Oriya- and Assamiya-speaking regions from united Bengal could have served that purpose. But the real purpose of the partition, was not only to weaken the hold of the Bengali *bhadralok* but also to prop up Muslims against Hindus – being a part of the well-tested policy of 'divide and rule'. The British also wanted to diminish the role of Calcutta in national politics and build up Dacca as an alternative centre of political power. It is also to be noted that in East Bengal the majority of the Muslim population were mostly landless labour and agricultural service providers. And they had a deep sense of resentment against the Hindu landlords and Hindu moneylenders. Thus playing on their deep-seated resentment, the British wanted to play the role of their benefactors, though the real purpose was to cut the national movement to its size.

Anti-Partition Swadeshi Movement

As noted earlier, the proposal of the partition of Bengal had evoked strong protests from the people since 1903. During 1903–05 widespread protest meetings were held, a number of memoranda and a large amount of publicity materials detailing critical points against the partition were submitted, printed and distributed. Besides, a number of papers and magazines like *Bengalee*, *Hitbadi*, and *Sanjibani* also launched a sustained and vigorous campaign against the partition. This was followed by a number of meetings to denounce and raise public opinion against it. But all these protests proved to be of no avail and ultimately the final decision for the partition was announced on 19 July 1905. Both at popular and leadership levels, it became distinctly clear that the traditional moderate methods of protest had proved to be totally ineffective. The conclusion was obvious: a new and more innovative and effective method of protest would have to be devised against the partition of Bengal. Such a realisation was followed by a number of public meetings in numerous towns of Bengal, pledging support for a programme of boycott of foreign goods and adoption of Swadeshi goods. But the Government stuck to its decision. The people countered this obduracy of the government by formally launching the Swadeshi Movement on 7 August 1905, with a clarion call to boycott foreign goods. The protests in various forms went on unabated. But the government persisted with its decision, and partition proposals were implemented on 16 October 1905. This brought immediate protests from the people: they not only struck work but also decided not to have fires in their hearths. Not satisfied with that, huge processions were taken out in the streets with *Bande Mataram* on their lips. Furthermore, people tied rakhis on each others' wrists to display heart-felt unity among the people of entire Bengal. At that stage, even the Muslim leaders like Abdur Rasul came in the forefront of the fight against the partition. Some of the prominent intellectuals of Bengal like Rabindranath Tagore, Aurobindo Ghosh and others joined the

वन्देमातरम्

सुजलां सुफलां मलयज शीतलां
शस्यश्यामलां मातरम् ।
शुभ्र ज्योतस्ना-पुलकित यामिनीम्,
फुल्लकुसुमित-द्रुमदलशोभिनीम्,
सुहासिनीं सुमधुर भाषिणीम्
सुखदां वरदां मातरम् ॥
सप्तकोटिकण्ठ-कलकल-निनाद कराले
द्विसप्तकोटिभुजैर्धृतखरकरवाले,
अबला केन मा एत बले ।
बहुबलधारिणीं नमामि तारिणीम्
रिपुदल वारिणीं मातरं ॥
तुमि विद्या तुमि धर्म्म,
तुमि हृदि तुमि मर्म्म,
त्वं हि प्राणाः शरीरे ।
बाहुते तुमि मा शक्ति,
हृदये तुमि मा भक्ति,
तोमारइ प्रतिमा गड़ि मन्दिरे मन्दिरे ।
त्वं हिं दुर्गा दशप्रहरणधारिणी
कमला कमल-दल-विहारिणी
वाणी विद्यादायिनी नमामि त्वां
नमामि कमलां अमलां अतुलाम्
सुजलां सुफलां मातरम्,
वन्दे मातरम्
श्यामलां सरलां सुस्मितां भूषिताम्
धरणीं भरणीम् मातरम् ॥

anti-partition movement. In a word, the anti-partition movement was massive, spontaneous and had cross-sectional support.

Such a massive anti-partition movement in Bengal soon captured the imagination of the people and leaders of the other parts of India. In fact, the entire character of the national movement was changed overnight. Lokmanya Tilak in Maharashtra, Lala Lajpat Rai in Punjab, Sayed Haider Raza in Delhi, and Chidambaram Pillai from Madras Presidency, soon joined the movement giving it a national character. The political atmosphere in the country was surcharged with anger and defiance: even the Moderate leadership of the Congress did not remain unaffected. The Indian National Congress annual meeting in

December 1905 at Banaras, presided over by a Moderate leader like Gokhale supported boycott and Swadeshi resolutions. However, the differences between the Moderate and the Extremist wings of the Congress also came to the fore: while the Moderates wanted the anti-partition movement with its emphasis on boycott and Swadeshi measures to be confined to Bengal, the Extremists favoured making it an all-India movement. They further differed on the ultimate objective of the movement. The Moderates' objective was the undoing of the partition, whereas the Extremists wanted it to be turned into a battle for Swaraj. In the initial stages, the anti-partition movement had cross-sectional popular support including participation by the Muslim masses. So much so that both the Central Mohammadan Association and Bengal Mohammedan Association supported the movement and Abdur Rasul, one of the prominent Muslim leaders, presided over a number of protests meetings, including one at Barisal.

All these events created a groundswell of popular support – so much so that when the Congress met in Calcutta 1906, it passed four resolutions on boycott, Swadeshi, national education and Swaraj. The atmosphere was so surcharged with national feelings that Dadabhai Naoroji, who presided over the Calcutta Congress (1906), made it clear that the political goal of the Congress was 'self-government' or Swaraj, like that of Canada and other colonies. This was a radical departure on the part of the Moderate leadership and it spoke volumes for the impact of the anti-partition movement on the thought-processes of the political leadership of India. Not only that, the Extremists became a dominant group at least in Bengal and they virtually got the anti-partition movement converted into a mass movement of non-cooperation, passive resistance and boycott. For example, the boycott did not remain confined to only boycott of foreign goods, but also engulfed schools, colleges, courts, titles and government services. Besides, processions, demonstrations and public meetings were being experimented as effective methods for popular mobilisation. Not only that, local *samities* were also set up in different parts of Bengal to mobilise people against the partition. The most prominent *samiti* work was done in Barisal under the leadership of Aswini Kumar Datta who developed a widespread network of *samities* in his district. A serious attempt was being made to reach out to the people through festivals, fairs and *Jathas*. It is also relevant to note that the Swadeshi Movement did not remain confined to political protests only. It also invaded and permeated the cultural life of the people. The songs of Rabindranath

Tagore and other poets became popular and touched the soul of Bengal. In the field of science, the scientists like Jagadish Chandra Bose, and P C Ray did some pioneering work. In the field of arts, Nand Lal Bose and Abanindranath Tagore revisited and revivified the Indian tradition of paintings. Some Swadeshi industries also cropped up during the Swadeshi Movement.

Several reasons led to the decline of the anti-partition movement. Repressive measures of the government partly contributed to the petering out of the movement: the press was gagged, some of the prominent leaders were deported, students were expelled from schools and colleges, imprisoned, fined and even flogged. There was always a limit to sustained sufferings imposed on the people by a ruthless government. Some of the prominent leaders of Bengal including Aswini Kumar Datta and Krishna Kumar Mitra were deported. Lala Lajpat Rai and Ajit Singh of Punjab and Chidambaram Pillai and Harisarvottama Rao of Madras Presidency were imprisoned. And Tilak was awarded six-years imprisonment. Thus the government used every means to break the back of the movement. But the government did not hesitate to dangle carrots to allure and entice away the Moderate wing of the Congress. Soon after the Congress resolution on self-government (Swaraj) at the Calcutta Congress (1906), there was an informal discussion between the Moderates and the government on the nature and structure of the constitutional reforms. What gave an impetus to the idea was the return of the Liberals in the British Government in whose generosity and sagacity the Moderates had always pinned their faith. The Moderates wanted to negotiate with the government on the issue of future constitutional reforms whereas the Extremists insisted on carrying out the Swadeshi movement to its logical conclusions. This led to the Surat-split which, in turn, gave a big setback to the national movement, including the Swadeshi Movement.

The constitutional reforms ultimately came in the form of the Indian Council Act of 1909, better known as Morley–Minto Reforms. Thus the British policy of repression and reform greatly contributed to the decline of the Swadeshi Movement.

A third contributory factor was the Muslim attitude to the Swadeshi Movement. It is true that in the initial stages of the movement, a section of the Muslim intelligentsia supported and participated in the movement. But later on, the government succeeded in winning them away. What precipitated the matter was the fact that Morley, the secretary of state for India, indicated in his budget speech of 1906 that some form of representative government was going to be introduced soon in India. That alarmed the Muslim leadership as they thought that they would be further marginalised in the new scheme of things. Thus a delegation of 35 delegates led by Aga Khan met the Viceroy Minto in Simla on 1 October 1906 and submitted a petition with a plea to treat Muslims as a separate community and grant proportional representation to them in the representative bodies, as well as in government employment. This was followed by the foundation of the Indian Muslim League on 30 December 1906, in Dacca, which aimed at protecting and promoting the interests of the Muslim community, as well as pledging loyalty to the British. In the formation of the Muslim League, and also in mobilising and organising pro-partition public opinion among the Muslims, Salimullah Khan, the Nawab of Dacca, proved to be the prime-mover. He used the Muslim League as an instrument to impress upon the Muslim masses that they constituted a separate political community and their interests would be better served if they co-operated with the British Government. The Muslim League widened the wedge between Hindu and Muslim masses on all conceivable grounds, including economic grounds. All this vicious propaganda resulted in communal riots in a number of towns of East Bengal between May 1906 and March 1907, including those in Mymensingh district where Hindu zamindars and moneylenders were targeted by the Muslim peasantry. This hiatus between the Hindus and Muslims went on widening. This major division in the national movement further weakened the Swadeshi Movement as the League was founded in the heartland of Bengal where the Swadeshi Movement was at its peak. The swadeshi movement in turn, also contributed to the ever widening hiatus between Hindus and Muslims.

Despite all this, the Swadeshi movement did not fail to make several distinct contributions to the cause of the national movement. In the first place, several new techniques like passive resistance, boycott and other effective methods of mass protests were evolved and experimented during the anti-partition movement, which were further refined and improved during the Gandhian era. The movement also led to the emergence of the trade union movement particularly in Railways and British-owned industries. Not only that, new forms of people's organisations like *samities* and railwaymen's union were also formed which proved to be quite an effective medium for popular protests. Second, the movement underlined the need and significance of institutions of national education, even though all of them did not achieve big success, except Tagore's Shantiniketan. But these national educational institutions did contribute to the swelling of the rank and file of the national movement including the revolutionary movement, as they turned out to be the recruiting ground of nationalists and revolutionaries like Aurobindo Ghosh. Third, on the economic front, though Swadeshi and boycott might not have broken the back of the British economy, these movements did lead to the decline of import of several British goods like cotton, salt, cigarettes and shoes. On the positive side of Swadeshi, there was revival of handloom, silk-weaving and other traditional crafts. Even attempts were made to promote some of the modern industries like cotton textile, porcelain, soap, matches and cigarettes and tanneries. All of them, however, did not succeed but they did underline the need to promote the industrial life of the country. Not only that, some attempts were made towards raising institutions in the field of insurance and banking. Punjab National Bank was one of the gifts of the Swadeshi movement. In Madras Presidency also, a Swadeshi Steam Navigation Company was set up by Chidambaram Pillai as a rival to British India Navigation Company. Fourth, it also contributed, though, ironically enough, to the coming of the Morley–Minto reforms of 1909, as the British had to pacify the Moderates at least half the way. Another side effect of the Swadeshi Movement was the emergence of a violent revolutionary movement. A number of young men engaged in the Swadeshi movement came to the harsh conclusion that the 'sword' of the British could be met with the Indian 'sword' alone, i.e. British violence could be contained only through violent means. The failure of the Swadeshi Movement did give birth to a more militant form of national struggle which, in turn, made its own contribution to the cause of our national movement. It could be fairly concluded that with all its limitations, the anti-partition Swadeshi Movement did make its own contributions towards furthering the cause of national independence.

> *We seek the fulfillment of our life as a nation. This is what the word Swaraj, which is a bugbear and terror to the Europeans, really means.*
>
> AUROBINDO GHOSH

9 The Extremists and the Indian Freedom Struggle

The Extremists of today will be the Moderates of tomorrow, just as the Moderates of today were the Extremists of yesterday.

BAL GANGADHAR TILAK

What is nationalism? Nationalism is not a mere political programme. Nationalism is a religion that has come from God, nationalism is a creed which you shall have to live. Let no man dare to call himself a nationalist if he does only with the intellectual pride, if you are going to be nationalist, if you are going to assent to this religion of nationalism you must do it in religious spirit; you may remember that you are the instrument of God. . . . Our ideal is that of Swaraj or absolute autonomy free from foreign control.

AUROBINDO

In the pre-Gandhian era there was yet another group which made significant contributions to the national movement both in terms of widening its political base and giving it a more militant character. They were called the Extremists or the militant nationalists. They came to be known as the Extremists because their political cousin, better known as the Moderates, were more mild and modest both in terms of political programme and action. The Extremists demanded more militant forms of struggle against the British. And they set Swaraj and Swadeshi as their goal, and boycott and passive resistance as their methods of struggle.

The prominent leaders of the group were Lala Lajpat Rai from Punjab, Bal Gangadhar Tilak (better known as Lokmanya Tilak) from Maharashtra and Bipin Chandra Pal from Bengal – a triumvirate of Lal, Bal and Pal. Later on, they were joined by Aurobindo Ghosh and a host of others leaders. Tilak (1856–1920) was well educated, both in terms of modern education and traditional learning. He authored famous works, viz., *Gita Rahasya* as well as *The Arctic Home in the Vedas.* In the Indian freedom struggle, he was better known for his thundering battle cry of 'Swaraj is my birthright and I will have it'. He believed in mass mobilisation and to that end he popularised Ganpati Puja and Shivaji Festival in Maharashtra. He relentlessly pursued his ideals and twice suffered imprisonment in the cause of the national struggle. He edited two newspapers – *Kesari* in Marathi and *Mahratta* in English – both of which he used for popularising the national struggle. He was the tallest among the national leaders in the pre-Gandhian era and became a symbol of militant nationalism.

Lala Lajpat Rai (1865–1928) came from Punjab, the Arya Samaj background founded by Swami Dayanand. As a militant nationalist he was active in the agitation against the partition of Bengal and was deported to a foreign country by the British Government. Subsequently, he went to the US and there too, he pursued his ideals and organised the 'Indian League of America' and edited *Young India*, to further the cause of Indian National Movement. After coming back to India he once again plunged into the national struggle. However, the greatest moment of his glory came when he was brutally assaulted by the British police while opposing the Simon Commission in 1928, which

Lal, Bal and Pal

caused his untimely death. Earlier, he was also active in the trade union movement. He also worked for the amelioration of conditions of the depressed classes.

Bipin Chandra Pal (1858–1932) came into prominence during the agitation against the partition of Bengal (1905–07). He was an excellent orator and virtually swept the country with his forceful explanation of the new concepts like swadeshi, swaraj, boycott and national education. He was externed from Madras Presidency in 1907, on account of what the British thought, 'inflammatory' and 'seditious' speeches. He was once deported and even imprisoned in the cause of agitation against the partition of Bengal. After 1908, he virtually retired from active politics.

Aurobindo Ghosh (1872–1950) was educated in England and came back to India in 1893 and worked in Baroda, Gujarat, till 1906. But Aurobindo, while studying in England, dreamt of liberating India from British rule and wrote a number of articles in *Indu Prakash* of Bombay in which he attacked the mendicant policies of the leaders of the Indian National Congress. He worked in Baroda in different capacities including that of a professor and acting Principal of Baroda College. He moved to Calcutta in June 1906 in the wake of the struggle against partition of Bengal and became the principal of Bengal National College. He soon became the chief editor of *Bande Mataram* – a journal started by Bipin Chandra Pal and inspired national leaders through his powerful writings. He was the first in India to declare publicly that the aim of political action was the total independence of the country. He joined hands with Tilak and Lala Lajpat Rai in Extremist politics. He also played a crucial role in formulating a policy of boycott and passive resistance including armed rebellion, if needed, in the cause of national independence. In May 1908, he was arrested in the Alipore Conspiracy Case and was acquitted in 1909. After being released from jail he tried to revive the nationalist movement and to that end he started two journals – *Karmayogi* in English and *Dharma* in Bengali. He soon realised that the nation was not yet prepared for such a movement. He went to Pondicherry in 1910 to pursue his spiritual goal and remained there until his death in 1950.

Reasons for the Growth of the Extremists

Before we discuss the role of the Extremists in the Indian national struggle, it would be expedient for us to trace out the factors responsible for their emergence and growth. Admittedly, the most significant factor leading to the emergence of the Extremists was the abject failure of the Moderates to snatch any substantive concessions from the British. By the end of the century, the Moderates were virtually at their tether's end. Aside from annual conferences of the Congress, which many termed as a 'three-day tamasha', there was hardly any other political activity for the rest of the year. Even Tilak's attempt to make the Congress adopt a new constitution with a view to making it a mass party was not much of a success, as it mostly remained on paper. Thus the Moderates were not measuring up to the task of radical politics which was becoming the crying need of the time.

Second, the hardening of the British policy particularly during the Viceroyalty of Lord Curzon (1889–1905) was another reason for the growth of Extremists among the early nationalists. Lord Curzon, who was an outright imperialist pushed through a number of administrative and legislative measures, viz., Calcutta Municipal Act (1899), Education Act (1903) and Indian Official Secrets Act (1904) to curb and control various institutions as well as the press. What added more fuel to the fire was the waste of scarce national resources on non-essential items like Delhi Darbar, Tibetan expeditions, etc. On the top of it, his refusal to reduce the land tax further alienated the people. His decision to partition Bengal on communal lines virtually proved to be the last straw on the people's patience, drawing strong reactions from all corners.

Some eventful happenings in the foreign lands were the third contributing factor in igniting the fire of extremism. People's struggles in Ireland, Turkey and China inspired the people of India to take their national struggle to a higher plane. Besides, the defeat of Italy at the hands of Ethiopia (1896) and Russia at those of Japan (1904) exploded the myth of 'whiteman's' supremacy, which emboldened our people to go in for a more decisive struggle. Fourth, the Extremists also derived their inspiration from the literary works of writers like Bankim Chandra Chattopadhyaya and religious leaders like Vivekananda and Dayanand. Bankim Chandra Chattopadhyaya not only eulogised Lord Krishna as an ideal man and a nationbuilder but also for his basic message of *Karmyoga* in *Bhagvad Gita*, which subsequently became a major source of inspiration and motivation for nationalist leaders. Besides, his novel *Anandmath* gave a new dimension and momentum to the emergence of cultural nationalism. Not only that, his homage to the motherland in the form of his hymn *Vande Mataram* proved to be so emotive that it virtually touched the soul of the people of India.

Similarly, in Maharashtra, Tilak's attempt at mass mobilisation against the Consent Bill of 1891, raising the marriageable age of Hindu girls, did lead to the consolidation of Hindu public opinion. Subsequently, his initiatives for the popularisation of Ganpati Puja and Shivaji festival were steps in the same direction. Dayanand Saraswati and his Arya Samaj also inspired militancy among some sections of our people. Lala Lajpat Rai, one of the stalwarts of the Extremist politics, came from Arya Samaji background. Similarly, Viveknanda's visit to the World Religious Conference in 1893 unleashed a new wave of militancy and boldness. His neo-Vedantism underlying the worldliness and service to the *Daridranarayan* also paved the way for a more militant mass politics. Fifth, the deteriorating economic conditions also led to widespread discontent among the people. Mass poverty and mass unemployment became the breeding ground of mass discontent. The advent of great famines followed by bubonic plague in Poona, further led to mass awakening. However, it was the callous attitude of the British towards the sufferings of the people that actually enraged the masses. On top of it, as the Plague Commissioner of Poona, Col. Rand's mishandling of the situation evoked extreme anger among the people, resulting in his murder by the Chapekar brothers , Damodar and Balakrishna, who were subsequently sent to gallows. It is relevant to note that the first imprisonment of Tilak was related to the same issue which further alienated the people.

The Extremists and the Partition of Bengal

Undeniably, it was the idea of partition of Bengal, first floated in 1903, by the British and finally implemented in 1905, which proved to be the most precipitous cause for the sudden spurt and popularity of the Extremist politics. It affected the entire nationalist leadership and even the Moderates started talking in the terms of 'Swaraj', 'self-government', 'Swadeshi', and boycott. But the real heroes of the anti-Bengal partition were Tilak, Bipin Chandra Pal, Aurobindo Ghosh and Lala Lajpat Rai. In fact, it was the fight against the partition of Bengal which gave a big fillip to the Extremist politics. A perusal of the proceedings of the Congress, both at Banaras (1905) and Calcutta (1906), makes it explicit that the Extremists came to occupy the centre-stage in the Congress politics pushing the Moderates in the background and even forcing them to toe their more militant line. The Calcutta Congress (1906), which was presided over by Dadabhai Naoroji, passed four resolutions on self-government, boycott, swadeshi and national education, primarily on account of the Extremists' ascendance in Congress politics. Earlier, at the Banaras Congress (1905), which was held in the wake of the partition of Bengal, the differences between the Moderates and the Extremists came to the fore. It is true that the Banaras Congress defined its political goal of India as 'self-government' like other colonies. The idea of self-government was further clarified by Dadabhai Naoroji in his presidential speech at the Calcutta Congress (1906), when he underlined the political goal of the Congress as 'self-government or Swaraj like that of Canada and other colonies'. And the same Congress passed a resolution demanding that 'the system of government obtaining in the self-governing British colonies should be extended to India'. It is true that except Aurobindo Ghosh, no other Extremist leader thought of 'Swaraj' in terms of total independence from the British. However, that does not mean that there was no difference of opinion between the Moderates and the Extremists on this score. Besides, it should be noted that the Moderates talked of 'self-government' under the compulsion of circumstances, whereas for the Extremists it was an article of faith.

A second concept, which became popular in the wake of the anti-partition movement was that of boycott. The Calcutta Congress passed a resolution underlining the fact that the boycott movement in Bengal, by way of protest against the partition of that province was legitimate. Soon the differences between the Moderates and the Extremists on the use of boycott as a method of forcing the government to undo partition came to the fore. The Moderates wanted the boycott movement to be confined only to Bengal whereas the Extremists really wanted to make it an all-India movement. Besides, the Moderates were satisfied with the boycott of British goods alone, whereas the Extremists included the organised resistance to the government too in its fold. Thus, for the Extremists, the organised passive resistance was the only 'effective means' to get control of our national life. Aurobindo Ghosh wrote a series of articles in *Bande Mataram* in April 1907, explaining the concept and meaning of passive resistance. He wrote: 'the essential difference between passive or defensive and active or aggressive resistance is this: while the method of the aggressive resistor is to do something by which one can bring about positive harm to the government, the method of the passive resistor is to abstain from doing something by which he would be helping the government'. He pleaded that the prevailing situation in India called for active resistance.

He, therefore, pleaded for an organised and relentless boycott of British goods, government educational institutions, the alien judicial system, police and other institutions of the executive, and ultimately total refusal to pay taxes as the final form of the passive resistance. Obviously, such a radical concept of boycott was not acceptable to the Moderates. Gokhale even ridiculed the idea of independence by saying that only mad men outside the lunatic asylums could think or talk of independence. The Moderates were still thinking in terms of political and constitutional reforms only.

Two other resolutions were also passed at the Calcutta Congress on swadeshi and national education. The Congress accorded support to the Swadeshi Movement by calling upon the people to make 'earnest and sustained efforts to promote the growth of indigenous industries by giving them preference over the imported commodities'. On national education, the Congress pleaded for organising a new system of education suited to the requirements of the country on national lines and under national control. The Extremists took the twin message of swadeshi and boycott as an effective method to force the government to make major political concessions to the people in the form of 'self-government with total autonomy'. For them, swadeshi and boycott were two sides of the same coin and the real effective means to achieve self-government. But for the Moderates, the Calcutta resolutions were too radical to be pursued relentlessly. In fact, at the Surat Congress they wanted to undo what had been achieved by the Extremists at the Calcutta Congress.

It is relevant to note that the concept of swadeshi was not entirely a new concept given by the Extremists in the wake of the partition of Bengal. Earlier, the Tagore family and a host of other nationalists like G V Joshi and Rajnarayan Basu had also talked of swadeshi, and made their own conceptual as well as practical contributions to it. But what the partition of Bengal did was to give a new dynamism and dimension to the concept of 'swadeshi'. Moreover, swadeshi and boycott, practiced together were proving to be a deadly combination against the British.

The Moderates, as such, were not much convinced about the use of boycott, and their acceptance of the Calcutta resolution was under the pressure of the Extremists and then-prevailing public opinion. Not only that, they wanted it to be confined to Bengal only. Soon they tried to wriggle out of it. On the other hand, the Extremists, particularly Aurobindo, wanted to take it to an all-India level. Besides, they wanted the boycott to be extended to schools, colleges, courts, government titles, government services and civil disobedience against unjust laws. Swadeshi was the other side of boycott. Boycott of foreign goods prompted our people to produce swadeshi goods, giving a great fillip to the cottage industries. The concept of swadeshi was further extended to the educational and cultural field. The Bengal National College was established with Aurobindo as the principal. Besides, the National Council of Education was established for the promotion of national education with the primary emphasis on regional languages being the medium of instruction. Bengal Technical Institute was also set up. P C Ray set up his Bengal Chemical Factory, followed by similar attempts in different areas. In Bengal, it also led to literary resurgence. Writers like Rabindranath Tagore, Rajanikanta Sen, and Mukunda Das lent a helping hand through their creative literary works.

Tilak and Lala Lajpat Rai took this movement to Maharashtra and Punjab respectively. Tilak arranged a big bonfire of foreign clothes at Poona. He also took the initiative in setting up a Swadeshi Vastu Pracharni Sabha which opened many stores of swadeshi goods. Tilak also started a picketing movement against liquor shops. Lala Lajpat Rai was in the forefront of the Swadeshi Movement in Punjab. He led a movement against the import of sugar, which was hampering the interests of the canegrowers of Punjab. Indeed, Lala Lajpat Rai put greater emphasis on swadeshi rather than on boycott. The foundation of Punjab National Bank by Lala Harkishen Lal was a big step in that direction. South India did not remain unaffected by the movement either. Chidambaram Pillai was the leader of the movement in the South. He floated a Swadeshi Steam Navigation Company as a rival to the foreign-owned British India Steam Navigation Company.

But soon the movement started losing momentum under the impact of the repressive measures taken by the colonial administration. A large number of people were jailed, thousands of students were expelled from their institutions and many people lost their jobs. Besides, like any other people's movement, it had reached the peak and was bound to slide down. What contributed to the weakening of the movement was the rift and division in the national movement. By now the Hindu–Muslim divide was also coming to the fore. After the formation of the Muslim League, the Muslim leadership was moving closer to the British. Of course, the British policy of 'divide and rule' played a crucial role in the process of divisive politics. The Moderates–Extremists divide was evident even during the Calcutta Congress and resolutions passed by it were in the nature of compromise between these two groups. But as the agitation against Bengal partition turned into a major movement, the Moderates started developing cold feet. Besides, with the Liberals coming to power in England, the expectations and hopes among the Moderates about new constitutional reforms were greatly heightened. The British lent a credence to their hope by floating the idea of the next round of reforms while following the policy of repression.

It was in such a state of confusion and acrimony that the Congress met in Surat in December 1907. What created distrust in the minds of the Extremists about the real intentions of the Moderates was the change of venue of the conference from Nagpur to Surat, which was supposedly the latter's stronghold. The real conflict between the two groups was that the Moderates wanted to scuttle the four resolutions adopted earlier at the Calcutta Congress (1906), whereas the Extremists wanted to retain them. Besides, the Extremists wanted Lala Lajpat Rai as the Congress President but he was not acceptable to the Moderates. Ultimately, the Moderates succeeded in getting Rashbehari Ghosh elected as the President for the Surat session. Tilak tried to address the delegates but was prevented from doing so. That led to some sort of pandemonium leading to what came to be known as the Surat-split. It is difficult to apportion the blame for the split between the two groups. But one thing is clear: Tilak regretted the split and, in fact, almost sent a letter of regret to the Congress President expressing his ardent wish to be back to the Congress. But for the Moderates it was a good riddance and hence they did not make any response to Tilak's political overtures. However, there is no denying the fact that the Surat-split weakened the strength of the national movement at a critical juncture of its history.

Things moved very fast soon after. At the annual session at Allahabad, the Congress came under the total domination of the Moderates. They framed a new constitution for the Congress and pledged their loyalty to the British and hoped that India would move towards self-government on the pattern of other self-governing colonies of the empire through constitutional means. In fact, they had high hopes about the next round of constitutional reforms, which finally came in the form of Morley–Minto Reforms of 1909. The Extremists, on the other hand, could neither sustain the momentum nor could they forge a new organisation. Soon they were hunted out by the colonial administration: Tilak was sentenced to six-years imprisonment in 1908 for his support to the Bengal Extremists, led by Aurobindo. Lala Lajpat

Rai voluntarily went for a long stay in USA. Aurobindo Ghosh, along with a number of people, including his brother Barindra Kumar Ghosh, were tried, for what came to be popularly known as the Alipore Conspiracy Case and spent a year behind bars. He was subsequently acquitted. And on his acquittal he left for Pondicherry to pursue his spiritual goals. Bipin Chandra Pal withdrew from active politics for the time being. With the big Extremist leaders out, the movement soon petered out. However, it paved the way for the emergence and growth of still more militant movements – the violent revolutionary movement which played a crucial role in subsequent years. When Tilak came back in 1914 from Mandalay Fort jail, he once again worked for Congress unity which led to a united Congress at Lucknow in 1916. Soon he launched his Home Rule Movement, a major mass movement having a distinct role in the history of our national struggle. Before making a critical assessment of the Extremists' contributions to the national movement, let us have a look at the major criticisms they have been subjected to.

The Extremists and Their Critics

The extremists have been subjected to a number of critical comments both by the Moderate leadership as well as by historians. In the first place, it is argued that the Extremists' new concept of nationalism, fired with religious fervour, created several problems. It smacked of the Hindu revivalist movement, which further alienated the Muslims. Thus it had been argued that it was during the ascendance of the Extremists that the All India Muslim League was founded in 1906. It is true that Sir Syed Ahmad Khan and his associates of the Aligarh school had earlier dissociated themselves from the Congress, but the religious nature of the new nationalism certainly contributed to further alienation of the Muslim leaders and masses.

A second line of attack on the Extremists has been that with all their fury and bravado, and personal sacrifices, they could not really build up a mass movement. It was only during the anti-Bengal partition movement that they were able to mobilise the masses on a reasonably respectable scale. This is further proved by the fact that after the Surat-split and in face of repressive measures against the big leaders like Tilak and Aurobindo, the new Nationalist Party almost petered out.

The third critical point raised against them is that they took an ambivalent attitude on the issue of violence. Aurobindo, of course, did not rule out the violent method. Even Tilak had consistently taken an ambivalent attitude on the issue of violence though he never openly supported violent methods. It is relevant to note that both his imprisonments during 1898 and again in 1908 arose from his indirect support to violent methods used by the Chapekar brothers (1897) and Bengal revolutionaries in 1908. Thus it is argued that the Extremists became the ideological progenitor of the violent revolutionary movement which subsequently emerged and occupied some of the space vacated by the Extremists in our national life. They were, in a way, responsible for inviting stringent repressive measures from the British against our people.

Contributions of the Extremists

Despite these criticisms, there is no denying the fact that they made several contributions to our national struggle. In the first place, they contributed significantly to the growth of a new concept of nationalism. It is relevant to note that the Moderates were primarily inspired by the European experience wherein the primary emphasis was on territorial nationalism, leading to the concept of the nation-state. In other words, nationalism in Europe emerged among the people of a particular region based on the commonality of history, culture, language and distinct geographical configuration. Obviously in such a scheme of things, the secular character of the nation-state was underlined. However, the Extremists made a departure by introducing new elements of religion, culture and some other primordial symbols. The Extremists' concept of nationalism developed around the notion of motherhood which underlined the inalienable relationship between a nation and her children. Thus, in their new concept of cultural nationalism they presented the country in the form of a mother. In Punjab and adjoining areas Arya Samaj also played a big role in creating strong nationalistic feelings based on the vedic way of life. All this created a sense of self-confidence among people as well as an intense anti-alien feeling. Lala Lajpat Rai, who had an Arya Samaj background, while explaining the new sense of nationalism commented: 'Our first want, then, is to raise our patriotism to the level of religion and to aspire to live or die for it.' However, it was in Bengal that an intense religious fervour was given to the concept of new nationalism. In Bengal, Bankim Chandra laid the foundation of new nationalism when he identified the nation with the mother goddess – the icon which evoked deep sense of emotions and sacrifice. This imagery of India as the mother in bondage and the sacred duty of her children to free her, continued to inspire generations of patriots. But it was Aurobindo and other revolutionaries who further perfected this imagery and made it almost a living symbol. As Aurobindo explained it: 'Nationalism is not a mere political programme; nationalism is a religion that has come from God; nationalism is a creed which you shall have to live'. Calling upon the youth of India, he further said: 'come, you who feel 'her' stirrings within you fling off the black veil of self, break down the imprisoning walls of indolence, help her with your bodies or with your intellect or with your speech or with your wealth, or with your prayers and worship, each man according to his capacity.'

This mother–son relationship was put on such a high pedestal that it became a fountainhead of inspiration for supreme sacrifice. As one of the popular songs in the Bengal countryside reminded the oppressors:

> You seek to make me forget my mother,
> By beating me, even, hanging me
> I am not that kind of son –
> Who will flee, leaving mother behind!!

A second contribution of the Extremists was the concept of 'self-government' or Swaraj. Aurobindo, of course, conceived it in terms of total independence. But where the Extremists collectively differed from the Moderates was that whereas the latter looked up to the British for guidance and support, the former favoured total autonomy for India without any real control by the British. Tilak's call for 'Swaraj as birthright', obliterated the finer distinction between 'total autonomy' as conceived by him and Purna Swaraj. In the popular mind swaraj became a synonym for freedom. Thus, on the whole, the Extremists took the national struggle to a higher pedestal by setting a higher national task, which in itself was a major contribution.

Aurobindo defined the goal of their political movement: 'There are some who fear to use the word freedom, but I always use the word because it has been the mantra of my life to aspire towards the freedom of my nation.' He continued: 'Our ideal is swaraj or absolute autonomy free from foreign control. We claim the right of every nation to live its own life by its own energies according to its own nature and ideals.'

A third contribution of the Extremists was that through their personal sacrifice and suffering they inspired a large number of people to work for the national movement. Tilak was first to defy the British by opposing its repressive policies and gladly suffered 18 months of rigorous imprisonment. This was the first major act of defiance from among the new political leaders and he was hailed overnight as 'Lokmanya' a symbol of defiant India. In due course he became an icon, a national hero who valiantly fought and suffered in the cause of our national struggle. Lala Lajpat Rai and Ajit Singh, the Extremist leaders from Punjab, were deported and their sufferings inspired a new revolutionary movement and the Ghadar Party workers. Aurobindo became a cult hero in Bengal and through his personal sufferings and indomitable will, inspired a number of people who sacrificed all that they could for the sake of the country.

The fourth contribution made by the Extremist leadership was about the means they sought to employ in the pursuit of their ideas. As Tilak himself said that it was not so much for their political goals but on account of their methods that they came to be known as the Extremists. Speaking in the Calcutta conference (1906) Tilak underscored the pivotal role of boycott in our struggle against the British, when he said:

> Boycott is our political weapon. We shall not assist them in fighting beyond our frontiers or outside India with Indian blood and money. We shall not assist them in carrying out the administration of justice. We shall have our own courts, and when the time comes we shall not pay taxes. If you can do (that), you will be free from tomorrow.

Aurobindo also pleaded for boycott as a weapon of national struggle, making it almost synonymous with total non-cooperation with the government.

Finally, with all their limitations it could not be denied that the Extremists took our national movement to a higher stage both in terms of its political goal and methods of struggle. On the ideological plane they made some seminal contributions in terms of new ideas like swaraj and swadeshi and anticipated some of the instruments of national struggle, like boycott and even the armed rebellion. As such, they became the ideological forerunners of the revolutionary movement, on the one hand and Gandhian politics on the other. Thus at a very critical stage of our national life they contributed a great deal both in terms of ideas and action.

> *Let all acts of construction go on, whatever they and their forms may be. Let no one be disheartened by his failures or sufferings in the cause of his work to attain Swaraj.*
>
> BAL GANGADHAR TILAK

10 The Home Rule Movement
An Appraisal

Home Rule has touched the ryots through his village life, where the present order presses hard upon him. . . . He wants the old panchayat back again; he wants that his village should be managed by himself and his fellows; and he wants to get rid of the tyranny of the petty-officials, who have replaced the old useful communal servants.

ANNIE BESANT

The Home Rule Movement led by Lokmanya Tilak and Annie Besant was an important landmark in the pre-Gandhian era of our national struggle. Since we have already introduced Tilak in earlier chapters, a word is called for about Madam Annie Besant. She, though born in Ireland, came to India in 1893 to work for the Theosophical Society with Adyar (Madras) as its headquarters. In England she had the reputation of being an exponent of radical Fabianism. While working as the World-President of the Theosophical Society, she had built up an impressive network of her followers, both in India and abroad. She joined the Congress politics in 1914 and founded and edited journals, viz., *Commonweal* and *New India* to propagate and translate her ideas of constitutional agitation to force the British to concede Home Rule to the Indian people. Thus along with Tilak, she emerged as one of the important leaders of the Home Rule Movement.

But before we discuss the details of the Home Rule Movement, it would be relevant to delineate the historical background of the movement. Let us recall that the First World War had given a big fillip to the feeling of nationalism all over the world, in general, and to the people of India in particular. The motive-force behind the War, as claimed by the allied powers, was high-sounding ideas like liberty, democracy and the principle of self-determination. All this had aroused unprecedented hopes in the minds of our people. Hence, they were receptive to the idea of the Home Rule. It is also worth noting that

Tilak was back from Mandalay Jail on 14 June 1914 and he immediately plunged into the national movement. His first and foremost task was to secure the entry of the Extremists in the Congress which they had left after the Surat-split in 1907. Annie Besant was also quite keen to lend her helping hand to the task of Congress unity. According to her, a united Congress, apart from ensuring the entry of a younger generation to the national movement, would also make it an effective organisation in the cause of our national struggle. Further, it would have a moderating impact on the Extremists and radicalising influence on the Moderates. Moreover, the War had given a real opportunity for a united national movement: the attack on Turkey had alienated the Muslims, who were already full of resentment against the British for the annulment of the Bengal partition in 1911.

The War had already prepared a background for the emergence of a united national struggle. What was more, the Irish Home Rule League provided a role model for the Indian nationalists, particularly for Annie Besant to launch a similar movement in India. In a word, all this had created a congenial atmosphere for launching a Home Rule Movement in the country. But both Tilak and Annie Besant were aware that the first and foremost task was to unite the Congress as a prelude to the launching of such a movement. Hence they tried their best to secure the entry of the Extremists in the 1914 Session of the Congress, but their efforts came to naught. However, they persisted with their effort and in the 1915 Congress session, the door was opened for the re-entry of the Extremists in the Congress fold. They actively joined it at the Lucknow Congress (1916) in good strength. Perhaps, what further facilitated their entry was the death of two prominent Moderate leaders – Pherozeshah Mehta and Gopal Krishna Gokhale in 1915, both of whom had opposed the Extremists' entry into the Congress. Perhaps even a section of the Moderate leadership was not quite happy with the state of inactive stalemate in the national movement. Hence, they easily consented to the entry of Tilak and his followers into the Congress.

The Formation of the Home Rule Leagues

In the 1915 Congress session, Annie Besant tried her best to get the Congress leadership to agree to her proposal of launching of a Home Rule League, to work for the cause of self-government for Indians. But being unsure of the Congress leadership, she persuaded the Congress to allow her to have her own League after September 1916, if the Congress failed to keep up its commitments. Since Tilak was not a party to Annie Besant's commitment to the Congress leadership, he started his own League in April 1916 itself. As the Congress failed to meet its commitment by September 1916, Annie Besant started her own Home Rule League with George Arundale, her associate in the Theosophical Society, as its organising secretary, which is why two Home Rule Leagues were founded in 1916 – one led by Tilak and another by Annie Besant. The basic objectives of both the Leagues were similar – to propagate and popularise the idea of Home Rule for Indians. As there was total understanding between Tilak and Besant, the separate existence of two Leagues did not create much leadership and organisational problems. In fact, there was almost a territorial division of the work: Tilak confining his activities to Maharashtra, Karnataka, Central Provinces and Berar, and Annie Besant in the rest of the country. In fact, they fully cooperated with each other and even shared political platforms for the propagation of their views.

Methods and Activities of the League

The strategy and tactics of the Home Rule Movement made a distinct departure from the earlier movement led by Tilak, viz., the Swadeshi Movement. New emphasis was given on educational rather than agitational aspects; the approach was not confrontationist but conciliatory; strategy was based on unity and all-inclusiveness rather than on divisiveness and differentiation; the methods were not sectarian and militant but pronouncedly non-sectarian, peaceful and non-violent. The reason for such a change in approach and methods of the new movement, in sharp contrast to those of *Swadeshi Andolan*, were not far to seek. Now, Tilak was a much more mature and mellowed leader and had immensely risen in stature and popular esteem. He had definitely emerged as the tallest leader of the national movement and, therefore, was more self-assured and self-confident. Annie Besant, coming from the background of Theosophy, was also temperamentally more suited to educational rather than agitational politics. Hence the combined effort of both Tilak and Annie Besant was to convince the British about the need and urgency to grant 'self-government' to the people of India. And to that end they wanted to educate the people with a view to building up a real mass movement. Thus, it was an ideal combination of persuasion and pressure, combining and transcending the earlier tactics of both the Moderates and the Extremists. They favoured the use of the vernacular language to move closer to the people. Annie Besant advanced a number of arguments in favour of the movement: the British had destroyed the village economy, its democratic institutions, industries and had kept the Indian people illiterate. But neither Tilak nor Annie Besant demanded total break up with the British, rather they were insisting on self-government for the people of India.

Organisational Activities of the Leagues

Tilak Home Rule had six branches – one each in Maharashtra, Bombay city, Karnataka, Central Provinces and two in Berar. Tilak extensively toured Maharashtra and explained to the people the rationale and need for Home Rule. He also printed pamphlets in Marathi, Kannada, Gujarati and English – explaining the need for the Home Rule Movement. The popularity of his literature could be gauged by the fact that 47,000 copies of these pamphlets were sold.

The main line of his argument was that the Indian situation was ripe for Home Rule. Without displaying any sense of rancour against the British, despite being jailed for six years, he pleaded the case for Home Rule with great sobriety. Earlier Tilak was known for his fire-eating speeches, but now he was more patient and persuasive. To sample this we may quote: 'India is like a son who had grown up and attained maturity. It is right now that the trustee or the father should give him what was his due'. Another change, also discernible in his new approach to the national politics, was that he was totally free from communal appeal. To elucidate this, we may quote: 'Alienness is not connected with religion, trade or profession, it is the question of interests. He who does what is beneficial to the people of this country, be a Muhammedan or an Englishman, is not an alien'. It is also relevant to note that Tilak, along with Jinnah, was one of the architects of the Lucknow Pact, which paved the way for a united national movement. Even some of the Moderate leaders in UP and Maharashtra joined as volunteers, going on lecture tours and bringing pamphlets in favour of the movement. What was more, even the members of Gokhale's Servants of India Society joined the movement. By April 1917, Tilak League alone had 14,000 members. He was so convinced about the need for national unity that during the Lucknow Congress he unequivocally declared: 'I am sure I represent the sense of the Hindu community all over India when I say that we would not care if the rights of self-government are granted to the Mohammedan community only. I would not care if these rights are granted to any section of the Indian community.'

The Lucknow Congress gave a big boost to the Home Rule Movement. At the end of the Lucknow Congress, a joint meeting attended by more than one thousand delegates of the two Leagues was addressed by Tilak and Annie Besant, which created a deep sense of enthusiasm among the Home Rule volunteers. Subsequently, both went on a long tour to educate the people about the issues involved in the Movement.

British Response to Home Rule Movement

When the Home Rule Movement started gathering momentum, the British were alarmed, though the movement was peaceful and lawful. In the last quarter of 1916, the government asked Tilak to furnish a surety of Rs. 60,000 and threatened to bind him for good behaviour for a period of one year. Tilak sought legal remedy but lost the case in the lower court. He went in appeal to the High Court which exonerated him in November 1916. That was a great morale booster for Tilak and his volunteers who went on declaring that their movement had got legal sanction. But that did not deter the Madras government from imposing an internment order on Annie Besant in June 1917. This infuriated even those leaders who had earlier kept away from the movement. A nationwide protest movement was launched, in which prominent leaders like Jinnah, Surendranath Banerjea, Madan Mohan Malaviya, Motilal Nehru, M R Jayakar, Tej Bahadur Sapru, C R Das and others participated to show their solidarity with Annie Besant. Tilak advocated passive resistance to get her released. There was almost a national upsurge in her favour. On the suggestion of Mahatma Gandhi, the signatures of one thousand men were collected, who were willing to defy the ban and march to the place of Besant's detention. Women participated in large numbers in the Home Rule Movement particularly in the South. Sir S Subranmaniya Iyer, Honorary President of All India Home Rule League, renounced his Knighhood when Ms Besant was interned. All this sent a stern message to the government and Annie Besant was freed in September 1917. She gained unprecedented popularity and was elected Congress President in 1917 at the initiative of Tilak.

Meanwhile, Montagu, Secretary of State, made his famous statement on 20 August 1917. As a sequel, the joint meeting of the

Congress and the League was held in October 1917. It was decided there to send a representative delegation to England to plead for the implementation of the scheme proposed after the Lucknow Pact.

The British government could easily gauge the mood of the people. And on 20 August 1917, Montagu made a significant declaration in the House of Commons. He promised an 'increasing association of Indians in every branch of administration and gradual development of self-governing institutions with a view to progressive realisation of responsible government in India as an integral part of the Empire'. Though there was no immediate promise of 'self-government', his declaration was certainly a distinct improvement on the act of 1909. Meanwhile, both the Congress and the Indian Muslim League were trying to impress upon the British about the need for constitutional reforms. That prompted a joint meeting of AICC and the Council of Indian Muslim League to push forward the constitutional reforms. It was also decided to send a delegation to England to impress upon the British about the need for constitutional reforms.

Montagu's declaration of August 1917 and subsequent publication of the reform scheme in July 1918, in a way, dampened the spirit of the Home Rule Movement. Moderates went with the government in support of new constitutional reforms and even Annie Besant virtually turned into a 'loyalist'. Tilak neither rejected the new proposals nor displayed any extra enthusiasm about them. But he had to go to England to fight a libel case, which necessitated his long absence from the Indian scene. As such, the Home Rule Movement lost its initial momentum.

Perhaps there were other attending reasons for the Home Rule Movement to lose its vitality and vigor. The most significant change that was taking place on the national scene was the gradual emergence of Mahatma Gandhi as a mass leader in his own right. He had his new ideas about national struggle which he had experimented in Champaran, Kheda and Ahmedabad during 1917-18. Besides, the issue of Khilafat had enthused the Muslim masses and added a new dimension to the national movement. All this demanded a new approach, a set of new national priorities and programmes, a new leadership. As such, the Home Rule movement was pushed to the background.

Achievements: It is true that the Home Rule Movement could not result in the kind of mass movement, the like of which we became familiar with during the subsequent Gandhian era. Besides, the movement did not aim at total independence – the kind of demand which was earlier raised by Aurobindo during the Swadeshi movement. Moreover, the tone and temper of the movement was a climb down from the earlier militant phase of the Extremists. Its main plank was education and persuasion. Despite these limitations, the movement did make some distinct achievements and certainly took the country further on the road to self-government. Thus, in terms of reaching out to different regions, and communities, it was certainly an improvement on the earlier movement, including Swadeshi in terms of popular participation. Annie Besant's League had 200 branches spread in major parts of the country, with a total membership of 27,000 and Tilak's League had 32,000 members by 1918. Not only that, how effective the publicity was could be gauged by the simple fact that more than three lac copies of pamphlets, pleading for home rule, in different languages, were sold. Another indication of the effectiveness of the movement was that Annie Besant was externed from Central Provinces and Berar during November 1916 and Tilak was externed from Punjab and Delhi during February 1917. All this speaks volumes for the effectiveness of the movement. Secondly, though there might have been other reasons for the Montagu declaration of August 1917, the fact that the Home Rule Movement had made its own contributions to that end could hardly be denied. Thirdly, Home Rule Movement reached out to new areas, new groups, and new generations, which in itself was no mean achievement. Major centres of the movement were located in Maharashtra, Madras, UP, Sindh and Gujarat. Fourthly, the movement contributed a great deal to the signing of the Lucknow Pact, which was a major milestone in our national struggle, as it is laid the foundation of a united national movement free from community, religion, caste and creed. In fact, many of the volunteers for Gandhian movements came from the background of Home Rule Movement. Besides, the movement had popularised the idea of self-government. In a word, the Home Rule Movement laid the foundation for a genuine mass movement, which Mahatma Gandhi later on capitalised.

> *The Home Rule Movement marked the beginning of the new phase in India's struggle for freedom. It placed before the country a concrete scheme of self-government, bereft of the verbiage with which the Congress led by the Moderates, surrounded their political goal.*
>
> R C MAJUMDAR

11 Lucknow Pact

It has been said by some that we Hindus have yielded too much to our Mohammedan brethren. I am sure I represent the sense of Hindu community all over India, when I say that we would not have yielded too much. I would not care if the rights of self government are granted to the Mohammedan community only. . . . When we are against the third party, it is important that we stand on this platform united, united in race, united in religion, united as regards all different shades of political creed.

BAL GANGADHAR TILAK

The Congress–League joint scheme, better known as the Lucknow Pact (1916), was one of the major landmarks in the history of the Hindu–Muslim relationship. This Pact heralded a new era of Hindu–Muslim bonhomie and also a joint front for achieving self-government for the people of India. The process was further strengthened by Khilafat and Non-Cooperation Movements.

Background

Let us first look at the circumstances which led to the signing of the Pact. It is relevant to note that both for the Congress and the Muslim League, a favourable political environment had emerged, making it possible for them to seek and work out a joint front. On the Congress front, much water had flown under its bridge after the Surat-split. The Moderates, who had pinned their faith in the British promise of constitutional reforms had been badly disappointed by the limited reforms under the 1909 Act. Two of its stalwarts, Gokhale and Pherozeshah Mehta had passed away in 1915. Others had lost their dynamism on account of advancing age. In fact, there was no Moderate leader who could now lead the Congress from the front. After the Surat-split, the Extremists, under the impact of the government repression had been in disarray with most of its prominent leaders either being imprisoned or deported. On the Extremists' front the only silver lining was Tilak's re-entry into national politics after being back from Mandalay Jail in June 1914. He, of course, was quite keen on his entry into the Congress fold as he looked at it as a prerequisite for giving a new push to the national movement in the form of the Home Rule Movement. Meanwhile, the Bombay Congress (1915), presided over by S P Sinha, passed a resolution demanding substantial measures of constitutional reforms, giving the people an effective control over their governance. The Congress further authorised the All India Congress Committee to work jointly with the All India Muslim League to evolve a scheme on constitutional reforms. Another important decision of the Bombay Congress was to partially open the door for the re-entry of the Extremists in the Congress by making suitable changes in its constitution. This was certainly a result of the efforts jointly made by Tilak and Annie Besant, since the release of Tilak in June 1914. In parenthesis, it could be said that Annie Besant who had joined the Congress in 1914, after many years of service in the cause of the Theosophical Society, had brought a new dynamism and wanted a reunited national movement to take India on the road of 'Home Rule'.

On the Indian Muslim League front, things were also not moving in the right direction. The euphoria created by the introduction of a separate electorate under the 1909 Act had died down, and annulment of the partition of Bengal in 1911 had dampened the pro-British enthusiasm among the Muslim populace. Furthermore, the British move against the Sultan of Turkey, who was also the religious head of Muslims, had further alienated them and had even created anti-British feelings among them. Moreover, a new leadership was getting active in the Muslim League which transcended the sectarian outlook of earlier leadership and was inspired by a broader vision of the national movement. Jinnah was emerging as a leader of the League and was committed to work for self-government for the people of India. In fact, he had joined the Muslim League in 1909 on the condition that the League would work for the self-government of the country. Not only that, on the initiative of Jinnah and others, the constitution of the Muslim League was amended in March 1913, committing the League to the goal of achieving self-government under the aegis of the British crown. Another repercussion of the First World War was that there was a widespread appreciation of the heroic deeds of the Indian soldiers who were fighting on the European front. In the words of Annie

Besant, India would look for the liberty for her people as a 'matter of right' and not as a 'reward for loyalty'. All this created a congenial background for the Lucknow Pact.

As agreed by the Bombay Congress, a joint committee consisting of the representatives of the Congress and the League was set up to frame a scheme for self-government for India. Accordingly, a draft proposal was prepared by the joint committee which was approved by the AICC in April 1916 and, subsequently, by a joint meeting of the AICC and the Council of the Muslim League in Calcutta in October 1916. In essence, this was a call for the government to grant dominion status to India. The agreement was sent to the Viceroy, signed by 19 members of the Supreme Council, including Jinnah, in November 1916. Finally, it was approved by the Lucknow Congress and the Indian Muslim League during the Congress session in December 1916, with some minor changes settling the quota of Muslim representation in the Punjab and Bengal provincial councils.

The following were the main features of the agreement:

1. Muslims should be represented through special electorates in the Provincial Legislative Councils in the following proportion of the total number of the elected members: Punjab: 50 per cent, United Province: 30 per cent, Bengal: 40 per cent, Bihar: 25 per cent, Central Province: 15 per cent, Madras: 15 per cent, Bombay: 33 per cent.
2. The total strength of the Imperial Legislative Council shall be 150, out of which 120 would be elected members and out of which 40 members would be Muslims.
3. No bill or resolution or any clause thereof, introduced by a non-official member, affecting one or the other community, shall proceed if opposed by three-fourth of the members of that community. This would be applicable both for the Imperial as well as the Provincial Councils.
4. The Imperial Legislative Council, however, shall have no power to interfere with the Government of India's direction of the military affairs, and the foreign and political relations of India, including in the matters of war, peace and treaties.

In essence, the Congress–League scheme, finally agreed at the Lucknow Congress, was an attempt to present a new vision of constitutional reforms which the dominant sections of the Indian political elite envisaged. Its primary significance lies in the fact that this was a high water-mark of Hindu–Muslim unity: whereas the Congress accepted separate electorates, the Muslim League expressed its willingness to join the mainstream of the national movement. The Muslim League also made concessions by accepting under representation in a Muslim majority area like Bengal, as a bargain for over-representation in Provinces like Bombay and United Provinces. Thus the interest of the Muslim political elite of UP got precedence over those of Bengal.

The Lucknow Pact had proposed quite radical constitutional reforms in respect of both provincial, and central governments as well as the relation between India and England. The following were other major demands put forward under the Pact:

1. A constitutional status for India similar to that of 'self-governing colonies'
2. Democratisation of the central as well as provincial legislative councils by providing four-fifth of its members to be elected on the basis of as wide a franchise as possible
3. The members of the Central as well as Provincial Executive Councils to be elected by their respective Legislative Councils
4. Autonomy for the Provincial Government
5. Grant of full measure of local self-government
6. The council of the Secretary of State should be abolished
7. Subordination of the executive to the legislature was to be ensured through the Legislative Councils.

It is evident that the acceptance of all these proposals could have resulted in substantial transfer of power to the Indian people. But except communal representation, no other demand was accepted by the Government under the Act of 1919.

The Lucknow Pact created a new hope for a united national movement as it marked a high-water mark in the process of Hindu–Muslim unity. But the subsequent developments belied the hopes created by it as the Hindu–Muslim unity was soon to elude the country. In retrospect, the Lucknow Pact had evoked several criticisms. Some of these criticisms are:

1. The Congress conceded the separate electorate system for the Muslims. This was not only a big climbdown for the Congress

but had long-term pernicious implications for the unity of the country and smacked of political opportunism. It encouraged the Muslims to be very conscious of their minority status and in all subsequent constitutional developments, the communal representation remained a constant theme on the part of the Muslims. The road from separate electorate to separate homeland for the Muslims was not distant. Both in the Centre and some provinces like UP and Bombay, the Muslims got more seats than was due to them on the basis of their population. Thus this was more than a compensation for their concession to accept 40 per cent seats in Bengal.

2. The provision that no bill or resolution would be passed if opposed by three-fourth of the community being affected, virtually gave a veto-power to the Muslims.
3. The Congress perspective was that the Lucknow Pact would lead to a united front in the cause of the national movement and would force the British Government to concede self-government to the people of India. But this proved illusory. By 1923-24 communal riots started occurring in the country. Even during the height of Hindu–Muslim bonhomie, the Moplah rebellion took place which involved attacks on the Hindus. Thus, Hindu–Muslim unity proved to be short-lived and illusory.
4. On the contrary, the Government of India took advantage of this agreement when the proposal for constitutional reforms was being considered. Though it conceded in principle that communal representation was 'dangerous' and obstructive of the 'unity and evolution' of nationalism in India, yet it was introduced in a much more accentuated form in the Act of 1919, under the plea that the Lucknow Pact had endorsed it.

In the long run the Lucknow Pact adversely impacted our national movement. Besides, it gave a handle to the British to pursue their policy of divide and rule more vigorously.

India's real progress could be achieved by a true understanding and harmonious relations between two great sister communities.

JINNAH

12 Khilafat Movement

The test of friendship is true assistance in adversity and whatever we are, Hindus, Parsees, Christians or Jews, we wish to live as one nation, surely the interest of any one of us must be the interest of all. We talk of Hindu–Mohammedan unity. It would be an empty phrase if the Hindus hold aloof from the Mohammedans when their vital interests are at stake.

MAHATMA GANDHI

Where God commands I am a Muslim first, a Muslim second and a Muslim last, and nothing but a Muslim. But where India's freedom is concerned, where welfare of India is concerned, I am an Indian first, an Indian second and an Indian last and nothing but an Indian.

MUHAMMAD ALI

The Khilafat Movement was one of the major movements in which Hindus and Muslims participated in a big way. In a way, this marked the highest watermark in the history of Hindu–Muslim unity and as such deserves an in-depth study. Besides, the Khilafat Movement has also been subjected to varying historical judgements. Some scholars have argued that the real seeds of partition were sown during the Khilafat Movement. The contrary view is that the failure of Hindu–Muslim bonhomie displayed during the initial stages of the movement led to the partition of the country.

Historical Background of the Khilafat Movement

The Khilafat movement was primarily concerned with the status of the Turkish Caliph, who happened to be the religious head of the

Muslim masses of the world. Interestingly, Indian Muslims have accepted him as their religious head on the promptings of the British. The British game behind it was to prop up Turkey, primarily with a view to contain Russian influence in the area. As the religious head, the caliph was also to look after Muslim religious places located in Arabia. Hence, his continuation as a caliph touched the religious sentiments of the Muslim masses. This was the primary issue which lay behind the Khilafat movement.

Several major political developments occurred during the second decade of the twentieth century, which laid down the foundation, as well as shaped the course, of the Khilafat movement. The First World War was one such major development. When Turkey joined the war against the Allied powers, the Muslims in India found themselves between the two horns of a dilemma: they had a religious affinity with Turkey and political affinity with the British. However, their task was made easier by the British promise of taking care of the Turkish interests including that of the Caliph. Indian Muslims, taking the British at their word, extended their support to the British war objectives. But once the war ended, it became common knowledge that the British would go back on their promises. Not only that, they would be a party to the Post-War settlement by which Muslim religious places would be taken away from the purview of the Caliph and even his own status would be adversely affected. With this surmise in Muslim minds the idea of Khilafat started gaining ground, leading to the formation of the Khilafat committee during 1919.

The second development which also affected the course and contours of Khilafat movement was Gandhiji's changed perception of the British rule. One might recall that Gandhiji had supported the British drive for recruitment of soldiers on the call of the Viceroy in 1918. Not only that, he himself worked so hard in Kheda district of Gujarat for the recruitment of soldiers that he ruined his health in the process. What changed his perception about the British rule, was the passage of the Rowlatt Act in March 1919. The Act sought to replace the defence of India Act, which, in itself, was a draconian measure. But the new Act had still sharper teeth: more stringent provisions like detention without trial and that too for as long a time as the government wished. The whole issue was summed up in a popular saying: 'No appeal, no *vakil*, no *dalil*'. This draconian measure had come in the context of the Allied powers' war time declaration that the war was being fought on the basic principle of self-determination. As such, it was a real anti-

Satyagraha Leaflet No. 16.

SUNDAY'S *HARTAL*.

ITS RELIGIOUS SPIRIT.

Brothers and Sisters,

To declare a *hartal* is no small matter. It requires strong reasons to support it. Let us therefore examine the justification for it. The citizens of Bombay are impatient to give some outward evidence of their deep affection for Mr. Horniman. They can provide it in a striking manner by means of *hartal*. Everybody's feelings will be tested thereby. Moreover, *hartal* is an ancient Indian institution for expressing national sorrow and we can therefore demonstrate through *hartal* our grief over the deportation and *hartal* is the best method of marking our strong disapproval of the action of the Government. It is a means, more powerful than monster meetings of expressing national opinion. Thus we serve three purposes by *hartal* and all of them are so great that we do not expose ourselves to the charge of exaggeration in declaring *hartal*.

This much is clear that none of the purposes above named will be served if suspension of business is brought about through fear of public opprobrium or physical pressure. If suspension were to be brought about by terrorism and if Mr. Horniman came to know it, he could not but be displeased and grieved by the knowledge, and such artificial *hartal* would fail to produce any effect upon the Government. *Hartal* forcibly brought about cannot be considered Satyagrahi *hartal*. In any thing Satyagrahi there should be purity of motive, means and end. I therefore hope that no man or woman who is unwilling to suspend business will in any way be interfered with, but that he or she will be guaranteed protection from any harm whatsoever. *I would far rather wish that people did not suspend business on Sunday in the city of Bombay and that the organisers were exposed to ridicule than that force was used upon a single person in order to make him suspend business.* In order to avoid all risk of commotion in Bombay on Sunday, the idea of holding public meetings has been discountenanced and all have been advised to, remain indoors. As all Satyagraha activity should be guided by the religious spirit, I have suggested that we should fast for twenty-four hours and devote the day to religious contemplation, and it is to be hoped that all the members of families including children and servants will take part in the religious observance. Hindus may have Bhagwadgita read to them. It takes four hours to read through it with clear pronunciation and other Hindu religious books might be read in addition or in place of it. The Mahomedans and others may have their own scriptures read to them. It will be a proper way of spending the day to read the stories of great Satyagrahis such as Prahlad, Harishchandra, Mirabai, Imams Hasan and Hoosein, Socrates and others. It will be opportune also to explain to family gatherings Mr. Horniman's title to our affection. The chief thing to be remembered is that we may not fritter away next Sunday in playing cards, *Chowpat*, gambling or in sheer laziness, but that it should be so spent as to make us better men and women for national service. Better placed and well-to-do families will, I hope, invite such of their neighbours as may be poor, solitary or ignorant, to participate in the religious devotion. A brotherly spirit is cultivated not by words but only by deeds.

Mr. Motilal Dahyabhai Zaveri of Kalbadevi Road has just dropped in and informed me that before the news of the declaration of *hartal* next Sunday, he had issued invitations for a wedding party on that day. He also said there were many such parties to be given on the same day. Mr. Motilal was most anxious that he and his friends should take part in the observance. I venture to advise that so far as the religious part of the wedding ceremonial was concerned, it should be gone through without disturbance, but that dinner parties and other rejoicings might be postponed to Monday. His patriotic affection for Mr. Horniman was such that he immediately accepted the advice and I tender it for the acceptance of those who may be similarly situated.

M. K. GANDHI.

6th May, 1919.

climax. Gandhiji spontaneously gave a call for Satyagraha and even set up a Satyagraha Sabha to carry on the struggle. The date 30 March 1919 was fixed as the D-day which was subsequently changed to 6 April. The people responded to his call in an unprecedented way and in their exuberance certain violent acts in Delhi, Ahmedabad and Amritsar were committed.

The people of Punjab came to the forefront in their fight against the Act. Gandhiji was arrested on 9 April 1919 and protest processions were taken out, which were fired upon in Amritsar resulting in the death of some people. In response, 13 April 1919 was fixed as a day of protests and people gathered at Jallianwala Bagh to lodge their protests. General Dyer, who had taken charge of the military contingent, ordered his forces to fire upon the unsuspecting, unarmed people without any warning. The firing was indiscriminate and altogether 1650 rounds were fired, which left 379 dead and 1137 wounded, as per official records. The non-official estimate ran much higher. There was virtually no escape route and the one that was available was blocked by military personnel. Firing was done with a view to kill people. People could not escape even if they wished to flee. Hence, it came to be known as the Jallianwala Bagh massacre. Not satisfied with that, martial law was declared in Amritsar and indiscriminate flogging and firing followed. At some places, people were even asked to crawl like reptiles. This was the greatest insult to the honour, dignity and self-respect of the people. Even the earlier brutal record of the British rule appeared as a party or free lunch as compared to the Jallianwala Bagh massacre. This further alienated the people and in fact infuriated them.

The Hindu–Muslim bonhomie and the Home Rule Movement led by Tilak and Annie Besant was another major development which prepared the background for the Khilafat movement. Their significance lay in the fact that they brought both the communities closer to each other. That paved the way for a united struggle against the British. But what really lent a helping hand to the Khilafat cause was the unsatisfactory nature of the constitutional reforms offered by the Act of 1919. For instance, Annie Besant found the reforms unworthy of England to offer and India to accept. However, some of the Moderates who had left the Congress supported the proposed reforms. Tilak looked at them as a 'sunless dawn'. It was in such a surcharged political environment that the Amritsar Congress met in December 1919. Despite certain voices of dissent, including that of C R Das and others,

Ali Brothers

Gandhiji, with the support of Malaviya and Motilal Nehru, carried the day. The Amritsar Congress, in spite of finding the reforms as 'unsatisfactory' and 'inadequate', expressed its willingness to give a trial to it. In fact, Gandhiji, despite his changed perception of the British rule, still had hopes from the British rule. This could be illustrated by the fact that despite the Jallianwala Bagh massacre, he neither supported Hasarat Mohani's boycott proposal at the November 1919 meeting of the Khilafat Committee nor did he totally oppose the reform proposals offered under the Act of 1919 at the Amritsar Congress (December 1919).

But two major developments took place in May 1920, which added further fuel to the fire of the people's resentment against the British. What was more, both these developments synchronised. These were: acceptance of the majority view of the Hunter Committee and the publication of the terms of the Treaty of Sèvres. It may be recalled that the Hunter Committee had been set up to enquire into the Punjab massacre after Rabindranath Tagore had renounced his Knighthood and Shankaran Nair had resigned from the membership of the Executive Council. The Congress, not being satisfied with the terms of reference of the committee, had set up its own enquiry committee with Gandhiji as one of its members. The Committee appointed by the Congress found the Jallianwala Bagh massacre as nothing but well calculated, and cold-blooded murder of innocent, unoffending, unarmed men, women and children, unparalleled for heartless and cowardly brutality in modern times. The committee had demanded adequate compensation for the families of the dead and the wounded. But the Government ignored this report and accepted the majority view of the Hunter Committee, in May 1920. The majority view of the Hunter Committee had exonerated all officials involved in the massacre. The Government defended General Dyer's brutal acts as an error of judgment and Sir Michael O' Dwyer, the Governor of Punjab, was allowed to go totally scot free.

It was a matter of coincidence that the Treaty of Sèvres was made public in May 1920 though it had been signed in August 1919. The net result of the treaty was that the Ottoman Empire was to be divided. Accordingly, it was to lose the entire rich area of Asia Minor. The Arab Provinces of the Turkish Empire were to be mandated territory under the British and French tutelage. And what was more, the Sultan was to be deprived of the leadership of the Muslim masses. Not only that, he was to become a virtual prisoner of the Allied High

Commission. Thus, the worst fears of the Muslim masses had come true and their resentment reached its climax by May 1920. The coincidence of the acceptance of the Hunter Committee Report and the publication of the Treaty of Sèvres turned out to be the proverbial last straw on the back of both Gandhiji and the Muslim leadership led by the Ali brothers. That turned Gandhiji from being a loyalist to a non-cooperator, as he himself admitted in the course of his trial in 1922.

At the end of the First World War fear gripped the Indian Muslims about the impending dismemberment of the Ottoman Empire. Consequently, the Khilafat Committee was set up in March 1919. In fact, the Khilafat Committee had two wings: the Bombay and the Delhi Group led by the Ali Brothers. The Bombay group favoured memoranda and delegation to press for its demands. The Ali brothers favoured agitational methods. It was this group which pressed for a countrywide non-cooperation movement when the All India Khilafat Conference met at Delhi in November 1919. Gandhiji tried to play a mediating role between these too warring groups. The Muslim leadership was all out to seek Hindu support for an All India agitation. They were also keen to have Gandhiji's support in particular. Gandhiji did not support Hasarat Mohani's proposal for the boycott of British goods. However, as referred to earlier, the acceptance of the Hunter Committee report and the publication of the Treaty of Sèvres changed the entire course of events. The Khilafat committee met in Allahabad in June 1920 to chalk out a plan for non-cooperation on an All India basis. This was attended by a large number of the Congress leadership including Gandhiji. They extended their unstinted support to the Khilafat proposal for the boycott of titles, civil service, police, army, schools and colleges. Subsequently, Gandhiji got the Congress Working Committee to extend support to the non-cooperation movement on three issues: Punjab wrongs, Khilafat injustice and the Swaraj. He followed it up by successfully seeking support for the same from the Calcutta and the Nagpur Congress.

The Course of the Khilafat Movement

The Khilafat Movement was carried out in a number of ways. In UP some Muslims took it as a general revolt against the authority, taking Khilafat in its literal sense of opposition. In Malabar, the Moplahs indulged in violence against the Hindu zamindars. The protest took yet another form when, in June 1920, 20,000 Muslims, *Muhajirin*, tried to do *hijrat* to Afghanistan in anger against the government over the issue of dishonouring their Caliph. Millennial hopes were thus aroused among the Muslim masses. For example, in August 1920, Zafar Ali Khan, editor of *Zamindar*, proclaimed from his house top that Mehandi, the Muslim saviour, was coming soon.

Subsequently, a deputation under the leadership of Dr Ansari called on the Governor-General to apprise him of the hurt feelings of the Muslims but nothing came out of it. In March 1920, the Ali brothers went to England and other countries to seek support for the cause of Khilafat but they returned empty-handed.

Soon the Khilafat Movement became a part of the Non-Cooperation Movement and along with Gandhiji, the Ali brothers emerged as prominent leaders of the movement. However, after the withdrawal of the Non-Cooperation Movement by Gandhiji, on 11 February 1922, the Khilafat Movement also lost its initial momentum. What gave it a big blow was the new leadership of Mustafa Kemal Pasha in Turkey who abolished the office of Caliph. Thus the very basis of the movement was taken away and the movement died a natural death.

Critical Appreciation of the Khilafat Movement

The Khilafat Movement, in general and Mahatma's unstinted support to it, had been faulted, both by academic historians as well as by his contemporaries, primarily on two counts. One, that the Muslim leadership was primarily inspired and guided by their pan-Islamic sentiments rather than the felt-need of Indian nationalism. It was, the critics aver, a tactical move on their part to seek the support of Gandhiji who had emerged as the uncrowned king of the Indian masses. When Khilafat became a non-issue in view of the abolition of the office of the Caliph by the Turkish leadership, more militant sections of the Khilafat leadership led by the Ali brothers and Maulana Abdul Bari fell out of the mainstream of the national movement and they even became critical of Gandhian politics. Thus, the tactical nature of the initiative of a section of the Khilafat leadership is conclusively proved by subsequent developments in Indian as well as in world politics. Second, in the course of the movement, the services of mullahs and maulavis were used in a big way for the popular mobilisation of the Muslim obscurantist masses leading to their consolidation based on Islamic religiosity. The forces, thus, unleashed by the Khilafat Movement retarded the growth of secular politics in India. Besides, it also became clear in the course of the movement that the Muslim's commitment to the principle of non-violence was more a matter of convenience rather than of conviction. Such a ground swell of Muslim consolidation, based on religious sentiments, provided a solid base for mobilisation of Muslim masses by the Muslim League after 1937, leading ultimately to the partition of the country. To sum up, a lot of religious passion was aroused among the Muslim masses during the Khilafat Movement which proved disastrous for the nascent Indian nationalism.

In defence of Gandhiji, it could be easily asserted that for him Hindu–Muslim unity had always remained as an article of faith since his South African days. Besides, the need for putting up a united fight against the British imperialism was so pressing that he looked at the Khilafat agitation as a God-sent opportunity to forge a Hindu–Muslim alliance on a national scale. He stuck to his faith till the end, which reached its apogee during the dark days of 1946-47. If the critics still persisted with their doubts about his secular credentials, his martyrdom completely vindicated him.

Some of his critics also point out that the Mahatma was primarily responsible for mixing up of politics and religion, which was actually experimented during Khilafat Movement. They further argue that it was this trend which ultimately culminated in the partition of the country. Once again, it must be borne in mind that Gandhiji was not the progenitor of the Khilafat Movement: he just lent his support to it. According to him, a religious perspective aimed at providing an ethical and moral base for politics. In the absence of a religious perspective, politics would become a mere power game. His principle of *sarva-dharma sama-bhava* hardly differed from a secular view of politics.

Nevertheless, there is no denying the fact that the Khilafat Movement did inject a lot of communal virus in the Indian body politic. But such a perception is based on our hindsight. During 1919-20, Khilafat had provided a rare opportunity to build up a united mass movement based on the rock-bottom of Hindu–Muslim unity. Yes, it failed but that does not mean the effort was not worthwhile. Success and failure are not the right criteria for measuring the just and righteous nature of a venture. As a poet said:

Not all who seem to fail have failed indeed
Not all who fail have therefore worked in vain;
For all our acts to many issues lead;
Out of honest purpose, pure and plain.

UNKNOWN POET

13 Non-Cooperation Movement

Proclaim to the government: you may hang us, you may send us to prison, but you will get no cooperation from us. You will not get it in jail, not get it on the gallows, not even in the regiments of army. You will not get it in legislative or in any department of the government service.

MAHATMA GANDHI

We have already delineated the historical background which led to the launching of the Khilafat and Non-Cooperation Movements. The deteriorating economic conditions in the post-war period had already generated a ground swell of anti-government feeling among the Indian masses. What gave an added momentum to the popular discontent were three immediate issues, namely, Khilafat wrongs, Punjab massacre and 'inadequate' nature of the reforms under the Act of 1919. What precipitated the issue was the publication of the Treaty of Sevres with Turkey, which demolished the position of the Sultan, almost reducing him to the position of a virtual prisoner in his palace. It further infuriated the Muslim masses who were already apprehensive about it despite the British assurances to the contrary. The publication of the Hunter Committee Report and acceptance of its majority view by the government, despite the Indian members' dissenting note, only added fuel to the fire that was burning in the hearts of the Indian people. It is also to be noted that the Indian National Congress had set up its own committee to enquire into the Punjab atrocities, which included Mahatma Gandhi as one of its members. The committee had held the British officials associated with the Punjab action guilty and had pleaded for strong action against them. The government ignored all this and accepted the majority view of the Hunter Committee, exonerating the Punjab officials. That sealed the fate of any rapprochement between the government and the people of India.

It is also relevant to note that the Khilafat Movement was already on. The Khilafat Committee held a meeting in November 1919, in Delhi, and its members reached a general consensus on launching a Civil Disobedience Movement. However, Mahatma Gandhi, who was present in that meeting, did not support Mohani's proposal of civil disobedience at that stage. He was still hopeful that good sense would prevail and the government would not ride roughshod over the people's sentiments. But this was not to happen and the government went ahead with its own plan. In April 1920, Shaukat Ali, one of the prominent members of the Khilafat Movement, had warned the government that if it failed to listen to the saner voice of the people of India, in general, and Muslims in particular, a joint Hindu–Muslim Non-Cooperation Movement would be launched under the leadership of Mahatma Gandhi. Soon after the acceptance of the Hunter Committee Report and publication of the terms of the treaty of Sevres in May 1920, the Khilafat Committee met at Allahabad during June 1–3 and decided upon a fourfold boycott programme. The programme included: (1) boycott of the titles offered by the government; (2) boycott of civil service, army and police; (3) boycott of schools and colleges, and (4) boycott of law courts. This virtually amounted to total non-cooperation with the Government. As Mahatma Gandhi himself, in his statement during his trial, put it: 'The Khilafat promise was not redeemed, the Punjab crime was whitewashed, the reforms were only a method of further draining India of her wealth and prolonging her servitude.'

At the Banaras meeting it was also decided to seek the opinions of the provincial Congress committees on the sensitive issue of non-cooperation. Gandhiji made it amply clear that he favoured launching of the Non-Cooperation Movement. Though there was general support in favour of non-cooperation among the provincial committees, but there was some reservation on the issue of the boycott of the Council election which was getting due under the 1919 Act. Earlier, when Gandhiji had approached Tilak, seeking his support on the issue of satyagraha, Tilak was sceptical about its efficacy, though he did not oppose it. Besides, Tilak was not very enthusiastic on the issue of support to the Muslims on the Khilafat issue, and he passed away on 1 August 1920. As decided earlier, the Non-Cooperation Movement was formally launched on 1 August 1920. Many fasted in the memory of Tilak and participated in the demonstrations and hartal as a part of the movement.

It was with this mixed bag of support that the special session of the Congress was held in Calcutta in September 1920, under the Presidentship of Lala Lajpat Rai. The old guards of the Congress like C R Das, Annie Besant, Madan Mohan Malaviya, Jinnah and Bipin Chandra Pal were opposed to the resolution favouring Non-Cooperation, moved by Mahatma Gandhi himself. But Gandhiji was determined to pursue his line of action and remained undeterred, even in the face of the old guard's opposition. Ultimately, he succeeded in getting his resolution, favouring the launching of the Non-Cooperation Movement, passed with a massive majority: 1886 delegates favoured his resolution while only 884 opposed it. The Calcutta resolution specifically stated: 'This Congress is, further, of the opinion that there is no course left open for the people of India but to approve and adopt the policy of progressive non-violent non-cooperation inaugurated by Mahatma Gandhi until the said wrongs are righted and swaraj is established'. The Congress favoured seven forms of boycott, namely, (1) boycott of titles and honorary offices, etc.; (2) boycott of the official and semi-official functions held by the government; (3) boycott of schools and colleges; (4) boycott of legal courts; (5) boycott of recruitment for service in Mesopotamia; (6) boycott of the Council's election and also boycott of voting, and (7) boycott of foreign goods. As an integral part of the Calcutta resolution on non-cooperation, there was also a programme of constructive work. An attempt was made to provide an alternative system while calling upon the people to boycott the government institutions. Thus, a national system of education, private arbitration courts, swadeshi goods, and hand-spinning and hand-weaving of clothes were to be supported and promoted.

The Calcutta conference heralded a new Gandhian era of combative and constructive politics. In pursuance of the Calcutta conference, there was a general boycott of the Council's election held in November 1920, both at the candidates as well as on the voters levels. The Congress met in its annual conference at Nagpur in December 1920 which highlighted certain important events. In the first place, Gandhiji gained further support, even from among the old guard of the Congress; both C R Das and Lala Lajpat Rai, who had earlier opposed the non-cooperation resolution at the Calcutta Congress, lent unstinted support to it. The Nagpur Congress accepted, in principle, the general dissociation from the Government at various levels along with the non-payment of taxes. However, it left the actual implementation of these programmes to be decided on a later date. Among other things, the Nagpur Congress supported the earlier programme of boycott along with its commitment to work for Hindu–Muslim unity, promotion of national education, raising a national fund, etc. However, this Congress really laid down a roadmap for democratisation of its organisational structure. It suggested a number of changes in its constitution. Some of these changes were as follows:

1. the formation of the 15-member working committee to look after the day-to-day work of the organisation;
2. to set up an All India Congress Committee (AICC) with 350 members;
3. Re-organisation of the Congress Provincial Committees on a linguistic basis;
4. the organisation of the Congress to be built at village, town, tehsil and district levels, along with the provincial and national levels; and
5. the Congress was to launch a membership programme with a symbolic fee of only four annas (one quarter of a rupee). This was the first major attempt to reach out to the common man.

Apart from organisational changes at Nagpur, the Congress also tried to change its creed and its goal. Its earlier goal of the 'attainment of self-government by constitutional means' was replaced by the 'attainment of swaraj by peaceful and legitimate means'. One obvious result of this new creed of the Congress was that non-violent satyagraha came to be accepted as the legitimate means under the new dispensation of the Congress. Thus, the Congress came very near to the Gandhian vision of the constructive and combative programmes and Mahatma Gandhi became its tallest leader.

Backed by the Nagpur Congress, the programme of non-cooperation soon gathered momentum. The people responded to the movement with a lot of enthusiasm. The Council election was successfully boycotted. Titles and honours were renounced on a massive scale. A number of prominent legal practitioners like Motilal Nehru, C R Das, Jawaharlal Nehru, Vallabhbhai Patel, Rajendra Prasad, C Rajagopalachari and a score of other legal luminaries left their legal practice. A number of institutions of national education like Gujarat Vidyapeeth, Bihar Vidyapeeth, Kashi Vidyapeeth and National College, Lahore came up to provide education to those young students who had earlier left their schools and colleges. Eminent persons like

Subhas Chandra Bose, Acharya Narendra Dev, Rajendra Prasad, Dr Sampurnanand and others became teachers at these national institutions.

In the background of such a massive response to its non-cooperation programme, the All India Congress Committee met at Vijayawada in April 1921. AICC decided to concentrate its attention on the collection of the Tilak Swaraj Fund, securing a membership of one crore Congress members and distribution of 20 lakh charkhas by June 1921. Once again there was a warm popular response to the Congress programme: The Tilak Swaraj Fund was oversubscribed, and 50 lakh Congress volunteers were enrolled. From July 1921 onwards the attention of the Congress shifted to the boycott of foreign clothes. It was also decided to boycott the visit of the Prince of Wales in November 1921. However, a final decision on launching of a mass civil disobedience movement along with the non-payment of taxes was postponed for the time being.

July 1921 was marked by an important development. Muhammad Ali was arrested as he had made a declaration that Muslims could never accept the fact of working in the British Army as it was against their religion. His arrest by the government led to widespread protests, and a large number of the Congressmen repeated the same statement forcing the government to ignore the whole issue.

But this was followed by an unfortunate development in August 1921 when the Moplahs of the Malabar attempted to establish a Khilafat kingdom. Soon it took a communal turn, and in the process a number of Hindus were killed and their properties were looted and seized by the Moplahs. It did not stop at that: some forcible conversion of Hindus to Islam also took place. The number of forcible conversions went up to 2,500 and the death-toll among Hindus went up to 600. Soon repressive measures by the government followed. A number of Moplahs were killed, and a large number of them were wounded. At one stage 45,000 of them were being held as prisoners. In November 1921, some Moplahs died, while being carried in a railway wagon, on account of asphyxiation. Strong measures, ultimately, resulted in the control of the situation.

During the visit of the Prince of Wales in November 1921, another unfortunate incident took place in Bombay. When the whole country was observing a strike on the eve of his visit, a section of Christians in Bombay tried to give him a warm welcome. This drew the wrath of some people and some Christians were attacked and assaulted. Gandhiji went around the city condemning these violent acts and even fasted for two days. All this must have convinced the Congress leadership that the country was not yet ready for mass civil disobedience. Thus in November 1921, All India Congress Committee authorised the provincial committees to start civil disobedience on their own responsibility.

Soon the government changed its strategy and went whole-hog in the use of repressive measures. It declared the Congress and Khilafat works as unlawful activities. Congressmen responded to this challenge and a large number of Congress workers and leaders like C R Das, Mualana Azad, Lala Lajpat Rai, Motilal Nehru, Jawaharlal Nehru and others courted arrest and were put behind bars. Altogether, 25,000 Congress and Khilafat workers were behind bars.

It was in such a surcharged atmosphere that the Congress met at Ahmedabad in December 1921 and it called up its members to suspend all other activities and volunteer themselves for arrest. Mahatma Gandhi was made its sole executive and things started moving fast. Meanwhile an attempt was made for a negotiated settlement with the government but it failed on the issue of the release of the Ali brothers from jail.

Gandhiji informed the Viceroy on 1 February 1922 that he intended to launch a civil disobedience movement in the Bardoli Taluka of Gujarat. He wanted to make Bardoli as a test case for a mass civil disobedience movement and no tax campaign. Hectic preparations were on for the Bardoli campaign. The seven-day notice which Gandhiji had delivered to Lord Reading was to end on 7 February 1922.

Meanwhile, on 5 February 1922 an unfortunate incident occurred at Chauri-Chaura village in the district of Gorakhpur in eastern UP. In the course of a peasants' march, some scuffles took place which led to police firing. In retaliation the people turned violent and 23 policemen were burnt in a police thana by the infuriated mob. Gandhiji was shocked beyond measure by the unfortunate turn of events and he withdrew the movement on 11 February 1922. Subsequently, his decision was endorsed by the Congress Working Committee. Soon after the withdrawal of the movement, Gandhiji was arrested on 22 February 1922 and was put on trial on 18 March 1922. He pleaded guilty to all charges and was awarded six-years imprisonment.

Criticisms of the Non-Cooperation Movement

The Non-Cooperation Movement and its undisputed leader, Mahatma Gandhi, had been subjected to severe criticisms on various counts. First, Gandhiji had been criticised for his decision to withdraw the movement on 11 February 1922 in the wake of the violent incident of Chauri-Chaura, both by his contemporary political leaders and also by some historians. Subhas Chandra Bose, one of the tallest among our national leaders, called it a 'national calamity'. R P Dutt, a Marxist historian, looked at the issue of the withdrawal of the movement in the light of 'class interest' and not on the issue of violence and non-violence. Even Jawaharlal Nehru expressed his 'amazement' at the decision of Gandhiji. And there is no doubt that the thousands of young men and women, who had put everything at stake in this first major battle for Swaraj, were thoroughly disappointed. More so, as the leader (Gandhiji) had earlier promised Swaraj within one year and the act of withdrawal came as a great anti-climax. Even some of the historians, who have tried to defend Gandhiji on this issue, looked at it more as a matter of strategy rather than that of principles. In their view, the continuation of the movement, after it turned violent at Chauri-Chaura, would have drawn sharp repressive measures from the government leading not to a decisive battle for Swaraj but futile sufferings, sacrifices and even demoralisation among the masses. However, for Gandhiji it was not a matter of strategy but rather an issue involving close affinity between the means and ends. As he himself put it 'I would suffer every humiliation, every torture, absolute ostracism and death itself to prevent the movement from becoming violent.' Thus for Gandhiji it was a matter of principle and not a matter of strategy.

Second, the movement and its leaders have been criticised on a more serious count of the mixing of religion and politics. It is argued that by lending support to the Khilafat Movement, Gandhiji unwittingly lent undeserved respectability to Muslim communalism, which ultimately led to the partition of the country. In this connection, it is further submitted that even Jinnah, who ultimately led the movement for Pakistan, was against the Khilafat–Non-Cooperation Movement as he, at that stage of his life, was opposed to the idea of mixing religion with politics. Gandhiji's support to the Khilafat Movement, ultimately, strengthened the forces of obscurantism and religious bigotry. In our view, the critics forget that Gandhiji was working to lay the foundation of a free, pluralistic and united India and for that goal, a united national movement was the basic need. Both the Khilafat and the Non-Cooperation Movements should be viewed in that larger Gandhian perspective. Besides, for Gandhiji, religion and politics were twins, deriving strength from each other, rather than being mutually exclusive.

Third, Rabindranath Tagore had his objection to the movement on a more fundamental level. He sensed a 'fierce joy of nihilism' in Gandhiji and even went to the extent of saying that the Mahatma was getting 'enamoured of his own doctrine' – which was nothing less than a 'dangerous form of egotism'. Commenting on the overall objective of the movement, Tagore described swaraj as a 'mist' which the Mahatma 'dangles before the country with the bait of getting dirt cheap and in double quick time'. He did not stop at that and pinpointed the consequences of the Gandhian style of work. He said: 'If nothing but oracles will serve to move us, oracles will have to be manufactured morning, noon and night for the sake of urgent needs and all other voices will be defeated.'

On his part, Gandhiji defended the idea of non-cooperation as a 'protest against an unwitting and unwilling participation in evil'. In parenthesis, one could say that these two great sons of India were looking at the problem in the light of their own perspective of truth and that is why they retained the high regard for each other, although each stuck to his own perception of truth.

Despite these criticisms, the Non-Cooperation Movement undoubtedly made significant contributions to further the ends of our national movement. Some of these contributions could be listed as follows:

The achievements of the movement on the economic front were quite spectacular. It gave a considerable boost to handloom and khadi industries, which was a positive development, both in terms of income and employment generation. It also led to a sharp decline of the quantum of the import of British goods. What was more, it paved the way for peoples-led self-help programmes like village reconstruction, village sanitation, and revival of handloom and khadi industries.

On the social front, the movement made still more significant contributions. Some of its programmes, like Hindu–Muslim unity and eradication of untouchability, were concerted attempts to strengthen the social fabric of the country, resulting in the emergence of a united national movement. Besides, multi-faceted prohibition campaigns brought a large number of women in the national movement – a group that started participating in the national movement for the first time in a big way. Besides, there was a remarkable spread of the national movement in geographical terms: new regions and new linguistic groups were brought into the national mainstream. New social groups and classes like the peasants, scheduled castes, scheduled tribes and women identified themselves with the national struggle. Not only that, a number of local movements, viz., Akali movement in Punjab, peasants movement in Midnapore in Bengal, Kanika in Orissa, Kheda in Gujarat, Gunter in Andhra, as the well as the peasant movement in Awadh in UP and that of north Bihar also got integrated as part and parcel of the national movement. All these led to widening of the base of the national movement, both in spatial and social-group terms.

On the political front also, the Non-Cooperation Movement made a departure in several ways. Swaraj became the battle-cry of the movement. It is true that swaraj was not yet well-defined but its mystique, along with Gandhiji's charisma, caught the imagination of even the common men and women. Not only that, the Congress, by committing itself to 'all peaceful and legitimate means' for the attainment of Swaraj, freed itself from the charges of political mendicancy. The people had an unprecederated sense of empowerment and even the lowliest of the low was now equipped with a new weapon of satyagraha. They, both individually and collectively, could challenge even the mightiest of the mighty. Thus, now the war for swaraj was on and losing or winning a battle here and there became immaterial for the people. As Mahatma Gandhi put: 'It is high time that the British people were made to realise that the fight that commenced in 1920 is a fight to finish whether it lasts for one month or one year or many years and whether the representatives of British re-enact all the orgies of the Mutiny days with redoubled force or whether they do not.'

These were not the words of mere bravado: they echoed and re-echoed in the hearts and homes of the millions of the people and that finally sealed the fate of the British Empire. Besides, the movement brought in thousands of young men and women who, virtually got wedded to swaraj and were ever more than willing to sacrifice all that they had for the sake of the country. In subsequent years, they proved to be the backbone of the national movement. Not only that, as the leaders of the old generation were fading out, the movement gave a new band of leaders who successfully led the country to independence in 1947. Leaders like C Rajagopalachari, Sardar Patel, Maulana Azad, Abdul Ghaffar Khan, Rajendra Prasad, Acharaya Narendra Dev, Jayaprakash Narayan, B C Roy, Shrikrishna Sinha, T Prakasam, Jawaharlal Nehru, Subhas Chandra Bose, G B Pant, Ravishankar Shukla, Jai Narayan Vyas, to name a few, were the products of the Non-Cooperation Movement. Some of them even played a crucial role in laying the foundation of a free and democratic India in the post-independence era.

On the cultural front also the movement was no less successful. A number of institutions of national education were founded, which became the mainstay of the national movement. Thus there was a great cultural resurgence in India: 'Indianess' became an idea, to have pride in and 'toadyism' became a term of ridicule and rebuke. Thus a new swadeshi spirit permeated throughout the length and breadth of the country. The movement also attempted to build up a bridge between the classes and masses. Gandhiji started wearing only a loincloth in the course of the movement. He became a symbol of peasant's simplicity, religious and spiritual humility, and political militancy – all these virtues blended in one. His trial and the bold fight put up by him became the symbol of new defiance, further exposing the iniquitous nature of the British rule. Thousands followed him and vied with each other in receiving imprisonment and other punishment with a sense of spiritual joy. All this made the people 'fearless' – and with that half of the battle for swaraj was won. As Jawaharlal Nehru put it: 'This little man of poor physique had something of steel in him, something rocklike which did not yield to the physical power, however great that might be'.

The people came to trust him, adore him and on his call, were more than willing to sacrifice everything they had. Truly, the Non-Cooperation Movement proved to be a real milestone on the road to our national struggle. The temporary setback which the movement suffered actually laid the foundation for a long and protracted battle for swaraj.

Truth for ever on the scaffold
Wrong for ever on the throne
yet that scaffold sways the future. . . .

JAMES-LOWELL

14 Swaraj Party

Ours is a purity movement, and as such is above diplomacy. To enter the Councils with the object of making them a failure is not only diplomacy but it is also diplomat's duplicity which every non-cooperator should disdain.

SARDAR PATEL

The Council's entry is and can be thoroughly consistent with the principle of non-cooperation as we understand that principle to be.

C R DAS AND MOTILAL NEHRU

The Swaraj party led by C R Das and Motilal Nehru, played a crucial role at a critical stage of our national struggle. But before we examine its genesis, its programme and policy and its working and contributions, it would be relevant to introduce its leaders: C R Das and Motilal Nehru. C R Das (1870–1925), after being educated at Presidency College, Calcutta, went to England and was called to the bar in 1893. He started his practice in Calcutta and soon became a leading legal practitioner of the country. He was associated with Congress politics from the beginning and soon became a prominent leader of Bengal. He was one of the leading members of the committee which was set up by the Congress to inquire into the Jallianwala Bagh massacre and other atrocities committed in Punjab. The committee had recommended compensation for the victims and punishment to the officials involved. However, the government rejected its recommendation and C R Das, along with other Congress leaders led by Gandhiji, came to the conclusion that non-cooperation with the Government was the only course open to them. When the Non-Cooperation Movement was launched he gave up legal practice and started a life of simplicity and self-denial. On the withdrawal of the Non-Cooperation Movement, he stood for changing the earlier decision of the Congress for Council boycott and strongly pleaded for a new policy of Council entry to wreck it from within. Subsequently, he along with Motilal Nehru founded the Swaraj Party and became its leader in the Bengal Assembly. Unfortunately, he died in 1925 at the comparatively young age of 55.

Motilal Nehru, the co-founder of the Swaraj Party, had a similar background. Born at Agra in 1861, he started his legal practice and soon became a leading practitioner of the country. He had a roaring practice and became associated with the Congress as early as in 1893 at the Allahabad Congress. Initially he was with the Congress liberal group. However, soon after becoming a member of the UP Legislative Assembly, in 1907, he started drifting away from liberal politics as he was becoming disillusioned with the British policy towards India. However, when Annie Besant was interned in 1917, Motilal Nehru came out openly against the British policy. In 1919, he brought out a paper called *Independent* and presided over the Amritsar Congress in the same year. In the wake of the Jallianwala Bagh massacre he joined hands with Mahatma Gandhi and on the call of the Non-Cooperation Movement he gave up his legal practice and also the membership of the UP Legislative Assembly. Not only that, he gave up his luxurious living and opted for a life of self-chosen simplicity. He founded the Swaraj Party, became its leader in the Central Legislative Assembly and played a glorious role in exposing the misdeeds of the colonial administration. He re-named his house at Allahabad as 'Swaraj Bhavan' and donated it to the country. He died in 1931 at the age of 70.

The Genesis of the Swaraj Party

The sudden withdrawal of the Non-Cooperation Movement by Mahatma Gandhi, in the wake of the Chauri-Chaura incident, created a crisis of confidence among the leaders of the movement. What further deepened the crisis was the arrest, trial and imprisonment of Mahatma Gandhi for a period of six years. The country was caught in a mood of despair and dilemma and was clouded with indecisiveness. There were contradictory opinions: some favoured the continuation of the Gandhian policy of non-cooperation and boycott, other like the liberals wanted to pursue the policy of cooperation with the Government. But even among the Congressmen there was a sharp division, particularly on the issue of the Council's entry. The entire leadership got divided on the issue. Even the Civil Disobedience Enquiry Committee, set up by the Congress in June 1922, and which submitted its report in October 1992, could not settle the issue. The Committee was evenly divided between two groups of the no-changers and the pro-changers, though it had unanimously recommended that the country was not ready for a mass civil disobedience movement. The real bone of contention was the Council's entry. While C Rajagopalachari, M A Ansari and S Kasturiranga Iyengar favoured the old Gandhian line of non-cooperation with greater emphasis on the constructive programme, Motilal Nehru, Ajmal Khan and Vithalbhai Patel favoured the Council entry. The Congress got ideologically divided in the two groups of 'pro-changers' and 'no-changers'. It was with such a divided house that the Congress met in annual session at Gaya in December 1922 with C R Das as its president. C R Das pleaded for the Council entry. But ultimately the no-changers led by Rajagopalachari had their way. Thus pro-changers were left with two options, either to submit to majority opinion or pursue their own independent line by floating a new organisation. They opted for the latter. C R Das resigned from the office of the president of the Congress in January 1923.

The Aims and Objectives of the Swaraj Party

Soon after leaving the Presidentship of the Congress in early 1923, C R Das, Motilal Nehru, and Vithalbhai Patel organised a new party which was called 'the Congress–Khilafat Swaraj Party'. They neither repudiated the leadership of Mahatma Gandhi nor did they go in for a total break up with the Congress. They did not even repudiate the policy of non-cooperation in totality. C R Das in his presidential speech at Gaya had explained his stand that through the Council entry they wanted to take the principle of non-cooperation 'from within' to expose the sham character of the reforms and tear off 'the mask' from the face of the British 'steel frame'. The contours of policy and programmes were contained in its policy statement as well as in the Election Manifesto issued in October 1923. A perusal of both documents reveals the broad framework of its policy and programmes. Some of them were:

1. The party reiterated its faith in the basic political goal of the Congress: the attainment of Swaraj by all legitimate and peaceful means.
2. Like the Congress, Swaraj for them meant dominion status within the British empire.

3. For them, the Council entry was needed: (a) to prove their popularity with the masses; and (b) to wreck this citadel of bureaucracy from within.
4. Their primary objective was to expose the 'sham' nature of the reforms offered under the Act of 1919 and make them totally unworkable. They underlined the fact that they would work for 'ending' or 'mending' the Act of 1919. Further, this was an extension of the principle of non-cooperation to the very citadel of bureaucracy. They made it clear that they wanted to pursue the objective of swaraj through parliamentary means, but if they would find it impossible, they would pursue a policy of 'uniform, continuous and consistent obstruction'. Their policy had both constructive and destructive planks. They insisted that it was on the ruins of the reforms of the Act of 1919 that a new edifice of swaraj could be built up. That is why they promised to work for the rejection of all anti-people programmes, policies, budgets and resolutions of the government with the ultimate objective of bringing the government machinery to a standstill. In pursuance of the same goal, they were committed to boycott all government bodies and all official functions. On the constructive side of their legislative work, the party was committed to push through proposals and resolutions to further the cause of constitutional development with an ultimate aim of achieving 'self-government' for Indians. They were also in favour of supporting Gandhian constructive programmes without making a fetish of them.
5. One of the major objectives of the Swaraj Party was to work for the acceptance of the right of the Indian people to make their own constitution. They insisted that so far all the reforms under the Acts of 1861, 1892, 1909 and 1919 had been passed by the British Parliament, and the Indian people had hardly participated in the process of their making. Thus, the Swaraj Party was the first to demand the right of the Indian people to make their own constitution based on their special needs and their own genius. Later on, the Indian National Congress put up this demand, first raised by the Swarajists, as a part of their own programme. That resulted in the setting up of the Constituent Assembly and subsequent adoption of a new constitution for our people in 1950.

Swaraj Party and the Indian National Congress

The relationship between the Congress party and the Swaraj Party always remained close and intimate. To underline its symbiotic nature, the founders of the party initially called it 'the Congress–Khilafat Swaraj Party' which subsequently came to be known as the Swaraj Party. Further, they neither repudiated the basic principle of the Indian National Congress nor the leadership of Mahatma Gandhi. The basic point of difference was the issue of the Council's entry. All members of the Swaraj Party continued to be active members of the Congress. Soon after the formation of the Swaraj Party, on the initiative of Maulana Azad, a political truce was brought about between the two parties wherein it was agreed that none of them would do much propaganda on the issue of the Council entry. This line of action was further extended when the AICC meeting in Nagpur agreed to suspend the earlier resolution of the Congress on the issue of the Council entry. The Congress further conceded the viewpoint of the Swarajists when the Congress meeting in a special session at Delhi, in September 1923, lifted the ban on the Council entry. This line of action was approved by the annual Congress session in December 1923 at Kakinada, Andhra.

Mahatma Gandhi was released in early 1924 on health grounds. He favoured the continuation of the old line on the Council boycott. But he did not show any personal animosity against C R Das and Motilal Nehru, and in fact praised them. Furthermore, when the Government moved against the members of the Swaraj Party in Bengal and arrested some of them, including Subhas Chandra Bose, Gandhiji extended his unstinted support to them. This further cemented their relationship and resulted in the personal meeting between Gandhiji, C R Das and Motilal Nehru, in November 1924. After the meeting, Gandhiji agreed that the members of the Swaraj party had the full liberty to pursue their work in the Council without any obstructions from the 'no changers' of the Congress Party. However, he reiterated that the Council's entry was inconsistent with the basic principle of non-cooperation. On their part, both C R Das and Motilal Nehru agreed for the 'thread spinning qualification' for retaining the membership of the Congress. This line of action was further approved by the Belgaum Congress held in December 1924. What brought Gandhiji closer to the Swaraj Party was the death of C R Das in June 1925. Soon the All India Congress Committee passed a resolution saying that the Swaraj Party would work as the legislative wing of the

Congress. This was followed by setting up of a separate organisation called All India Spinners Association to carry on the Khadi work. Moving ahead on the same road, the practice of spinning qualification for the membership of the Congress was dropped and the old system of four annas membership was restored.

The Swaraj Party the Council's Election of 1923 and 1926

The Council's elections were held in November 1923. The Swaraj Party contested the election and came out of it with flying colours. The Swaraj Party got a clear majority in the Central Provinces and a dominant position in the Central Assembly as well as the Bengal Provincial Assembly: It got 45 out of 145 seats in the Central Assembly. In the Central Assembly Motilal Nehru became the leader of the Party and C R Das in the Bengal Assembly. Motilal Nehru managed to defeat the Government on many occasions in the Central Assembly. He forged an alliance with Madan Mohan Malaviya and Jinnah for that purpose. Similarly, in Bengal, C R Das managed to get the support of Muslim members through the Bengal Pact and made the working of dyarchy come to a standstill by refusing to accept the ministerial responsibility as provided by the Act of 1919. Not only that, the Bengal Council passed many resolutions on the issue of the release of prisoners and repeal of repressive laws. Besides, it rejected a number of grants and demands for salaries of ministers. Dyarchy was virtually made unworkable in Bengal.

In the Central Provinces the task of the party was much easier as it had the absolute majority. Thus dyarchy was made totally unworkable there too. All this created a great embarrassment for the government. In the Central Assembly the leader of the Swaraj Party managed to secure the support of the Independents and the Nationalists and embarrassed the government on many occasions. The most historic occasion was when Motilal Nehru managed to get through a resolution in the Assembly in February 1924, calling upon the government to take steps to amend the Act of 1919. It further urged the government to hold a Round Table Conference to make recommendations for a new constitution of India. This exposed the government's hypocritical attitude towards the issue of 'self-government' for Indians, as the government summarily rejected the resolution. In response to it, the Swaraj Party managed to get a number of demands, made in the Finance Bill of 1924, rejected. This was followed by the rejection of budgets in subsequent years and each time the Governor-General had to use his extraordinary power of certification which was extremely embarrassing for the government. Not only that, many resolutions on the initiative of the Swaraj Party were passed even in the face of stiff opposition from the government. It was followed up by boycott of government functions and several walk-outs from the Assembly.

The government tried to pacify the Nationalists and made an announcement in February 1924, regarding appointment of a committee to report on the working of dyarchy with Sir Alexander Muddiman, as the Chairman. Motilal Nehru, however, refused the offer of the government for the membership of the committee. The committee failed to produce a unanimous report. The majority report suggested only minor changes as it did not find anything inherently wrong with the basic principles of dyarchy; but the minority report rejected the very basic principles of dyarchy. In September 1924, the government pressed for the acceptance of the majority report. Motilal Nehru got it rejected by moving an amendment to it, which was accepted by an overwhelming majority. Similarly in September 1924, the Lee Commission Report on the Superior service came up for consideration before the Central Assembly. Motilal Nehru got it rejected through moving an amendment to it. The Swaraj Party played a crucial role in the legislatures both at the central and provincial levels.

The Work of the Swaraj Party Outside the Legislature

Though the Swaraj Party was founded on the issue of the Council entry, they never rejected the importance of constructive programmes as enunciated by Mahatma Gandhi. In fact, they had faith in major Gandhian programmes: Hindu–Muslim unity, Khadi work and removal of untouchability. Both Motilal Nehru and C R Das had impeccable secular records. Motilal Nehru managed to secure the support of independent members through Jinnah in the Central Assembly. Similarly, C R Das managed to enter into a pact with Muslim members of the Bengal Council. It came to be called the Bengal Pact which made dyarchy unworkable in Bengal. Even on the issue of Khadi work, they were not opposed to it in principle. What they were opposed to was the idea of making a fetish out of it. It was through their effort that spinning qualification for the membership of the Congress was dropped and the old qualification of four annas membership was restored. On the issue of the removal of untouchability, they were second to none in their commitment. On the initiative of C R Das, Tarakeshwar temple in Bengal was handed over to a public trust and its gates were opened for all including the 'untouchables'. Not only that, they also lent their support to the Vaikom Satyagraha (1924-25) in Kerala, which was launched to get the gates of Hindu temples opened for the untouchables. In a word, the Swaraj party played a creditable role outside the legislatures also.

Decline of the Swaraj Party

A number of factors led to the decline and final re-integration of the Swaraj party in the Congress. In the first place, their policy of 'uniform and continuous obstruction' was quite successful in the initial stages and also in establishing the credentials of the members of the Party as the genuine representatives of the people. However, gradually it lost its initial sheen and reached some kind of dead end. The Party members themselves realised its futility. Even C R Das, shortly before his death, while addressing the Bengal provincial Congress at Faridpur, hinted that the cooperation with the Government was possible if real responsibility was transferred to the people. His death in June 1925 only hampered the process of 'responsive cooperation' with the government.

Another factor that led to its decline was the internal schisms and bickerings in the party. Acceptance of membership of various government committees by the Swarajists, further complicated the matter. Some of the Swarajists accepted the membership of the Steel Protection Committee. In 1925, Motilal Nehru himself became a member of the Skeen Committee, which was set up to inquire into the possibilities of Indianising the Indian Army. Vithalbhai Patel became the Speaker of the Assembly. In the Central Provinces the situation was worse: S B Tambe, a prominent leader of the Party, became a member of the Executive Council despite Motilal's opposition. And when Motilal Nehru threatened him with disciplinary action, there was a virtual revolt in the Party: N C Kelkar and M R Jayakar supported Tambe. All this weakened the Party, which was reflected in the Council election held in 1926. As compared to the 1923 election, the Swaraj Party lost seats in every Province except in Madras and Bihar. Even in the Central Assembly their strength was reduced as they got only 35 seats as against 45 in the 1923 election.

There were other contributory factors: the Indian political scene was changing fast; the period of Hindu–Muslim bonhomie was over and communal riots started occurring in the country. The communal organisations like the Muslims League, Hindu Mahasabha, and RSS became active in pursuing their communal lines. This also led to breaking up of the alliance politics in the Central Assembly. Malaviya and Lala Lajpat Rai took their own stand and Jinnah took his own. All this weakened the effectiveness of the Swaraj Party led by Motilal Nehru in the Central Assembly.

The appointment of the Simon Commission in 1927 perhaps made the separate existence of the Swaraj Party untenable. This brought about universal opposition. Lala Lajpat Rai was beaten while leading a demonstration against the Simon Commission, which resulted in his premature death. The basic idea behind the opposition to the Simon Commission was that the British Government had no right to impose any constitution on the Indian people. One result of the opposition to the Simon Commission was that in an all-parties' conference, a committee was set up under the chairmanship of Motilal Nehru to frame a constitution for India. The committee did a good job and produced a constitution for India, which came to be known as the Nehru Report. This was the first major attempt to frame a constitution of India by the Indian leadership and it left its impact on the 1935 Act as well as on the new constitution of India in the post-independence era. But the government did not evince any interest in the Nehru Report. Thus by 1928, the country was moving towards another mass movement and the Swaraj Party went back to its parent organisation – the Indian National Congress.

The Swaraj Party had a lifespan of six years, i.e. 1923–28. It did suffer from an inner contradiction in its main policy of continuous obstruction. It failed to bring the machinery of the Government both at the provincial and Central level to a standstill. Besides, they did indulge a lot in the finer distinction between cooperation, 'responsive cooperation' and non-cooperation. It is this inner contradiction which led to internal bickering in the Party.

However, that does not mean that the Swaraj Party played no fruitful role in the freedom struggle. It came at a time when the policy of non-cooperation as conceived by Mahatma Gandhi had practically failed. In such a situation the constructive programme of Mahatma Gandhi alone was not enough to enthuse the masses and some stiff opposition to the government was the need of the hour. And there can be hardly any doubt that the Swaraj Party played the role of the opposition brilliantly. The Swarajists succeeded in exposing the unresponsive nature of the colonial administration. Second, they proved the inadequacies of the Act of 1919 and it was on their persistent demand that the Muddiman Committee and even the Simon Commission was setup to inquire into the inadequacies of the Act of 1919. Third, the Swarajists were the first to underline and demand the right of the Indian people to make their own constitution. That was a very revolutionary demand which later on became one of the major demands of our national struggle. Not only that, one of its leaders, Motilal Nehru, heading an all-party committee produced a constitution for India which came to be known as the Nehru Report. That was the first attempt at constitution-making by the Indian leadership. Thus through the effort of the Swaraj Party the question of constitution-making was put on the national agenda. Lastly, the sincerity and commitment of the Swaraj Party was also proved by the fact that when the time came for mass struggle in the wake of the Simon Commission, they did join the mainstream of the national struggle. In a word, at a very critical junction of our national movement, the Swarajists played a crucial and constructive role. Their return to the Congress, like a prodigal son, really disproved what the poet wrote about British Whigs, long ago:

> *But bees on flowers alighting cease their hum*
> *So settled upon the places, 'Whigs grow dumb'.*
>
> THOMAS MOORE

15 Simon Commission

When a commission was wanted the British Government would not give it; but they would impose upon the Indian people a commission which is not wanted, and when it is not wanted.

S. SRINIVASA IYENGAR

We have already seen that Indian public opinion was clamouring for a drastic revision of the Act of 1919, with a view to gaining self-governance for the people of India. But the British Government was insisting that, as per the Act of 1919, such a Commission could not be appointed before 1929. However, in November 1927, the government suddenly set up the Indian Statutory Commission, which subsequently came to be known as the Simon Commission after its Chairman. The nationalist public opinion interpreted this volte-face on the part of the Government in terms of the Conservative's fear of the Labour Party coming to power after the general election of 1929. Additionally, what prompted the British Government to predate the Commission was the growing militancy of the youth in India as well as the division and disarray of the nationalist movement.

The Composition of the Simon Commission

The Simon Commission consisted of seven British members of Parliament. The fact that no Indian was considered good enough to be associated with the Commission, which was to decide the political fate of India, was too much of a national insult to be taken lightly. Besides, its sudden appointment also created a deep sense of doubt regarding the very motive of the British Government. The government tried to justify its composition by saying that only the members of the British parliament could become its members. The Nationalist leadership countered it by pointing out the eligibility of Lord S P Sinha in joining the Commission as he was already a member of the British Parliament. Another argument advanced by the Government was that in view of divisions and fissures in the Indian national movement, it was not possible to associate any Indian without offending another section of the Indian public opinion. If this was so, our leadership argued, then why was no attempt made to find a consensus candidate/candidates from among the Indian people. All these British arguments were laboured attempts to justify its composition. The crux of the matter was that there was an absence of sincerity on the part of the British on the issue of the self-government for the people of India. The association of any Indian with the Commission's work could have exposed its insincerity, with all its glaring implications.

However, for Indian leadership, apart from its all-white composition, there were other deeper reasons to reject and boycott the Simon Commission. The Indian National Congress took its well-known stand that the people of India had a right to make their own constitution. This was a consensual national viewpoint as evidenced by the passage of two resolutions (February 1924 and September 1925) by the Central Assembly, reiterating the same demand. Besides, as the Congress president, S Srinivasa Iyengar argued any enquiry to the fitness of the Indian people for self-government was nothing but a direct affront to our national respect. All that was needed, he further argued, was a direct negotiation between the people of India and the British with a view to grant self-government to us. There was an unprecedented unity among the Indian political leadership leading to universal condemnation of the Commission. Apart from the Indian National Congress, other parties and groups, viz., the Indian Muslim League, Liberal Federation of India, Hindu Mahasabha, and Khilafat Conference, also joined the chorus of the national condemnation of the Commission. Jinnah described it as 'butchery of our soul', while Tej Bahadur Sapru called it 'the worst challenge to Indian nationalism'. Not only that, on the initiative of Lala Lajpat Rai, on 16 February 1928, a resolution was passed by the Central Assembly expressing 'its lack of confidence in the Parliamentary Commission'. But the strongest stand against the Commission was taken by the Indian National Congress. In its Madras Congress (December 1927) it passed a resolution calling on the people of India to boycott the Commission by organising demonstrations against it on its arrival in India. It further called upon all members of Indian legislatures, including the non-official members, not to associate with the Commission's work in any manner. Mahatma Gandhi was echoing the sentiments of the Indian people when he called for befitting 'action' and not mere 'declaration' and 'speeches' against it.

Boycott of the Commission: The People's Action

There was a groundswell of opposition when the Commission landed at Bombay on 3 February 1928. An all-India strike was observed on its arrival. There were protests all over India and the sky echoed with the slogan of 'Simon! Go back'. Mass rallies, black flag demonstrations, and processions became the order of the day. There was hardly any town in India where anti-Simon Commission demonstrations were not held. In Madras, the situation took an ugly turn when there was police firing resulting in the death of three people. Madras also witnessed a death-defying act on the part of T Prakasam – a prominent Congress leader, who bared his chest for being shot, on being prevented from reaching the place of police firing. In Calcutta, there was a similar confrontation between students and the police. In Delhi, the Commission was greeted with hostile demonstrations. Placards and banners carrying the slogan 'Go Back, Simon', flooded its streets. In Patna, the scene

Demonstration against the Simon Commission

was not different: Over 50,000 people gathered to demonstrate against it and even when the entire city was invaded by the police force, the people refused to be cowed down. In Lucknow, even Jawaharlal Nehru and Govind Ballabh Pant were subjected to lathi-blows. There was also a more innovative and comic scene: thousands of black kites carrying slogans of 'Simon! Go Back', flooded the sky of Lucknow city. But the most heart-rending scene took place in Lahore when Lala Lajpat Rai was showered with lathi-blows on 30 October 1928, while demonstrating against the Simon Commission. While receiving lathi-blows at the hands of police officer Saunders, Lala Lajpat Rai, the lion of Punjab roared: 'The lathi-blows that are hurled at me will one day prove as nails in the coffin of the British empire'. It is relevant to recall that it was in response to the beating of Lala Lajpat Rai that Bhagat Singh and his comrades attempted to kill Saunders in December 1928. In brief, the year 1928 was marked by political agitations against the Simon Commission. Demonstrations, burning of foreign clothes, strikes, and mass processions became the order of the day. It amply demonstrated people's readiness for a new mass movement. It also marked the return of Mahatma Gandhi to active politics.

The Report of the Simon Commission

As noted earlier, the job of the Commission was to enquire and recommend whether India was ready for further constitutional progress and to what extent and in which direction. In its own way and despite strong Indian protests, the Commission took its job seriously. It made two long-stretched visits to India from March 1928 to October 1928 and in April 1929. It toured various parts of the country extensively and made its own consultations. Finally, in May 1930, it submitted its report, with the following major recommendations:

1. First, it recommended scrapping of the dyarchy at the provincial levels as provided under the 1919 Act, to be replaced by a responsible government within a federal framework. It further recommended for the enlargement of the strength of the provincial Legislative Assemblies with a minimum of 200 members and the maximum of 250. But there was a rider to the general principle of provincial autonomy: the Governors had to have some special powers to safeguard the interests of the minorities and to maintain peace and tranquility.

2. Second, the Commission was not for any drastic change at the central level: it was not willing to introduce even the much-despised system of dyarchy therein, not to talk of responsible government. It did not favour a system of unitary government at the centre in the long run. Instead, it favoured a federal government, including Princely India.
3. Third, the commission was for enlargement of franchise, though it did not favour general adult franchise at that point of time. However, it assented to raising of franchise from 3 per cent to 15 per cent of the population.
4. Fourth, despite a lot of obfuscation on the general principle of representation, it finally favoured the system of communal representation.
5. Fifth, it recommended separation of Sindh from Bombay, Orissa from Bihar, and Burma from India.
6. Sixth, the Commission stood for framing of a really elastic constitution which would develop in course of time and thus avoid periodical parliamentary enquiries.

Simon Commission: An Appraisal

The Commission, from its very inception, on account of its composition as well as its terms of reference, was a suspect in the eyes of the Indian people. Its recommendations only proved the worst fears of our national leaders. Hence, it was faulted on various counts. First, neither did it seriously consider the question of self-government for the Indian people, nor did it favour Dominion Status as the future political goal of India. Second, it favoured a fully non-responsible government at the centre with a non-representative central legislature which looked like being 'retrogressive' and 'anti-people'. Third, its recommendation favouring communal representation was a replica of the old policy of 'divide and rule'. Fourth, even the provincial autonomy was hedged by the special powers of the Governor. Its recommendation for a meager expansion of franchise did not give a big push to democratisation of Indian polity.

In fact, by the time the Commission made its recommendations, a lot of political change had already taken place both in India as well as in England. There was a change of the Government in England with the Labour Party in the saddle, which did not augur well for its recommendations. Besides, Indian people had already produced an outline of a new constitution, known as the Nehru Report after its Chairman Motilal Nehru. Besides, the Calcutta Congress (1928) had already opted for Purna Swaraj in principle and had given an ultimatum to the government in this regard. This ultimatum was a compromise formula to which the young radical leaders like Subhas Chandra Bose and Jawaharlal Nehru also agreed. On 31 October 1929, the Government made a declaration that a round table conference would be held to discuss the question of dominion status under the Act of 1919. But by December it was clear that the British Government was not serious about the issue and hence the Lahore Congress (December 1929) under the leadership of Jawaharlal Nehru adopted the historic resolution on Purna Swaraj. That set the stage for the next round of struggle under the leadership of Gandhiji. This sequence of events made it quite clear that by the time the Simon Commission made its recommendations, they had lost all their practical utility due to the change in the political environment.

In retrospect, it appears that the Commission and its recommendations had only twofold practical utilities. One, some of its recommendations worked as building blocks of the Act of 1935. Two, it gave a big fillip to the national movement as the opposition to it became a rallying point for the national movement. Thus, though inadvertently, it contributed to the strengthening of the national movement and prepared the ground for the next British experiment of parliamentary federalism in India.

> *It is impossible to think of a single movement in which Lalaji (Lala Lajpat Rai) was not to be found. His love of service was insatiable.*
>
> MAHATMA GANDHI

16 Nehru Report

This Congress having considered the Constitution (Nehru Report) recommended by All Parties' Committee Report welcomes it as a great contribution towards solution of India's political and communal problems and congratulates the Committee on virtual unanimity of its recommendations . . . approves the constitution drawn up by the committee as a step in political advance speedily as it represents the largest measure of agreement attained among the important parties in the country.

THE CALCUTTA CONGRESS (1928)

The Nehru Report was a landmark in the history of constitution-making in pre-Independence India. It may be noted that although all the constitutional Acts might have come as a British response to the Indian demand for self-government, but in their actual making, the Indian people had hardly any real hand. In sharp contrast to these Acts, the Nehru Report of 1928 was a wholly Indian attempt at constitution-making. What was more, it had cross-sectional support and its major contours were not a product of any one individual or group. Moreover, some of its recommendations had a far-reaching impact on the Act of 1935, as well as on our new constitution of India. In view of this, a detailed study of the Nehru Report is called for.

Historical Background

Before discussing its major provisions and their long-term implications, let us delineate the historical backdrop to the Nehru Report. We have already seen that there was almost a consensus among our leaders that the Act of 1919 was 'inadequate' and hence needed drastic revision for taking India on the road towards self-government. And for this a new constitution for India made by the Indian people themselves was needed. Several resolutions were passed by the Central Assembly, containing all these demands. But the British hardly paid any attention to it. On the contrary, Lord Birkenhead, while announcing the setting up of the Simon Commission, ridiculed and even challenged the Indian leaders to produce a constitution acceptable to all political sections in India.

The British understanding of the situation was that on account of sharp division among different political groups, the Indian leadership would never succeed in producing a constitution acceptable to major sections of the Indian society. But the opposition to the Simon Commission was so universal in India that the Congress was encouraged to take up the gauntlet thrown down by Lord Birkenhead. Consequently, the Madras Congress (December 1927) directed its Working Committee to hold a special convention to work out a constitution in consultation and cooperation with other political groups as well as the elected members of Central and Provincial legislatures. Fortunately, the idea was also approved by the Indian Muslim League as well as the Indian Liberal Federation. Thus a special convention consisting of representatives of different political formations was held at Delhi in February 1928 under the chairmanship of Dr M A Ansari, a prominent Congress leader. As a result, a committee headed by Motilal Nehru was set up to draft a constitution for India. The other prominent members of the Committee were Tej Bahadur Sapru, Sardar Mangal Singh, S Quareshi, Sir Ali Imam and N M Joshi. This Committee, after making a strenuous effort, produced a draft constitution for India which was subsequently approved by All Parties' Conference held at Lucknow in August 1928. The major recommendations of the Nehru Report were as follows:

(i) India should be granted dominion status forthwith.
(ii) Responsible government should be introduced both at the central as well as at the provincial levels.
(iii) There would be a bi-cameral Parliament. The upper house, to be known as the Senate, would consist of 200 members to be elected by the provincial legislatures. The lower house, known as the House of Representatives, would consist of 500 members who would be elected directly by the people based on adult franchise.
(iv) The Report accepted the basic principle of general adult franchise: every person who had attained the age of twenty-one, unless disqualified by law, would enjoy general adult franchise.

(v) Fundamental Rights, more particularly relating to freedom of conscience, freedom of religion and profession should be an integral part of the constitution.

(vi) Powers between the Provinces and the Centre were to be divided on the basis of the lists of subjects covered at both levels. However, residuary powers were to be vested in the centre.

(vii) Some precautions were taken to provide stability to the government. For instance, it was provided that the Central as well as Provincial cabinet could not be removed during the first three years except on the specific charges of corruption. However, it was suggested that after three years the government, both at the Centre and at the Provinces, would have to resign if a vote of censure was passed by the two-third majority of the lower house.

(viii) Similarly extremely cautious measures were suggested in respect of defence. A committee for defence was to be set up comprising the prime minister, defence minister, foreign minister, the commander-in-chief and two other experts with advisory functions in the defence matters. The defence budget was subject to the approval of the lower house, but in case of foreign aggression, real or threatened, the Government was given authority to incur expenditure on defence.

(ix) The report disfavoured the principle of separate electorate and provided for joint or mixed electorate. However, it did provide for reservation of seats for Muslims where they were in minority and similarly reservation of seats for non-Muslims in the North-West Frontier Province. The reservation of seats would be on the basis of population and for a fixed period. However, the community with reserved seats should have the right to contest the general seats. There would be no reservation of seats for Muslims in Punjab and Bengal.

(x) The Supreme Court would be made the final court of appeal and all appeals to the Privy Council would be stopped.

(xi) Princely India was to hasten the process of introduction of responsible government and ultimately an All India Federation was to emerge, also covering Princely India.

The Report was approved by the All Parties' Committee at Lucknow in August 1928, though a section of the delegates favoured Purna Swaraj and were not satisfied with its recommendation for dominion status.

However, the unanimity displayed at the Lucknow conference turned out to be short-lived. For, when the Report was put before the All Parties Convention, held at Calcutta in December 1928, Jinnah expressed his strong reservations on the recommendations and suggested a number of changes which were as follows:

(i) The Muslims must have one-third representation in the Central legislature.
(ii) Till adult franchise was accepted, Bengal and Punjab legislatures should have Muslim representation on the basis of population.
(iii) Residuary powers should be vested in the Provinces and not in the Centre.
(iv) The separation of Sindh from Bombay should be carried out forthwith.

There was a fierce debate on the amendment moved by Jinnah. Tej Bahadur Sapru tried to save the situation by pleading for Jinnah's proposal of one-third Muslim representation in the Central legislature. However, a number of people led by M R Jayakar were deadly against it. Ultimately, Jinnah's amendments were put to vote and were lost. For Jinnah, it was 'parting of the ways'. It is relevant to note that earlier, Jinnah had agreed on the principle of joint electorate and even split the Indian Muslim League on this issue, when the other group led by Muhammad Shafi and Aga Khan stood by the principle of separate electorate for the Muslims. The rejection of Jinnah's proposal at Calcutta led to a Delhi convention of Muslims in January 1929, which supported the principle of separate electorate. Besides, the Delhi convention also adopted an expanded version of Jinnah's earlier demand submitted at All Parties Convention at Calcutta in the preceding year. Subsequently, it came to be known as Jinnah's fourteen-point proposal. Some of the new points covered under the proposal were:

(i) Religious, cultural, educational, social and political liberty should be guaranteed to all communities.
(ii) Adequate share to the Muslims in all the services of the state and self-governing bodies.
(iii) No cabinet, either Central or Provincial, should be formed without granting atleast one-third seats to Muslims.
(iv) The system of separate electorates should continue.
(v) No constitutional amendment could be carried out unless

approved by four-fifth majority of either house sitting separately or both houses voting jointly.

This was not the end of the road for the Nehru Report. During the Congress session at Calcutta (December 1928), the report faced stiff opposition from younger leaders, led by Subhas Chandra Bose and Jawaharlal Nehru, who favoured Purna Swaraj and not dominion status as provided by the Nehru Report. And it was only with the

Nehru and Bose: Main Advocates of Purna Swaraj

intervention of Mahatma Gandhi that a compromise formula was evolved, by which the Congress gave an ultimatum to the government: either accept the Report by December 1929, lest the Congress would go in for Purna Swaraj, backed up by a mass movement.

Despite its innovative features, the Nehru Report faced criticism from several quarters. The Indian Muslim League ultimately rejected the major recommendation of the report on the issue of communal representation. Many people have argued that acceptance of Jinnah's proposal for one-third Muslim representation in the central legislature was not too much of a price to be paid for the sake of Hindu–Muslim unity. The Nehru Report, despite its best efforts, failed to tackle the communal problem as it could not evolve a consensus on the issue of Muslim representation. In fact, it missed the bus of communal amity at a critical juncture of our national life. As noted earlier, the Report also faced stiff opposition from young, radical leaders like Nehru and Bose, who favoured Purna Swaraj and were not happy with the provision of the Report on dominion status. The Marxists found in the report an open support for the propertied classes.

But all these criticisms did not take away the sincere effort on the part of the committee, which formulated the report, to work out an India-made constitution. Besides, the committee did find an agreed solution on the question of communal representation and even carried the nation on the road of national amity. It was Jinnah's obduracy that, ultimately, sabotaged their assiduously worked-out formula to bury the virus of communalism.

However, the political scene in India was moving so fast that within a year the Nehru Report lost its sheen. The Lahore Congress (1929) discarded the Nehru Report as the Government failed to accept it by the deadline of December 1929. The Congress went in for Purna Swaraj followed by the Civil Disobedience Movement. However, there is no denying the fact that the Nehru Report was a milestone in our constitutional history, if for nothing else at least for its home-made nature. Although the Lahore Congress bypassed the Nehru Report, it did accept its essential formulation that no constitution would be acceptable to the Indian National Congress that failed to give full satisfaction to the minorities.

> *I venture to suggest that the Report (Nehru's) satisfies all reasonable aspirations and is capable of standing on its own merits.*
>
> MAHATMA GANDHI

17 Civil Disobedience Movement

The call of 1920 was a call for preparation. The call in 1930 is for engaging in the final conflict.

MAHATMA GANDHI

As we have already seen that by 1928 the country was slowly but surely, moving towards a new mass movement. At the Calcutta Congress (December 1928), the Indian National Congress had given an ultimatum to the Government either to accept the Nehru Report granting India dominion status at once or face a mass movement on a heightened national goal of Purna Swaraj. Meanwhile the country was getting politically heated. A number of political workers like Dr Satya Pal of Punjab, Mr Annapurnayya of Andhra and a host of other political leaders were being arrested; Bhagat Singh and his comrades had been sentenced to transportation for life in the Assembly Bomb Case and they were also being tried in the Lahore Conspiracy Case. They had gone on a hunger strike demanding just and humane treatment for the prisoners. That led to the death of Jatindra Nath Das (also known as Jatin Das) on the 64th day of hunger-strike in September 1929. Earlier the Government had arrested 31 trade union leaders, mostly of communist ideology, who were being tried under the Meerut Conspiracy Case. In a word, the political environment in the country was getting over-heated.

However, the coming of the labour government headed by Ramsay MacDonald in England did raise a glimmer of hope, which was further heightened when Lord Irwin, after his London visit made a statement to the effect that the natural issue of India's progress, as contemplated in the declaration of 1917, was the attainment of dominion status. He further promised to hold a round table conference once the Simon Commission Report was in hand. However, hopes aroused by Lord Irwin's statements were soon dashed to the ground as it became clear that the goal of dominion status was only for the future, and not on the immediate agenda of the government. This created a deep sense of anger and resentment, which also led to a new militant atmosphere in the country.

Besides, there were a number of other contributing factors leading to a new confrontation between the people and the government. The Simon Commission had evoked universal condemnation, leading to mass protests resulting in the death of many patriots, including Lala Lajpat Rai. Even inside the Congress, a lot of rethinking on the basic strategy was going on. Mahatma Gandhi, who had maintained a low political profile for a few years, was back to the mainstream of national politics. The Swaraj Party had also gradually come to realise the futility of its policy and was willing to join a new battle for Swaraj. There was also a surge of the left-wingers inside the Congress, led by Jawaharlal Nehru and Subhas Chandra Bose, who were primarily responsible for conceiving and spreading the idea of Purna Swaraj through the Indian Independence League. There was also an economic dimension to the problem: the Great Economic Depression (October 1929) had also afflicted the Indian people. Some of the classes, like the peasantry and working class, were its worst victims and thus were willing to lend their shoulders for the national struggle. The Bardoli Satyagraha led by Sardar Patel was a symbol of growing peasant's militancy. The All India Trade Union Congress presided over by Jawaharlal Nehru in 1929, committing itself to work for the independence of the country, was a pointer to the same direction.

All this became more distinct when Gandhiji met Lord Irwin and impressed on him to make a categorical statement that the promised Round Table Conference would proceed on the basis of full dominion status and not on its mere promise for the future. Lord Irwin refused to make any definite promise on the issue of dominion status.

Against the backdrop of this, the Lahore Congress met, towards the end of December, and passed its historic resolution of Purna Swaraj. It read: 'This Congress, therefore, declares that the word Swaraj in the article of the Congress constitution shall mean complete independence.' In furtherance to this objective, the Congress called upon all concerned to abstain from participating directly or indirectly in future elections and even directed the present Congress members to relinquish their seats. It further authorised the AICC to launch a 'programme of civil disobedience including non-payment of taxes'. The timing and nature of action was left to the discretion of the AICC.

Thus, the stage was set for a new confrontation with the Government. As decided by the Lahore Congress, 26 January 1930 was celebrated as the Independence Day. On that day a pledge of independence was taken by thousands of people all over the country, who took it 'to be crime against man and God to submit any longer' to a rule which had ruined India in every possible way.

As usual, Gandhiji wanted to negotiate with the Viceroy and as such submitted an eleven-point demand to the latter. Some of these demands were: (i) 5 per cent reduction of land revenue; (ii) abolition of salt tax and the end of Government monopoly on salt; (iii) cut in army expenses; (iv) release of political prisoners and total prohibition, etc. Many Congress leaders, including Jawaharlal Nehru, did not appreciate Gandhiji's proposal. The government also took a negative attitude to his proposal. After a lot of spiritual churning and heart-searching, Gandhiji decided to launch, what came to be known as the Salt Satyagraha. For Gandhiji, salt tax affected the poorest of the poor and as such was inhuman, causing an unnecessary burden on them. Besides, it was the greatest common denominator that affected every hearth and home including those of *daridranarayana*. In his letter to the Viceroy dated 2 March 1930, Gandhiji conveyed his decision and also reiterated some of his earlier demands. And he made it clear that if no positive response came by 11 March 1930, he would proceed along with his Ashram co-workers to break the provisions of the salt laws.

Dandi March

As there was no positive response from the Government, Gandhiji decided to start his march from Sabarmati Ashram to Dandi – a place 240 miles away from Ahmedabad on the Arabian sea-coast. Seventy-eight of his Ashram inmates were to be his companions in this historic long march – a march in broad daylight, which was an act of total non-violent defiance. The entire distance was to be covered in 25 days. Gandhiji and his companions started their march on 12 March 1930. His Ashram inmates who accompanied him were drawn from different region and religions. In a word, it was a mini-India marching under the leadership of the twentieth-century apostle of truth and non-violence. For many, it was reminiscent of the last journey of Jesus Christ, marching towards Jerusalem along with his twelve disciples. Here, with Gandhiji, there were 78 followers who stood by him like a rock. Historically speaking, the Dandi March had an edge over the long-march in China led by Mao Zedong in the late 1930s as Mao's army was equipped with all kinds of weapons, whereas Gandhiji and his companions had only non-violence and truth as their weapons.

The Dandi March was well planned and executed with consummate skill and determined will. In no way was it a sloppy affair. The entire march was covered in 25 days. On the way, people flocked around the marchers as the news spread like wild fire. Every village, family, and even individual surrounding the march route tried to contribute their bit to welcome their liberator, the 'greatest son of India after Lord Buddha' as described by Rabindranath Tagore. There was no secrecy, no legal quibbling, no demagogic oratory: it was an act of total defiance of 'lawless law'. The marchers were greeted with welcome banners, flags, festoons, banana leaves and flowers all the way. Many people were spinning their yarn, others plied their charkha as Gandhiji and his companions passed from village to village. Many people could see a historical parallel when Maryada Purushottam Ram went to the forest to liberate the good from the evil hands. While Ram had been banished by his father Dasarath to the forest, for Gandhiji it was a self-imposed penance. Yet others were reminded of Purna Avatar Krishna marching with his Yadavas clan from Mathura to Dwarka, in the process earning the title of Ranchhorji (one who turns away

I want world sympathy in this battle of Right against Might.

Dandi M.K.Gandhi

5.4.30

from the battlefield), but here was Gandhiji marching to join the battle for swaraj.

The marchers reached Dandi on 5 April and rested and prayed for the day. The next day, i.e. on 6 April 1930, came the historic occasion when Gandhiji picked a handful of salt from the sea – signalling total defiance of the salt law. Lo and behold! This handful of salt shook the foundation of the mightiest empire of the world.

Meanwhile, hectic preparations were on for joining the battle of Swaraj by people all over the country. There were frantic activities in respect of fund-collection, recruitment of volunteers, the mobilisation of masses, public meetings, and identification and selection of sites for breaking the salt laws, etc. In a way, the entire nation was on the move, aroused, expectant, determined and battle-ready, waiting with bated breath for Gandhiji's *Shankhnad.* And that came on 6 April 1930 when Gandhiji picked up a handful of salt from the sea. The people joined the battle instantaneously; thousands defied the 'lawless law' all over the country. The movement was not confined only to breaking of the salt laws alone. People also joined, rather enthusiastically, the other programmes of the movement, like picketing of liquor shops, burning of foreign clothes, refusal to pay taxes, and the boycott of Government schools and colleges and legislatures. In response to the call of the Congress by February 1930, 172 members of legislatures had resigned their memberships, including 21 from Central Assembly and the rest from the provinces like Bengal (34), Bihar and Orissa (31) CP (20), Madras (20), UP (60) Assam (12) Bombay (6) and Punjab (2) and Burma (1).

But the real battle for swaraj started when Gandhiji broke the salt law on 6 April 1930. Thousands joined the movement all over the country and there were dramatic demonstrations of defiance in many places. In Madras, C Rajagopalachari led a column of salt satyagrahis from Trichinopoly to Vedaraniyam on the Tanjore coast. He was arrested on 30 April 1930 but the flag of the satyagraha was kept flying even in his absence. In Malabar, K Kelappan, the hero of the Vaikom Satyagraha and his companions staged a march from Calicut to Paynnur for breaking the salt laws. In the far North-East, salt satyagrahis marched all the way from Sylhet in Assam to Noakhali on the Bengal coast for making salt. In Andhra, Satyagrahis marched from village to village, spreading the message of Swaraj to reach the coastal area for making salt. In the North-West Frontier Province, Khan Abdul Ghaffar Khan and his band of *Khudai Khidmatgars* proved to be real heroes of the Civil Disobedience Movement. On 23

April, some of the leaders including Ghaffar Khan were arrested, which was followed by a massive demonstration. War-liking Pathans demonstrated their absolute faith in non-violence, which moved the soldiers of Garhwal Rifles so much so that they refused to fire on them and in turn invited their own imprisonment.

Earlier in Calcutta, J M Sen Gupta, the Mayor of Calcutta, publicly read out from seditious literature in defiance of the law of sedition and invited imprisonment. Even before the Dandi March had started, Vallabhbhai Patel tried to educate and prepare the village-folk on the route of the Dandi March for an ensuing big battle of swaraj. He was soon arrested and imprisoned. In Allahabad, Motilal Nehru gave away his palatial house, Anand Bhawan, which was renamed Swaraj Bhavan, to the country. He even tried to make salt in the streets of Allahabad. Jawaharlal Nehru was arrested on 14 April and gave his clarion call to the people: 'Who lives if India dies and who dies if India lives'.

Apart from these dramatic events in several parts of the country, at the grass roots level the movement was widespread and took different forms. In Gujarat a number of village Patwaris relinquished their posts and joined the movement. In the Central Province, people defied unjust forest laws and started cutting trees. In some parts of Gujarat no-tax campaign was launched. In zamindari areas, movement for non-payment of chaukidari tax also gathered momentum. Different sections of the people participated and made their own contributions to the movement. Traders and businessmen also participated by boycotting foreign clothes, evidenced by the fall in the imports of British clothes from 26 million yards in 1929 to 13.7 million in 1930. Revenue on liquor excise also went down in a significant measure. The working class also participated, as evidenced by strikes by Sholapur, an industrial town of Maharashtra, in May 1930. The participation of Muslims in the North-West Frontier province was quite impressive.

But one of the marked features of the movement was the large-scale participation of women. When Gandhiji started his march, thousands of women flocked around him to welcome him on his way to Dandi. Not only that, they participated in the movement all over the country. They particularly took the lead in picketing liquor and foreign clothes shops. They launched their own 'Purda Hatao' (Remove the veil) Movement in which the women, drawn from all sections of society, participated. Thus, if for nothing else, the Civil Disobedience Movement would go down in the history of women's liberation as a new milestone. The Press gave wide coverage to the march of Gandhiji, comparing it with the great march of Moses with the Jews towards the promised land. In fact, people looked at the Dandi march as a march to the promised land of swaraj.

But the movement was still to enter a more decisive phase. Gandhiji, in his letter to the Viceroy in early May expressed his intention of raiding the salt depots located at Dharasana in Surat district so as to break the government monopoly over salt. However, before he could take his volunteers to Dharasana, he was arrested on the night of 5 May 1930 and was sent to Yeravada jail. Afterwards the Government let loose its repressive machinery in a big way. More than 1,00,000 people were arrested all over the country. Properties of a number of the satyagrahis were confiscated. Many people lost their jobs. But more heroic deeds were yet to come, on the part of the satyagrahis. Gandhiji's arrest, instead of working as a deterrent, inspired them to make greater sacrifices. On 21 May 1930, the satyagrahis attempted to takeover the Dharasana salt depots. Pyarelal, Sarojini Naidu and Manilal Gandhi were leading them from the front. Web-Miller, a United Press Correspondent, and an eyewitness, gave a vivid description of the whole scene: the satyagrahis faced blows with steel-shod lathis on their bare heads and not one of them even raised his hands to protect his head. Each one of the satyagrahis went ahead till he was beaten unconscious and then another batch came facing the same fiery ordeal.

There was no fight, no struggle, and no resistance but total non-violent non-submission. As Louis Fischer later on commented: 'The British beat the Indians with batons and rifle-butts. The Indians neither cringed nor retreated. That made England powerless and India invincible'.

In fact, the Dharasana struggle inspired many such satyagrahas. For instance, a crowd of 15,000 carried away all the salt from Waddla salt-work in a suburb of Bombay, despite deployment of heavily armed mounted police. In Karnataka, a crowd of 10,000 satyagrahis invaded Sanikatta salt-work and faced lathi blows and police firings. So was the case in Madras. In Bihpur, Bhagalpur, a large crowd of satyagrahis were lathi-charged, in which Dr Rajendra Prasad was seriously hurt. Altogether, more than one hundred people lost their lives and more than a thousand were wounded.

Despite governmental repressive measures, the movement touched the soul of India and a stern message did go to the government that the Indian people were no longer willing to remain slaves. The government, despite its outward belligerent postures and repressive measures was also unnerved, as it never expected such massive support from the people. In July 1930, Lord Irwin started talking in terms of holding a Round Table Conference towards the end of the year. Not only that, the services of liberal leaders like Tej Bahadur Sapru and M R Jayakar were enlisted to work out a compromise formula, leading to a truce. But nothing came out of their efforts as both sides stuck to their guns. Hence the struggle continued. Meanwhile, the First Round Table Conference was held from 12 November 1930, in London, which was boycotted by the Congress. A realisation dawned on the government that any Round Table Conference without the participation of the Indian National Congress would not be productive. There was some re-thinking on the part of the government. This was evidenced by the statement of the British Prime Minister at the end of the RTC that an attempt would be made to 'enlist the services of those who were engaged in civil disobedience at present'. As the Movement was losing its momentum towards the end of 1930, some rethinking was also probably being done by the Congress leadership. Madan Mohan Malaviya, Tej Bahadur Sapru and Shrinivas Shastri did play behind-the-scenes roles to work out a new rapprochement between the Congress and the Government. All this bore its fruit on 25 January 1931, when the Government decided to release the members of the Congress Working Committee, along with the withdrawal of the legal ban on the Congress. Consequently, the members of the Congress Working Committee were released on 26 January 1931. There was a prolonged negotiation between Mahatma Gandhi and Lord Irwin which resulted in the Gandhi–Irwin Pact of 5 March 1931. Consequently, the Civil Disobedience Movement was withdrawn as the Government agreed to release political prisoners and restore the properties seized during the Satyagraha.

Many people on the side of the Government as well as that of the Congress were not happy with the terms of the Gandhi–Irwin Pact. More conservative elements on the side of the government took it as surrender on the part of Lord Irwin, whereas more militant leaders like Subhas Chandra Bose and others of the Congress also looked at it as an act of surrender on the part of Mahatma Gandhi. However, the Pact was ratified both by the Working Committee and the Karachi Congress. Mahatma Gandhi agreed to participate in the Second Round Table Conference which was to be held in London from 7 September 1931. However, a lot of political change had taken place between the period of the Gandhi–Irwin Pact (March 1931) and the Second Round Table Conference (September 1931). In England, the labour Government was replaced by a National Government, though still to be headed by Ramsay MacDonald, who was expelled by the Labour Party for his act of betrayal. As a result of this change of the government, Samuel Hoare had assumed the office of the Secretary of State for India and Lord Irwin was replaced by Lord Willingdon, both well known conservatives. The new team was much less sympathetic to the Indian cause than the earlier one. Gandhiji, despite his initial hesitation, went to London to attend the Second Round Table Conference, which was held from 7 September 1931. Meanwhile, as a result of general election, a fully Conservative Government came to power in October 1931. Despite his best efforts and his utmost sincerity, Mahatma Gandhiji could not achieve a breakthrough on the issue of communal representation during the Second Round Table Conference. What further added to his discomfiture was the hardened attitude of the new British team for India, which was not only unsympathetic but openly hostile. All this resulted in the situation of 'parting of the way' between the British Government and Mahatma Gandhi at the end of the Second Round Table Conference.

Second Round of the Civil Disobedience Movement (1932–34)

When Gandhiji came back to India after the Second Round Table Conference on 28 December 1931, he found the condition of the country very tense. The government had adopted a no holds-barred policy against the movement. In three provinces the situation had crossed all limits. In the North-West Frontier Province, the Khan Brothers were behind bars and there had been firing and lathi-charges galore on the peaceful processions. In the United Provinces, the peasants were on the receiving end and the Congress' call for suspension of ruthless rent collection was not heeded, and a number of people including Jawaharlal Nehru were put behind bars. In Bengal, in the name of tackling the 'terrorist' problem a reign of terror had been let loose. In all these provinces new anti-people repressive ordinances were proclaimed, reminding people of the sufferings and repressions of the days of the Swadeshi Movement. The Simla Agreement between Gandhiji and the Viceroy, promising enquiry into any excesses committed by the officials was being openly violated. Thus, the Congress decided on the resumption of Civil Disobedience. However, on 31 December Gandhiji sought an interview with the Viceroy which was refused. Not only that, soon after on 4 January 1932, Gandhiji was arrested and a number of new ordinances were evoked to suppress the movement.

The civil liberty of the people was given a go by and most of the national leaders were put behind bars. The people responded with lot of anguish and more than a lakh of people were put behind bars. The Congress and all its front organisations were declared illegal. Lathi-Charge became the order of the day. Prisoners, including women, were even beaten in jails. Rigorous imprisonment was awarded on flimsy grounds and properties of the satyagrahis were seized and sold away at throw away prices. Press was gagged; nationalists literature was banned; punitive actions were taken against a number of journals, journalists and printing presses. In this way, within a few months the government apparently crushed the movement with all such barbaric measures. The movement continued, though its pace slowed down by the later part of 1932.

To make the situation worse, the Communal Award was announced unilaterally by Ramsay MacDonald in August 1932. The Communal Award was an attempt on part of the government not only to widen the Hindu–Muslim hiatus but also to divide the Hindu community by giving separate electorate to the depressed classes. Gandhiji was deeply concerned and on 20 September 1932, he went on a fast unto death to resist the separate electorate for the depressed classes. Ultimately, with the persuasive intervention of some prominent Indian leaders, the Poona Pact was signed with Dr Ambedkar, the leader of the depressed classes. The Poona Pact provided for reservation of seats for the depressed classes instead of the separate electorate. On the termination of the fast on 26 September 1932, Gandhiji turned his attention towards the problems faced by the Harijans.

The Civil Disobedience did continue and the Congress held its two sessions, Calcutta (April 1932) and Delhi (April 1933). Gandhiji went on self-purification fast of 21 days on 6 May 1933. The purpose of the fast, in Gandhiji's own words was 'purification of me and my associates for greater vigilance and watchfulness in connection with the Harijan cause'. In spite of the government's decision to set him free on 8 May 1933, Gandhiji continued his fast. But defying all speculations, Gandhiji survived the self-imposed ordeal of 21-day fast. He advised the Congress President M S Aney to suspend the movement for one full month or even six weeks. He also appealed to the Government to release all the civil resisters if it sincerely wished to restore peace in the country. But he made it clear that the Civil Disobedience Movement could not be withdrawn so long as civil resisters including the Khan brothers, Jawaharlal Nehru and Vallabhbhai

Patel were behind bars. The Congress president suspended the movement for six weeks. But the government refused to respond unless the threat of the resumption of the movement was totally taken back. The Congress president extended the suspension by another six weeks.

Subsequently, in July 1933, an informal meeting of some of the Congress leaders decided to authorise Gandhiji to approach the Viceroy for a honourable peace. And it was also decided that mass civil disobedience and individual civil disobedience would be undertaken only if permitted by the Congress high command. But on being approached by Gandhiji, the response of the government was totally negative. Gandhiji inaugurated the individual Satyagraha and even offered to give up Sabarmati Ashram to the government, which was refused by the latter. Consequently, he handed over the Sabarmati Ashram to the Harijan movement. Thus, on the night of 31 July, Gandhiji along with his 34 inmates was again arrested. He was released on 4 August but was asked not to leave Poona, which he refused. He was again arrested and imprisoned. This was followed by the arrest of hundreds of Congress leaders. After his imprisonment in August 1933, he went on fast once again to protest against the non-granting of facilities, which he was having before May 1933, in connection with his Harijan work. And, he was ultimately released on 20 August 1933. Subsequently, Jawaharlal Nehru was also released on 30 August as the condition of his mother was serious. Both of them met and discussed the political situation of the country. Meanwhile Gandhiji went on a tour of ten months from November 1933 in connection with Harijan work. This was the period when a new thinking was growing in a section of the Congressmen that there was a need once again for the entry into the Council. Accordingly, a conference was held in Delhi in March 1934, which decided to revive the All India Swaraj Party with a view to participate in the ensuing Council's election. After consultation with Gandhiji, ultimately, the Civil Disobedience Movement was withdrawn on 20 May 1934 and the Congressmen were permitted Council entry.

> *The latest act of Mahatma Gandhi in suspending Civil Disobedience Movement is a confession of a failure. We are of the opinion that the Mahatma as a political leader has failed. The time has come for a radical reorganisation of the Congress on new principles with a new method for which a new leader is essential.*
>
> VITHALBHAI PATEL AND SUBHAS CHANDRA BOSE

18 The Gandhi–Irwin Pact

But the truce was made not because we were tired out, but it was imperative. He who will fight on because he can fight on is no satyagrahi; but a conceited person guilty before God.

MAHATMA GANDHI

The Gandhi–Irwin Pact, signed on 5 March 1931 marked a landmark in the history of our freedom struggle. The fact that it came in the midst of the Civil Disobedience Movement gave it a special significance as it was the first, and perhaps only, formally negotiated and signed pact between the Mahatma and the Viceroy of India. Besides, it also underlined the centrality of the Indian National Congress in general and that of the Mahatma in any future political settlement for India. However, the Pact did not remain untouched by criticism. But first let us look at the historical background in which it emerged.

As noted in the earlier pages, the Congress had launched a Civil Disobedience Movement in early 1930 under the leadership of Mahatma Gandhi. Subsequently, the movement demonstrated that it had mass support despite all repressive measures by the Government. Meanwhile, the publication of the Simon Commission Report in May 1930 only added fuel to the fire of the movement as it did not even recommend full-pledged dominion status not to talk of Purna Swaraj. During July–August 1930 some attempts were made by liberal leaders like M R Jayakar and Tej Bahadur Sapru to bring about a truce between the government and the Congress, but it came to a naught.

Meanwhile, the government went ahead with the First Round Table Conference to discuss institutional arrangements for India from November 1930 to January 1931. The Congress had boycotted it. But at the end of the conference, it became crystal clear to everybody that any negotiated settlement for India without the Congress would be like Hamlet without the prince of Denmark. It was this realisation on the part of the British Government that prompted the British Prime

Minister, the chairman of the RTC, to express a hope that the Congress would be associated with it in the next round of the dialogue.

This was followed by some persuasive interventions by liberal leaders like Jayakar, Sapru and Malaviya, both with the Congress leaders as well as with the Viceroy of India. Ultimately, the members of the Congress Working Committee were released on 26 January 1931. Subsequently, some of the Indian Leaders who had earlier participated in the RTC succeeded in arranging a meeting between Mahatma Gandhi and Lord Irwin, the Viceroy of India on 17 February 1931. After protracted negotiations between Gandhiji and the Viceroy, an agreement was reached between the two on 5 March 1931 which subsequently came to be known as the Gandhi–Irwin pact.

The Main Provisions of the Pact

Both sides made concessions as it happens in any negotiated settlement. On the part of the Government, the main concessions given were as follows:

- (i) Release of political prisoners.
- (ii) Withdrawal of draconian ordinances.
- (iii) All declarations regarding all associations, including the Indian National Congress, making them unlawful during the movement were to be taken back.
- (iv) All pending/prosecution proceedings related to the Civil Disobedience Movement would be withdrawn except those directly related to violence.
- (v) All petitions/proceedings moved by the Government against all legal practitioners will be dropped, except those which relate to the acts of direct violence. However, proceedings/prosecutions against police and armed personnel would not be covered by this clause.
- (vi) All civil disobedience prisoners would be released except those directly related to violence. This amnesty was not to cover the soldiers and police personnel.
- (vii) All fines not yet realised were to be remitted. All moveable property seized during the movement would be returned. The same rule would apply to the seized immoveable property, including land, except in those cases in which District Magistrate was convinced otherwise. However, all properties moveable or

immoveable, which had been already sold by the government would not be returned.

(viii) All those who had resigned from their posts during the movement and wished to revert to their jobs would be reinstated, except relating to all those posts which had been filled up on a permanent basis.

(ix) Except permitting the inhabitants of the coastal area to collect or make salt, there would not be any substantial modifications in the salt laws.

(x) Picketing would be permitted only in respect of liquor shops and intoxicating materials.

On the side of the Congress two major concessions were made: (a) that the movement would be withdrawn, and (b) it would participate in the forthcoming Round Table Conference. The key and most controversial clause in the Agreement related to the further discussion around constitutional reforms already discussed at the First Round Table Conference. It inter-alia read: 'of the scheme there outlined, federation is an essential part, so also are Indian responsibility and reservations and safeguards in the interest of India, for such matters, as for instance, defence, external affairs, the position of minorities, the financial credit of India and the discharge of obligations'.

The Gandhi–Irwin Pact evoked mixed feelings. Many, including the Congressmen were dismayed by Gandhiji's consent to withdraw the movement at a very critical stage without achieving its basic objectives. Some of them pointed out the following basic lacunae of the agreement:

(i) That the concessions granted by the government were primarily formal and apparent rather than substantial. In support of the above contention the critics cited the following points. Release of prisoners did not cover the Sholapur prisoners or Garhwali regiment prisoners. The government even had rejected Gandhiji's request for remission of the death sentence awarded to Bhagat Singh, Rajguru and Sukhdev.

(ii) The land and other moveable and immoveable properties already sold were not to be returned.

(iii) No enquiry was to be held in respect of excesses committed by the Government, which Gandhiji had insisted on all along.

(iv) On the constitutional issue, the government did not make any substantial concessions and clauses like reservations and safeguards in the interest of India relating to defence, foreign affairs and position of minority, were always subject to ominous interpretations going against the interest of the Indian people.

(v) This agreement was not in keeping with the pledge which Gandhiji himself had taken while starting his Dandi March that the Civil Disobedience Movement, once begun, could not be and must not be stopped so long as there was a single civil resister left free or alive.

(vi) Throughout, Mahatma Gandhi had kept the members of the Congress Working Committee abreast with the course of negotiations but the final agreement was reached by him alone. Many were inclined to ask Gandhiji what happened to the pledge of Purna Swaraj. All this provoked Jawaharlal Nehru to record his reactions in his autobiography in the following moving words: 'So I lay and pondered on that March night and in my heart there was a great emptiness as if something precious had gone beyond recall . . . this is the way the world ends, not with a bang but with a whimper.'

(vii) A contrary view was taken by the British Conservative leader, Winston Churchill. He said: 'it was alarming and nauseating to see Gandhiji – late Inner Temple Lawyer, now a seditious fakir, striding half-naked, up to the steps of the Viceroy Palace to parley on equal terms with the representatives of the King-Emperor.'

However, Gandhiji issued a long statement on 5 March, defending the terms of the agreement in his own characteristic way. He reminded his critics that suffering of the people had its well defined limits and it would not be a wise step to prolong it. Besides, he reiterated that there was nothing in the agreement to prevent the Congress from pursuing its goal of Purna Swaraj on the forum of proposed RTC or any other forum. On the issue of prisoners, seized property and picketing, he defended the agreement both on practical and principled grounds. Despite these political reservations and murmurings, Gandhi–Irwin Agreement was approved by the Working Committee as well as the Karachi Congress which met subsequently.

In retrospect, it seems that the Gandhi–Irwin agreement, with all its limitations, underlined one undeniable fact, that the British had to negotiate with Gandhiji on equal terms which was even resented by the Conservatives among the British public opinion including Winston Churchill. The very fact that soon after the change of the Government in England and with a new India team, the Government started going back on the commitment made under the agreement, speaks volumes for its positive implications for the Indian people. After all, it was a compromise and as such was not expected to meet all the Indian demands at one stroke. It did give a respite to our people so that after a while they could march on the road of freedom with renewed enthusiasm and vigour.

The Karachi Congress: A Quantum Jump Towards Welfare State

The Karachi Congress (March 1931) has a special place in the history of our national movement. In fact, its resolution on fundamental rights and economic programme and policy could be described as nothing short of being historic. If the Lahore Congress (December 1929) had committed itself to the idea of Purna Swaraj, the Karachi Congress tried to give concrete contents to it. But before we go into the details of the Karachi resolution on the people's rights and duties, it would be expedient to note that the Karachi Congress met in the aftermath of the Gandhi–Irwin pact and the execution of three young and brave sons of India, Bhagat Singh, Rajguru and Sukhdev just a week before the Congress. The people were shocked beyond measure by these executions and even Gandhiji had to face black flag demonstrations on his way to the Congress. The fact that he had failed to save their lives was heavily weighing on his conscience. It was on his initiative the Congress passed a resolution which looked at these executions as nothing short of an act of 'wanton vengeance' and a total disregard for 'universal demand for their commutation'. Thus the Congress, while dissociating itself from any act of 'political violence' recorded its admiration for these martyrs for their 'bravery and sacrifice'. No less moving was the resolution on the martyrdom of Ganesh Shankar Vidyarthi who had been earlier assassinated during communal riots at Kanpur. The Karachi Congress also approved the Gandhi–Irwin pact after some initial opposition.

However, the Karachi Congress really became memorable for its resolution on fundamental rights and economic policy. In fact, it was the first attempt of the Congress to give concrete contents and shape to the concept of Purna Swaraj which had become the political goal of the country, as enunciated by the Lahore Congress. The Karachi resolution was in three parts. *Part I* dealt with the fundamental rights and duties of the people, while *Part II* dealt with labour and *Part III* with economic policy and programme. The resolution on the fundamental rights promised that every citizen of India would enjoy the rights of freedom of expression, free association, peaceful assembly, freedom of conscience and religion. Besides, every citizen was also assured that he could not be deprived of his life and liberty except through the due process of law. The state was to desist from offering any titles but would strive to provide free and compulsory free education. The citizens were also assured of a system of universal adult franchise and their right to property and their free movement in every part of the country.

The working class including industrial workers were assured of minimum wages, better working conditions, including regulated hours of work. Women workers were assured of maternity leave and equality in respect of wages, etc. Children were to be barred from being employed. Besides, peasants and working class were given the right to form unions for the protection of their interest. Small peasants were assured of reduction of land revenue and rent and their exemption, if found necessary.

In another section, the resolution promised to protect textile and other indigenous industries. The State was to own key industries and services, mineral resources, railways, waterways, shipping and other means of public transport. The resolution also promised relief in respect of agricultural indebtedness and control of usury. The citizens were to be given right to bear arms subject to public regulations. In brief, the Karachi resolution presented a concrete and comprehensive picture of citizen's rights in respect of civil, political, and economic liberty. And, it is indeed the Karachi resolution that did work as a reference point when the provisions regarding Fundamental Rights and Directive Principles of State Policy were being formulated in our constitution. It was also made clear that in any future negotiation in respect of constitutional arrangement the Congress would insist upon these demands.

In sum, the Karachi Congress would go down in the history of our national movement for presenting to the people a charter of their rights as well as the contours of social order conceived by our people.

Kafir hai to talwar pe karta hai bharosa
Momin hai to be-teg bhi larta hai sepahi

(The man without faith relies on a sword,
the man of faith fights without a sword).

UNKNOWN POET

19 The Round Table Conference

I have often wondered myself what we are going to do at the Conference when we know that there is such a gulf between what we want and what has been as yet offered at the Conference. But the considerations of a satyagrahi decided me.

MAHATMA GANDHI

Three round table conferences held between November 1930 and December 1932, have their important place in the history of our constitutional development. It is relevant to note that the very idea of holding round table conferences, with a view to thrash out a new constitutional framework for India, was first mooted by the Swaraj Party. On the initiative of Motilal Nehru, the leader of the Swaraj Party, the Central Assembly passed a resolution as early as 1924, in this regard. This was reiterated by a similar resolution in the Central Assembly in 1925. But, on both occasions, the government failed to take any notice of the demand. Instead, it set up the Simon Commission in 1927 to review the working of the Act of 1919 and suggest appropriate changes based on its findings. But the Simon Commission was rejected by the Indian political leadership from its very inception and a boycott movement was launched against it. This was followed by the Civil Disobedience Movement, in early 1930. Meanwhile, the retrogressive recommendations of the Simon Commission came in May 1930, adding fuel to the fire, which further intensified the movement.

In July 1930, the government, unnerved by the intensity of the movement, offered a Round Table Conference, to be held by the end of the year. An attempt was made to rope in the Congress but the negotiation collapsed on the issue of Purna Swaraj. Thus the Congress decided to boycott the conference, but the Government went ahead with the proposed round table conference which was inaugurated on 12 November 1930 by Ramsay MacDonald, the then Prime Minister, and lasted till 19 January 1931. It had altogether 86 delegates, 16 from Princely India, 57 from British India and remaining 13 were from different British political parties. The Prime Minister made some proposals which formed the basis of discussion. One, he proposed a federal form of government for India which would include both British and Princely India. Two, the Provinces would be given full autonomy with some safeguards. Three, a kind of dyarchical system could be introduced at the centre where the principle of responsible government would be recognised, but the defence and external affairs would be kept in reserved categories. The Governor-General would have special powers in respect of peace and tranquility of the state and also in regard to financial stability. It was made clear that the Government neither favoured immediate grant of the dominion status for India nor the introduction of a full-fledged parliamentary system.

The conference set up a number of committees to work out details in different areas. The federal structure committee, in its report, pleaded not only for a limited responsible Government at the centre but also favoured special powers for the Governor-General in respect of external affairs and defence. The Indian delegates welcomed the idea of introduction of responsible government, even if it was limited by the special powers and responsibility of the Governor-General. But the real problem arose in respect of minority communities. Initially, hope was aroused when some of the Indian delegates suggested that the problem could be ultimately sorted out by the Indians themselves. However, soon, it became clear that it was not acceptable to Jinnah and other Muslim delegates. They insisted on communal representation and made it clear that no constitution would be acceptable to them without adequate safeguards for their interests. What complicated the matter further was the insistence of the leaders of the depressed classes, as well as those of Sikhs, who also insisted on separate electorates for their communities. Thus, separate or joint electorate became the real bone of contention among the Indian delegates, though the principle of reservations of seats for minorities was acceptable to the delegates of the general categories.

When the conference met in its plenary session, it appreciated the work done by various committees and decided to continue the work in future. In a valedictory speech, the British Premier said that the view of His Majesty's Government was that responsibility for the

Government of India should be placed upon the legislatures, subject to such guarantees as are required by minorities to protect their political liberties and rights. But he also hastened to add that the reserved powers so framed and exercised were not to prejudice the advance of India through the new constitution to full responsibility for her own government. He expressed the hope that the Congress might be persuaded to participate in future discussions. The conference ended on a hopeful note.

The Second Round Table Conference

When the first Round Table Conference ended, things were looking up. Soon the Gandhi–Irwin agreement in March 1931 was announced and despite some doubts and initial hiccups, the agreement was ratified by the Karachi Congress. The Karachi Congress also proved to be historical in yet another sense: a resolution listing the fundamental rights of the people was also adopted by it. Interestingly, the Karachi resolutions greatly influenced the framers of the Indian constitution in respect of fundamental rights and directive principles of state policy. Thus, for a while the sailing looked good for the Congress and the country. But in subsequent months the tide turned against the people of India. The execution of Bhagat Singh and his comrades cast a shadow on the political map of the country as it resulted in a groundswell of resentment against the government. This was followed by communal riots in Kanpur in which Ganesh Shankar Vidyarthi, a staunch secularist, lost his life. To make the matter worse, Lord Irwin was replaced by Lord Wellingdon, a staunch conservative and another anti-Indian hand, Samuel Hoare took over as the Secretary of State for India. Thus, gradually the Gandhi–Irwin agreement started being undermined.

In such a situation, Gandhiji started having doubts whether any useful purpose would be served by his participation in the Second Round Table Conference in the light of the divided nature of the national movement and the new hostile attitude of the British officials. Gandhiji tried to find a solution for the minority problem. In May 1931, he met the representatives of Muslim conference and Muslim nationalists. But nothing came out of it. Meanwhile, the All India Muslim conference, in April 1931, had almost reiterated the 14 point programme of Jinnah, including separate electorate for the Muslims and one-third representation of Muslims in the Central Legislature. In

July 1931, the Congress Working Committee announced a scheme for the minorities. That included a system of joint electorate with reservation of seats for the Hindus in Sindh, the Muslims in Assam, the Sikhs in Punjab and NWFP. Besides, it provided reservation of seats for Hindus and Muslims, wherever they were less than 25 per cent in population. And in federal and other provincial legislatures they were to be given seats on the basis of population, with the right to contest additional seats. Thus, the Working Committee virtually conceded all demands of the Muslim leaders except one-third representation in the Central Legislature. As such, in 1931, the Congress was willing to make concessions to Muslims, which it was not willing to do in December 1928, at Calcutta. An All India Muslim Nationalist conference held at Lucknow on 15 April 1931, had pleaded for joint electorate but now the die was cast in favour of a more militant Muslim line by raising its status from a minority to a nation as conceived by Muhammad Iqbal. Admittedly, Gandhiji and the Congress had failed to find a solution for the minority problem. The prospect for the implementation of the Gandhi–Irwin Pact was no better. There was a large scale harassment of the people in the United Provinces, Bombay and North-West Frontier Province. After his meeting with the Viceroy in Simla on 25 August 1931, Gandhiji was satisfied as the Gandhi–Irwin Pact was reaffirmed and the principle of holding an enquiry into complaints was conceded. As a sequel to that, Gandhiji started his journey on 29 August for London to participate in the Second Round Table Conference.

The Second Round Table Conference was to be held in a new atmosphere: the Labour government had been replaced by the national Government, and Samuel Hoare, the new secretary of state for India was hostile to the Indian sensibilities. The main problem was the Hindu–Muslim problem. In the Minority committee, Gandhiji made a powerful speech in his attempt to allay the fears of minorities and pleaded with them to work unitedly for the independence of India. But he failed to persuade them, as other minorities like scheduled castes, the Anglo-Indians, Christians and non-Brahmin groups also joined hands with the Muslims to assert that without adequate safeguard of their interests, no constitution for India would be acceptable to them. As the minority problem was not being solved, the conference turned out to be a big flop. This failure provoked Gandhiji to say that the 'parting of the way' had come. The Prime Minister put up a brave face and declared that the communal difference would not be allowed to come in the way of further constitutional arrangements. But he also made it clear that if no agreement among the different sections of Indian people could be reached on the minority issue, he would announce his own award on it.

Why did the Second Round Table Conference fail to achieve substantial progress? In retrospect, several factors seem responsible for it. In the first place, the composition of the Muslim delegates was such that they were more committed to the Muslim cause rather than the cause of independence. Second, the Labour Party Government, primarily responsible for the First Round Table Conference and the Gandhi–Irwin Agreement, had been replaced by the national Government which was virtually dominated by the conservatives. Not only that, it was in the midst of the conference that the Conservative Party was swept to power in October 1931, which further emboldened them to take a more anti-Indian stand. Even the stiff stand taken by the Muslim delegates at the Conference was the result of this changed attitude of the Government, which was more than willing to play the 'the crescent card' against the Indian people.

Third Round Table Conference

The Second Round Table Conference almost ended in a fiasco as it failed to find an honourable solution for India, primarily on account of the obstinacy of the Muslim delegates and the hostility of the government. But the situation in India had vastly changed for the worse. On his arrival from London on 29 December 1931, Gandhiji found that repressive measures under various anti-people ordinances were rampant, particularly in UP, NWFP and Bengal. Jawaharlal Nehru in UP and the Khan brothers in NWFP were behind bars. In Bengal, the worst repressive measures were being taken under the pretext of dealing with the emerging terrorism. The Gandhi–Irwin Pact, for all practical purposes, was dead as a dodo. All attempts by Gandhiji to revive its spirit failed as he was not even given an interview by the Viceroy. More than anything else, there was a radical change in the attitude of the new dispensation as compared with one under Lord Irwin. While the old dispensation treated Gandhiji and the Congress with respect, the new one was out to humiliate them by showing them their place. Thus, the Congress was hardly left with any other alternative but to revive the mass Civil Disobedience Movement with renewed vigour. But renewed movement invited the worst repression from the government. More than that, there was fundamental change in the attitude of the Government after the collapse of the Second

Round Table Conference. The new idea was to make British Parliament the sole arbiter of the political fate of India in place of the old idea of making Gandhiji and the political groups, particularly the Indian National Congress as an equal partner.

It is relevant to note that towards the end of the Second Round Table Conference, a number of committees had been set up to make recommendations after holding a proper enquiry. One of the major committees was the consultative committee, headed by the Governor-General, to consider the reports of other committees and send them to London with their own comments. But in the light of the new policy even the liberals like Sapru, Jayakar and Joshi resigned from the committee, which the government was happy to accept. The new idea was that the reports of other committees should go directly to the British Government instead of being mediated through the consultative committee in which Indians had some role to play.

Meanwhile, as promised at the end of the Second Round Table Conference, Ramsay MacDonald announced his communal award on 10 August 1932. This award was a big blow to Indian nationhood and was designed to further fragmentation, as it extended the principle of separate electorate to many Indian religious and caste groups. Gandhiji reacted sharply and went on a fast unto death on 20 September 1932. However, with the intervention of Madan Mohan Malaviya and other leaders an agreement was reached that subsequently came to be known as the Poona Pact. It restored the principle of joint electorate with reservation of seats for the depressed classes, which was accepted by the British Prime Minister.

It was in this background that the Third Round Table Conference was announced. This was a part of window dressing, as both the purposes as well as the composition of the conference was radically changed. Most of the Congress leaders were behind bars. Princely India had lost its earlier enthusiasm and hence they were represented only by officers and ministers. The Labour Party refused to join it. Jinnah was excluded. From India, only liberals and communalists were invited. Altogether only 46 delegates participated in the conference. Thus, it comprised handpicked delegates from both India and England. The conference met from 17 November 1932 to 24 December 1932. It considered the reports of the committees and even the reasonable suggestions of the Indian delegates, like a Bill of Rights for the Indian citizens was ignored. Even Tej Bahadur Sapru's sane advice that the proposed constitution would have meaning only if it was acceptable to the people of India, was not given due consideration. Based on the committee reports some broad framework for a new constitution was delineated. Subsequently, the government published a White Paper on 15 March 1933, apparently based on the proceedings of the Third Round Table Conference, which gave an outline of a new constitution. In certain respects, this was more retrogressive as there was no mention of dominion status for India. But even this was not acceptable to die-hard Conservatives like Winston Churchill, who condemned it. Soon after, in April 1933, a joint parliamentary committee was appointed which submitted its report on 19 December 1934. Finally, a Bill was introduced in the British Parliament which was passed on 4 August 1935 and became the India Act of 1935. The main feature of the India Act of 1935 was provincial autonomy. But this was still hedged by the discretionary power of the Governor, giving him considerable scope for manipulation, particularly in the Provinces where there were weak and divided political parties. The Act did provide for a federation comprising British India and the Princely India. However, there was no provision for responsible government at the Centre. This part of the Act never came into force in account of the divided political opinion in the country.

In retrospect, it seems that to the journey, which started with a demand for a round table conference to re-examine and review the Act of 1919, ended with a new Act of 1935. This Act evoked hostile sentiments from Indian public opinion as it failed to meet their democratic aspirations. However, the Indian national struggle had covered a vast ground – Nehru Report, Civil Disobedience and three Round Table Conferences, each constituting a new milestone in its own way. Now, India was really knocking at the British door to take its affairs in its own hands. But the British seemed reluctant to concede it. That goal was reached only in August 1947. But by August 1935, India had covered a vast ground towards its independence.

Charti hai jab ishq ki san pe teg-i-khudi
Ek sepahi bhi zard karta hai kar-i-sepah

(When the sword of individuality is sharpened on the whetstone of love, the stroke of a single soldier does the work of an army).

UNKNOWN POET

20 Communal Award

I felt angry with him (Gandhiji) at his religious and sentimental approach to a political question, and his frequent references to God in connection with it. He even seemed to suggest that God had indicated the very date of the fast. What a terrible example to set!

JAWAHARLAL NEHRU

The communal award (August 1932) was one of the most baneful challenges, which the Indian National Movement was confronted with, in the post-Khilafat Non-cooperation period. As noted earlier, the country was rocked by a number of communal riots in the post-Khilafat period. Many attempts were made to exorcise the demon of communalism but it refused to die. Even Gandhiji's fast at Muhammad Ali's house at Delhi, in 1924, failed to make any permanent impact. There was a temporary reprieve during the boycott of the Simon Commission, and serious attempts were made to tackle the problem through the All Parties' Conference and the Nehru Report. But once again the attempt failed and the virus of communalism got a new lease of life. The Muslim League, not only got revived but also adopted a more militant posture. Jinnah's fourteen-point-demand and Muhammad Iqbal's advocacy for a separate Muslim federation in the North-Western Provinces gave further momentum to Muslim communal politics. Even during the first two Round Table Conferences (1930-1) it was the minority problem which proved to be the main stumbling block to any constitutional development in India. It was during the Second Round Table Conference that British Prime Minister Ramsay McDonald had made an announcement that in case of the failure of the Indian leadership to come to a solution, he himself would announce a scheme in this regard. Some attempts were made by the Indian leadership to find an amicable solution, but in the end nothing much came out of these deliberations. Accordingly, on 16 August 1932 Ramsay McDonald gave out a scheme which, subsequently, came to be known as the Communal Award. In fact, it was more of an order rather than an award as the Congress Party was never a party to rendering any authorisation to McDonald in this regard. Perhaps, this is why it was made clear by him that in case Indian political groups would succeed in finding an all-agreed scheme, the award would be withdrawn and suitably substituted by it.

Main Provisions of the Award

Ramsay MacDonald, the British Premier, announced the Communal Award on 16 August 1932. According to this award, the right of separate electorate was not only given to Muslims but also to all minority communities in the country. The primary aim of this award was to further fragment the body politic of India, as it sought to allot a number of seats to each minority community in the provincial legislatures to be elected on the basis of separate electorate. Thus each community was to be treated as a separate constituency for the purposes of election for its representatives. In other words, a Muslim could be elected only by the members of his community and the same principle would apply in case of other minority communities. Ten communities were identified as minorities: (i) Muslims, (ii) Depressed classes, (iii) Backward areas representatives, (iv) Indian Christians, (v) Anglo-Indians, (vi) Europeans, (vii) commerce and industry, (viii) Land holders, (ix) university and (x) the labour. However, the award did not cover the Central Legislature as the question of Princely India's association in the federation and its actual size and composition was still under consideration.

Nevertheless, it was made clear that while deciding the composition of the Central Legislature, the question of adequate representation of all communities would be kept in mind. The actual distribution of seats in the provincial legislatures differed from province to province. It was based on which of the ten minorities comprised its population and their actual strength as well. However, in actual calculations, careful consideration was given by the Award to safeguard the British imperial interests. This became evident as the entire scheme was not based on the actual strength of each community in each province. The award, in fact, was an extension of the old British policy of 'divide and rule' and propping-up of Muslims, Europeans, and Anglo-Indians beyond their actual strengths. Besides, it was carefully designed to cut to size the dominant Hindu community.

An understanding of criteria of seat allotment to different communities would go a long way to support the above observations. For instance, in a number of provinces where Muslims were in a minority, undue weightage was given to them, though similar consideration was not given to Hindus in the Muslim-majority areas. For instance, in Madras, UP, Bihar and Central Provinces, the Muslims were given 29, 66, 42 and 14 seats respectively. But if they were to get seats in all these provinces based on the strength of their population, they would have got only 17, 35, 20 and 5 seats. On the other hand, in a Muslim-majority province like Bengal, Muslims constituted 55 per cent of the population and Hindu 43 per cent and others were only two per cent. But in the distribution of seats, as given by the award, European and others got 20 per cent seats whereas Hindus got only 32 per cent seats. Such an arrangement was made in Bengal with a view to protecting the interest of the British capital as well as to maintain cleverly a balance between Hindus and Muslims. In Punjab, a slightly different stratagem was adopted: the Sikhs, though constituting only 13 per cent of population were given 18 per cent of seats, i.e. 32 seats out of total troughs of 175. But no weightage was given to Hindus (unlike the Muslim in the Hindu-majority areas) as they were given only 50 seats of 175, which was almost in accordance with their population.

The entire scene becomes clear if we look at the total picture: out of 1488 seats in all the 9 provinces, Hindus got only 776 (715 general seats + 61 for the depressed classes) which was a little more than 50 per cent of the total seats, whereas the Muslims got 489 which was more than 33 per cent. If we bear in mind that Muslims at best constituted not more than 25 per cent of the population, the British game becomes clearer. But the Muslims were not being propped up at the cost of the British imperial interest. This was evidenced by the fact that both in Bengal and in Punjab, they were not allowed to have a majority of seats, even though they constituted a majority of the population in both the provinces. In Punjab, they were given 86 seats out of a total of 175 and in Bengal 119 seats out of a total of 250. This was done to keep them tightly under the British clutches.

Let us look at the arrangements for the depressed classes, which were still more curious. An attempt was made to create a façade that they were not totally and permanently cut off from the general Hindu community. Thus, the members of the depressed classes were to have two types of seats – one for the general constituency and the other for an own special constituency. The special constituencies were to be created where the population of the depressed classes was in a large number. Except in Madras, these special constituencies were not to cover the entire area of any other province. In Bengal, special constituencies were not to be created as the depressed class constituted a majority even in some general constituencies. In any case, not less those 10 per cent seats would have to be given to the depressed classes in the Bengal Legislature. In the North-West Frontier Province, the depressed classes were not given any seat as their population was supposed to be negligible. It was also declared that special constituencies for the depressed classes would come to an end after 20 years.

The communal award was no doubt a plan for real balkanisation of India. It would give a big blow to united nationalism, as it would force various sections of Indian society to think only in terms of their community interests rather than the national interest. In fact, the principle of separate electorate as an instrument of divisiveness in Indian politics was even accepted in the legal reports of the various governmental committees and commissions. That it was an obstacle to the emergence and growth of healthy nationalism in India was never contested by sensible leaders, including the ones from the British establishment. But as a part of their policy of divide and rule, they conceded it under the Act of 1909, which was also accepted by the Act of 1919. What gave them sanctity was its acceptance by the Congress under the terms of the Lucknow Pact. The report of the Simon Commission also favoured its retention. The communal award was a further extension of the principle of separate electorate, covering other communities which had so far remained untouched by its virus. Thus it was a very retrogressive step. Besides, it tried to divide the Hindu community by taking away the depressed classes from its fold. Not only that, it did not have any governing principle: the weightage given to the Muslims in the Hindu-majority areas was quite substantial though no such weightage was given to Hindus in the Muslim-majority areas. What was more, the British did not even trust the Muslims in the Muslim-majority areas as they did not allow them to have a majority without seeking British support. In brief, the communal award was nothing but an extension of the policy of 'divide and rule'.

The Poona Pact

For Mahatma Gandhi, the award threw a big challenge. It is relevant to note that since the days of the Non-Cooperation Movement, Harijan uplift had become one of the major components of his constructive programmes. Besides, he had made it clear during the Second Round Table Conference and in the subsequent period that he would resist any attempt to snatch away the Harijans from the fold of Hinduism, as it would not do any good to them either. In fact, he had made it clear that any such arrangement would not only harm the larger Hindu interests but also those of the Harijans. The moment the award was announced, he made his decision to go in for a fast unto death, though he was in prison during those days.

As per his past commitment, Mahatma Gandhi started his fast unto death on 20 September 1932. Early morning he received a telegram from Tagore conveying his heart felt appreciation for his (Gandhiji's) sublime penance. He was in the Yervada Jail and the government expressed its intention to release him on the first day of the fast itself. He reiterated his firm intention to continue his fast even if he was released. This created a big stir in the country. The day was observed as a day of fasting all over the country. Initially, Dr B R Ambedkar, the leader of the depressed classes, did not take Gandhiji's fast seriously. But the country felt otherwise as a number of leaders, viz., C Rajagopalachari, Madan Mohan Malaviya, M C Rajah, Rajendra Prasad and others took the initiative with a determination not to leave a single stone unturned to find an amicable solution. Madan Mohan Malaviya made strenuous effort to impress upon both Hindu and depressed classes' leaders to come to an agreement and ultimately B R Ambedkar was brought on the line. An agreement was signed, which subsequently came to be known as the Yeravada Pact or Poona Pact.

It is relevant to note that the Congress and Mahatma Gandhi, though opposed to the principle of separate electorate, had always favoured adequate representation of seats in the legislatures for the depressed classes. The real apple of discord was the separate or joint electorate. The depressed classes led by Ambedkar insisted on the principle of separate electorate whereas the Congress and the Mahatma were committed to the principle of joint electorate. Ultimately, the depressed classes' leaders agreed to give up their demand for separate electorate in lieu of adequate reserved seats under joint electoral system. The main provisions of the agreement were as follows:

(i) Seats would be reserved for the depressed classes out of the general electorate. There would be 148 reserved seats in different provincial legislatures instead of 71 as provided under the

Communal Award. Thus, the depressed classes got more than double the seats than they could have got otherwise under the Award. Under the agreement they got 30 seats each in Madras and Bengal, 20 each in the Central Provinces and the United Provinces, followed by 18 in Bihar and 15 in Bombay and Sindh. This was a substantial gain for them.

(ii) A procedure was also worked out for the election to these reserved seats. The members of the depressed classes in each reserved seat would first elect a panel of four candidates.

(iii) The same procedure would be adopted in the case of election to the Central Legislature and 18 per cent of the seats allotted to the general electorate in British India would be reserved for them.

(iv) Such a system of representation for the depressed classes, in case of both provincial and Central Legislatures, would continue till it would be terminated by the mutual agreement of the communities concerned. However, the system of election of the primary panel would came to an end after the first ten years.

(v) Every effort would be made to secure fair representation of the depressed classes in regard to the election to local bodies as well as in their appointment to public services.

(vi) An adequate sum, out of the educational fund of every province, would be earmarked for providing educational facilities to the members of the depressed classes. This agreement was signed not only by prominent national leaders like Madan Mohan Malaviya, C Rajagopalachari, Rajendra Prasad, and G D Birla, but also by prominent depressed classes leaders like B R Ambedkar and M C Rajah.

The British Prime Minister immediately accepted these points of the Poona Agreement, which were relevant to the award already announced by him.

Many people were critical of Gandhiji for his fast unto death at a critical juncture of the Civil Disobedience Movement. It was argued that his fast diverted people's attention from the national struggle to the problem of representation for the depressed classes. Even a leader and close follower of Gandhiji, Jawaharlal Nehru was not very happy with his fast on the same ground. But for Gandhiji it was not a 'non-issue' as conceived by many other people. He justified his fast on various

Superintendent,
Yeravda Central Prison,
(Poona).

Dear Gurudev,

It is just now 1-45 A.M. and I think of you and some other friends. If your heart indorses contemplated fast, I want your blessings again.

my love and respects

Yours

M.K.Gandhi

2-5-33

grounds. One, it was undertaken in deference to the 'still small voice within' which was an integral part of his life's philosophy. Second, the fast was intended to 'sting the Hindu conscience' for right religious action. Third, separate electorates would not remedy Harijan's degradation, rather it would perpetuate the practice of untouchability for ever.

Many people were also unhappy with Gandhiji for ignoring the equally dangerous and divisive provisions of the communal award for separate electorate for many other communities. Mahatma Gandhi had made it clear in his letter to the British Prime Minister that there were many other parts of the Award which could not have his approval. But his conscience had not warranted self-immolation as it had done in the case of depressed classes. Gandhiji often acted on being prompted by that 'still small voice within' which was very basic to his belief system. True, it did involve an element of subjectivity but the voice of his conscience was that of a purified soul. It was never a tactical step for him and that he demonstrated during the entire stewardship of the national movement. Thus, if judged as an act of a politician it has many limitations, but if looked at as an act of a purified soul it has many justifications. The country had to decide whether or not it wanted his leadership. But once it decided to take him as the leader, it could not grudge his freedom to act on the basis of his 'still small voice within'. That he was committed to the cause of the Harijan uplift since the days of non-cooperation was a well-known story and his decision to risk his life was in consonance with his lifelong commitment

Gurudev and Mahatma

to it. Moreover, he followed it up by solid work by undertaking a journey of 12,500 miles including a long 'padyatra'. That only demonstrated his sincerity and commitment. He followed it up by starting the 'All India Anti-untouchability league' (September 1932) and a journal called *Harijan* (January 1933). That only proved his commitment to the cause, which remained an article of faith with him till his death.

Some other scholars have faulted his work for Harijan uplift on the ground that he concentrated more on social reforms like access to wells and ponds, temple entry, removal of untouchability and other humanitarian works. But he never took up their economic cause, like redistribution of land. Nor did he attack the very basis of *varnaashram*. In fact it was on this basis that B R Ambedkar refused to send a message for the *Harijan* – a journal started by Gandhiji. In defence of Gandhiji, it could be said that he always wanted to judge one's commitment on the basis of deeds rather than mere words. Even in the field of Harijan uplift, he demonstrated his sincerity and commitment through his small work and not merely by big and brave words.

In retrospect, the sagacity of the Poona Pact could be judged by the fact that even independent India followed the same system with minor modifications, in which B R Ambedkar had a big role to play. Another thing to be noted is that through his epic fast and subsequent work among the Harijans, he brought them, in a big way, to the political mainstream of the national movement. In the process, he made the national movement voice the hopes and aspirations of one of the most dispossessed sections of Indian society.

A Critical Evaluation of the Civil Disobedience Movement

The critics of the Civil Disobedience Movement found a number of loopholes, both in respect of its overall strategy and its aspectual decisions. First, Gandhiji's decision to enter into an agreement with Lord Irwin in 1931, his decision to go on a fast unto death on the issue of the communal award and the decision to convert the movement from mass civil disobedience to an individual satyagraha, leading to its final withdrawal in May 1934 – all these aspects have been subjected to severe criticism even by some of the followers and the participants of the movement, including stalwarts like Subhas Chandra Bose and Jawaharlal Nehru. The main points of criticism have been twofold. First, when the people were engaged in a battle of life and death with the British empire, Gandhiji more often than not, took his decisions mostly on the basis of his 'inner voice' which often could not be explained on rational grounds. For many of his critics it appeared more as acts of compromise rather than his tactical retreats. Not only that, more often than not, he hardly gave the Congress and other participants of the movement any other choice than to accept his decisions. Thus, judged on an ordinary scale, it sounded undemocratic, nay even autocratic, at times. But these critics forgot that Gandhiji was subjected to harsh criticism during every national movement he launched, but when the time came for the next round of struggle, the entire country, including the Indian National Congress, had to lean on his shoulders for launching and guiding it. For, of all the leaders he alone had the uncanny knack to feel the pulse of the people. Hence, willy-nilly the country had to look up to him for leadership.

Second, many critics from the left have criticised him for his rejection of the theory of class struggle which he replaced by theory of class conciliation. These critics never ask as to why they themselves, even with their more radical and pro-poor, pro-peasant policies and with working-class ideological moorings, could not produce either a single mass leader of great stature or lead a mass movement on any massive scale. Any sectarian leader whether working for a class or caste or a particular religious group, could any day, appear more radical and even more revolutionary in course of the espousal of their sectional cause. This is why Jinnah, Ambedkar and S A Dange could always appear more revolutionary in the eyes of their followers than any other national leaders like Gandhiji, who had to carry the entire nation with him reconciling various groups with varied conflicting interests. In fact, that is the real strength of Gandhiji, whatever the left critics might obfuscate.

However, one front where the Civil Disobedience Movement really failed was the problem of Hindu–Muslim unity. Whereas the Non-Cooperation Movement marked the highest watermark of Hindu–Muslim bonhomie, by the time the Civil Disobedience Movement was launched, things had changed drastically. The Indian Muslim League had been revived, communal riots had started occurring in various parts of the country, and the Muslim intransigence on the issue of separate electorate had reached a point of no return. And with a prospect of a new constitution with greater amount of democratisation, the bugbear of Hindu domination had gripped the minds of the Muslim leadership. Gandhiji made several attempts by organising a unity conference and All Parties Conferences to find an amicable solution, but he could not succeed. That did remain a glaring failure and the Civil Disobedience Movement widened the hiatus rather than bridging it up. But his effort to bury the demon of communalism could not be doubted, and if he failed it was more on account of circumstances and the Muslim leaders' intransigence rather than the lack of his sincere efforts.

Despite all these weaknesses, the Civil Disobedience Movement marked a decisive phase in the history of national struggle. There is no denying the fact that on a number of counts, its achievements were spectacular. In the first place, it exposed the brutal face of the British Empire in full public glare, which even the international community did not fail to notice. In the same vein, it established the moral basis of the Indian struggle as well as its mass support base. Third, it took the battle of Swaraj to the doorsteps of the most dispossessed sections of the Indian people – tribals, Harijans, backward classes and women. Fourth, the economic impact of the movement was not less impressive. The import of the British cotton goods fell from 1248 million yards, during 1929-30 to 376 million yards during 1931-2. Fifth, the movement remained peaceful and non-violent despite the worst provocations from the British Government, which vindicated Gandhiji's faith in truth and non-violence.

And above all, the movement changed the quality of the will of the people. It strengthened people's will to resist the British Empire, inviting sufferings without raising even their own hands in self-defence. And it was amply demonstrated during the Dharasana raids. '*Na Marenge Na Manenge*' (Neither will we kill, nor we would accept injustice) became a battle cry, which held India in good stead and attracted the attention of the world public opinion towards its uniqueness.

> *I would far rather like that Hinduism died than that untouchability lived. I will not bargain away their (Harijans) rights for the kingdom of the whole world. . . . I would say with all the emphasis I can command that if I was the only person to resist this thing, I will resist it with my life.*
>
> MAHATMA GANDHI

21 The Act of 1935 and the Indian Freedom Movement

After all, we framed the constitution . . . of 1935 because we thought . . . it was the best way . . . to hold India to the Empire.

LORD LINLITHGOW

The Government of India Act 1935, in its own way, was a distinct milestone on the road to constitutional developments. Despite its obvious limitations, under this Act, responsible governments were introduced at the provincial levels and a promise of an Indian federation, comprising both the British Indian Provinces and Princely India, was conceived and concretised in a constitutional document passed by the British Parliament. It is quite relevant to mention that the Act of 1919 had failed to satisfy the rising political aspirations of the Indian people. The Non-Cooperation Movement had decisively proved that the people of India were determined to achieve substantial transfer of power to their hands. The Swaraj Party, in a way, working as a legislative wing of the Congress Party, became a major protagonist for securing a new constitution for India. It was in response to its persistent demand that the Simon Commission was set up towards the end of 1927. Not only that, it was under the leadership of Motilal Nehru that a framework for the Indian constitution was produced, which subsequently came to be known as the Nehru Report. The Nehru Report had the support of the All Parties Conference.

Indian constitutional development reached a turning point when in October 1929, Lord Irwin, the Viceroy of India, declared that full dominion status would be the natural political goal of the Indian people. Subsequently, the Simon Commission Report submitted in June 1930 had recommended the introduction of a fully responsible government at the provincial level by abolishing the then prevailing dyarchical system. However, it did not suggest any major change at the central level. The Lahore Congress' categorical demand for Purna Swaraj followed by the Civil Disobedience Movement, had given a new momentum to the demand of the Indian people for a new and radical constitutional arrangement.

An attempt was made through the round table conferences to carve out the new contours of constitutional development in India, which tried to underline the ideas on Indian federation, responsible government and safeguards for the minorities. Ultimately, nothing concrete came out of these conferences as the minority issue turned out to be insurmountable.

After the ascendance of the Conservative dominated government in England in September 1931, the situation took a turn for the worse. The third Round Table Conference held in December 1932 hardly made any contribution towards the removal of roadblocks to a new constitutional initiative created by the Communal Award of August 1932.

Henceforward, the British Government moved on its own and published a white paper on the constitutional issues in 1933, which was subsequently referred to the joint Select Committee of the British Parliament for being processed. No worthwhile consultation with the Indian leadership took place and finally the Government of India Act 1935 came into being after receiving Royal assent in August 1935.

The Government of India Act 1935, was a comprehensive document consisting of 321 Sections and 10 Schedules. It provided for a new constitutional arrangement both at the central and the provincial levels. At the provincial level, the most significant change that was brought about was the abolition of the much-maligned system of dyarchy and its replacement by a responsible government. Another redeeming feature of the federal structure was that greater autonomy for the provinces was provided under the new Act. However, the nature and structure of the responsible government was hedged and marred by various discretionary powers granted to the provincial governors. Therefore provincial ministries failed to receive the kind of autonomy and freedom, which was usually available to such a government in any parliamentary system. Provincial governors not only retained certain responsibilities to be discharged in their individual judgement but were also given a number of discretionary powers. For example, a provincial governor was given special power in respect of minority rights, safeguard of

British business interest and privileges of civil servants. Besides, the governor could also take over the provincial administration under certain special circumstances. What made the position of the governor more formidable was the fact that 40 per cent of the provincial budget was beyond the purview of the provincial ministries. The governor also enjoyed the power to restore the budget even if it had been rejected by the legislatures. It was also the special responsibility of a provincial governor to ensure adequate representation of minorities in the cabinet. As such, a provincial governor enjoyed a pivotal position in the provincial administration. Therefore, it was difficult to reconcile the needs of a responsible government with autocratic powers of the governor.

So far as the constitutional arrangements at the central level were concerned, the Act conceived of a federal structure comprising both British Indian provinces as well as Princely India. However, states were given full freedom whether or not to join the federation. Not only that, the federation was to come into being only if more than 50 per cent states decided to join it. The Act, however, did provide for three lists, federal, provincial and concurrent. It also made provision for a federal court, which was entrusted with the task of adjudicating the disputes, if and when they arise, between the federation and the federating units.

The Act conceived a plan for a dyarchical system of the government at the central level. To that end, it provided for two categories of the subject list: reserved and transferred. The reserved list included defence, external affairs, tribal administration and ecclesiastical affairs. The Governor-General was to administer the subjects of the reserved category with the help of his executive councillors. The transferred subjects were to be administered by the Governor-General with the help of the ministers. The ministers were to be appointed by the Governor-General from among the persons enjoying the confidence of the Central Legislature. But he was also to include representatives of the Princely States in the ministry. Besides, he was to coordinate the work of the councillors and ministers.

The Act also provided for a bicameral legislature at the centre – the lower house to be known as the House of Assembly and the upper house as the Council of State. The House of Assembly was to comprise 375 members – 250 members from the provinces and 125 members from the states. These 250 members from the provinces were to be divided in the following different groups: Hindus (104), Muslim (83), other minorities (26), industries and commerce (11), labour (10), landlords (7) and women (9). Regarding the upper house, the provisions for its composition were as follows: The total strength of the house: 260, out of which 104 from Princely India and six members to be nominated by the Governor-General. The distribution of the remaining seats were to be as follows: General category (75), Schedule castes (6), Sikhs (4), Muslims (49), Women (6) and Anglo-Indian (10). The members of the House of Assembly were to be elected by the members of the Provincial Assemblies by the system of proportional representation with a single transferable vote basis. So far as the composition of the Council of State was concerned, 104 members were to be nominated by the rulers of Princely India. Six members were to be nominated by the Governor-General. The remaining 150 members were to be elected directly by voters with high property qualifications. The electorate was further based on communal lines.

Major Criticism of the Act of 1935

The Government of India Act 1935 was subjected to criticisms from various quarters, both in India as well as in England. One major criticism was that it was autocratic in nature. Jinnah described it as 'rotten, totally unacceptable and absolutely unworkable'; the Hindu Mahasabha characterised it as 'reactionary and obstructive to the growth of nationalism and democracy'. Jawaharlal Nehru criticised it by saying that 'Britain retains power without responsibility, there is not even a proverbial fig leaf to cover the nakedness of autocracy' (Autobiography). Clement Attlee found it based on the 'keynote of distrust'; whereas in Professor Laski's opinion, it contained 'the worst features of the worst modern constitution. Second, the Act of 1935 was actually retrogressive as even Britain's earlier promise of the grant of the 'full dominion status' was missing from its provisions. In fact the imprint of the Conservatives in the British Parliament led by Winston Churchill, was quite pronounced in the provisions of the Act. Third, even the granting of provincial autonomy and the installation of responsible government at the provincial level was too about hedged by the autocratic nature of the powers of the governor. All provisions relating to 'safeguards reserved and discretionary powers' were made under the pretext of providing protection to minorities. But actually, the real intention behind the Act was to safeguard the British interests and, above all, the safety and continuation of the British imperial rule. Even the introduction of responsible government at the provincial level was a part of that larger strategy of the British.

If at all, there were any silver linings in the Act, they were: the ideas of federation, covering the entire country and the introduction of the responsible government at the provincial level. Hence, when the Constituent Assembly engaged itself in the task of constitution-making for independent India, the Act of 1935 came as a very handy and helpful document for the founding fathers of our constitution.

Implementation of the Act of 1935

As discussed earlier, the Act had provided for constitutional schemes both for the central and the provincial levels. However, the federal part was never implemented, primarily on account of the reluctance of Princely India. It is interesting to note that though the Princes had evinced a lot of interest in the idea of federation during Round Table Conferences, but by 1935 they had lost all interest in it. Perhaps, the rising tide of the *Praja Mandal* movement led by the All India States People's Conference supported by the Congress, proved a red-herring to the princes. Consequently, they felt threatened in respect of their autonomous, and in some cases, even their autocratic rule. However so far as the British rulers were concerned, the non-implementation of the federal scheme did not create much of a problem. There was a provision in the Act that in case the federal part fails to take off, British India could continue to be governed by the Act of 1919, with some minor modifications. However, at the provincial level, the Act was subsequently implemented and elections were held in February 1937. The Congress demonstrated its electoral clout and secured a majority in most of the provinces, except in Bengal, Assam, NWFP, Punjab and Sindh. For a while, there was a tussle with the government on the issue of the freedom of provincial ministries. After some clarification from the government, popular ministries took over in July 1937. Soon, Congress-led ministries were also installed in Assam and NWFP. It was in the course of the ministry formation that Jinnah wanted a coalition government, particularly in UP and Bombay. That was rejected by the Congress on ideological grounds. The spurned Muslim League went for rapid communalism, which in the opinion of some scholars, ultimately led to the partition of the country. The Congress ministries took a number of popular measures in respect of civil liberty as well as those relating to peasants, working class and other weaker sections of the society. Besides, they presented a creditable record on the questions like primary education, prohibition, tenancy laws, agricultural indebtedness, etc. However, the Muslim League kept on accusing them of pursuing an anti-Muslim policy. The left parties and their front organisations like trade union and the Kisan Sabha also went on expres-sing their dissatisfaction with the overall performance of these ministries.

Meanwhile, the Second World War broke out in early September 1939 and the Viceroy dragged India into the War without any proper consultation. The Congress was stunned and demanded a concrete assurance in respect of Indian independence, which the government refused to give. As a protest, the Congress ministries resigned in October 1939. Thus the popular rule in the Congress-ruled provinces came to an end and the government once again resumed its autocratic rule. That once again set the stage of another mass movement which was to engulf the country in the form of the Quit India Movement in 1942. In the next chapter, we shall undertake a detailed study of the Quit India Movement, which shook the foundation of the British Empire to its depth.

The sham constitution (the Act of 1935) will only add to the burdens of tax-payers and will forge fresh chains for our enslavement.

ACHARYA NARENDRA DEV

22 Quit India Movement

Here is a mantra, a short one, that I give you. You may imprint it on your hearts and let every breath of yours give expression to it. The mantra is: Do or Die. We shall either free India or die in the attempt; we shall not live to see the perpetuation of our slavery.

MAHATMA GANDHI

The Quit India Movement (*Bharat Chhoro Andolan*) was the biggest mass movement ever launched in the course of our national struggle. Even in terms of its ideological import, it had subtly made a departure from earlier Gandhian movements: It was a kind of open people's rebellion, in which participants were free to use all means at their disposal except overtly causing physical violence to the wielders of the imperial power. Though non-violence was to be its guiding norm, the people were not supposed to make a fetish of it. Even in terms of impact, it stood out from all earlier movements as it virtually gave a death-blow to the British rule in India. In brief, it occupies a unique place in the annals of our freedom struggle and as such it deserves a detailed study.

First, let us trace out the historical background of the movement. In the wake of the outbreak of the Second World War, in September 1939, and the Viceroy's unilateral decision (without any consultation with the Indian leadership) making India a party to the war, the national leaders found themselves between the two horns of a dilemma. Any unconditional support to the British would further boost its stranglehold over the Indian people; but any blind opposition to it would result in strengthening the forces of Nazism and Fascism. Besides, it also brought about a division among the Indian leadership: Subhas Chandra Bose favoured all-out opposition to the British, whereas the dominant section of the Congress was willing to offer conditional support to them. The Congress demanded an immediate declaration of the British war aims and their specific applications to the Indian situation. But the Viceroy was not willing to go beyond saying that after the war an attempt would be made in consultation with the Indian leadership to give a fresh look at the Act of 1935 and to seek its modifications, if needed. As it fell far short of the Congress demand, the Congress provincial ministries resigned towards the end of October 1939. The stalemate, however, continued.

Meanwhile, the war in the European arena was going against the allies. To break off the impasse, in July 1940, the Congress offered to support British war efforts on two conditions: (a) the Indian people's right to self-determination should be recognised forthwith; and (b) a provisional government responsible to the Central Legislature should be set up soon. But all that the Viceroy was willing to offer were: (a) a dominion status and constitution-framing body after the war; (b) expansion of the Executive Council; and setting up of a War Advisory Council. This was an offer which was too little and too late and the Congress immediately rejected it. This led to the launching of the individual Satyagraha which continued from November 1940 to December 1941, when it was finally withdrawn. It was an attempt to lodge a strong protest against the British reluctance to take any concrete step towards India's independence, without impairing British war efforts. Meanwhile, with Japan joining the war against the allies, the situation was becoming critical on the eastern front. That led to the setting up of the Cripps Mission in March 1942. The Mission did make some efforts to bring about a rapprochement between the British Government and the people of India, but ultimately it failed.

The failure of the Cripps Mission created doubts in the minds of our leadership about the basic sincerity of the British Government. They veered around the view that the basic purpose behind the Cripps Mission was to assuage the feelings of its war allies, viz., China and USA: it had no intention of working out a plan for substantial transfer of power to Indian hands. This suspicion led to deep-seated resentment in the minds of our national leaders, which prompted them to plan a concrete and positive course of action. What gave an added urgency to this course of action was the deteriorating war situation on the eastern frontiers of India. As the Japanese invasion of India appeared imminent, a feeling grew that at the critical moment the British authorities might just leave the Indian people to their fate. Though some difference of opinions existed among the Congress leadership about the actual course of action, it was evident that total inaction might prove suicidal. As on earlier occasions, Gandhiji could always see the light at the end of the dark tunnel and inspire the people to a new course of action. On 26 April 1942, he wrote in *Harijan* in a ringing voice: 'whatever the consequences to India, her real safety and that of Britain too lie in orderly and timely withdrawal from India'.

Subsequently, he made it clear that if the British failed to do so, he would not hesitate to launch a mass movement. This was the context in which the Congress Working Committee, followed by the All India Congress Committee, met at Allahabad (April-May 1942) and proposed a programme for non-violent non-cooperation with the Japanese army. And, it simultaneously called for a speedy British withdrawal from India. Once again Gandhiji accepted the leadership of the Congress, as it had broadly veered around his views. Gandhiji started preparing for a new mass movement. The Congress Working Committee, on 14 July 1942, passed a resolution calling upon the British to withdraw from Indian soil, failing which it would be 'reluctantly compelled to utilise all the non-violent strength it might have gathered since 1920'. It was also decided to hold the AICC meeting on 7 August 1942. The government remained adamant making it clear that it would not tolerate 'any interference with defense measures'. When the AICC met in Bombay on 7 August, Gandhiji gave a clarion call by coining a new slogan of 'Do or Die'. The message was loud and clear. 'We shall either free India or die in the attempt; we shall not live to see the perpetuation of our slavery'. Gandhiji wanted to negotiate with the Viceroy but the government did not even wait for the movement to be launched formally. All the top leaders were arrested in the early hours of 9 August 1942 and taken to different prisons. This was followed by the arrest of a large number of political workers all over the country. Besides, all Congress organisations were declared unlawful and their funds were confiscated. Not only that, defence of India Rules, along with a number of other ordinances, were issued to impose strict control over all walks of our national life.

The sudden arrest of our national leaders, followed by other draconian repressive measures, miserably failed to dampen the freedom-spirit of our people. On the contrary, it had an electrifying impact on the minds of our people: virtually left leaderless, each man felt free to act in the light of his own understanding of the situation. The response of our people was instantaneous and spontaneous. For a few days, particularly in many urban areas, public life came to a standstill as strikes, demonstrations and processions became the order of the day.

The lack of space does not permit us to even summarise the broad contours of the movement. Thus we have no choice but to underline some of its highlights. Region-wise, the movement was very widespread in eastern UP, Bihar, Maharashtra, Bengal, Orissa, parts of Karnataka, Kerala, Tamil Nadu and Andhra Pradesh. It is true that the first response to the government's repressive measures came from the urban areas. Apart from the general public, the working class came openly in support of the movement. In places like Lucknow, Kanpur, Bombay, Nagpur, Ahmedabad, Madras, Delhi, and Jamshedpur the working class struck work as they favoured a national government. The textile mills of Ahmedabad and the Tata Steel Mills of Tata Nagar were closed for quite some time in support of the movement.

Students played a crucial role in spreading the message of the movement to the masses as well as leading demonstrations from the front. Students spread the message of 'Quit India' by writing slogans on the walls, and even on the trees. They organised mass meetings, distributed leaflets, pamphlets and other revolutionary literature. They boycotted schools and colleges and at many places hoisted our national flags by pulling down the Union Jack. In the course of their attempts to hoist the national flag on the Patna secretariat on 11 August 1942, seven students were shot dead, which further led to the intensification of the movement in that part of the country. Subsequently, Pandit Punyadeo Sharma, a prominent freedom fighter, succeeded in hoisting the national flag on the Patna Secretariat. In Banaras, the army was called to quell the revolutionary spirit of the students of Kashi Vidyapeeth and Banaras Hindu University. In Etawa (UP), Arjun Singh Bhadauria continued armed rebellion through his Lal Sena for a long time. In Bombay, Yusuf Meherally, a socialist leader, exhorted the student community to paralyse the administration of the province.

Another new feature added to the movement was that in a number of places parallel governments were set up, replacing the British administration. Ballia in Eastern UP, Midnapore in Bengal, and Satara in Maharashtra were the three places where parallel governments earned prominence. For some time they took over the administration and virtually ran the government. Though they could not be sustained for a long time in the face of excessive use of force by the imperial administration, but for people's morale their psychological impact was tremendous. Chitoo Pandey of Ballia and Nana Patil of Satara, became folk heroes overnight.

A new dimension to the movement was given by the leaders of the Congress Socialist Party led by Jayaprakash Narayan (J P). They organised an underground movement to paralyse the British administration. In October 1942, along with a number of co-prisoners, J P scaled down the 62-feet-high walls of Hazaribagh prison and they escaped, to lead an underground movement against the government. These death-defying and dare-devil acts created a new enthusiasm among the Indian people and inspired them to attempt new heroic deeds. The prominent socialist leaders who were in the forefront in underground resistances were Rammanohar Lohia, Ram Nandan Mishra, Basawan Singh, Achyut Patwardhan, Usha Mehta and others. In Bihar, they organised Azad Dasta under the active leadership of Nityanand Singh and Suraj Narayan Singh, which played a crucial role in cutting communications and paralysing the British oppressive machinery. In Bombay, Usha Mehta and Rammanohar Lohia organised a secret Radio Station to broadcast the message of the movement. Jayaprakash Narayan's letters to All Fighters of Freedom was a clarion call which inspired the freedom fighters to keep the flag of the movement flying, even in the face of the government's repressive measures.

Yet another feature of the movement was an attack on the symbols of the government like police stations, courts, post offices and railway stations. A number of people lost their life in the course of these attacks. At a number of places, railway tracks were removed so that the Government could not move men and material for the suppression of the people. In Bihar and eastern UP, the slogan of *Thana Jalao* and *station phoonko* caught the imagination of the people. The idea spread in other parts of the country also. According to the official assessment, 208 police stations, 1,300 Government and public buildings, and 273 private buildings and 382 railway stations were destroyed. Besides, 664 bomb explosions, 474 cases of sabotage to the roads, 411 cases of track destruction and 66 cases of derailment were also reported. That was not all: 945 post offices were destroyed and 12,286 incidents of sabotage to telegraph departments were also recorded. In all these heroic deeds, people faced police batons and guns, which spoke volumes for their earnestness for the freedom of the country.

A number of other heroic deeds were reported from different parts of the country. At Dumraon, in Shahabad district of Bihar, four people led by Kapil Muni were shot dead in the course of their attempt to hoist the national flag on the Dumraon police station.

Gandhiji's Fast

Since the beginning of the movement, the Government was squarely blaming the Congress for all the violence that was let loose in the country. It did not even spare the apostle of non-violence, Mahatma Gandhi and invariably accused him of inciting violence. The Government let loose a battery of propaganda not only in India but also abroad. From the very beginning of the movement, Gandhiji tried to explain that the movement was designed to remain non-violent. Therefore, for any violence the blame must go to the government's door. When he failed to convince the Government that the people's violence was in response to 'leonine' violence of the Government, he decided to undertake a 21 days fast, which started from 10 February 1942 and ended on 3 March 1942. There was great apprehension in several quarters that Gandhiji might not survive this self-imposed ordeal. The government had even made preparations for his cremation. But he did survive. Tremendous pressure was brought on the Government to release Gandhiji while he was on fast, as it had evoked worldwide interest in India's cause. Inside the country, many people returned the honours conferred to them by the Government: Prominent among them was Allah Baksh Khan, the Premier of Sindh. Subsequently, he was dismissed by the Government on that very count. Three members of the Viceroy's Executive Council, namely, H P Modi, N R Sarkar and M S Aney followed suit and resigned. But the Government stuck to its position and refused to release Gandhiji. The Government brought out a pamphlet 'Congress Responsibility for the Disturbance of 1942-43' blaming the Congress and its leader Mahatma Gandhi for violence during the movement. However, Gandhiji's fast gave a new momentum to the movement as it inspired a number of freedom fighters to keep the flag of the movement flying. Besides, it put the case of Indian independence on the world agenda. Subsequently, Gandhiji was released on 6 May 1944 on health grounds. An attempt was made to revive the Congress activities through constructive programmes. The government kept a strict watch even on these aspects of the Congress activities. Meanwhile, the War took a turn in favour of the allied powers. Most of the Congress leaders were released in June 1945 to enable them to participate in the Simla conference called by the Viceroy to find a way out of the political deadlock. That marked the end of the movement.

The Government Response

Even before the Congress resolution of 7 August, the government had made elaborate preparations for the suppression of the movement. The Government was not prepared to enter into any kind of dialogue with the Congress and Gandhiji. This is fully demonstrated by the fact that a number of newspapers, including *National Herald* and *Amrita Bazar Patrika* were banned. Special courts were set up to deal with the criminal cases. Some of them were even referred to the military courts. As per the government's own admission, nearly 25,000 people were convicted and were sentenced to various periods of imprisonment. About 50 people were awarded the death sentence. In face of such massive repression, it was not surprising that the Government succeeded in suppressing the major chunk of the movement by the end of 1942. Thereafter, the movement went underground. The government did not wait even to know the exact plan of the movement, not to talk of entering into any negotiations. All prominent leaders were put behind bars, even before the movement was formally launched. In fact, the Government let loose a virtual reign of terror. All kinds of forces including firing by machine-guns from the air were used against the people. According to the Government's own records police firing was resorted to on 601 occasions in which hundreds of people lost their lives. According to unofficial estimates, at least 10,000 people lost their lives in the course of the movement. Besides, the government imposed collective fines on 173 occasions, collecting over Rs one crore in fines from the people. More than hundred thousand people were put behind bars in the course of the movement. Not only the Congress committees were banned, but even newspapers and journals were not spared.

The Government did not stop at police and military action alone. On the political plane, it spared no effort to isolate the Congress by building a countervailing force in the form of the Indian Muslim League led by Jinnah. It is also to be noted that once it became clear to the Government that the Congress would go for a mass movement, it tried to counter it by expanding the Viceroy's Council. On 2 July 1942, the Viceroy's Executive Council was expanded from 11 to 14 members. Obviously, this was an attempt to gather public support from some sections of the Indian people. The new membership was distributed as follows: 4 Hindus, 4 Muslims and one each from the European, Scheduled Castes and Sikh community and the remaining three were officials. In view of the Congress and the Muslim League's refusal to participate, virtually every member was handpicked by the Government. Therefore, it is not surprising that the first act of the Executive Council was to order the arrest of the Congress leaders on 9 August 1942.

Critical Appreciation of Quit India Movement

The critics of the Quit India Movement have tried to find several faults even on practical grounds. In the first place, they argued that the movement provided the government with a golden opportunity to promote and prop up the Indian Muslim League and virtually made its leader, Jinnah as the sole spokesman of the Muslim masses. After the resignation of the Congress ministries towards the end of 1939, the British support enabled the Muslim League to spread its tentacles in the Muslim-majority areas which were its real Achilles' heel. It is relevant to note that till March 1942, Jinnah and his Muslim League did not have support among the Muslim-majority provinces. All the Premiers of the Muslim majority provinces like Sindh, Punjab, and Bengal did not belong to the Muslim League. Even NWFP was controlled by the Khan Brothers, who were allied to the Congress and the Khan ministry resigned along with the Congress in 1939. The Cripps Mission had enhanced the standing of Jinnah among the Muslim masses, as it virtually conceded the idea of Pakistan. But, very soon, the Muslim-majority provinces were handed over to Jinnah. For instance, in Sindh, Premier Allah Baksh Khan was dismissed and replaced by Ghulam Hussain Hidayatullah, a Muslim Leaguer. In Bengal, Premier Fazlul Haq was forced to resign by the governor and in April 1943, he was replaced by Khwaja Nazimuddin of the Muslim League. In Punjab, after the death of Sikandar Hayat Khan in December 1942, the new premier Khizer Hayat Khan came under the clutches of the Muslim League, though he continued to keep the façade of the Unionist Party. In North-West Frontier Province, after the resignation of the Khan ministry, Aurangzeb Khan, a Muslim League member, headed the ministry with the blessings of the British. In Assam also, Mohammad Saadullah, another Muslim Leaguer, headed the ministry. Thus, all the five provinces came under the domination of the Muslim League, making Jinnah virtually the uncrowned king of the Muslim masses. This was one of the unavoidable consequences of the Quit India Movement and the leaders could hardly do anything to prevent it. But the critics continue to point out that the Quit India Movement brought the British and Jinnah closer to each other, which resulted in Jinnah emerging as the sole spokesperson for the Muslim masses. But they forget that the acceptance of the Cripps Mission would have resulted in not one partition but several partitions of the country. In fact, its acceptance could have resulted in the total dismemberment of the country. Besides, Gandhiji was still hopeful of independence with unity for India and hence he could not have accepted Cripps proposal.

Second, the spread of the movement was uneven. The movement was weak in Madras Presidency and Punjab. Except in Mysore, the movement was also weak in Princely India. Besides, the movement was opposed by a large section of the political elite, viz., the, Communist Party of India, Akali Dal, Liberal Party, the Unionist Party, Ambedkar led Scheduled Caste Federation, the Indian Muslim League, and even by the Hindu Mahasabha.

The Quit India Movement is also faulted on the ground that it was unorganised and spontaneous. Therefore, it petered out soon, as it lacked organised coordination in the absence of a central agency. Looked at from another angle, its spontaneous and unorganised character was also to be taken as its strength. As we know that it was not supposed to be a Congress movement, but a people's movement and as such it was bound to be marked by spontaneity and disorganisation. This was anticipated by Gandhiji much before the movement started and, hence, he asked every Indian fighting for independence of the country 'to be his own guide'.

Another question that has been raised is whether the Quit India Movement deviated from the Gandhian path of truth and non-violence. In fact, this is precisely the charge which the British Government made against the Congress party and Mahatma Gandhi. In support of this charge, the government pointed out several overt and covert acts of violence indulged by the people in the course of the movement. Besides, its underground nature also went against the Gandhian principle of non-violence and truth. It was also pointed out that not only did Gandhiji refused to condemn violent acts of the people but he even eulogised leaders like Jayaprakash Narayan who was leading an underground movement. All this, the critics point out, went against the Gandhian principle of satyagraha based on truth and non-violence. There is no denying the fact that some violent acts were committed by the freedom fighters. But it should not be forgotten that the initiative for violent suppression of the movement came from the government and at some places people paid it in its own coin. The Government's refusal to negotiate and subsequent arrest of all national leaders were grave provocations, and in such a mass movement everybody was not trained as a non-violent activist. Hence, different people reacted in different ways. Considering the size of the country, the large number of people involved, and the kind of reign of terror unleashed by the government one can safely conclude that despite some minor deviations here and there, on the whole, the movement did maintain its non-violent character.

It is true that the movement could not force the British to quit India at once, but it certainly demolished the very foundation of the British rule in India. It cut asunder the British myth that they were opposed by a few and liked and supported by many. The movement gave a loud and clear message to them – pack up and go home by the first available plane. Second, the movement put the Indian struggle on the world agenda. The Indian struggle, standing on a high moral pedestal, turned out to be the trailblazer for the oppressed and the enslaved people of the world. It is not for nothing that Indian independence started a process of decolonisation leading to the freedom of a large number of enslaved people in the post-war period. By any standard the Quit India Movement would remain a glorious chapter in the annals of our freedom struggle.

> *No empire intoxicated with the red wine of power and plunder of weaker races has yet lived long in this world and the British Empire, which is based on organised exploitation of physically weaker races of the earth and upon a continuous exhibition of brute force, cannot live, if there is a just God ruling the universe.*
>
> MAHATMA GANDHI

219

23 Mahatma Gandhi's Contributions to the Freedom Struggle in India

And then Gandhiji came. He was like a powerful current of fresh air that made us stretch ourselves and take deep breath; like a beam of light that pierced the darkness and removed the scales from our eyes; like a whirlwind that upset many things, but most of all the working of people's mind. He did not descend from the top; he seemed to emerge from the millions of India, speaking their language and incessantly drawing attention to them and their appalling condition.

JAWAHARLAL NEHRU

The role of the individual in the historical process has been a subject of debate in the social science discourses for a long time. In the Marxian lexicography, it is characterised as the relative role of 'subjective' and 'objective' forces in shaping the social history of man. Marxist scholars, while not totally rejecting the contribution of the individual (subjective forces) have assigned a much larger role to social/objective forces in the historical process. Similarly, there are scholars and thinkers who, while not totally rejecting the role of objective forces, have, nevertheless, underlined the role of the individual in social history. Perhaps both viewpoints contain some truth. History is witness to the fact that both types of forces impinge upon each other and both together play crucial roles in shaping the pattern and texture of history. A similar question was raised in the *Mahabharata* in the context of the relative role of the 'King' (Raja) and the 'Time' (Kal) and it is rightly asserted there too that both, the King and the Time, impinge upon each other and are influenced by each other.

In the case of the Indian freedom struggle, a section of scholars do believe that violent movements led by revolutionaries like Bhagat Singh and Subhas Chandra Bose, the revolt of the naval and air force sections of the Indian army, and fear of general uprisings in the Indian armed forces, actually forced the British during 1946-47, to transfer power to the Indian hands. On the other hand, the very fact that Mahatma Gandhi is recognised as the father of the Indian nation underlines his centrality in the whole process. There is no dearth of historical facts and arguments supporting each contention. Perhaps, the debate could be fairly summed up by saying that there were always contributory streams augmenting and strengthening and even shaping the contours of the mainstream but they can neither replace nor undermine the latter's centrality. And undoubtedly, the Indian National Congress under the leadership of Mahatma Gandhi constituted the mainstream of our national movement. With these preliminary remarks, let us try to make a critical evaluation of Gandhiji's contributions to the freedom movement in India.

Born on 2 October 1869 at Porbandar in Gujarat, Mohandas Karamchand Gandhi was educated both in India and in the UK. What distinguished him from his fellow students was not his brilliance or studiousness but his truthfulness and a deep sense of rectitude. But what, in fact, changed his own fate, as well as the fate of Indian people, was his visit to South Africa, in 1893, to pursue a legal case on behalf of one of his clients. That was the time when racial discrimination against the Indian community, was at its worst. And the Indian community, comprising primarily indentured labour, low-grade servicemen and some businessmen, was hardly in a position even to raise their voice, not to talk of offering any resistance to it. In the course of his travel, Mohandas himself was subjected to racial discrimination but unlike other Indians he refused to pocket personal insults. Instead, he decided to resist it irrespective of its costs and consequences. He did not take it only as his personal insult, instead he interpreted it as a direct attack on the dignity of the entire Indian community. He organised the Indian community and launched many struggles against racial discrimination. It was in the course of one of these struggles that he 'invented' and perfected the instrument of satyagraha. Ultimately, on the face of a long-drawn struggle, the South African Government conceded some of the major demands of the Indian community.

The South African experience and his prolonged stay and struggle therein enriched his life in several ways. He had found a new weapon (satyagraha) to resist injustice both at the individual and societal level;

learnt the art of leading a life of an exemplar; developed a unique capacity to feel the pulse of the people and prepare them for self-suffering and sacrifice. And he also developed a deeply held secular outlook despite being rooted in religious and spiritual experiences. With such a rich and varied experience, he was back to India in January 1915. On the advice of his political Guru, Gokhale, he spent a year travelling throughout India to familiarise himself with the people of India and their problems. He attended the Lucknow Congress (1916) but had hardly any big role to play there. Meanwhile, his name and reputation earned during his South African struggle had not gone unnoticed in the country. His speech at Banaras Hindu University in 1916, in which he condemned the entire Indian elite including the Indian Princes for leading a life of ease and opulence when the people are being grinded in poverty, had reached every nook and corner of the country. Soon Gandhiji was invited to Champaran, Bihar, and he himself witnessed the conditions of peasants suffering at the hands of the Indigo-planters of European origin. Having examined their problems, he launched a struggle which ultimately resulted in some relief for the Champaran peasantry. Subsequently, he led two more local struggles – Kheda peasant satyagraha and Ahmedabad mill-worker's strike. In all these local struggles, he successfully demonstrated the efficacy and effectiveness of the weapon of satyagraha. This was followed by the Rowlatt Satyagraha in 1919, which was the first national struggle led by Gandhiji and that brought him at the national scene. He was greatly moved by the Jallianwala Bagh massacre and also by the genuine grievances of the Indian Muslims against the British, for their mishandling of the Turkish Caliph question. All these events provided the background to the launching of the Khilafat and Non-Cooperation Movements in 1920. Gandhiji dominated the Indian political scene like Colossus from 1920 to 1947 and led India to her independence. In between he led three major national movements – the Non-Cooperation (1920–22), the Civil Disobedience (1930–34) and the Quit India (1942–44). Gandhiji's role in the freedom struggle, can be clearly understood under the following eight sub-headings:

(i) Unmasking of the ugly face of British imperialism;
(ii) Satyagraha as a new weapon for national struggle;
(iii) Secular foundation of Indian nationhood and Hindu–Muslim unity;
(iv) The Congress in a new avatar;

(v) Constructive work: a new dimension of revolution;
(vi) Work through legislatures and local self-government bodies;
(vii) A dream for a new India; and
(viii) A dream of new civilization.

Unmasking of the Ugly Face of British Imperialism

It is true that ever since its inception in 1885, the leaders of the Congress were engaged in the task of disrobing British imperialism to its nakedness. They attempted to pull down three pillars which held the edifice of the British rule in India: benevolence, rule of law and its invincibility. One of the basic justifications of the British rule in India was its supposed benevolent character as ordained by providence. The early nationalists like Dadabhai Naoroji, M G Ranade, R C Dutt and Gopal Krishna Gokhale were the first to refute this British claim. And they, through their writings and speeches, proved beyond any reasonable doubt that the British rule had brought nothing but misery and mass pauperisation in its trail. In the light of their exposure, the British rule looked more like a curse rather than a boon from the hands of Providence. It was another matter that the liberals did not translate their intellectual investigation into actual political demands. This was followed by the Extremist's bold tactics to expose the facade of the British rule being based on the pillar of the rule of law. Tilak, Aurobindo, Lala Lajpat Rai and Bipin Chandra Pal and other Extremist leaders, through their self-invited sufferings, exposed the brutal and lawless character of the British Rule. Whenever these leaders were awarded long-term imprisonment or were deported from the country, the illegal character of the British system stood exposed and self-condemned, making its claim of ruling India by law to appear as a sham. But, perhaps despite their best efforts, the Extremists could not take the battle of Swaraj to the court of the common people. The armed revolutionaries pulled down the third pillar of the British claim of their being invincible. A small band of armed revolutionaries challenged the mightiest Empire on earth, and through their death-defying acts instilled a sense of deep fear among the British rulers, while injecting at the same time a sense of fearlessness among our own people. Thus, through their daring acts, they exposed the soft underbelly and the Achilles' heel of the British Empire. But their activities were confined to certain pockets of the country and there too only among a small section of the society. They could not establish live contacts with the larger masses.

Then came Mahatma Gandhi like a political hurricane and shook all the above-mentioned three pillars of the British imperial rule to their foundation. During the period from 1919 to 1922, he thoroughly exposed the brutal, authoritarian nature of the British 'lawless laws'. What was more, he brought the masses along with him to see the ugly face of the British Empire. By all-round exposure of the British ugly face, he weakened the moral fibre of the British rule and limited its capacity, to a great extent, to indulge unashamedly in acts of oppression and suppression. That limitation of the British 'steel frame' and Gandhiji's utter defiance instilled a sense of fearlessness among our people. That was demonstrated by the fact that in every subsequent national movement more and more people participated – making self-invited suffering and defiance as an order of the day. The benevolence, rule of law and invincibility, the three pillars of the British imperial rule, were shaken by Gandhiji to their foundation. Thus, he made the British rule appear both morally and materially untenable.

Satyagraha as a New Weapon for the National Struggle

As we have seen earlier, in the pre-Gandhian era that there were three major schools of thought, each using its brand of armoury against the British. Law, popular pressure and guns were the three weapons being used by the Moderates, the Extremists and the armed revolutionaries respectively. By 1918–19, all three weapons used by different schools had lost their cutting edge. By the end of the war the revolutionary movement had been curbed, controlled and tamed by the strong armed tactics and use of brutal force by the British. The liberals were virtually in disarray and, in fact, lost all their sheen as they appeared as a willing partner in the implementation of half-hearted and half-baked measures of self-government, i.e. the Act of 1919. Tilak's Home Rule Movement had failed to take a popular form and was primarily confined to certain pockets of western India. By 1918–19, Annie Besant had started dragging her feet and was avoiding a head-on collision with the British. In brief, the country was groping for a new leader and new sudarshan chakra. What gave urgency to this national need was the national disillusionment caused by the inadequacies of the Act of 1919 and brutalities displayed by Rowlatt Act and subsequent Punjab happenings.

It was in such a situation that Gandhiji appeared on the national scene with his sudarshan chakra of satyagraha in his hands. Besides, he was no greenhorn political activist. He was an old warhorse with an experience of two decades of struggle in South Africa. Having invented, experimented and perfected his own sudarshan chakra of satyagraha he had the self-confidence of a master-warrior of non-violent struggle. Thus, in the eyes of the people he entirely fitted the bill of a new saviour of the nation. For Gandhiji, satyagraha was based on truth and non-violence. It was much more than boycott or passive resistance. It was to posit soul force against the brute force. It was no weapon for the weak. It was a weapon of the strong, willing to undergo self-invited sufferings but not to accept any act of injustice. The underlying idea behind it was that one will resist every act of injustice, irrespective of cost and consequences: (neither will we kill nor will we accept any act of injustice). The beauty of satyagraha is that it leaves behind no trail of bitterness and personal animosity, as it is based on the principle of 'Resist the Evil but not the Evil-doer'. Thus, it uplifts all the parties involved in a disputation both morally and spiritually. It puts a limit on the ferocity of counter-attack. If the other party crosses the *Lakshman Rekha* of oppression, it would fall in its own eyes. What is more, it can be used by the lowliest of the low and the weakest of the weak against the highest of the high and the mightiest of the mighty. Gandhiji used his sudarshan chakra of satyagraha in all national struggles as well as at the local level – at Champaran, Kheda, Ahmedabad, Bardoli and many other places. Gandhiji never considered satyagraha as a stale and stagnant concept: it was a dynamic and growing phenomenon ever acquiring new dimension and new meaning. Examine this: The same Gandhiji who withdrew the Non-Cooperation Movement on the issue of violence at Chauri-Chaura refused to condemn people's violence during the 'Quit India Movement'. He even refused to censure Jayaprakash Narayan who was leading an underground movement, which went against the Gandhian principle of open defiance and resistance. It is this ever-growing and ever-dynamic aspect of satyagraha, which had made it so popular all over the world. It has remained as the *brahmastra* of all those who might be physically and materially weak but strong and invincible spiritually.

The point of non-condemnation of people's violence during the Quit India Movement needs a little more elucidation. To that end, one can raise a number of direct questions. Was the Mahatma losing his faith in the efficacy of non-violence or was he willing to take to another path as a part of his *apatdharma* (contingency) and more than willing to deviate from his *nityadharma* of non-violence. The answer to these questions is an absolute negative. For him non-violence was a part of his being. On a personal level, there was no question of deviation from the path of non-violent resistance. It may be recalled that even while launching civil disobedience in 1930–32, he had made it clear that stray cases of violence would not make him withdraw the movement. That was truer of the Quit India Movement which was being launched in the nature of a people's rebellion, unlike the Non-Cooperation Movement which he withdrew after the Chauri-Chaura incident. But, the Quit India Movement, was not to be the Congress-led movement, but a people's movement. He knew it more than anybody else that the entire population could not be made to develop absolute faith in non-violence. Hence, the only alternative was not to launch any movement till the entire population was trained in non-violent

Mahatma Gandhi and Frontier Gandhi

resistance. This was an impossible proposition. Besides, the primary aim of the Quit India Movement was nothing less than independence of the country. The same was made clear when he addressed the AICC meeting of 8 August 1942, which endorsed the Quit India Movement. Giving a clarion call to his countrymen he said: 'Every one of you from this moment consider yourself a free man or woman and act as if you are free. I am not going to be satisfied with anything short of complete freedom. We shall do or die. We shall free India or die in the attempt'.

It is clear from the above statement that the nature, dimensions and the objective of the Quit India Movement radically differed from the earlier Gandhian movements. It was nothing less than a call for total rebellion within the broad framework of non-violent resistance. Besides, the government unleashed tremendous violence against the people who responded to this unprecedented challenge in whatever way they could. And that is why the Mahatma blamed the government and its 'leonine violence' for people's acts of resistance which might not be considered non-violent, which is why he refused to condemn the people and their leaders who took to violent resistance. He was so convinced of the Government's responsibility for unleashing violence during the Quit India Movement that when it came out with a pamphlet 'Congress responsibility for the disturbances during 1942-43', he challenged the Government to initiate trial of the detenus and produce evidence so that they could defend themselves and prove their innocence in the court of law. As an unimpeachable proof of his total faith in non-violence, he undertook a 21-day fast during February–March 1943 to resist the false propaganda of the government that the Mahatma and his Congress had bid goodbye to the principle of non-violence during the Quit India Movement. The letter which he wrote to the Viceroy on the eve of his epic fast is worth quoting:

> It (the fast) is on my part meant to be an appeal to the Highest Tribunal for justice which I have failed to secure from you. If I don't survive the ordeal I shall go to the judgement seat with the fullest faith in my innocence. Posterity will judge between you as a representative of an all powerful government and me as a humble man who had tried to serve his country and humanity through it.

It is clear from the above analysis that the Mahatma had not lost his faith in non-violence. Nor was he willing to take to other means as a part of his *apatdharma*. So convinced was he about the 'leonine violence' of the government that he refused to censure his compatriots for any deviation from the non-violent path as a response to leonine violence of government.

A question is often asked whether the weapon of satyagraha could be used against a more authoritarian and totalitarian regime like those of Hitler and Stalin. Admittedly, it would be much more difficult. But in our view if there is a group of determined satyagrahis, no power on earth, however brutal and inhuman it might be, can withstand their moral onslaught on their unjust system. Thus satyagraha has the potential to be used in all conditions and all eventualities, the only pre-condition being a pure will and an iron determination to use it.

Secular Foundation of Indian Nationhood and Hindu–Muslim Unity

The Indian National Congress, from its very inception was committed to lay down a secular foundation for Indian nationhood. It tried to encompass and represent all communities in the country. In fact, no one raised any doubt against the secular credentials of the Moderates. Even Tilak, whose secular credentials were doubted primarily on account of his mass mobilisation techniques of Ganesh Puja, joined hands with Jinnah to sign the Lucknow Pact, which started a new era of Hindu–Muslim bonhomie.

Gandhiji took Hindu–Muslim unity to new heights. He had impeccable secular credentials since his South African days even though he always asserted that he was a Sanatani Hindu. In fact, his religious world-view was that if one is rooted in his own religion, it provides a good base for respecting others' religion. After coming to India he virtually made Hindu–Muslim unity as one of the basic principles of his belief system. Thus, in his *Ashram Bhajanawali* he picked up relevant passages from scriptures of different religions, which used to be recited during his prayer meetings. When the Indian Muslims initiated the Khilafat Movement, he extended whole-hearted support to their cause. Muslim leaders like Muhammad Ali and Shaukat Ali enthusiastically participated in the Non-Cooperation Movement launched by Gandhiji. For a while it seemed that a firm foundation for Hindu–Muslim unity had been laid down. But soon things took a new turn and communal riots started visiting the country during 1923–24. Gandhiji made Herculean efforts through the All Parties' Conference and the Nehru Report to find an amicable solution for the communal tangle. But ultimately nothing much came out of it. And Jinnah ended as a Muslim communal leader by presenting a 14-point package for the Muslim community. Gandhiji made another attempt at the Second Round Table Conference to thrash out a solution for the communal problem but he failed on account of the intransigence of the Muslim leadership. The poor performance of the Muslim League in 1937 and its failure to enter into a coalition government with the Congress, made Jinnah more intransigent, and in 1940 he ended by propounding the two-nation theory and demanding a separate homeland for the Muslims. Soon after his release from jail in May 1944, Gandhiji entered into a serious dialogue with Jinnah and even went to the extent of accepting the idea of Pakistan based on Rajagopalachari's (CR) formula. But this was not acceptable to Jinnah and hence the talks ended in a fiasco. The Cabinet Mission Plan tried to keep the country united but it ultimately collapsed on the issue of compulsory grouping of Provinces and the sovereignty of the Constituent Assembly. This plunged the country into the the biggest communal carnage. Gandhiji rushed from one place to another, viz., Calcutta, Noakhali, Bihar, and Delhi in a singular effort to extinguish the fire of communal carnage. That was the highest water-mark of his secular credentials. He was assassinated by a Hindu fanatic on the ground that he favoured Muslims. If secularism became one of the main pillars of the Indian constitution, Gandhiji's life and work was perhaps the greatest contributory factor to it. In brief, Mahatma Gandhi played a singular role in laying the secular foundation of our country. He lived and died for it.

The Congress in a New Avatar

Gandhiji was aware that a re-organised and re-vitalised Congress was a precondition for launching the Non-Cooperation Movement on the national scale. He knew that the Congress since its inception had been, what one of prominent leaders had called, a three-day *tamasha*. As such it had hardly any organisation at the grass roots level and hence its capacity to mobilise the people for any struggle was limited. Hence at the Nagpur Congress held in 1920, Gandhiji proposed a number of changes in the Congress both at its ideological and organisational levels. The new objective of the Congress was 'the attainment of Swaraj by peaceful and legitimate means'. Thus it underlined the inherent right of the people to agitate and even defy laws so long they could remain peaceful and would be willing to pay the price for defying the laws. But a much more important question was how to make the

Congress a fighting organisation in the absence of which no programme, however radical it might be, could be implemented. On the initiative of Gandhiji, the Nagpur Congress made major changes in the structure and the nature of the Congress organisation. Some of these changes were as follows:

(i) The provincial Congress committees were to be organised on a linguistic basis and not on the basis of British-made Provinces, which more often than not, were conglomeration of a number of linguistic groups.
(ii) The total strength of membership of the All India Congress Committee was increased but a ceiling of 350 memberships was also imposed.
(iii) For a better deliberation of the issues, it was decided to hold the Subject Committee meeting two or three days before the general session. That would contribute towards a better decision-making process in the general session.
(iv) A Working Committee comprising 15 members including the president, secretary and treasurer was to be constituted, which would carry on the day-to-day work of the Congress. Besides, it would also ensure continuity of work.
(v) The Congress was to be organised from the grass roots level to the national level with regular active membership. To enable even the poorest of the poor to apply for the membership of the Congress, only a nominal fee of four 'annas' (a quarter of a rupee) was introduced.

All this resulted in the complete overhauling of the Congress organisation making it a fit and fighting organisation. Besides, the Congress was made a fully democratic organisation in which everyone had a right to present and press for his particular viewpoint. Mahatma Gandhi maintained a peculiar relationship with the Congress. On many occasions, particularly during the national struggle, he would get authorisation from the Congress to take all major decisions on his own. Even after 1934, when he, on his own, ceased to be a Congressman, it was he who would decide about the timings as well as issues on which the national struggle would be fought. And for taking such decisions on his own, he primarily depended on his 'inner voice' rather than formal decisions of the organisation. But this was no authoritarianism as his 'inner voice' was not based on his whims and fancies but based on a well-thought out strategy and real will of the people. As he had the uncanny knack of feeling the pulse of the people as well as the Congressmen spread all over the country, his decisions were never off the mark. Whether it was the Civil Disobedience Movement or the Quit India Movement, millions responded to his call and participated in his movements risking all that they had. It was his unique leadership quality which always held him in good stead making people repose their faith in him. Even those who differed with him could never challenge his integrity and sincerity. Another issue he tackled was that of finding the wholetimers for the national work. The people who left schools, colleges, law courts and services became the mainstay of the national movement. Many of them did not care to earn their livelihood or raise a family. It is they who worked as the standing army of the national movement. In brief, we may say Mahatma Gandhi took the Congress to the grass roots level, revitalised it at every level, built up an army of whole-time workers and imbued them with a deep sense of purpose and commitment to the national cause. By any standard, this was an unparalleled performance in historical terms.

Constructive Work: A New Dimension of Revolution

One of the basic problems of the Marxian revolutionary movement is how to bring about social change till the state power is captured by the working class. The Marxists have solved this problem by asserting that all reformist programmes are reactionary, as they divert the attention of the working class from the main task of smashing the bourgeois state and, thereby, capturing the state power. The basic weakness of the Marxist thinking is that all attention is focused on the institution of the state which, ultimately, results in the emergence of the totalitarian state. What is more, in the process the sinews of civil society are weakened, virtually giving the wielders of the state power total freedom to act as they wish. Gandhiji was sceptical of the institution of the state. For him, the state as by its very nature smacks of authoritarian violence posing a serious threat to the liberty of individuals. In fact, he stood for a weak state and strong civil society. In keeping with his basic principled stand, he assigned a big revolutionary role to the constructive programmes both in the pre-revolutionary and post-revolutionary period. In the wake of the withdrawal of the Non-Cooperation Movement, he came out with a string of constructive programmes: Khadi work, development of village industries, national education, the removal of untouchability and Hindu–Muslim unity. Subsequently, he set up a single purpose organisations like All India Spinner Association, Adimjati Sevak Sangh and Harijan Sevak Sangh and a host of other organisations. He also encouraged and helped in setting up of thousands of Ashrams largely manned by constructive workers. Gandhian constructive programmes played a crucial role in the national movement in several ways. In the first place, the string of constructive programmes extended support and succour to the thousands of freedom fighters, particularly when the national struggle was at its low ebb. In fact, during the pause, they were resting, recuperating and gathering strengths as well as establishing live contacts with the people through various programmes. Thus, constructive programmes were of great help in consolidating as well as expanding the national movement. Second, they provided hardcore cadres at the time of the national struggle. In any mass movement, the common masses come and fight for a while and then go back to look after their hearths and homes. Thus, the real strength of any mass movement is sustained by whole-time workers. But that raises the question of their maintenance and new opportunities for continuous work. Mahatma Gandhi, through his constructive work-related institutions and Ashrams, not only succeeded in raising a big army of workers but also trained them and made them real vanguards of the movement. Third, constructive programmes significantly contributed to uplift of the weaker sections of the society. In the process they strengthened the social fabric of civil society, while making solid contributions to social revolution.

Work Through Legislatures and Local Self-Government Bodies

Mahatma Gandhi himself was no great admirer of legislative work. Hence, even after the withdrawal of the Non-Cooperation Movement, he insisted on the continued boycott of the legislative bodies. But soon after 1924-25 he accepted the initiative taken by C R Das and Motilal Nehru, who had earlier set up the Swaraj Party. The Swaraj Party was permitted by the Congress to pursue their work in legislatures which, in turn, performed an outstanding work by making the dyarchy almost dysfunctional for a while. In fact, there was an inherent contradiction in the basic policy of the Swaraj Party. In their struggle with the 'no-changers' who favoured the continued boycott of the legislature, the Swarajists did argue that their primary motivation for the Council's entry was to take the battle of Swaraj to the enemy's camp with the ultimate objective of wrecking the system from within. However, the lure of the office, ultimately, led to its split and decline. But, the credit goes to the leadership of Motilal Nehru that the Swarajists were back to openly join, the battle of Swaraj under Gandhiji's leadership. Subsequently, the Congress itself, with the blessings of the Mahatma, participated in the 1937 elections and even formed governments in a number of Provinces. But Congressmen refused to be co-opted by the Establishment and, in fact, they used their power position either to expose the iniquities and injustices inherent in the system or to extend help or relief to the people. But when the time for struggle came, those engaged in legislative work, without any hesitation, plunged into the movement putting their heart and soul in it, even by sacrificing their ministerial positions. In fact, through their enhanced stature, acquired through their legislative work, they not only drew more people to the movement but also forced the British to deal with them with greater respect, partly out of fear and partly out of genuine respect.

A Dream for a New India

In the pre-Gandhian era, there was not much clarity about the kind of India our people would like to build up in the post-independence era. One of the major contributions of Mahatma Gandhi was that he had a vision and dream for a 'new' India. For him a radical social transformation leading to a revolutionary change in the status and living conditions of the *Daridranarayan* was to be a real touchstone for the India of his dream. He was firmly of the opinion that in such an India there would be no distinction of the rich and the poor, and the high and the low. Besides, there would be no discrimination on the basis of caste, creed, religion, region and sex. It would be a society totally free from exploitation of man by man. He was so much committed to the principle of equality among men that he was totally opposed to any distinction between mental and physical work. In fact, he propounded his theory of bread labour which, in plain language meant that everybody, whatever may be his educational and professional qualifications, would have to put in some amount of physical labour to earn his bread. He stood for a self-sufficient village republic, looking after its needs to the maximum extent. Being a philosophical anarchist, he favoured the concept of minimal state so that it did not infringe upon the liberty of the individual. He did not favour total abolition of the institution of private property, and, in fact, favoured a system of trusteeship in which the rich would retain their property but would look upon themselves as the trustees rather than the owners of these properties. He did not favour big machines, though he was not opposed to machines per se. In a word, India of Gandhiji's dream would be what he called Ram Rajya. As such, he stood for a millennial change. It is a different matter that independent India took a different road to development. But now sensitive people all over the world are rediscovering him and finding some of his ideas rather more relevant for the twenty-first century.

A Dream of a New Civilisation

In his *Hind Swaraj* and even in his subsequent writings Gandhiji was critical of the Western civilisation which he called 'Satanic'. For him vices like violence, exploitation, materialism, capitalism, inequality, ecological imbalances, racialism, consumerism and imperialism were inherent in the very nature of the Western civilisation.

After rejecting the modern civilisation he attempted to present an outline of a counter-culture, which he called Ram Rajya. Ram Rajya is self-rule of an individual. For that, man has to reduce his needs to the bare minimum. Many people have not fully grasped the deeper meaning of Ram Rajya as conceived and conceptualised by Gandhiji. For him, Ram Rajya was not the rule of any king. In fact, it has nothing to do with the state. For Gandhiji, Ram Rajya meant rule of Dharma, rule of justice. And above all it meant self-rule by an individual upon himself. For that man has to reduce his needs to the bare minimum. In fact, he never talked of Ram as an individual; for him Ram is a metaphor and an abstract concept, which stood for justice, equity, self-sacrifice, concern for others, etc. He always maintained that in every human heart both Ram and Ravana live. Ravana stands for selfishness, subjugation of others, naked show of strength, grabbing worldly things to the maximum extent. On the other hand, Ram stands for selflessness, sacrifice, self-denial, self-rule and a deep sense of justice.

In spite of the clear enunciation of the secular nature of the concept of Ram Rajya by Gandhiji, it always remained an anathema, nay even a red-rag, to the Muslim communalists. They deliberately gave it a Hindu connotation to beat Gandhiji with a communal stick. Even the fact of immense popularity of the Ramayana story among the Muslim masses of Indonesia did not deter them from imputing to it a communal tinge. For Gandhiji it was nothing but a mythical symbol of good, just, and equitable rule. In other words, it was a real people's rule with the promise of justice for every body.

As we have seen in the preceding pages, Mahatma Gandhi made a number of contributions to the Indian struggle for independence. But there was no dearth of his critics even during the days of the freedom struggle. Though Hindu–Muslim unity ever remained as a basic article of his faith, yet he had his critics from both the sides of the line. According to Jinnah and the Muslim League he was an ardent Hindu and a thorough Congressman who wanted to dominate and subjugate the Indian Muslims. On the one hand, Jinnah totally rejected Gandhiji's secular credentials; on the other, Hindu fanatics attacked him for being pro-Muslim and primarily responsible for promoting Muslim communalism in India. They even held him responsible for the partition of the country. In fact, one of the Hindu fanatics, Nathu Ram Godse, assassinated him on this very count. In our view, these biased attacks from both sides of the line, only prove his secular credentials. Jinnah divided the country because Gandhiji was nothing but a Hindu and Godse killed him because he favoured the Muslims. His impeccable secular record during 1946-47, his death-defying courage to stand in the midst of the communal carnage without making any discrimination between Hindu and Muslim crowds is a living witness to the courage of his convictions nay, his undying faith. He lived and died for communal amity.

A second line of attack comes from the Marxists. The nitty-gritty of their criticism has been that Gandhiji had a class-bias in favour of the rich and propertied classes. They further argued that his theory of trusteeship is nothing but a clever ploy to help the propertied classes. They also accuse him of being soft on British imperialism, always ready to compromise, including the last one for the independence of the country. They also attack some of his basic ideas like self-sufficient-village, minimal state, theory of trusteeship, his concept of bread labour, etc., either as too idealistic or too backward-looking. The Marxists including the Communist Party of Soviet Union and the Comintern revised their own assessments of Gandhiji several times. Not only that, the Communist Party of India at times came to the fold of the national movement and at other times it drifted away from it. At times, they even openly opposed it, as in the case of the Quit India Movement. These inconsistent stands and their changing assessments of the Gandhiji–led national movement took away much of the sting from their criticisms. Some of the problems which Gandhiji identified in the Marxist line of thought like the totalitarian nature of the state and total suppression of individual liberty, have been proved to the hilt by subsequent developments of the communist societies. Gandhiji's view that mere abolition of private property would not necessarily result in an exploitation-free social order, has also been proved by historical developments.

The fact of the matter was that Gandhiji was leading a mass movement in which every section made its own contribution. As we have seen that Gandhiji wanted a millennial change – a society free from vestiges of all forms of exploitation. And hence the Marxist attack on his class-bias is off the mark. In his personality as well as in his ideas he had transcended all these limiting categories, of class, caste, region and religion. With the passage of time some of his ideas are appearing to be more and more relevant. To sum up, Gandhiji made seminal contributions not only to our freedom struggle but also to a new world civilisation. Perhaps, a poet was thinking about the life and work of a great man like Gandhiji when he wrote:

There is no failure for the good and wise
What though their seed should fall by the way side,
And bird snatch it – yet the birds are fed,
Or they shall bear it far across the tide
To give rich harvest, after thou are dead.

AN UNKNOWN POET

A Russian poet Boris Pasternak expressed the same view in more memorable words:

It is not revolutions and upheavals
That clear the road to a new and better days.
But revelations, lavishness and torments
Of someone's soul, inspired and ablaze.

BORIS PASTERNAK

PART III

The Minor Streams of the Indian National Movement

The Untouchables need a movement if they are to remain conscious of their wrongs and if the spirit of revolt is to be kept alive amongst them. They need a movement because the Caste Hindus have to be told that what is the tragedy of the Untouchables is their crime.

DR B R AMBEDKAR

I, who have rocked the cradle, I who have sung soft lullabies – the emblem of Mother India – am now to kindle the flame of liberty. . . .

SAROJINI NAIDU

The dominant leadership of the Congress associated with Gandhiji called off the movement (non-cooperation) because they were afraid of the awakening mass activity; and they were afraid of the mass activity because it was beginning to threaten those propertied class interests with which they themselves were still, in fact, closely linked.

R P DUTT

24 Role of the Communist Party of India in the Indian Freedom Struggle

Life is like a tattered coat of a beggar.
To which, everyday a new rag of pain is added.
But the epoch of cruelty is coming to an end
Be patient a little longer, our salvation is at hand

FAIZ AHMED FAIZ

That the Indian Left had its own distinctive contributions to India's struggle for independence could hardly be overemphasised. While maintaining their separate identity and at times even respectable distance from the mainstream of the national movement led by the Congress, the Left, nonetheless had a role in affecting the latter's ideological colour, contours, and character. It is true that the Left was hardly any match for Gandhiji in terms of mass mobilisation, but through their sectional mobilisation, they also brought the masses to the national movement in their own way. Moreover, in the crucial moments of the national movement, these Left parties contributed greatly in sharpening the striking power of the national movement. In this section we will primarily concentrate on the study of the Communist Party of India and the Congress Socialist Party, leaving out their splinter groups.

The Communist Party of India

The formation of the Communist Party of India (CPI) during 1924-25 was preceded by a number of historic events which greatly contributed to its emergence. In this connection, two major events deserve special mention. The first was the Russian Revolution of 1917, which had put state power in the hands of the working class for the first time in human history. The second event, which also had a role in the process of the emergence of the Communist Party, was the disillusionment caused by the withdrawal of the Non-Cooperation Movement in the wake of the Chauri-Chaura incident. It was the hype created by Gandhiji's promise of Swaraj within a year at the time of the launching of the movement, that led to a high level of disappointment, particularly among the youth. Perhaps some other contributory factors were: the deteriorating economic condition of the people of India and the formation of the All India Trade Union Congress in 1920 – the first major all India working class organisation. The working class militancy was on increase as they were faced with the problems of wage cut as well as unemployment, forcing them to launch strikes in various parts of the country. This was the socio-economic context in which the Communist Party of India was subsequently founded.

In the beginning, a number of people were making individual efforts in the formation of communist groups at different places. In this respect, Naren Battacharya, who later on became famous by the name of M N Roy, deserves special mention. His baptism in Marxist ideas started with his role in the formation of the Mexican Communist Party in 1919, in collaboration with M Borodin. Subsequently, he crossed swords with Lenin when he challenged the latter's thesis on the Marxist support to the national liberation movement led by the bourgeois leadership. He propounded his own counter-thesis and pleaded for Marxist dissociation from the bourgeois-led movement and taking to an independent path. In October 1920, M N Roy succeeded in setting up an Indian Marxist group in Tashkent with the help of a number of Indian émigrés. During the same period, some other Marxists were also trying their hands on it in various parts of India. S A Dange in Bombay, S Chettiar in Madras and Muzzaffar Ahmad in Calcutta were the prominent individuals, who were trying to create their groups in the area of their operations. All of them were critical of the Indian National Congress, though some of them had participated in the Non-Cooperation Movement. In fact, it was in April 1921 that S A Dange wrote a pamphlet called 'Lenin vs Gandhi' in which he sought to establish the superiority of Lenin over Gandhiji. Undoubtedly, M N Roy continued to be the main source of ideological inspiration for all these groups.

The British Government was already keeping a watch over the activities of these groups. In 1924, some of them, namely, S A Dange, Shawkat Usmani, Nolini Kanta Gupta and others were hauled up and charge-sheeted in what came to be known as the Kanpur Conspiracy Case. But it failed to dampen the spirit of the Communist workers. Subsequently, the Communist Party of India was formally founded in December 1925. Some of the prominent founding fathers of the CPI were S V Ghate, S A Dange, Muzzaffar Ahmad and others.

The main political objective of the Party was complete independence from British rule and the establishment of a political system based on the lines of the USSR. Initially, the primary tactical line of the CPI was to work closely with the Indian National Congress, with a view to transform it into a mass-based militant organisation. Hence, they did not have much hesitation in working in the Congress organisation. But simultaneously they were also trying to organise the peasants and the working classes by setting up a number of organisations. Muzzaffar Ahmad, in collaboration with Kazi Nazrul Islam set up the Labour Swaraj Party in Bengal, in November 1925. Thus, within a few years of the formation of the CPI, there was a mushroom growth of Marxist-led political front organisations in different parts of the country. The Congress Labour Party in Bombay, Kirti Kisan Party in Punjab and Labour Kisan Party of Hindustan in Madras, belonged to the same group. Besides, communist workers were active among the textile workers of Bombay and railway workers of Kharagpur. All these local initiatives ultimately led to the formation of the Workers and Peasant Party (WPP) in 1928. The WPP primarily sought to radicalise the Congress, while it went on organising peasant and working classes. Its primary objective was to achieve independence as well as socialism.

The colonial administration was fully alive to these communist-led initiatives. Consequently, it launched yet another conspiracy case, known as the Meerut Conspiracy Case, in March 1929, in which 32 prominent communist and trade union leaders, including three members of the Communist Party of Great Britain were involved. The Meerut Conspiracy Case did give some setback to the Marxists but also led to the popularisation of Marxian ideas in the country.

Perhaps, a more momentous development, which greatly affected the policy and programmes of the Indian Communists, was the decision of the Comintern in 1929 to dub all bourgeois-led national movements as agents of imperialism. Hence, the communists all over the world were called upon not only to dissociate themselves from such movements but also to oppose them actively. In the light of the Comintern policy guidance, the Communist Party of India, in 1929, adopted a new policy denouncing the Congress as the party of the bourgeoise and as such the Indian communists would have nothing to do with it. It is quite interesting to note that when the Congress was taking a leftist position under pressure from Jawaharlal Nehru and Subhas Chandra Bose and getting committed to Purna Swaraj (Lahore Congress 1929) and some kind of socialism (Karachi Congress 1931), the Indian Communists were condemning it as a bourgeoise-led party, though they had previously worked under its banner. But then they had hardly a choice for independent thoughts: they had to toe the political line drawn by the Comintern. As a result, the Communist Party completely dissociated itself from the Civil Disobedience Movement – which was in itself, a major mass movement. But the CPI, with its new policy orientation had rejected non-violent forms of political struggle and committed itself to the policy of armed struggle against British imperialism. The new policy made it clear that the organisational structure of the party would be centralised, independent and illegal. It also committed itself to follow the policy guidelines laid down by the international communist movement. The Communist Party put forward a number of demands including abolition of zamindari, nationalisation of banks, tea gardens and shipping industries and a host of other radical programmes. In keeping with the new policy line, it not only dissociated itself from the Civil Disobedience Movement but also denounced the Gandhi–Irwin Pact as an act of the betrayal of the Indian people.

It is true that the petering out of the Civil Disobedience Movement by 1934, once again created a new wave of disillusionment with Gandhiji's leadership, particularly among the youth. Some of these young people, namely Jayaprakash Narayan, Acharya Narendra Dev, Rammanohar Lohia, Minoo Masani and others joined hands and founded the Congress Socialist Party – a party committed to both independence and socialism. This was the time when there was another policy change on the part of the international communist movement: once again it reversed its policy and asked the Indian communists to extend support to the bourgeois-led national movement under its new policy of the united front. Earlier in 1934, the Communist Party had been banned by the colonial administration. With the new policy of the united front, the communists came back to the national movement. They started working closely with the Congress. They also came back to the All India Trade Union Congress. Most of them started working through the Congress Socialist Party and some of them also became its members. Working through the united front policy, the Indian communists still sought to transform the Congress as a thoroughly anti-imperialist organisation, though they accepted its predominant position in the struggle against imperialism. The policy of the united front and its working in close collaboration with the Congress and particularly with the CSP soon started paying them rich political dividends. Communist workers got protection while working through these organisations as there was a ban on the CPI. Besides, it also provided them with an opportunity to influence the contours and character of the national movement. It also helped them in getting a pre-dominant position in the All India Trade Union Congress and All India Kisan Sabha and in influencing the cadres of these organisations with their ideological moorings. But above all, it was through the policy of the united front that it could establish a strong foothold in the organisational structure of the Congress Socialist Party. At some stage, they even planned to takeover the entire organisation of the CSP – lock, stock and barrel. Ultimately, when their plan came to the notice of some of the CSP leaders, the communists were expelled and the policy of united front came to an end. But it had served their major purpose: in Kerala and Bengal it walked away with a number of CSP cadres, including some of the leaders like E M S Namboodiripad. In Bengal and Kerala they could establish a strong base as a result of their united front policy.

With the declaration of the Second World War in September 1939, India was unilaterally made a party to the War by the Viceroy without consulting the Indian leadership. This presented a challenge before the Indian leadership. But it also created a rupture in the national movement. Any unconditional support to the British would have meant strengthening the tentacles of British imperialism, but the total opposition to it might have strengthened the hands of the Axis powers, whose ideology was not acceptable to the Indian people. Thus, the Indian leadership found itself caught in the dilemma: to support or to oppose the British – both the lines of action creating its own problems. Ultimately, the Congress offered to support the British war effort provided the latter set a definite roadmap for Indian independence. Like Subhas Chandra Bose, the Communist Party of India was also for a policy of total opposition and confrontation with the British. This brought about major policy differences within the national leadership and even created a crisis in the united front policy of the Indian communists, which they had pursued since 1935. It may be of interest to recall that this was a honeymoon period between Hitler and Stalin, who had signed a Pact of mutual interest, in August 1939. Thus, in keeping with the new Pact, the Indian communists declared the War as 'an imperialist war' and hence the need of total opposition to the British war efforts. The CPI formulated a new policy statement known as 'Proletariat Path' through which it committed itself to open rebellion against the British rule in India by organising a 'general strike' in the major industries along with 'a no rent, no tax campaign'. Not only that, it also wanted to make an open attack on all symbols of the British authority including police and army structure. In pursuance of this new policy, they organised a major strike in the textile mills of Bombay in March 1941.

But when in June 1941, Hitler invaded Russia, the Communists changed their earlier characterisation of the Second World War as the 'imperialist war' to the 'people's war'. Now, the Communist Party of India wanted the Indian people to play a 'people's role' in this people's war! As such, the Indian communists decided to extend all support to the British war efforts. So much so that subsequently they not only opposed the Quit India Movement but also openly worked against the nationalist leaders by cooperating and collaborating with the British colonial administration.

In retrospect, it seems that in the initial stages of the War, when the CPI sought to offer total opposition to the British war measures, this was more out of their support to the Hitler-Stalin Pact rather than on account of their anti-imperialist commitment. This turncoat role of the CPI also brought about a change in the British policy towards CPI. In July 1942 they lifted the ban imposed on it, in as early as in 1934. It started functioning openly as a preferred ally of the colonial administration in India, making a total reversal of its role from being anti-imperialist to becoming a 'pro-imperialist'. During the Quit India Movement, the Communist Party in its new 'avatar' worked as an imperialist's agent and even collaborated with the British police, including its CID branch. On the industrial front, they used their dominant position in the AITUC for the creation of an environment of industrial peace so that no obstacles were put in the path of the British war effort. Not only that, in keeping with Stalin's views on the 'nationality question' it soon adopted Adhikari's thesis' – 'Pakistan and National unity'. It not only supported the idea of Pakistan but also tried to cover many other such nationalities. This was nothing but a call to balkanisation of India. This collaborative role with the British brought about rich political dividends for CPI: it got a fillip both in terms of swelling membership and regional expansion, including trade union movement. It also tried to reach out to the *bhadralok* through the Indian People's Theatre Association (IPTA), which was successful in roping in such cultural figures as Balraj Sahni, Khwaja Ahmad Abbas, Kaifi Azmi, Salil Chaudhary and others. They further strengthened their stranglehold over AITUC and All India Kisan Sabha. Working through Kisan Sabha, the Communist Party got a good foothold in the countryside, particularly in the areas where the Quit India Movement was not that strong. Consequently, Kisan Sabha made significant gains in Punjab, Kerala, coastal areas of Andhra, Telangana and North Bengal.

Once the war ended, there was another shift to the policy of the Communist Party of India. Along with the Congress and other parties they openly joined the nationwide agitation against the trial of the INA men – whom they had opposed tooth and nail, even calling their leader Subhas Chandra Bose a traitor and an agent of the Axis powers.

During the 1946 election the Communist Party tried to raise the issue of the new composition of a Constituent Assembly based on universal adult franchise and even pleaded for a Congress–League–Communist's United Front and for a last battle against the British rule. But all this did not help them in making any spectacular gains during the 1946 elections except in Andhra and Tamil Nadu. The Indian communists also started opposing the process of negotiations among the League, the Congress and the British in the wake of the Cabinet Mission Plan. Taking advantage of their strong presence in North Bengal and Telangana, they launched major peasant movements in both the regions. In North Bengal, they organised the share-croppers and launched what came to be known, as the 'Tebhaga Movement'. The main demand of the movement was that the share-croppers would give only one-third of their produce to the landlords and not one-half, as was the practice till then. This movement ultimately fizzled out in the absence of cross-sectional support. Similarly in the Travancore state, the CPI had a strong support base among coir factory workers, fishermen, toddy-tappers and landless labour. In January 1946, the Dewan C P Ramaswami tried to impose an American model of the government in which the assembly was to be elected by the people based on universal franchise. However, the executive headed by the Dewan was to be appointed by the Maharaja. The Communists were in the forefront of the agitation against the proposal, which ultimately forced him to give up his plan and also finally contributed to the integration of Travancore state in the Indian Union. In the Telangana area of Andhra, during the war period, the communists had built up a strong social base in the villages. During 1946–47, it led to an armed uprising which continued even after independence. The Indian communists were opposed to the idea of any compromise with the British during 1946–47. And when independence came in August 1947, they even went to the extent of describing it as 'sham'.

After making a brief survey of the activities of the Communist Party of India during the freedom struggle, one is called upon to make a critical evaluation of its contributions. In retrospect, it appears that since its inception during 1924–25, the communist movement of India suffered from a number of infirmities and limitations, including ideological confusion. In the first place, it failed to carve out an independent and indigenous ideological framework, based on a realistic assessment of the Indian situation. It tried to live on borrowed ideas and ideals without understanding whether or not they were in consonance with the historical experiences of the Indian people. For example, it tried to posit the weapon of armed struggle against the non-violent struggle led by Gandhiji. This attempt was based on the experiences of the Russian and Chinese revolutions whose cultural milieu were entirely different from those of Indian people. The net result of such theoretical and borrowed policy was that it failed to strike a sympathetic chord in the hearts and minds of the Indian people. Hence, it always remained on the periphery of the Indian National Movement. Second, the Communist Party of India was so deeply attached to the apron-strings of the Communist Party of Soviet Union (CPSU) that it could never dream and dare to act independently. As we have seen earlier, it continued to change its policy in accordance with the needs and dictates of the Comintern, which was basically a handiwork of the CPSU. The overnight policy change in characterising the Second World War from 'imperialist war' to a 'people's war' was a case in point. This was nothing less than the command performance at the behest of CPSU. Third, the Indian communists could never make a correct and realistic assessment about the Indian National Movement and its leader Mahatma Gandhi. They even failed to realise that Mahatma Gandhi was the biggest mass leader that India ever produced and he alone had the capacity and competence to mobilise millions. Consequently, more often than not, they found themselves on the wrong side of the national movement which prevented them from emerging as a mass party. Fourth, Indian communists could not work jointly and honestly with other Indian left-groups. They never went the whole hog with Nehru – a prominent left wing leader of the Congress.

Their relationship with Subhas Chandra Bose, another left winger, soured so much during the Second World War that they even raised a question mark about his patriotism. In fact, they did not hesitate to even call him a traitor and an agent of the Axis power. Even when they joined hands with CSP, it was more out of their tactical line rather than a desire for honest partnership. Thus, they could not earn the goodwill of any left group of India and ever remained at the periphery of the national movement.

But it would be unfair not to acknowledge their contributions in the cause of our people. They made several contributions which have to be acknowledged. In the first place, through their work among the peasantry, working class, youth, student community and the under-privileged sections of the Indian society, they impacted the Indian national movement and, to some extent, were responsible for giving it a leftist slant and direction. Undoubtedly, they did contribute to the radicalisation of the Indian National Congress, making it take a left slant. Second, they succeeded in raising people's organisations, representing the interests of the different sections of Indian society, viz., All India Trade Union Congress, All India Kisan Sabha, Indian People's Theatre Association, All India Students Federation, Progressive Writers Association and All India State People's Conference. All these organisations had their own contributions in raising political consciousness among the people as well as in espousing the people's causes.

In brief, with all its limitations, the Communist Party of India did make its own contribution to the cause of the national movement.

> *The Third International nowadays formulates policies which seem simply an extension of domestic policy of Russia.*
>
> ACHARYA NARENDRA DEV

25 The Congress Socialist Party and the Indian Freedom Struggle

Socialism wants to free the world and remove all social obstacles to the development of individuality. Socialism aims at fostering real liberty, equality and fraternity through the creation of an exploitation-free society, and by removing the present state of slavery, inequality and intolerance.

ACHARYA NARENDRA DEV

The Congress Socialist Party (CSP) played the role of a catalyst in the last phase of our national struggle. In fact, it is the socialist leaders who became prime-movers and real people's heroes of the Quit India Movement. Once the top-echelon of the Congress leadership was arrested in the initial stages of the Quit India Movement, they took over its leadership and kept the fire of the movement burning, even when it had reached its lowest ebb.

But before we discuss its policy, programme and working, it would be relevant to discuss the circumstances and political situations which led to its formation. The Civil Disobedience Movement (1930–34) had attracted a large number of youthful leaders who had risked all that they had and participated in the movement with a lot of enthusiasm and fervour. They had pinned their faith in the leadership of Gandhiji and hoped that through this movement, they would be able to give a mortal blow to British imperialism. Their high hopes were dashed to the ground when the Civil Disobedience Movement, despite massive people's response, came to a naught. What gave them a further shock was the attempt to revive the Swaraj Party in a bid to revive the parliamentary politics. All these political developments came as a rude shock to a number of left-wing leaders like Jayaprakash Narayan,

Rammanohar Lohia, Acharya Narendra Dev, Achyut Patwardhan, N G Goray, Minoo Masani, Yusuf Meherally and a host of others. But they were not the kind of people who would throw up their hands and be caught in the slough of despond. In fact, they thought of setting up of a new organisation of their own to carry forward the task of national struggle against British imperialism while simultaneously

14th June, 1934.

My dear Masani,

I have read the questions you left with me as also the Congress Socialist Party's programme.

I welcome the rise of the Socialist Party in the Congress. But I can't say that I like the programme as it appears in the printed pamphlet. It seems to me to ignore Indian conditions and I do not like the assumption underlying many of its propositions which go to show that there is necessarily antagonism between the classes and the masses or between the labourers and the capitalists, such that they can never work for mutual good. My own experience covering a fairly long period is to the contrary. What is necessary is that labourers or workers should know their rights and should also know how to assert them. And since there never has been any right without a corresponding duty, in my opinion, a manifesto is incomplete without emphasising the necessity of performance of duty and showing what that duty is.

You would not want me at this stage to examine your programme clause by clause, but if you so desire and if you do not mind consulting my convenience, I would appoint for you a time when I could discuss with you, and those whom you may wish, the whole of your programme in detail.

Yours sincerely,

M K Gandhi

fighting on the home front against capitalists and vested interests on behalf of the downtrodden people. The idea of such a new organisation cropped up during their discussion in Nasik jail where some of them were lodged as the participants of the Civil Disobedience Movement. Some of these leaders involved in the Nasik dialogue were Asoka Mehta, Achyut Patwardhan, Jayaprakash Narayan, N G Goray, Minoo Masani and Yusuf Meherally. Some drafts were prepared, discussed and circulated. When these leaders were released in 1934, they pursued the idea of a new organisation with greater vigour. In May 1934 in Patna, the foundation of the Congress Socialist Party was laid down, though it was formally launched in Bombay during 21–22 October 1934. Between Patna and Bombay conferences, a number of regional conferences were held in different parts of the country to mobilise and unite all socialist–nationalist minded people and knit them under the banner of a single organisation. It would be of interest to recall that the formation of a Bihar socialist group had preceded the Patna conference by a few years, in which people like Ganga Saran Singh, Jayaprakash Narayan, Rambriksha Benipuri and a number of other people were involved.

The leaders of the Congress Socialist Party had a well-thought-out strategy behind the idea of organising a left-oriented separate party and yet keeping it inside the fold of the Congress. While the separate existence of the party enabled them to have greater ideological manoeuvrability, the association with the Congress enabled them to derive strength from the latter and particularly from Gandhiji's mass appeal. If pursued with tact and perseverance, they could have a rare opportunity of having the cake and eating it too. Theoretically, what they tried to achieve was to transform the Congress into a radical organisation and ultimately persuade it to accept a socialist programme and even a socialist leadership. They were convinced that such a strategy would succeed if they were able to mobilise the masses, particularly the peasants and the working classes, and bring them under their organisational and ideological fold. Hence, their immediate emphasis was on organising the peasants and workers by raising their demands in a big way. They even dreamt of bringing the Congress under the socialist leadership. The Meerut thesis of the party clearly mentioned that the primary objective of the party was to replace the present leadership of the Congress by a socialist leadership. But soon they had a better grasp of the ground realities and started thinking in terms of a composite leadership to broaden the mass base of the national movement as well as to retain its cross-sectional support. Inside the Congress they looked up to both Subhas Chandra Bose and Jawaharlal Nehru as the source of inspiration for their socialist ideology. It may be of interest to recall that in the wake of the withdrawal of the Civil Disobedience Movement in 1933-34, Nehru was not only critical but also had openly expressed his socialist leanings. And, when Nehru was elected the Congress President in 1936, he included three socialist stalwarts in his working committee, namely, Jayaprakash Narayan, Acharya Narendra Dev and Achyut Patwardhan. Not only that, Subhas Chandra Bose was also elected as the president, both at the Haripura and Tripuri Congress, drawing support from the Indian socialists. But at the time of voting on Pant's resolution, which sought to reiterate the supremacy and centrality of Gandhiji's leadership, the Indian socialists by abstaining themselves made it possible for the resolution to be passed so easily.

That brings us to their relationship with Gandhiji. The Mahatma reacted adversely when the Congress Socialist Party was founded in 1934. In fact, he cited this as one of his reasons for resigning from the Congress in September 1934. The socialists, in their turn, were critical of Gandhiji's leadership and his style of working. But both had high respect for each other's sincerity and patriotism. Besides, soon, the socialists became convinced that no major movement could be launched in India without Gandhiji's support. As the war clouds started gathering in Europe, they moved closer to Gandhiji and even tried to impress upon him the need for a decisive battle against the British. Perhaps, that was the reason why they, ultimately, refused to go the whole hog with Subhas Chandra Bose at Tripuri and moved closer to Gandhiji. Thus, their initial dream of capturing the leadership of the Congress was replaced by their decision to work as a left-oriented pressure group inside the Congress. But they were aware that all would depend upon their own strength. Hence, they went on building-up mass organisations of peasants and workers.

In keeping with their broad policy of fighting both on the anti-imperialist front as well as on the front of socialism, they concretised the fourfold basic objectives of their party: (i) total independence from the British rule; (ii) the right of the Indian people to frame their own constitution; (iii) the foundation of a socialist society in the post-independence era; and (iv) abolition of the institution of private property leading to a society free from the exploitation of man by man. In brief, nationalism and socialism were two basic and driving principles of their political philosophy. In keeping with this basic philosophy, the Indian socialists insisted on the need for bringing the peasants, workers and other deprived sections of Indian society into the mainstream of the national movement. Simultaneously, they also tried to impress upon the downtrodden masses of India that their participation in the national movement would, ultimately, serve their interests as it would lead to the establishment of a socialist society.

Soon they formulated a 15-point programme in furtherance of their basic political philosophy. The points of the programme were as follows:

1. Transfer of all powers to the producing class.
2. The state to play a decisive role in the planned development of the country.
3. Nationalisation of all prominent national industries.
4. State monopolistic hold on foreign trade.
5. Role of co-operatives in production, distribution and public credit system.
6. Abolition of zamindari, and Princely system without any compensation.
7. Re-distribution of land among the peasants.
8. State support for cooperative farming.
9. End of people's indebtedness.
10. Right to work for the people.
11. Need-based distribution of goods.
12. Introduction of universal adult franchise.
13. Establishment of a secular society.
14. Equal rights for women.
15. Abolition of so-called public debt.

An analysis of the above programme reveals that they produced an exceptionally radical programme to cater to the needs of the downtrodden sections of society. Besides, in keeping with the spirit of their time they also envisaged a very big role for the institution of the state. This was in keeping with their Marxist moorings. They also tried to create an organisational structure of the party in the light of their basic objectives. It was supposed to be a cadre-based party and its membership was also restricted. Only those who were the members of the Congress Party and who would pin their faith in the socialist ideology as enunciated by the CSP could be given its membership. The day-to-day activities of the party were to be carried by an executive committee elected during the annual conference of the party. However, the ultimate power of policy formulation was vested in the annual conference which would have participation from the provincial units.

Soon after the party was launched in 1934, its cadre and leaders got engaged in the task of expanding its base among peasants, workers and other deprived sections of the Indian society. They struck strong roots among the peasantry in Bihar and Andhra where Swami Sahajanand Saraswati and N G Ranga had already laid sound foundations. It also developed some roots in the UP Congress where a large number of leaders came to its fold also on account of factional fights in the Congress. In UP, the Indian socialists raised some of the issues such as regulation of land tax, abolition of illegal levies on tenants, cancellation of debts of the tenants, etc.

The Congress Socialists were totally dissatisfied with the provisions of the Act of 1935. As such, they sought to wreck the Act of 1935 and make it totally inoperative. They thought of a strategy to capture the legislatures by participating in their elections and then to create a total political deadlock by refusing tó form the governments. They firmly believed that such a strategy would force the government to suspend the Act of 1935. They submitted a memorandum signed by prominent UP. Socialist leaders like Sampurnanand, Narendra Dev, Rafi Ahmed Kidwai, C B Gupta and others, to the Congress high command to propagate their viewpoints. They even moved a resolution to that effect in the Lucknow Congress (1936) which, however, was not accepted. Consequently, they participated in the elections but campaigned against the move towards office acceptance. Ultimately, however, the Congress accepted office after assurance of non-interference, by the Governor, in the day-to-day working of the government. Subsequently, some of socialist leaders like Sampurnanand, Rafi Ahmed Kidwai and Vijayalaxmi Pandit joined the government, which caused a great deal of resentment and embarrassment among the socialist leaders. The next issue the Indian socialists took up in a big way was the release of political prisoners. They organised meetings, agitations on the streets and even moved resolutions in the Congress forums to secure the release of the political prisoners. The CSP also observed All Indian Andaman Day on 14 August 1937, demanding not only the release of prisoners but also the closure of the Andaman jail. Ultimately, most of the political prisoners were released in the subsequent year, for which CSP could rightly take much of the credit, along with Gandhiji. Similarly, the Indian socialists were very active in the agitation against the Princely States through All India States People's Conference.

Another highlight of the political strategy of the Indian socialists was their attempt to forge a united front with the Indian Communists. Initially the CSP and the Communist Party of India were not on very good terms with each other. During the Civil Disobedience Movement, the CSP leaders were for a militant action and took part in the movement wholeheartedly, whereas the Communist Party kept itself aloof from it. Besides, though the CSP was set up essentially on Marxist principles, it had differences with the Communist Party on several counts. In the first place, it was totally opposed to the CPI policy of being attached to the apron-strings of the CPSU and virtually doing a command performance at the behest of the Comintern. This was totally against the CSP attempt to strike roots, both ideologically as well as organisationally, in the indigenous soil. Second, though both these parties were dissatisfied with the dominant section of the Congress leadership, yet there was a difference of opinion between the two parties on this point as well. The CPI always failed to make independent assessment of the Indian national movement and its leader Gandhiji. At times, the CPI denounced both in totality and at other times it embraced them as a part of its tactical line. On the other hand, the CSP, despite being critical of the Congress including Gandhiji, was convinced that they alone enjoyed widespread popular support. As such, no meaningful anti-imperialist struggle could be launched without them.

However, in 1935, the CPI extended its hands of friendship to the CSP (CPI had been banned in July 1934) and the latter grasped it with warmth and enthusiasm. Consequently, a large number of the CPI cadre and leaders joined the CSP and started working together in organisations like All India Kisan Sabha and All India Trade Union Congress. The CPI not only returned to the AITUC but started dominating it. Soon, the All India Kisan Sabha was also launched in 1936 under the leadership of Swami Sahajanand. With Jawaharlal Nehru as the Congress president, the left was in the ascendant. Under the garb of the united front policy the CPI surreptitiously strengthened its stranglehold over the organisational structure of the CSP. By 1938 the socialist leaders did realise the real game of the CPI, but by that time much water had flown under the bridges of Hugli, Krishna and Godavari. By the time CPI members were expelled from the CSP in 1940, they had virtually gobbled up the Andhra, Kerala and Bengal units of the CSP, including such stalwarts as E M S Namboodiripad and A K Gopalan. Thus, in actual terms, the policy of united front paid rich dividends to the CPI, whereas for the CSP it resulted in the net loss of its organisational strengths.

Indian Socialists and the Quit India Movement

The participation of Indian Socialist's leaders in the Quit India Movement was the most glorious chapter of their political life. Before the Quit India Movement was launched, there was some confusion in the minds of some prominent Congress leaders, including Jawaharlal Nehru, regarding opposition to the British when they were engaged in

Jayaprakash and Lohia

a battle of life and death with the Axis powers. But the socialist leaders were quite clear that the British must be opposed tooth and nail, as they were unwilling to take any concrete measures towards the independence of India. They moved closer to Gandhiji and egged him on to lead a decisive battle against the British. When Gandhiji decided to launch the Quit India Movement after the failure of the Cripps Mission, the socialists were really very close to him. In fact, it is the socialist leaders like Jayaprakash Narayan, Aruna Asaf Ali, Rammanohar Lohia, Ram Nandan Mishra, Basawan Singh, Suraj Narain Singh, Yogendra Shukla and others, who not only sustained the movement but also organised a network of underground resistance by organising the *Azad Dasta* of freedom fighters. They were not only in the forefront of the national struggle but also widened the concept of non-violence by taking the position that attacks on government properties and symbols of imperial authority could not be construed as a part of violent struggle. Jayaprakash Narayan, Rammanohar Lohia and Ram Nandan Mishra were imprisoned in Lahore fort and were subjected to the worst kind of mental and physical torture. They were the last to be released. In popular eyes they were the real heroes

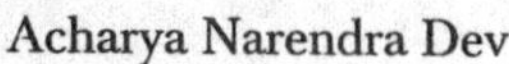

Acharya Narendra Dev

Rammanohar Lohia

of the Quit India Movement. Thus, it was not surprising that when Jayaprakash Narayan reached Patna after his release from the Lahore fort, lakhs of people greeted and hailed him at Gandhi Maidan in Patna where the national poet Ramdhari Singh 'Dinkar' recited his famous poem 'Jayaprakash' in which he exhorted him by saying that today the 'whole sky was yours'.

No study on the Congress Socialist Party would be complete without discussing its relationship with Gandhiji. Initially, they had a lukewarm attitude towards each other. In fact, the CSP opposed the Gandhian policy of compromise and conciliation. Gandhiji, on his part, was not happy about the prospect of the socialists having a dominant position in the Congress organisation. In fact, when he resigned from the Congress in September 1934, he cited the formation of CSP as one of the reasons for his resignation.

In the course of time, however, Indian socialists and Mahatma Gandhi moved closer to each other. What brought them together was their mutual respect for each other's sincerity and commitment to the purpose. And above all, it was their opposition to the British rule which knitted their heads and hearts together despite some differences in methods and strategy. The socialists were virtually itching for a fight with the British. Gandhiji, with an experience of more than fifty years of his struggle against the British, had a tremendous amount of patience and had developed a rare knack of choosing the right moment and the right issues for the national struggle. In the fight against the British, Indian socialists were like the foot-soldiers of the national movement – always more than willing to move forward and join the battle and became extremely resentful if asked to retreat from the battlefront. Gandhiji, on the other hand, as the commander-in-chief of the non-violent army, always had a better overview of the battlefield. He knew how best to deploy his forces, knew when to strike, and strike hard, and even knew when to retreat for tactical reasons. For him, any retreat was the first preparatory steps towards the next battle and his one step backward was always followed by two steps forward. Indian socialists were always conscious of the fact that Gandhiji stood head and shoulders above every other leader. When, by the middle of the Second World War, their opposition to the British imperialism reached a stage of crescendo, they moved closer to Gandhiji, who had also arrived at the same conclusion. Thus, from the days of the Quit India Movement to the day of his martyrdom, they stood like a rock by his side. Not only that, every offer of the British from the Cripps Mission to the Mountbatten Plan, including the Cabinet Mission, was opposed by them. For them, every act of compromise was an act of betrayal for the national cause. Indian socialists consistently opposed every plan for partition of the country. Even when the Congress decided to accept the partition of the country under the force of circumstances, both in the Working Committee and AICC, they opposed it. If they did not finally vote against the resolution accepting the partition in the AICC meeting, it was more out of deference and respect for Gandhiji who had finally acquiesced in the Congress acceptance of the partition. So far as the Indian socialist leaders relationship with Nehru was concerned, it went into reverse gear. It began with a lot of mutual admiration so much so that the socialists looked up to Nehru as their leader and he in turn appreciated their socialist initiatives. He also admired them and was the first Congress president to take three of the socialist leaders in his Working Committee. But gradually they drifted away from each other, more so in the post-war-period when Nehru along with Patel accepted partition and moved to the seat of power. The socialists gradually drifted away from Nehru and moved closer to Gandhiji.

Before we make an overall assessment of the contributions of the Congress Socialist Party to the national movement, let us point out the major limitations it suffered from. First, they initially underestimated the moral force behind the Gandhian idea of purity of means and symbiotic relationship between the ends and the means. The Indian socialists, in their Marxian exuberance and overenthusiasm, started with the formulation that ends justify the means. Ultimately, they veered around to Gandhiji's idea of close relationship between the ends and the means. As such, one can point out a crisis of consistency in their ideological and strategic stance. Second, they hastened to join hands with the Communists and pursued the united front policy which the communists used to dominate them and, ultimately, took away some of their major local units. The pursuit of a united front policy proved to be a very costly affair for the Indian socialists both in ideological and organisational terms. A little more prudence could have saved them from this disaster. Third, despite their virulent opposition to the idea of the partition and their firm commitment to the unity of the country, they could hardly do anything concrete to ward off this disaster. Fourth, despite their attempt to build up a 'Desasth' (indigenous) Socialism, they failed to carve out a real ideological niche for themselves. In fact, ideologically they fell between the two stools: the Congress and the Communists. It was not for nothing that the Congress, ultimately, succeeded in grabbing their ideological ground. In fact, it even succeeded in occupying their ideological space and took a number of their leaders into its fold.

But despite these limitations, the Indian socialists contributed towards the growth and enrichment of the Indian national movement in several ways. In the first place, they took an uncompromising stand against British imperialism and even played a vanguardist role in the Quit India Movement. But for their acts of courage and sacrifice, the Quit India Movement might not have acquired the depth and dimension it actually did. Second, it goes to their credit that they consistently stood for a secular and united India. Even when Nehru and Patel dithered on the issue of Indian unity and, in fact, gave in to Jinnah's demand for Pakistan, the socialist leaders refused to compromise and held on to their position till the last. Third, despite their Marxist orientations, they refused to work as the drum-beater boys of either the CPSU or the Comintern. Soon they became critical of Stalinist excesses. In fact, they pursued an independent line both in organisational as well as ideological terms and consistently refused to live on borrowed thinking. This boldness to strike a lonely ideological furrow speaks volumes for their independent thinking. Moving on the same line, they came to a point where human liberty became the first and the last article of their faith. Fourth, they made a small contribution in widening the concept of non-violence: by taking an ideological position during the Quit India Movement that violence against property is no violence. However, they always retained their faith in the sacrosanct nature of human life. Fifth, they underlined the revolutionary role of peasantry and rural proletariat in their political philosophy and in the process they brought thousands of peasants and the rural poor to the mainstream of the national movement. They even forced Swami Sahajanand Saraswati, the fiery Kisan leader, to agree to their demand of zamindari abolition which, initially, he was not willing to accept. Leaders like N G Goray, Indulal Yagnik, Ram Nandan Mishra, Yadunandan Sharma, Rammanohar Lohia and others, played a glorious role in raising the cause of the peasantry at the national level and launched and led a number of agitations in support of their demands.

Finally, it could be concluded that their record in the freedom struggle was outstanding, as they led some of these movements from the front. Besides, even if they failed to carve out a very distinct ideological niche for themselves, the very fact that they attempted to do it, much before any other socialist group in the world, speaks a lot for their innovative and independent thinking.

> *The reasons why the party (CSP) is within the Congress are not far to seek. The party came into existence as a result of a group of Congressmen in the course of struggle. They came under the impact of the socialist thought of the world . . . the dire necessity of anti-imperialist struggle led to their conversion and they quite rightly desired to develop the Congress platform for an anti-imperialist struggle.*
>
> ACHARYA NARENDRA DEV

26 Peasant Movements and the Indian Freedom Struggle

Who made him dead to rapture and despair,
A Thing that grieves not
And that never hopes,
Stolid and stunned, a brother to the ox.

UNKNOWN POET

Little do the town-dwellers know how the semi-starved masses of India are slowly sinking to lifelessness. Little do they know that their miserable comfort represents the brokerage they get for the work they do for foreign exploiters, that the profits and the brokerages are sucked from the masses. . . . No sophistry, no jugglery in figures can explain away the evidence the skeletons in many villages present to the naked eyes.

MAHATMA GANDHI

Indian peasantry played a crucial role in India's struggle for independence. In fact, the Marxist scepticism about any revolutionary role for the peasantry was belied in the Asian countries including Marxist-led revolutions in China and Vietnam. In the case of India, the revolutionary record of the Indian peasantry was impeccable so far as the freedom struggle was concerned. In fact, there was a very concrete reason for peasantry playing a significant role in the Indian freedom struggle: they were the worst victims of the British colonial rule, which had led to their mass pauperisation and penury. It was the anti-peasant aspect of the British colonial policy which had resulted in high land revenue, rural indebtedness and emergence of a class of small peasants, landless labour and moneylenders. Besides, destruction of the Indian handicrafts, both in rural and urban areas, further contributed to the already overstretched rural resources, primarily based on land. It was not surprising that Indian rural areas were marked by a number of peasant uprisings during the nineteenth century. The colonial rule became the real cause of their poverty and sufferings and hence they rose in spontaneous revolts without much preparation and organisation. One of such major peasant revolts which deserves special mention was the Indigo Revolt of 1859–60 in Bengal. The revolt had its genesis in the indigo planters, mostly of European origin, who indulged in unabashed use of fraudulent contracts with the local peasants. In the process, they compelled them to sell their products at a price which hardly met the cost of production. Unabated exploitation of indigo groups resulted in a revolt in September 1859. Some of the villagers gave up indigo cultivation and physically resisted attempts by planters and their henchmen to force them to go back to indigo-growing. This revolt subsequently engulfed wider areas in 1860 and virtually spread to all indigo-growing districts of Bengal. It forced the indigo-planters to close their shops by the end of 1860. The revolution of 1859–60 got the support of the Bengal intellectuals. Dinabandhu Mitra's play 'Neel Darpan' portraying the suffering and helplessness of the indigo-growers, was widely performed and discussed. Ultimately, the government came out with a declaration in November 1860 that peasants could not be compelled to grow indigo and the planters also saw the writing on the walls and virtually closed their shops.

The same militancy was displayed by the peasants of Pabna district of east Bengal during the 1870s when the zamindars tried to force them to pay enhanced rent. The peasants resisted the move and the movement soon spread to other parts of east Bengal. This ultimately forced zamindars to concede to them the occupancy rights and non-payment of enhanced rent. The rights of the tenants were also supported by the intellectuals like Surendranath Banerjea, Ananda Mohan Bose Dwarakanath Ganguli and a host of others. Subsequently, a similar peasant movement struck its roots in some districts of Maharashtra, like Ahmednagar and Poona. Here the enemy symbol was the village moneylender who charged exorbitant interest on the loans extended to peasants, which was required by them to pay high land revenue. That revolt ultimately resulted in the passage of the Deccan Agricultural Relief Act of 1879. The movement was supported by the Poona Sarvajanik Sabha led by Justice Ranade. Similar revolts among the Indian peasantry occurred in other places. In Punjab there was the Kuka Revolt led by Baba Ram Singh during the 1870s. In Assam also peasant revolts took place during 1893–94.

It is true that these peasant rebellions were more spontaneous than organised and were not directly challenging the authority of the British. Rather they were directed against local landlords. The real significance of these movements, however, was that peasants displayed a deep sense of sacrifice and defiance, and even organisational abilities and secular credentials. True, these movements were localised and did not have an all India character. But they brought out the sufferings of the peasantry and put their problems on the national agenda.

Some of the early national leaders extended their support to the peasant cause. For instance, Gokhale raised the issues of peasants' indebtedness and illiteracy. But he could hardly do anything concrete to mitigate their sufferings. But peasants, on their own, did rise in revolt in some parts of Rajasthan in the early years of the twentieth century. They even refused to cultivate land on account of high incidence of different kinds of taxes and even tried to migrate to other areas. Similarly, in some parts of Darbhanga district of Bihar, during 1919–20, they protested and ultimately succeeded in getting some concessions from the Darbhanga Raj.

Mahatma Gandhi was the first major political leader of India who systematically and specifically underlined the need for bringing peasants into the fold of the national movement. Not only that, he soon got involved in the agitation against the indigo planters in the Champaran district of Bihar. He visited Champaran at the invitation of Rajkumar Shukla, a local peasant leader, and held a detailed inquiry about the problems of the indigo-growers. Ultimately, the government was forced to set up an enquiry committee to study their problems and suggest remedial measures. It was during the Champaran struggle that he picked up illustrious co-workers like Rajendra Prasad, J B Kripalani, Brajkishore Prasad and a host of others who came to play a major role in India's struggle for independence. The real issue in the Champaran struggle was that peasants were forced to grow indigo on 3/20 parts of their land and had to sell it to the British planters at a non-remunerative price fixed by the British planters. Ultimately, on account of Gandhiji's struggle, the Tinkathia system (3/20) was abolished when the government enacted the Champaran Agrarian Act of 1917. This was followed by another movement known as Kheda Satyagraha. The peasants of Kheda, a district of Gujarat, protested against the land revenue collection as crops had failed. The government tried to take aggressive measures, but ultimately due to Gandhiji's intervention, it was forced to make a retreat and offer some concession to the peasants.

The real momentum to the peasant movement was given by the launching of the Non-Cooperation Movement, led by Mahatma Gandhi, in 1920. One of the major parts of the Non-Cooperation Movement was non-payment of taxes and land revenue. Thus, the peasantry could visualise the battle of Swaraj with the coming of a no tax-regime. That brought peasants in large numbers to the Non-Cooperation Movement. It is true that the UP Kisan Sabha had been set up in February 1918 with the blessings of Madan Mohan Malaviya. However, by 1920 Baba Ramchandra, emerged as the most prominent leader of the UP Kisan Sabha. He was soon able to rope in Jawaharlal Nehru, who established live contacts with the Kisan Sabha. Baba Ramchandra was arrested during August 1920. The peasants protested and soon Baba Ramchandra had to be released. On account of some differences with Madan Mohan Malviya, a new organisation known as Awadh Kisan Sabha was subsequently set up, which called upon Kisans not to offer *begar* (free labour) and also to solve their disputes through panchayat. A big demonstration of peasants was held at Ayodhya and Faizabad in December 1920. All this led to the passage of the Oudh Rent (Amendment) Act, which though modest in real offering, nevertheless raised high hopes among the peasants of Oudh. This was followed by the Eka movement, which covered a number of districts, including Sitapur and Barbanki. In the Eka movement, peasants insisted that they would pay the recorded rent in cash only. They also demanded a right to graze their cattle on the forest land. On account of government repression, the Eka movement was virtually over by December 1922.

It was in the later part of the 1920s that a number of peasant-organisations started being raised. A number of regional Kisan Associations came up in Punjab and UP during 1925–28. The Andhra Provincial Ryots Association was formed in 1929. The formation of Workers and Peasants Party (WPP) in 1928 was one of the major developments in this direction. The Moplah rebellion was another important peasant uprising which occurred in the middle of the non-cooperation movement. Moplahs, located in the Malabar area, had a long history of resentment against their Hindu landlords for their exploitative exactions. What gave them a new sense of confidence was the support extended to them by the Khilafat Movement and the visits of leaders like Gandhiji, Shaukat Ali and Maulana Azad. Ultimately, most of the prominent leaders including K Madhavan Nair, Yakub Hasan and others were arrested in February 1921. In August 1921 some volunteers were arrested from a mosque but the rumour spread that the Mambrath Mosque had been destroyed by the British army. That inflamed the Moplah rebellion in a big way. Initially, it was an anti-British movement but soon assumed a form of forced conversion of Hindus. Hindu landlords were attacked. The government declared martial law. By December 1921, the rebellion was suppressed and in the process 2,337 Moplahs lost their lives. The non-official figure estimated more than 10,000 killed and more than 50 thousand captured. In the course of the rebellion, a number of police stations were destroyed and 600 Hindu landlords were killed and 2,500 Hindus were converted to Islam. The worst incident took place when 66 bodies of Moplah prisoners were recovered in a railway wagon, on 20 November 1921 at Podanur railway station.

The Bardoli Satyagraha (1928–31) was another very significant movement which had a distinct place in the history of the peasant's protest movement in India. Earlier, Bardoli Taluka had shot into prominence when during the Non-Cooperation Movement, Gandhiji had selected it for an intensified Civil Disobedience Movement. Soon it became a centre of constructive programmes of Gandhiji and a number of prominent constructing Gandhian workers emerged from the area. Prominent among them were two brothers Kalyanji and Kunverji Mehta. They worked among the poor sections of the society. Thus, when the government wanted a 30 per cent increase in land revenue, a hue and cry was raised and the Bardoli enquiry committee was set up, which submitted a report in July 1926 and found that the proposed increase was unjustified. This was followed by a protest movement, as a result of which, the government agreed to bring down the increase to 22 per cent. This was too meagre a concession and hence a new movement under the leadership of Sardar Patel was launched in 1928. The main issue was that peasants were to refuse to pay the enhanced rent until the government accepted the earlier amount as full payment and appointed an independent enquiry committee. Sardar Patel displayed his rare organisational skills and his ability to mobilise the masses during the Bardoli satyagraha. And it was here that the people gave him the title of Sardar. Women were mobilised in large numbers and they became the mainstay of the movement. The Bardoli satyagraha attracted support from different organisations from all over the country. Gandhiji himself camped in Bardoli in August 1928. Ultimately, the government was forced to reduce the enhanced rent from 30 per cent to the tune of a mere 6.03 per cent.

The peasant movement got a boost when the Civil Disobedience Movement was launched in 1930. The Great Economic Depression also contributed towards worsening of the living conditions of the peasantry, as the prices of agricultural goods came down heavily. Thus, there was a direct linkage between the peasant movement and the Civil Disobedience Movement. As in many parts of the country, the Civil Disobedience Movement took the form of a no-tax, no rent campaign. A number of peasant movements sprang up in provinces like Andhra, Gujarat and Karnataka. In Gujarat, Bardoli peasants refused to pay rent and 80,000 peasants migrated to Baroda state. The government seized peasant land on a large scale but the peasants continued to protest, which ultimately led to restoration of their land. This was a rare display of grit and determination on the part of Bardoli peasants. In UP, a no-rent campaign was launched, which

Swami Sahajanand Saraswati

was supported by prominent leaders like Mahatma Gandhi and Jawaharlal Nehru. In Andhra, Punjab, Bihar and Bengal, the peasant movements took different forms but the basic issue was the suffering of the peasants caused by unjust revenue laws. In Bihar and Bengal it took the form of anti-chaukidari tax. In Punjab, the main demands took the form of reduction of land revenue and water charges. In Maharashtra, CP and Bihar, unjust forest laws were the main target of attack. In Andhra, it took the form of an anti-zamindari movement.

The major breakthrough on the front of the peasant movement came with the formation of the All India Kisan Sabha, in 1936 under the dynamic leadership of Swami Sahajanand Saraswati as its president. The other prominent leaders were Indulal Yagnik from Gujarat, N G Ranga from Andhra and Yadunandan Sharma, Karyanand Sharma and Punyadeo Sharma from Bihar. It had the support of national leaders like Jawaharlal Nehru, Jayaprakash Narayan, Rammanohar Lohia and others. Earlier, after the formation of the CSP in 1934, peasant movements had got a real boost. Subsequently, the CPI also joined the Bihar Kisan Sabha. Ellore Zamindari Ryots Conference in 1933 and the Indian Peasant Institute in Andhra, started by N G Ranga, were precursors of the foundation of All India Kisan Sabha in 1936. The basic objective of the Kisan Sabha was to secure complete freedom from economic exploitation and achievement of full economic and political power to the peasants and workers. Subsequently, a Kisan Manifesto was prepared which greatly influenced the issues which were raised and incorporated in the 1937 election manifesto of the Congress. The issues raised in this manifesto were security of tenure for tenants, a living wage for agricultural labourers, a moratorium on debts and 50 per cent reduction in land revenue and rent.

With the formation of the Congress ministry in several provinces, the peasant movement got a major boost. The period from 1937 to 1939 was a remarkable phase in the life of the peasant movement. Some major agrarian reforms like debt relief, restoration of lands lost during earlier movements, and security of tenancy were introduced. The Kisan organisations mobilised the peasantry for more radical measures. In the wake of this mobilisation, a significant peasant movement emerged in Kerala under the banner of the CSP – which demanded reduction in tax, debt-relief and stopping of victimisation of tenants. It also demanded the amendment of the Malabar Tenancy Act of 1929 which resulted in the passing of a debt relief law by Madras legislature in 1938. In Andhra also, a powerful peasant movement emerged under the leadership of N G Ranga, who led many agitations against zamindars. One of the novel methods of peasant mobilisation adopted by the Andhra Kisan Sabha was the long march in 1938 in which 2,000 peasants covered a distance of 1,500 miles. On the way they interacted with a large number of Kisans and on 27 March 1938, presented a petition to the Madras provincial legislature which, among other things, demanded debt-relief. Consequently, the Madras legislature, set up a zamindari enquiry committee. In Andhra, another novel way introduced was study classes which were addressed by prominent leaders. Thus, Andhra became a main centre for peasant mobilisation.

Another area of active peasant movement was Bihar. Under the leadership of Sahajanand, the Bihar Kisan Sabha had earlier demanded abolition of the zamindari system in 1935. In 1938, a massive peasant demonstration was held to popularise the demands of the Kisan Sabha. The Bihar Congress ministry passed a resolution for reduction of rent and restoration of Bakasta land. Bakasta land was that land which cultivators had lost to zamindars on account of non-payment of rent but continued to cultivate as share croppers. The proposal of the government that tenants had to pay the half price of the auction did not satisfy the Kisan Sabha leaders, and it became a major bone of contention between the Government and the Kisan Sabha. Bakasta movement gathered momentum in Gaya, Monghyr, Darbhanga and Saran districts. The prominent leaders of the movement were Ram Nandan Mishra, Kishori Prasanna Sinha, Punyadeo Sharma, Rahul Sankritayayan, Yadunandan Sharma and Karyanand Sharma. The movement finally ended in 1939, when some concessions were granted to the peasantry.

In Punjab, where peasants were earlier mobilised under the banner of Naujawan Bharat Sabha and Kirti Kisan Congress the Akalis got a boost when the Punjab Kisan Committee was formed in 1937. The Punjab peasants were mobilised around the main demands of reduction of taxes and moratorium on debts. The immediate issue was increase in water tax, which lead to the Lahore Kisan Morcha in 1939, in which thousands of peasants courted arrest. In the districts of Multan and Montegomery, the movement was organised against feudal levies being imposed on the tenants. Central Punjab, mostly comprising Sikh peasantry, was the main centre of agitation. In Punjab, some of the important leaders were Baba Sohan Singh, Teja Singh, Baba Raj Singh, and Master Harisingh. Similar movements also occured in Assam and Uttar Pradesh.

During the Second World War, a dissension overtook the Kisan Sabha, when the Indian communists adopted a pro-British war line, when Hitler attacked Russia in June 1941. Thus, there was a split in Kisan Sabha and some of it's leaders left the organisation, which considerably weakened it.

Once the process of the transfer of power was on, the peasants raised their major demands like abolition of the zamindari system and higher wages for agricultural labour. In Bengal in 1946, the Tebhaga struggle was a major movement. The main demand of the movement was that share-croppers would give only one-third of their produce to the landlords and not one-half as was the practice then. Besides, the share-croppers also insisted that they would store the crop in their own godowns and not in *jotedars.* Meanwhile, the Muslim League-led ministry published a Bengal Burgadars Temporary Regulation Bill in January 1947, which recognised the rights of Burgadars. This further gave a fillip to the Burgadars movement. This resulted in major clashes between the burgadars and *jotedars* men. But the process of the Bill could not be completed as the ministry subsequently lost interest in it.

After this brief survey of the peasant movements in pre-Independent India, it remains for us to make an evaluative study of their contributions to the national movement in general and to the cause of the peasants in particular. Let us first consider that in India, with its staggering diversity, it was no easy task to build up a powerful All India Kisan Movement. Besides, on account of the scattered nature of the peasants and wide spatial horizons, it is always a daunting task to mobilise and organise peasantry under the banner of a single organisation. Second, the peasants are always reluctant to integrate in their movement the demands of the agricultural labourers, as in certain ways, they were also the employers of these landless labourers. Third, most of their leadership came from the middle classes though some of them did have some rural moorings and linkages but not many of them were from actually cultivating classes.

Despite these limitations, the peasant movement made a number of major contributions to the cause of the national movement as well as that of the peasantry. In the first place, they raised the issues affecting the peasants, mobilised them and launched agitations around these demands. In this way they put the problems of the peasants on the national agenda. Hence, the entire nation became aware of the plight of the peasantry and sympathised with them. Popularisation of peasant's demands, which caught the imagination of the Indian people, is not a minor contribution of the peasant movements. Their demands clearly brought out iniquities and injustices inherent in the system and paved the way for future radical agrarian reforms like zamindari abolition acts, share-croppers acts, land distribution acts, the issue of homestead land acts, etc. They pointed to the road ahead and worked as the sappers and miners of the peasant cause.

Second, the peasant movement by and large, remained non-violent, using methods of mobilisation like meetings, conferences, demonstrations, etc. They pointed to a peaceful way to tackle peasant problems, and popularised the non-violent methods of struggle. In the process they became a major partner in the national struggle. This close linkage between peasant movement and national movement reinforced each other. This widened and strengthened the base of the national movement by bringing a large number of people to it. In turn, the national movement extended moral, intellectual and material support to the cause of the peasants. In fact, it was a relationship in which both reinforced each other. Third, like any other sectional movement, they made the Congress include their demands as a part of the larger national movement. And in the process it contributed to the radicalisation of the national movement.

Their struggle might not have solved all their problems, but it did force the government to take some measures to alleviate the conditions of the peasantry. In fact, some of the important pieces of legislation came in the wake of the peasant agitations. Some of them were: Debt Relief Acts (UP) 1934, Regulation of Account Act (Punjab) in 1934, Moneylenders Act (Bengal) in 1933 and the Relief of Indebtedness Act in 1935. They were not as radical the peasant leaders might have wished, but certainly they had a mitigating impact on the suffering and plight of peasants. In brief, the peasant movements, in their own way, made contributions to the national cause.

The Kisan organisation is therefore necessary to exert revolutionary pressure on the Congress to adopt more and more demands of peasants.

ACHARYA NARENDRA DEV

27 Trade Union Movement and the Indian Freedom Struggle

I have always said that my ideal is that capital and labour should supplement and help each other.

MAHATMA GANDHI

The Trade Union Movement in India also had an important role in our freedom struggle. It not only supported the call for national struggle at critical junctures, but also impacted its course and character in several ways. It made the national leaders to integrate and articulate some of the sectional demands of the working class as an integral part of the national agenda for struggle. In fact, the emergence and growth of the working class organisations and our national movement was so closely interlinked that both almost grew together. But before we discuss the role of the working class in the freedom struggle, let us have a look at its early history.

There is no denying the fact that the emergence of the industrial working class as a group and their problems came up in the process of industrialisation, which started in the later part of the nineteenth century, when the British capital started getting invested in India in a big way. Initially, tea plantation, railways and textiles were three such major sectors. Perhaps, one of the primary attractions for the British capital was the availability of abundant raw material and of cheap labour in India. The Indian workers employed in the British industries were subjected to the worst kind of exploitation and even forced to work under most inhuman and unhygienic conditions. As such, their extreme suffering and miseries touched the souls of many sensitive Indians. One such sensitive Indian philanthropist was Sorabjee Shapoorji Bengalee from Bombay, who was the first social activist to take up the workers' cause. In 1878, he introduced a bill in the Bombay Legislative Council which sought to limit the working hours of the labour. A little earlier in Bengal, a similar initiative was taken by Sasipada Banerjee, who started a working mens' club in 1870 and even brought out a journal known as *Bharat Sramjeebi* for discussing the problems confronting the working class. Another person who did pioneering work in this area was Narayan Meghajee from Bombay, who even started a weekly paper called *Dinbandhu*, totally devoted to the cause of the working class. He also set up the Bombay Mill and Millhands Association in 1890.

It is clear that these were some of the stray efforts of some sensitive persons and were not a part of any organised trade union movement as such. Besides, these pioneers hardly had any connection with contemporary national leaders. Early nationalists leaders were equally concerned about the mass poverty of our people. But they were not keen to build up any class organisation as such and mostly raised their voices on national issues. Perhaps, the early nationalists wanted to maintain the unity of the national movement and hence did not favour class organisations. There was another reason for not taking up the cause of the working class. It might have hurt the interests of Indian factory owners, which they were not willing to do. There was also an irony in the whole situation. Some of the British textile producers were demanding more radical labour law in India which, they thought, would cut the quantum of profitability of Indian textile producers, making their own products more competitive in the Indian market. The Indian leaders were also aware of this aspect of the problem. Besides, they also favoured quick and rapid industrialisation in India, and hence, were hesitant to take any step which might thwart this process. The early nationalist leaders tried to meet the challenges of the situation by devising a wise strategy. They would support the cause of those workers who were employed in British industries and not of those who were working in Indian industries. Thus, they did not have any hesitation in extending support to the tea-plantation workers in Assam, who were being treated no better than slaves. Similarly, when there was a strike call by the workers of great Indian Peninsular Railway, it received wide support from the national leaders including Tilak and Pherozeshah Mehta.

A change in the attitude of national leaders towards the problems of working class took place during the initial years of the twentieth century. Some of the leaders like G Subramaniya Aiyer from Madras and Bipin Chandra Pal from Bengal now started taking the position that the working class must unionize and fight for its rights. It was indeed the Swadeshi Movement (1905–08) which brought about a real change in the attitude of our leaders: they started seeing the advantage of a close linkage between the working class and the national movement. Some of the leaders even undertook the task of organising the workers employed in the government press, railways and jute industry – where either foreign capitalists or the colonial government were the employers. There was also a radical change in the attitude of the working class as they started taking a keen interest in national problems. Perhaps, this attitudinal change, on the part of the national leaders as well as on the part of the working class, was brought about by the mutual need and experiences of the Swadeshi Movement, which had emerged in the wake of partition of the Bengal. For instance, the workers of Burn Company struck work when they were not granted leave to attend a meeting of a prominent Swadeshi leader. Far South in Madras, when Chidambaram Pillai, a prominent leader, was arrested in 1908, the working class struck work in his favour. In Bombay when, Tilak was sentenced to six-year imprisonment in 1908, the Bombay working class went on strike in his support. Similarly, in Punjab when Ajit Singh and Lala Lajpat Rai were being deported, railway workers went on lightning strike to express their support and solidarity with them.

Like in any other field, the advent of Gandhiji on the political scene of India marked a new milestone on the road of the trade union movement. He was deeply concerned about the suffering and misery of the common people and that prompted him to set up the Ahmedabad Textiles Workers Association in 1918. And he even launched movement in the support of their demands. Not only that, in the course of the Rowlatt Satyagraha and Khilafat – Non-Cooperation Movement, the workers went on strike on several occasions in the support of the national cause. When Gandhiji was arrested in April 1919 in the course of his Rowlatt Satyagraha, the textile workers in Ahmedabad struck work. Not only that, the workers of the North Western Railway also gave a call for an all India strike on the same issue. Similarly, when the Indian National Congress decided to boycott the Prince of Wales's visit in November 1921, the Bombay working class expressed their support by going on strike. In sum, a close linkage between the national movement and the working class started getting connected. In 1920, the All India Trade Union Congress (AITUC) was set up with Lala Lajpat Rai as its first president and Dewan Chaman Lal being its first General Secretary. Bal Gangadhar Tilak also extended his heartfelt support to the new organisation. The AITUC manifesto underlined the close linkage between the working class and the national movement. There was another change in our leaders' attitude; they started refusing support to the Indian capitalist class if they tried to ignore the interests of the working class. The other prominent national leaders who took keen interest in the working of AITUC were C F Andrews, J M Sen Gupta, Subhas Chandra Bose and C R Das. The Indian National Congress also welcomed the formation of the new organisation.

The formation of the Communist Party of India in 1925 also gave a big boost to the trade union movement in India. The communists became active in AITUC but also set up their own trade unions like Girni Kamgar Union (GKU) which led a six-month strike in the Textiles Mills of Bombay in 1928. This was preceded by the Bombay Textiles Mills strike in March 1924 and the north-western railway strike in June 1925. The communists also had set up the Workers and Peasants Party with branches in many parts of the country. When the country decided to boycott the Simon Commission in 1928, the working class also supported the national move by staging a big demonstration against the Commission. Besides, this was the period in which Bhagat Singh and the Hindustan Socialist Republican Army were getting interested in the working class, as they were gradually moving towards the Marxist position of the primacy of the working class in any revolutionary movement. Bhagat Singh even tried to define revolution in the terms of the 'dictatorship of the proletariat'.

The government was not unaware of these developments: It adopted a two-pronged strategy of coercion and concessions. As a part of its coercive strategy, it tried to push through draconian measures like the 'Public Safety Act' and 'Trade Disputes Act', which provoked Bhagat Singh and Batukeshwar Datta to throw bombs in the Central Assembly, creating a big stir in the country. As the part of their coercive strategy, the government launched the Meerut Conspiracy Case against some of the communist leaders. To assuage the feelings of the working class, it decided to set up the Royal Labour Commission to look into their problems. During this period, sharp differences of opinion emerged in the All India Trade Union Congress. One of the issues was whether or not to boycott the Royal Labour Commission, earlier set up by the government. A second bone of contention was about sending representatives to the International Trade Union located at Geneva. All this led to a split in AITUC in 1929. A number of trade union leaders led by N M Joshi left AITUC and formed their trade union called Indian Trade Union Federation. Subsequently, under the new policy dictated by the Comintern, asking Indian communists not to associate with the national movement, the communists also drifted away from the AITUC and formed a separate organisation called the Indian Red Trade Union Congress. But, despite the dissociation of the Indian communists from the Indian national movement, the working class participated in the Civil Disobedience Movement in a big way. The workers of Sholapur Textiles Mills not only struck work but also virtually took over the town for a few days in March 1930. Similarly, the Great Indian Peninsular Railways workers struck work when Gandhiji broke the salt law on 6 April 1930.

With yet another change in the policy of the Comintern, the Indian communists initiated a new policy of united front. They not only came back to AITUC but started working in the Congress through the Congress Socialist Party. All India Trade Union Congress supported the Congress party in the 1937 elections. With the formation of the Congress ministries there was a new upsurge in the trade union activities. When the Second World War broke out in September 1939, the working class of Bombay staged a massive anti-war demonstration on 20 October 1939. Soon after Hitler's attack on Russia in June 1941, the Communists again changed their policy and started extending support to the British Government. In the process, they became the greatest advocates of maintenance of industrial peace.

But despite the non-participation of the communists in the Quit India Movement, the working class did not lag behind in extending its support to it. The Tata Steel Plant in Tata Nagar was closed for 13 days during the Quit India Movement and Ahmedabad Textiles workers also struck work for a month.

This close linkage between the working class and the national movement continued even in the post-war period. The working class took part in demonstrations against the INA trial and the Calcutta Dock workers refused to load supplies, which were being sent to suppress the national movement in Indonesia. In February 1946, Ratings of the Indian Royal Navy revolted. A glorious chapter in the history of the working class was added as they came out openly in support of the rebellion. The Army was called in. They had to fire on the people in which 250 workers laid down their lives.

In the post-war period, another development on the trade union front was the split in its ranks. The communists succeeded in fully controlling the All India Trade Union Congress, which led the Congress to form its own trade union wing in 1947 called the Indian Trade

Union Congress. Subsequently, Indian socialists also decided to have their own trade union body and established the Hind Majdoor Sabha.

Finally, let us make an overall assessment of the role of the Indian trade union movement in India's struggle for independence. It would be expedient for us to first look at some of their limitations. In the first place, on account of the low level of urbanisation and industrialisation in India, the working class could play only a marginal role in our national life. India, basically being an agricultural country, the working class could not be expected to play the kind of dominant role which Karl Marx had envisaged in respect of the highly industrialised European countries. Therefore, Mahatma Gandhi had rightly envisaged a much bigger role for Indian peasantry instead of the working class. Second, since the Indian communists were major players in the Indian trade union movement, the lack of independent thinking in their ranks greatly hampered the growth of the trade union movements in India. A section of the Indian trade union movement could not participate fully in the freedom struggle on account of its being attached to the Comintern and its policy. That, in a way, limited the role of the trade union movement in India's freedom struggle. Third, the Indian trade union suffered from internal divisions. All India Trade Union Congress, Indian Trade Union Congress, Hind Majdoor Sabha and a host of other trade union organisations, more often than not, competed and fought with each other, which greatly hampered a sound growth of the trade union movement in India.

Despite these limitations, the trade union movement did play a role in the freedom struggle. They participated in many of the Gandhian movements and even the movement supporting the RIN rebellion and INA. Second, they also affected and influenced the mainstream of the national movement, making it adopt a more radical line. Third, they underlined the need for building up of society which is free from the exploitation of man by man. Fourth, they also raised the issues concerning the working class and forced the government to take some measures to alleviate the suffering of the working class. In a word, the working class of India had its own role in our freedom struggle.

> *The workers should participate in the anti-imperialist struggle led by the Congress. In India, unlike Russia, a proletarian weapon of strike has not yet been the signal for mass action, but the working class can extend its political influence only by using the weapon of general strike in the service of the national struggle; it can impress the petty bourgeoisie with the revolutionary possibilities of a strike.*
>
> ACHARYA NARENDRA DEV

28 Tribal Movements and the Indian Freedom Struggle

Liberation! Liberation! Liberation!
Liberation for the Pariahs, the Tiyas and the Pulaiyas,
Liberation for the Parayas, the Kuravas and the Maravas.

SUBRAMANIA BHARATHI

Like many other sections of the Indian society, the tribal people also made their own contributions to the growth of our national movement. But, before we discuss their role, it would be expedient to have an overview of the tribal people and their territorial location in the country. Though different tribal groups were scattered all over the country, the bulk of them were located in Assam, Bengal, Bihar, Orissa, Central Provinces, Rajasthan, Maharashtra and Gujarat. In these provinces also there were certain pockets where the tribal population was densely located. In south India, they were located in Vizagapatnam (Visakhapatnam) and also in certain pockets of east Godavari district of Andhra Pradesh. In Punjab there were located in the northern areas. Some of the Princely States had a considerable number of the tribal population.

Tribal people constituted around 8 per cent of the total Indian population. The governance of these tribal groups was controlled by the scheduled District Act of 1874, which subsequently was replaced by the Act of 1935. Under the Act of 1919, the tribal administration was put under reserved subjects and was under the control of the provincial governor. The British policy was to keep these tribal groups isolated. Whether or not any provincial legislation would be applicable in respect of the backward tracts wherein the bulk of the tribal population was located, depended on the discretion of the governor. Even Indian citizens had to have special permission to travel inside the inner line. The Act of 1935 did not drastically change the pattern of tribal administration, except that tribal groups residing in partially excluded areas were given an extremely restricted right to vote for the provincial legislatures.

It is also relevant to note that the tribal groups were, perhaps, one of the worst victims of the British rule in India. Prior to the British occupation, the tribal people had lived in inaccessible hinterlands for centuries and had enjoyed the control over local resources including forest land and its produce. Besides, being in the close proximity of nature they had enjoyed a carefree life – a life of ease and freedom. Their lifestyle was not affected by commercial values.

But the coming of the British brought about a major change in their earlier pattern of life. The British occupation of India led to the opening of the hinterland. The development of modern means of communication helped the new rulers to reach out to the tribal population, gradually bringing them under their colonial rule. In the process, the tribal people started losing their control over the local resources including their land and forest produce. In the course of time, the colonial rule also brought outsiders, whom the tribal people started calling Diku, who became the symbol of exploitation, exactions and forced labour, as they started occupying their land by intimidation, manipulation and even treachery. In the process, the tribal people, on account of their alienation from forestland and its produce, were being reduced to sub-tenants, share-croppers and agricultural labourers. Against the backdrop of these developments, the tribal revolt of the nineteenth century against the British rule began. Three of these tribal revolts have been subjected to detailed historical studies. The Bhils were one of the earliest tribal groups to revolt against the British. They were located in the hilly ranges of Khandesh in Maharashtra. The Bhils had come under British control by 1818 and in the very next year, viz., 1819 they revolted, which was of course crushed by the British, by the deployment of huge forces.

However, the fire of Bhil rebellion kept smouldering till 1831, when their leader Umaji Raje was captured and executed. During 1831–32, a similar revolt took place among the Kols who were located in the Chhota Nagpur region. This was also subdued by superior British forces. Santhals were another group who rose in revolt. They were located in and around Raj Mahal hills in Santhal Paragana and were being subjected to the worst kind of exploitation: not only was their land being leased out to the outsiders, they were also being subjected to the worst kind of repressive measures by the colonial administration. All these developments led the Santhals to rise in rebellion during 1855. Thousands of them, armed with bows and arrows, started an open rebellion against the government and other exploiting groups. Initially, they succeeded in controlling a vast territory from Bhagalpur to Raj Mahal, but they could not hold on as the superior forces unleashed by the government indulged in the worst kind of oppressive measures including burning of their villages. Two prominent leaders of the Santhal rebellion were Sidhu and Kanhu, who were more than convinced that God was on their side. Sidhu was captured and killed in 1855 while Kanhu was arrested in 1856. One positive result of the Santhal rebellion was that Santhal Paragana was organised as a separate administrative unit with a view to tackle the problems of Santhals more effectively.

Mundas were another group which rose in rebellion during 1899–1900 under the leadership of Birsa Munda, who subsequently came to be called Birsa Bhagavan. Mundas, like the other tribal groups, were being subjected to exploitation by *jagirdárs*, contractors and the colonial administration which prompted them to rise in rebellion. Birsa was convinced that he was a divine messenger and the Mundas also accepted him as their messiah. In 1899, Birsa mobilised a force of 6,000 Mundas and a rebellion ensued. However, he was captured in 1900 and subsequently died in jail.

The tradition of tribal rebellion continued unabated during the second decade of the twentieth century. For instance, in 1910, a big tribal revolt took place in Jagdalpur, against the Raja of Bastar. Here, the real cause of rebellion lay in new forest laws, which sought to ban shifting cultivation along with the free use of forest produce. The rebels tried to besiege Jagdalpur town, but ultimately this was also suppressed. A similar movement took place among the Khonds of Orissa in 1914, who thought that the First World War had provided them with a golden opportunity to establish their own Raj. The British took immediate repressive measures and soon succeeded in suppressing the Khond rebellion. Similar sentiments were prevailing among the Oraons of Chhota Nagpur in the initial stages of the war. In 1915, the Oraons rose in rebellion as they thought that the war had provided them with a new opportunity to assert their traditional authority. But their movement was also suppressed. In the east, in 1917, the Kukis revolted and even used guerrilla tactics to continue their rebellion against forced labour and the ban on shifting cultivation. In the west, among Bhils around Banswara, Govind guru, a local Bhil leader, had started a reformist movement. In 1913, an attempt was made to set up Bhil

Raj, which was suppressed by the British, resulting in the death of 12 tribals as well as their arrest in large numbers.

All these tribal rebellions were the byproduct of the extreme exploitation of tribals under the British colonial rule, which incidentally also paved the way for the massive entry of the Diku – (outsiders) in the tribal area. In a way, Diku and the colonial officials joined hands for subjecting the tribals to extreme exploitation.

In the pre-Gandhian era, Indian nationalists did not take much notice of the problems confronting the tribal people. As it was basically a middle class movement, the poor and the dispossessed and their problems did not yet form an integral part of our national agenda. Hence, it is not surprising that the early nationalists did not take much notice of the problems confronting the tribal people. Only when Mahatma Gandhi appeared as a Colossus on the Indian political scene during the early 1920s, did tribal people and their problems came on the national agenda. His concept of *daridranarayan* and his solemn promise to 'wipe out every tear from every eye' had greatly touched the souls of the dispossessed of India. And a number of them joined the Non-Cooperation Movement launched by Mahatma Gandhi. But despite the Mahatma's message of non-violence, the old tradition of armed rebellion by the tribal people still continued to dominate their psyche. Thus, in the wake of the Non-Cooperation Movement the first armed rebellion by the tribals took place in Andhra Pradesh. The leader of that rebellion was a tribal leader. Alluri Sitarama Raju, who himself was inspired by Mahatma Gandhi's clarion call not to submit to any act of injustice. He was the leader of a tribal group that inhabited Nallamai hills located in the north Godavari areas. Here the roots of rebellion lay in some of the old acts of injustice and exploitation, namely, retrogressive forest laws, exploitation by moneylending classes, and the system of forced labour (*begar*). Raju, despite being inspired by Gandhiji, pinned his faith in violent methods and led a guerrilla contingent which resulted in the death of some British officials in September 1922. The rebellion continued for some time but ultimately it was suppressed by the government. Raju himself was captured and shot dead on 6 May 1924, which virtually marked the end of the rebellion.

But the Mahatma's dream of millennial change had created a stir among the tribal people and his method of satyagraha had also made some dent in the old tribal tradition of armed rebellion. In the Mewar region of Rajasthan, some of the Gandhians like Hari Bhau

Upadhyaya and Manakya Lal Verma inspired a Bhil movement on the issue of landlord exploitation as well as imposition of some new tax and the system of *begar*. They applied the Gandhian method of non-violent satyagraha, virtually creating a new tradition of non-violent struggle among the tribal people. This was followed by a movement in Garhwal in UP, which was led by Badridutt Pandey of Almora. He led a movement against the system of *beth-begar* (the forced labour). Similarly, in the Midnapore district of Bengal, a movement was led by a local leader Sailjan Sen. This movement was directed against the colonial administration as well as against the European landlords.

In all those movements certain new characteristics emerged, which marked a departure from earlier tribal revolts. The new tribal movement came to be led by non-tribal nationalist leaders and the methods mostly used were non-violent satyagraha. Besides, new movements succeeded in establishing a new linkage between local issues and the rising wave of national consciousness. In fact, there was a reason why the Gandhian movement struck a sympathetic chord in the hearts of some of the tribal groups. Some of the tribal groups had their conversion to Vaishvanism and had developed a new leadership, who came to be known as Bhagats. The birth of a new tradition, of Tana Bhagats among Oraons, the Harilal movement among Bhils and the Rajmohini movement among the Gonds had already created an intellectual acceptance of millennial change marked by a new religious fervour. The Gandhian movement stirred some of the tribal groups namely, Santhals, Oraons, Gonds and Bhils, as they could visualise a new hope for returning to their old way of life and even establishing a tribal Raj. Some of them joined the Gandhian movement and participated both in combative and constructive programmes launched by Gandhiji. Some of them could even identify the Gandhian concept of Ram Rajya with the tribal Raj.

Some of the Gandhian constructive workers like Amritlal Thakkar, better known as Thakkar Bapa, in fact, dedicated their lives for the uplift of the tribal people and established a number of Ashrams among the tribal regions. For instance, Vedachi Ashram was established by some of the Gandhian constructive workers in the Surat district of Gujarat. Here, a group of Gandhian workers led by Jugatram Dave popularised a new concept of abstinence from liquor, and meat-eating, bringing both the tribals and non-tribals on the same platform. Besides, Vedachi Ashram became a centre for popularisation of khadi, spinning and spread of education among the tribals. Besides, these Gandhians did not hesitate to take up some of the radical programmes like debt-relief and tenancy reforms.

Apart from the Vedachi Ashram experiment, the Gandhian constructive programmes also influenced other tribal groups. A number of tribal leaders participated in the freedom movement and they also actively participated in the movements launched by Praja Mandals and Kisan Sabha. For instance, the Khonds of Orissa took part in the Praja Mandal agitation in 1939, seeking more equitable agrarian and forest laws.

During the Civil Disobedience Movement, the tribal participation in the movement became more and more pronounced. Tribal protests took the form of forest satyagraha, particularly in some parts of Karnataka, Maharashtra and the Central provinces. Thousands of tribal villages defied the forest laws, at places led by the tribal leaders themselves. For instance, in Betul in the Central Provinces, Ganjan Korku, a Gond, emerged as a big local leader as a result of the forest satyagraha. The forest satyagraha was against iniquitous forest laws which had taken away grazing and other rights from tribals. At times, the movement even tended to take a violent form, despite its overall non-violent character.

Once the Congress came into power in the wake of the 1937 elections, the tribal participation in the national movement assumed larger dimensions, both through national movement as well as Praja Mandal movement. The tribal groups like Bhils, Gonds, Kharwars, Oraons, Mundas and Khonds had got activated due to the Gandhian movement. Thus, Khonds of Orissa participated in a big way in the Praja Mandal agitation in 1939. In 1938, a reformist movement among the Bhils was led by Gula Maharaj, who himself was a Bhil. In a number of Princely States like Nilgiri and Dhankanal of Orissa, the tribals broke the forest laws in an open defiance during the Quit India Movement. But more dramatic was the movement led by Luxman Naiko around Malkangin and Nawrangpur. He had openly declared the demise of the British rule. He led a no-tax campaign in August 1941. Luxman Naiko was subsequently arrested and was hanged to death in 1943.

What about the north-eastern regions where the tribal population was quite sizeable? Here there were lesser activities than among the tribals of the central India. As early as in 1931, a Kabul Naga revolt had taken place in the area bordering Manjpur and North Cachar, which was led by Guidillieu – a woman who had claimed divine magical power for herself. However, two more tribal movements from the north-east deserve special mention. One was led by Jadunag, who was essentially a reformer, taking Gandhiji as his main source of inspiration. He, as a Naga Leader, was active around the Chachar area. Gradually, his movement assumed a more pronounced political dimension. He led a movement against the forced labour and unjust laws and impressed upon his followers to stop paying taxes. His followers were convinced that the British Raj is coming to an end, ushering in a new Naga Raj. He was subsequently captured and hanged to death on 29 August 1931. His movement covered the period of 1929–32. Another notable tribal movement in the north-east took place during 1942-43, the period when the country was stirred by the Quit India Movement. Like Jadunag, Ratanmani also started his career as a socio-religious reformer and was taken as a guru by his people. He pleaded for the direct election of the tribal headmen and even tried to set up a pro-poor alternative government. Soon he was arrested by the British for his involvement in the Indian National Army and he died subsequently.

Apart from their participation in the national movement, there was another stream of the tribal movement. Some of the tribal groups started demanding political autonomy, and even their own Raj. For instance, when the process of constitutional reforms started gaining momentum in the wake of the First World War, in the eastern India a Naga Club was set up. The Naga Club did put forward a number of demands including the direct rule of the British on the Naga people before the Simon Commission. Similarly, during the last phase of the British Empire, a proposal for founding a 'Crown colony' for the Nagas was put forward, which was opposed by another local Naga group. However, the tribal movement for a separate state for the tribals in Chhota Nagpur region was better articulated and better organised. Here, Christianity also played a role, which had a wide network of institutions in the area. Besides, it has played a significant role in the spread of literacy among the tribals. Here, the tribal community was more concentrated in a distinct area, making their case for an autonomous state more relevant and meaningful. And that is why the Chhota Nagpur Unnati Samaj was set up in as early as 1920. Till 1938, their demand was confined to better employment and educational opportunities for tribals and reservation of seats in services as well as the legislative bodies. By 1937–38, the Adivasi Mahasabha took over the cause of the tribals under the dynamic leadership of Jaipal Singh. The Adivasi Mahasabha started demanding their own state, taking the adjoining areas of Bengal and Orissa. But in the 1946 election, the Mahasabha could not demonstrate its hold on the region. The Congress emerged out of it with flying colours. Subsequently, the movement took the form of a demand for a separate Jharkhand state which came into being only around the turn of the twentieth century.

There were several trends seen in the tribal movements ranging from armed rebellion to peaceful constructive programmes. The problems of the tribal groups came to constitute an important segment of our national agenda. The Gandhian movement, both constructive and combative, drew the tribal groups towards the mainstream of the national movement. However, due to several reasons, an Ambedkar-like leadership could not develop among the tribals. Perhaps they were too divided among several sub-tribal groups, making it more difficult for any leader to claim the allegiance of all sub-groups. Some of the other factors that prevented tribals from playing a more crucial role in the national movement were lack of education and their physical inaccessibility. Hence, they could not demand a more equitable share in the national cake. They continue to suffer and have been reduced to penury. They had hardly benefited much from the development process. They have in fact provided a strong social base for the Naxal Movement in post-independent India.

The toad beneath the harrows knows
Exactly where each tooth-point goes
The butterfly upon the road
Preaches contentment to the toad.

UNKNOWN POET

29 Role of Women in the Indian National Movement

Therefore, I charge you, restore to your women their ancient rights. . . . Educate your women and the nation will take care of itself; for it is true today as it was yesterday, and will be to the end of human life. The hand that rocks the cradle is the power that rules the world.

SAROJINI NAIDU

Indian women had fought shoulder to shoulder with their menfolk in the battle of Swaraj and earned a well-deserved recognition for their glorious role in the national movement. However, earlier they were being appreciated for their supportive rather than a direct participatory role: their role as family-provider when their men were behind bars, their courage in offering shelter and succour to many fugitive freedom fighters and above all, their role as being the main source of inspiration for their menfolk to suffer and sacrifice. Of late, however, there is a paradigm shift in appreciation of their role in the freedom struggle. Now, they are being recognised for their direct participation in the national struggle. In the heyday of our renaissance, it was underlined that in ancient India the women enjoyed a high status and had greatly contributed to the enrichment of our cultural heritage. The case of Maitrei from the Upanishadic age was often cited as a case in point. She crossed intellectual sword with her husband Rishi Yajnavalkya, which is recorded in *Brihadaranyak Upanishad*. She raised and debated over some of the most fundamental questions of the human situation, almost on equal intellectual footing with her husband. In course of time, the status of women in the Indian society was downgraded and *Manusmriti* even clubbed them with shudras and outcastes both of them being denied access to Vedic knowledge. In fact, the *Manusmriti* prescribed a social system in which a woman was to remain within the protective wings of her father, her husband and her son during different stages of her life. In the course of history the womenfolk were pushed within the four walls of their hearths and homes. An ideal woman was to be *asuryampashya* (one who has not seen the sun). Her role was confined to raising a family and looking after its needs, and in the process she had to remain as a living embodiment of sacrifice and sufferings. Some scholars are of the opinion that the Islamic occupation of India also played a role in the process of the decline of the status of the Indian woman. Though a number of other scholars contest this on the ground that in the Mughal courts, a number of women played a crucial role in the decision-making process. But purda (veil), undoubtedly, is an Islamic contribution which certainly reflected the inferior position of women in Indian society. Second, the system of child-marriage also became popular during the Islamic period as that was considered the only way to protect the young girls from the lecherous eyes of a marauding crowd.

Keeping aside this debate, the fact remains that by the time the British consolidated their position in India, the status of the Indian woman was no longer high. Child marriage, female infanticide, widow-burning, social ban on widow remarriage and widespread women's illiteracy were some of the social maladies afflicting the Indian society. That became an anathema as much to the colonial administration as to the modernising Indian elite. Consequently, both joined hands in the task of ameliorating the condition of the Indian women. As a result of joint efforts, female infanticides and widow burning was banned and widow-remarriage was legalised.

It also became clear that the spread of education among women was one of the preconditions for bettering their conditions. The socio-religious reforms movement going around the country in the nineteenth century were pioneers in the field. Keshav Chandra Sen of Brahmo Samaj, M G Ranade of Prarthana Samaj, Annie Besant of Theosophical Society and Swami Dayanand of Arya Samaj took up the cause of women's education in their respective areas. The colonial administration also started getting favourably disposed towards women's education. Consequently, some funds started flowing towards institutions engaged in spreading education among women. Thus, visible progress did occur in this area in the course of time.. However, the problem of the emancipation of women faced some roadblocks as well. Tilak's opposition to the Age of Consent Bill (1891), which tried to push the age for consummation of marriage for Hindu girls from 10 to 12 years, was a case in point.

Some citizens also earnestly took up the women's cause including their education. Iswar Chandra Vidyasagar, one of the pioneers of Bengal renaissance, deserves a special mention in this regard. He campaigned for widow remarriage, spread of education among women and launched a strong movement against polygamy. Besides, some of the prominent women like Pandita Ramabai from Maharashtra, Sister Subbalaksmi in Madras and Begum Rokeya Sakhawat Hossain and Tarabai Shinde from Berar occupied a pride of place for their pioneering work. Some of them tried to carve out a niche for women in the public life, though they were not successful in this regard. Theirs was a cry in wilderness, as the Indian women were still expected to play the role of ideal wives and ideal mothers.

In Maharashtra, Jyotiba Phule and his wife Savitri Bai also worked for women uplift. They found a direct linkage between caste hierarchy and low status of women in the Indian society. The Young Women's Christian Association (YWCA) was established in Calcutta as early as in 1875, which became a national body by 1896. Subsequently, Sarladevi Chaudhurani from Bengal founded *Bharat Stree Mahamandal* in 1904. Despite these bold but stray efforts, women and their problems were far away from occupying the central attention of early nationalists. Indian women were expected to play their role in their hearths and homes and very little public space was, as yet available to them.

In Bankim Chandra Chattopadhyaya's *Anandmath*, the mother-goddess became synonymous with mother India. Its famous song *Bande Mataram* became a source of inspiration for a number of nationalists. India, being pictured as a mother, became a very powerful imagery for a call to be given to her children to break off the chain of slavery and rescue her from her tormentors and enslavers. The new mother symbol of nationhood was effectively used during the struggle against partition of Bengal (1905), which also came to be known as the Swadeshi Movement. There was some actual mobilisation of women during the Swadeshi Movement and their role went much beyond, being the source of inspiration. They directly participated in the demonstrations and processions and were willing to face every eventuality. Not that that their role as being the source of inspiration for revolutionaries ceased, it did not even diminish. For instance, most of the prominent revolutionaries of Bengal like Satish Chandra Mukherjee, Jatindranath Mukherjee, Jibantara Haldhar and a host of others were inspired by their mothers and sisters to fight relentlessly against the British Empire. But there was a perceptible change in the role of women during the Swadeshi revolutionary movement. Now, some collective action also started taking place on the part of the women of Bengal. For instance, when Bhupendra Nath Dutta, brother of Vivekananda, was convicted for his revolutionary activities, a number of women visited his mother, Bhubaneshwari Devi and expressed their sympathy and solidarity with her. Some of the women also did not fear to extend shelter and succour to the fugitive revolutionaries. Some of the prominent women of Bengal who deserve special mention here are Bagalasundari Devi, Kailashbasini Devi and Jagat Tara Devi.

Subsequently, women started playing a still greater and more active role in the revolutionary movement of the country. They started directly participating in the revolutionary movement. They fought, absconded, were captured and were even imprisoned. For instance, Nanibala Devi not only sheltered fugitive revolutionaries in her house, but also absconded and was captured in Peshawar and was subsequently convicted. Similarly, Dakoribala Devi of Birbhum was awarded a two-year imprisonment for her revolutionary activities. Recalling limitations arising out of the conservative social milieu of their times, one is really impressed by their grit and determination. They defied not only colonial the political system but also their conservative social system. They really stood out in their acts of political and social defiance.

When the second phase of revolutionary movement started in around 1925–26, the role of women in the revolutionary movement became more prominent and pronounced. There were reasons for it. By that time, the spread of female education had started gaining momentum, raising their level of political consciousness. Besides, the advent of Mahatma Gandhi on the political scene, of the country and subsequent participation of women in the Non-Cooperation Movement also had a liberating impact on the women of India. This was also reflected in the emergence of a number of women's organisations in different parts of the country. Leelavati Nag founded Deepali Sangh in Dacca (1923) and Kalyani Das and others set up Chatri Sangh in Calcutta University in 1928. This was followed by a number of women's organisations even in the district towns. Not only that, woman revolutionaries were active both in Yugantar and Anushilan groups of Bengal. Both these groups recruited, trained and assigned specific roles to the women participants in the cause of revolution. For instance,

Kalpana Datta was directly involved in the Chittagong Armoury raids led by Surya Sen. But she was not a lone woman revolutionary. Two young women revolutionaries, Santi Ghose and Suniti Choudhury were involved in the murder of the District Magistrate of Comilla in 1931. This was followed by Bina Das's attempt to assassinate the Governor of Bengal in 1932. Preetilata Waddedar led an attack on the European Club in Chittagong in 1932, and in the process made supreme sacrifice. Stree Sangh, established by Leelawati Nag in Dacca, played a crucial role in the recruitment and training of women revolutionaries in Bengal.

There was a perceptible change in the role of women revolutionaries between the first phase (1905–18) and the second phase (1925–34) of the revolutionary movement of India. In the earlier phase, their role was supportive rather than participatory. But during subsequent phase of revolutionary movement, they directly participated as comrade-in-arms. In the process, they also played a liberating role in loosening the rigid, restrictive and stratified social system.

Women's Participation in India's Freedom Struggle During Gandhian Era (1920–1947)

The role of the Indian women in the freedom movement entered yet another decisive phase with the advent of Gandhiji on the Indian political scene. Gandhiji was no greenhorn political activist even in the field of women's mobilisation: he had a lot of field experience from his South African days. In 1913, in South Africa he had experimented with women's participation in demonstrations on a massive scale, and since then he was convinced of their potential in pursuing a non-violent struggle. He put the domestic and public role of women in continuum rather than in a dichotomous relationship. He picked up Sita, Damyanti and Draupadi as role models for the Indian women and underlined the fact that all of them combined and reconciled in their personality their domestic and public role. Gandhiji was fully convinced that women had to play a big role in the battle for Swaraj. What others considered their weakness – their passivity, their immense capacity for suffering and sacrifice, he took it as their strength as it made them ideal satyagrahis. But initially he encouraged them to take up a number of constructive programmes – Khadi, swadeshi, service to the downtrodden, etc. But launching of the Non-Cooperation Movement had a great liberating impact for Indian women. They were no longer expected to live within the confines of their house. They came out, many of them got rid of purda, worked beside men without much social embarrassment. For instance, Lady Amman, the mother of the Ali brothers, addressed several meetings in the course of the Khilafat Non-Cooperation Movement by removing her veil. Not only that, in Bombay in the course of the boycott of the Prince of Wales' visit in November 1921, women demonstrators played a leading role. In Calcutta, Basanti Devi, wife of C R Das, came out on the Calcutta streets and courted arrest. In Prayag Mahila Samiti of UP, Rameshwari Nehru was an active member of the organisation since its inception in 1909. She was editing *Stree Darpan*, a magazine committed to the women's cause. Subsequently, during Non-cooperation days, few other women of the Nehru family like Uma Nehru and Vijayalakshmi Pandit also joined the struggle.

In south India, apart from Annie Besant, Margaret Cousins and Muthu Lakshmi a number of other women like Durgabai, better known as Durgabai Deshmukh, and Duvvuri Subbamma also played a leading role in the Gandhian movements. Durgabai took over the leadership when T Prakasham was arrested during the salt satyagraha. On the eve of independence, Durgabai became a member of the Constituent Assembly and subsequently played a bigger role at the national level. She had also founded Andhra Mahila Sabha and a number of other institutions to serve the women's cause. From Bihar Prabhavati Devi, wife of Jayaprakash Narayan, devoted her life to Gandhian work and a number of other women like Manorama Devi wife of Pandit Punyadeo Sharma, Bhagwati Devi, sister of Dr Rajendra Prasad, Vindyavasini Devi, Kamakhya Devi and hundreds of other women played a prominent role in the freedom struggle.

Gradually the number of women participants in the Indian struggle swelled and started playing a more diversified and militant role. By the time the Civil Disobedience Movement was launched, women activists were already playing a bigger and more militant role. In the course of Gandhiji's Dandi March, thousands of women thronged him on the way, expressing their solidarity with his cause and displaying a rare determination to throw all that they had in the cause of national struggle. In the course of the movement, thousands of women discarded purda. They broke salt laws, picketed liquor vends and foreign goods shops and joined prabhat pheries. A number of women courted arrest and went to jail. After the arrest of Gandhiji, Sarojini Naidu led the raid on Dharasana Salt Depot, which was a historic demonstration of the power of non-violent satyagraha. When the Congress came to power in the wake of the 1937 elections, a number of women changed their role from law-breakers to law-makers. Some of them became legislators, councillors, and members of district and local boards. During the Quit India Movement a large number of women participated in the movement and some of them led the movement, even from the front. For instance, Sucheta Kripalani was the moving spirit behind non-violent mass struggle, whereas Aruna Asaf Ali, a prominent leader of the Congress Socialist Party, played an equally important role in organising an underground movement.

Women's participation was also quite pronounced in the communist movement. A number of young girls were also active in the All India Students Federation – a youth front organisation of the Communist Party of India. Under the banner of the Communist Party, a Tebhaga Movement was launched in 1946 with the major demand that tenants would give only one-third produce to the land-owners and not half as was the prevailing practice. A number of women, particularly drawn from the dalit and tribal group were in the forefront of the struggle and some of them even made supreme sacrifices. Similarly, in the Telangana movement, led by the Communist Party, a number of women activists participated with great verve and enthusiasm.

But more spectacular was the role of women participants in the Indian National Army led by Subhas Chandra Bose. When he re-organised the Indian National Army in South-East Asia, women played a crucial role in raising the funds required for the Army. They handed over their savings, including their own ornaments, for supporting the armed struggle for the liberation of India. Putting his immense faith in the capacity of the Indian women for sacrifice, he organised a women's Regiment called Rani Jhansi Regiment – in the honour of the legendary figure from 1857 rebellion. It was led by a lady Laxmi Swaminathan. A large number of women joined the regiment, went through rigorous training and participated in actual fighting. They were drawn from different sections of our society. What was more, they refused to be satisfied with non-combatant role and insisted upon taking part in the actual fighting. On their persistent demand, they participated in the Imphal campaign of 1945 and put up quite an impressive record. In the course of time, there was an unprecedented expansion of the role of women in our national struggle. Starting with a supportive role, they covered a lot of ground by actual participation in armed struggles.

To sum up, Indian women had a glorious role in our freedom struggle. They started with a passive and non-active supportive role, but ended as actual comrades even in armed struggles. But in terms of number and sustained work, their role in the Gandhian movement was most impressive. A large number of women left the cosy corners of their homes and participated in the national struggle by putting all that they had at the altar of the national movement. Kasturba Gandhi, Manu Behan Patel, Raj Kumari Amrit Kaur, Basanti Devi, Prabhawati Devi, Sarojini Naidu, Durgabai Deshmukh, Kamla Nehru, Vijayalakshmi Pandit, and Swarup Rani, are well known names as they led the national movement from the front. But thousands of other women, who suffered and sacrificed for the sake of freedom of the country remained unknown and unsung.

Women's Organisations

No study of the women's participation in our freedom struggle would be complete without referring to their attempt to build their own organisations. In this respect, Sarla Devi Chaudhurani played a pioneering role as she set up the *Bharat Stree Mahamandal* as early as 1904. Subsequently, the Women's Indian Association was set up by Margaret Cousins and Annie Besant in Madras in 1917. During those days, women's organisations were primarily struggling for getting female franchise along with universal franchise. In 1917, Sarojini Naidu led a delegation to impress upon the Constitutional Reforms Committee the need for granting of adult franchise. Soon, in the wake of the 1919 Act, a number of provincial legislatures granted the right to vote for women, though the entire system of franchise was still limited. In 1925, at the initiative of Lady Tata, the National Council for Women, as a national chapter of the International Council for Women was set up. This was soon followed by the formation of the All India Women's Conference in 1927. Margaret Cousins was the prime mover behind this new organisation. Initially, this new organisation was primarily committed to women's education. But in the subsequent years, it was drawn to the national movement and got involved in issues like women's franchise and other rights of women including laws relating to labour and marriage. In Bengal, a number of women's organisations like Bangiya Nari Samaj, Bengali Women's Education League and All Bengal Women's Union started raising all kinds of issues related to women, including the demand for legal steps against trafficking of women. Most of these organisations sought and received support both from the national leaders as well as the colonial administration. As a result of their initiative, the women's franchise was granted by the provincial legislatures during the 1920s – an issue which had been left unsettled by the Act of 1919. When there was a general increase in the quantum of franchise, women were also its beneficiaries.

In the 1937 election, a number of women participated not only as voters but also as contestants. Apart from these developments on the political front, even on the social front, a number of laws, including the Sharda Act of 1929, were passed to provide relief to Indian women. It is a different matter that these laws failed to drastically change the situation on the ground in favour of women. The classic example was that of the Sharda Act which failed to make a substantial dent in the number of child-marriages, in the absence of popular support. However, the efforts of these women's organisation had an impact on the course of the national movement. The Karachi Congress demand for fundamental rights also featured a demand for universal franchise, including women's franchise. The All India Women's Conference even sent a women's delegation comprising Radhabai Subrayam and Begum Shah to the First Round Table Conference to represent and plead for the women's cause. This was followed up by a committee led by Sarojini Naidu to the Second Round Table Conference, which demanded universal franchise, including women's franchise. In Southern India, the Theosophical Society led by Annie Besant had earlier played a crucial role in raising the level of women's political consciousness and spreading a wave of new awareness among them. *Stree Dharma*, the journal run by the Women's Indian Association (WIA) led by Margaret Cousins, also played a prominent role in espousing the women's cause. One of the leading lights of the Women's Indian Association, Dr S. Muthu Lakshmi, as the first woman member of the Madras Legislative Council, played a leading role in favour of the women's cause. When Ramaswamy Naicker, better known as EVR, started his self-respect movement around 1925–26, he put the issue of women's rights high on his radical agenda.

To sum up, considering the kind of social system prevailing during the freedom struggle, the role played by women participants in the national movement appears quite creditable. As outlined above, whether it was revolutionary movement or the Gandhian movement, the women of India had always made their presence felt. They did not even hesitate to take up guns and fight on the action-fronts when the situation so demanded. Apart from this, they also promoted the cause of the national movement by quietly suffering when their menfolk were in jail or they were running as fugitive revolutionaries. As sister and mother, and even as comrades, they remained a constant source of inspiration to their men who were fighting for Indian independence.

One big question raised by many scholars is that all these women's organisations never succeeded in putting the issue of women's emancipation on the centre-stage of the national movement. Besides, they could not succeed in getting their share in the political power. As Sarala Devi Chaudhurani once put it that men prefer women as 'the lawbreakers but and not as lawmakers'. There is some truth in Sarala's lament as even the issue of 33 per cent reservation for women in the legislative bodies is still hanging in the air. Besides, it is also a reflection on our national movement that in the wake of the partition of the country, women became its worst victims: thousands of them were raped, maimed and mutilated. All this speaks for a serious flaw in our male-dominated society.

However, this should not be taken as a reflection on the courageous role played by women participants and their organisations in our national movement. If the issue of women's emancipation could not be put on the centre-stage of our national agenda, it was not because of the lack of effort on the part of women participants. Besides, it is also unfair to judge their contributions in the light of the issues which became prominent only a few decades back. The issues like relative role of patriarchy and matriarchy are being raised only recently and should not be transported to the age when they did not exist. In fact, for that generation of women freedom fighters, the issues of national liberation and women's liberation were in continuum rather than in a dichotomous relationship. Besides, the process through which the women freedom fighters went through was in itself a liberating experience for them. Thus, while contributing to the process of the national liberation, they also contributed to their own liberation. Some of them not only played a critical role in the freedom struggle but also an equally important role in the nation-building process. The emergence of Indira Gandhi, Sucheta Kripalani, Sarojini Naidu, and Vijayalakshmi Pandit were not mere historical accidents. They were the by-products of a long process of struggle which the Indian women had engaged in the course of our national struggle. In brief, Indian women did play a role in the course of our national struggle, which can make any nation proud. It is a different matter that a lot remains to be done for them including a fair share to them in the political process of the country.

What is she to me, not a wife nor a mistress
nor any daughter of mine,
why then, ah, why does her sorrowful image,
Leaves me till morning to pine.

UNKNOWN POET

30 The Backward Classes, the Depressed Classes Movement and the Indian Freedom Struggle

The touchable and the untouchable cannot be held together by law, certainly not by any electoral law substituting joint electorate for separate electorate. The only thing that can hold them together is love. The salvation of the untouchables will come only when the caste Hindu is made to think, and is forced to feel that he must alter his ways. I want a revolution in the mentality of the caste Hindus'.

B R AMBEDKAR

The *varna* system has been one of the unique features of the Indian social structure. In plain language, the system is marked by the fourfold division of the society comprising Brahmins, Kshatriyas, Vaishyas and Shudras, the hierarchy being in descending order with Brahmins on the top and Shudras at the bottom and Kshatriya and Vaishya in the middle. The system was marked by hierarchy and holism. Traditionally, there has been close linkage between the *varna* and professions – Brahmins looking after the intellectual and spiritual needs of the society; Kshatriyas its defence, administrative and proctorial needs, Vaishyas engaged in the task of wealth creation and other production-related works and Shudras performing the physical tasks of the society. This is usually supported by a passage of the Purush-Shukta of the *Rig Veda* which mentions that Brahmins came from the mouth of Brahma, Kshatriya from his arms, Vaishyas from the thighs and the Shudras from his feet. In the eighteenth chapter of the *Bhagvad Gita*, Lord Krishna gave a detailed description of the nature of the tasks assigned to each *varna.* Many scholars and social reformers, including Mahatma Gandhi, support the *varna* system on the ground that one's varna was not based on one's birth, but on one's innate tendencies and proclivities. In other words, in its original pristine form the *varna* system was not by *Janmana* (not by birth) but was by *Karmana* (by profession). Besides, it was not hierarchical and the question of one being high and other being low did not arise. Not only that, the system had a very stabilising impact on society as everyone got a sense of fulfilment by pursuing a particular profession based on his innate qualities and proclivities.

When and how the system degenerated into innumerable castes and sub-castes is again a matter of debate among scholars. Perhaps in the course of historical developments, the *varna* system degenerated into the caste system through the slow process of social stratification. Be as it may, the new system of birth-based caste was marked both by hierarchy and pollution. It did not remain confined to the fourfold division of the society, but degenerated into hundreds of divisions, each claiming to be higher in hierarchy than the other, and even the system of pollution was followed by the lower caste against each other. Only the top position of the Brahmin remained intact. There are many scholars who believe that even when the system degenerated into the castes, initially it was not marked by total atrophy: there was enough scope for upward social mobility by migrations, which provided an opportunity to a group of people to upgrade their ritual ranking by moving to a new territory and in a new environment. The Rajput caste is a case in point. Many upwardly mobile castes integrated themselves and swelled the Rajput population. There is also a consensus among the scholars that Islam, despite its message of universal brotherhood, did not contribute to the loosening and liberalising of the caste system. Ironically, it contributed to a greater regimentation and stratification of the caste system, as the traditional Indian society was put on the defensive and the only way it could protect itself was by making it more inward-looking and regimented.

The coming of the British to India did not bring about any marked change in the traditional social order. Ideally, it did open the gate for everybody for its newly available power positions. However, for historical reasons, the bulk of the new positions that were made available in the field of law, civil services and in the army were grabbed by the upper castes, particularly the Brahmins who had taken to the new system of English education with enthusiasm and alacrity. Consequently, the people located at the lower rung of the society were left behind, both in terms of education and employment. Thus, the colonial rule, in a way, further strengthened the traditional social system. Some of the British ethnographers even injected a racial angle by saying that 'fair-skinned and sharp-featured' sections of the Indian society had the Aryan background whereas 'dark-skinned and crude-featured' sections belonged to the original inhabitants of the country. Even the theory of Aryan invasion of and subsequent destruction of pre-Aryan civilisation of Mohenjo-Daro and Harappa was a part of the same thinking. This gave a further boost to the game of identities. It was further strengthened by a new system of enumeration of caste, their location in the social hierarchy and ritual ranking in the 1871 census reports. The system continued till the 1931 census.

The system of caste enumeration with social ranking in the census reports led to an emergence of a number of caste associations, each competing and clamouring for a higher ritual ranking. Strangely enough, the colonial state, though claiming to be secular and even providing equal opportunities both at group and individual levels, unwittingly, contributed towards greater social atrophy and stratification. But in another way, the principle of equal opportunity, transcending the traditional caste hierarchy and de-linking of one's caste and profession, had a limited positive result as well. It brought the entire discourse from the sacred to the secular field. As a result, these caste associations also started raising secular issues and started playing a modernising role both in intra- as well as inter-caste discourses. Subsequently, the non-Brahmin section of the Indian society soon became conscious of its inability to take full advantage of the new opportunities offered by the colonial state, both in the field of education and employment. Consequently, a clamour for affirmative action started being made, though it lacked the verve and vehemence of the present era. Some of the Princely States were first to pick up the gauntlet: States like Mysore and Kolhapur introduced the system of reservation in the services for the non-Brahmin castes. In the course of time, the colonial state also became conscious of the social and educational handicaps faced by the depressed classes. Certain steps were taken to make special grants available for the education of the depressed classes.

Meanwhile, Maharashtra and south India soon witnessed a new kind of movement which sought to challenge the very basis of the existing social order. In the Maharashtra region, it was Jyotiba Phule who challenged the very basis of the *varna* system and its domination by the Brahmins. For him the real problem of the non-Brahmin section of the society arose from Brahminic domination in all walks of life.

He sought to unite all non-Brahmin sections including dalits. To pursue his ideas, he set up the *Satya Shodhak Samaj* (Society of Truth-seekers) in 1873. Towards the end of his life, Phule concentrated more on the mobilisation of his own 'Kunbi' caste and working for giving the Marathas a Kshatriya identity.

This led to the alienation of the Dalit in Maharashtra from the non-Brahmin movement. Soon the non-Brahmin movement developed cracks and started displaying two divergent tendencies. The radical section led by *Satya Shodhak Samaj* persisted in pursuing its radical programmes in terms of bi-polarity between the Bahujan Samaj on the one hand and Shethji-Bhatji (Bania and Brahmin) on the other and also insisted that their interests are mutually exclusive. Another part of the non-Brahmin movement comprising a rich section among the non-Brahmins used their collectively-mobilised strength to move closer to the British. In the wake of the Act of 1919, which had provided new political opportunities to the Indian political elite, they even organised a new political party called the Non-Brahmin Association which pledged loyalty to the British. The Non-Brahmin Association joined hands with the leaders of the Liberal Federation for the implementation of the provisions of the Act of 1919.

However, once Gandhiji took over the leadership of the Indian National Congress, the Non-Brahmin Association started moving closer to the Maharashtra Congress. The Congress, led by Gandhiji identified itself with the peasants in a big way, which made a tremendous impact on the peasant masses, including the Maratha peasantry. Besides, a new leadership in the Congress led by N V Gadgil emerged, which was also more sympathetic to the non-Brahmin cause. By 1938 N V Gadgil and Keshavrav Jedhe, a leader of the Non-Brahmin Association, joined hands and in the process the Non-Brahmin Association merged with the Congress which greatly broadened the base of the national movement.

In the Madras region, the issues leading to the genesis of the non-Brahmin movement were slightly different, though the Brahmin domination remained the common issue. In the beginning, it was the Vellalas who constituted the social base for the non-Brahmin movement. The main grouse of the Vellala elite was the contempt with which the Brahmins of the Tamil region looked at the Tamil language. This not only angered the Vellala elite, but also prompted them to make a deliberate display of their Dravidian identity towards the end of the nineteenth century. Indeed, prior to that, some of the Christian missionaries had also underlined Dravidian identity and had even asserted that, of all the languages in India, Tamil alone owes nothing to Sanskrit and even does not belong to the same family. Not only that, they had also argued that the caste system was alien to Dravidian culture and hence Vellalas and other non-Brahmins could not be put in the category of the Shudras. In the process, anti-Brahmanism, anti-Aryanism and anti-North became the main mobilising slogan for the common non-Brahmin masses. On the positive side, the focus was on respect for Dravidian identity and Tamil language.

The non-Brahmin movement in that part of the country got a new forum when in 1916, the Justice Party was set up by a group of Tamil activists. A non-Brahmin manifesto was also issued, underlining the major thrust of the non-Brahmin movement. The Justice Party launched a virulent and relentless attack on the Congress Party, describing it as the party of Brahmins. It demanded separate communal representation for the non-Brahmins in the Madras Legislative Council, on the pattern of the Muslims. The Justice Party's opposition to the Congress and its loyalist base helped it, as separate representation for non-Brahmins was conceded under the Montagu–Chelmsford Reform of 1919. And non-Brahmins got 28 reserved seats in the Madras Legislative Council under the Act. Not only that, the Justice Party vehemently opposed the Non-Cooperation Movement launched by the Congress, including its call for boycott of the Council. The Justice Party contested the 1920 election for the Madras Council; won 63 out of 93 seats and even formed the government under the dyarchy system. But very soon the Justice Party started losing its sheen because the power game and not the reformist agenda, became its motive force. Perhaps, one reason for its decline was that from its very inception it was organised on a negative programme of anti-Brahminism. Brahmins became the main enemy symbol for the mobilisation of non-Brahmins under the banner of the Justice Party. In fact, it was not entirely the poor and the downtrodden that provided the social base of the Justice Party: the bulk of its support base was constituted by the richer sections of the society like, Vellalas of the Tamil region, Reddis, Kapus and Kammas of Telugu areas, and Nairs of Malabar. It also had its roots in some of the trading communities like Beris-Chetis, Balija, and Naidus which were scattered all over the south region. Soon the power game had better hold on the Justice Party and the concern for the poor and the deprived was pushed to the background. Consequently, the depressed classes got alienated from the Justice Party, prompting one of their prominent leaders, M C Rajah, to leave the Party. All this weakened the Justice Party and it was no surprise when it got a crushing defeat at the hands of the Swaraj Party in the 1926 election. That put the Justice Party in disarray and both in the 1937 and 1946 elections, the Congress Party won in Madras, hands down.

Another development which contributed to the decline of the Justice Party was the emergence of a new and more dynamic movement in the Tamil region under the leadership of E V Ramaswamy Naicker, also called Periyar. The new movement led by Periyar came to be known as the 'Self-Respect Movement'. E V Ramaswamy had participated in the Non-Cooperation Movement as a Congressman. But he left the Congress in 1925, alleging that the Congress Party had little political space for the non-Brahmins. He launched a cultural movement, which had both its negative and positive programmes. On the negative side, his movement was anti-north, anti-Brahmin, anti-Hindi and anti-Aryan. For him all these were nothing but the different aspects of the ploy used by the Brahmins to subjugate the Shudras and the women. On the positive side, he wanted the non-Brahmins to take pride in the Tamil language and Dravid culture. He launched a virulent attack on Brahmins as a caste and Sanskrit as a language, both of which, according to him, were out to subjugate the Adi-Dravid. He further argued that self respect was a precursor to self-rule. Since the self-respect movement shared the common social base of the Justice Party, the latter lost some of its ground to it, leading to the latter's decline and its final demise. In subsequent years, Ramaswamy Naicker adopted a much more virulent attitude towards Brahmins and other symbols of Aryan culture. He called upon his followers to burn *Manusmriti*, to boycott Brahmin priests for marriage and other religious ceremonies, and even launched a movement for forcible temple entries. Not satisfied with that, he also led anti-Hindi, anti-North agitations. He even started talking in terms of a separate state of 'Dravidnadu' and took hold of the Justice Party in 1940s and rechristened it as Dravid Kazhagam (DK), which was committed to securing a separate non-Brahmin state of Dravidnadu. However, this demand was dropped by the new political parties of DMK and AIDMK which came into being after a split in the DK.

The Depressed Classes Movement

The depressed classes were another segment of the Hindu society who organised themselves and raised their voices against the caste system. In fact, the Dalits, as they subsequently came to be known, had been the worst victims of the *varna* system for millenia. The caste system was challenged both by Buddha and Mahavir, who revolted against it by pointing out its pernicious impact. But Buddhism and Jainism lost their sheen after Hinduism bounced back through the singular effort of Adi-Sankaracharya. The *varna* system again had its heyday. In medieval India, the Bhakti Movement again picked up the gauntlet against the caste system and did make some impact. But even the Bhakti poets failed to uproot it lock, stock and barrel, though people like Guru Nanak Dev, Kabir, Ravidas, and others did make some impact in certain areas. Subsequently, Christian Missionaries tried to intervene and even worked for their religious conversion to Christianity. Attempts were also made to extend special help to educate the children of the depressed classes. Not only that, even some of the socio-religious reform movements of the nineteenth century also joined the battle against the caste system. Subsequent years saw the birth of the socio-economic reform movements among the Dalits. Some of these movements were: Shri Narayan Dharam Paripalana Yogam among the Ezhavas of Kerala, Adi Dharam Movement among the *Chamars* of Punjab, *Adi* Movement among the *Chamars* of UP, Satnam Panth among the *Chamars* of Chattishgarh and Balahari Movement among the Hadis of Bengal. All these movements tried to underline the dignity of the Dalits and challenged the Chaturvarana system by refusing to accept their low position under it. But all these efforts were within the confines of the religious domain.

So far as the secular field was concerned, the colonial state, except taking some half-hearted measures in the field of education, hardly took any radical measures to improve their conditions. Even the Indian National Congress did not take up their issue in any significant way till Mahatma Gandhi appeared on the political scene of India, towards the second decade of the twentieth century. In the course of the Non-Cooperation Movement, he made it clear that total elimination of the curse of untouchability would be a necessary precondition for the attainment of Swaraj. He followed it up by including it in the agenda of his constructive programmes.

Among the Dalits, the first major move was made when a conference of All India Depressed Classes (All Bhartiya Bahiskrit Parishad) was held at Nagpur in 1920, presided over by the Raja of Kolhapur. This was a very modest attempt and the conference primarily ended by taking stock of the situation for the depressed classes. The next move was much more substantive, when, in 1926, the All India

Dr B R Ambedkar

Depressed Classes Leaders Conference was held at Nagpur. This resulted in the formation of the All India Depressed Classes Association with M C Rajah of Madras as its first elected President. Dr B R Ambedkar was elected as its Vice-President, though in absentia. Subsequently, he resigned from the conference, and in 1930, he set up a separate organisation called the All India Depressed Classes Congress. During the conference, Ambedkar made a frontal attack on the Congress Party, though he had much less harsh things to say on the British rule. Prior to that, Ambedkar had come into prominence when he burnt a copy of *Manusmriti* in 1927 on the ground that it had given a religious sanctity to the inhuman system of untouchability. During the same period he had created a stir by launching a movement at Mahad against the denial of the right to Dalits to drink water from the village pond reserved for the upper-castes. It is also interesting to note that B R Ambedkar refused to accept the Congress programme for the boycott of the Simon Commission and even made a presentation before it. He demanded a separate electorate for the Dalits in view of the absence of the adult and universal franchise. He again reiterated his position on the separate electorate during the First Round Table Conference. Soon after that, the All India Depressed Classes Leaders Conference endorsed his position on the separate electorate during its meeting in Bombay on 19 May 1931. Armed with this support, Ambedkar took a very strong stand on the issue of a separate electorate during the Second Round Table Conference and even had a major confrontation with Mahatma Gandhi during the same conference.

However, there was no unanimity even among the top Dalit leaders, as in February 1932, M C Rajah-led All India Depressed Classes Association had favoured joint electorate and even condemned Ambedkar's demand for a separate electorate. In fact, M C Rajah had signed an agreement with Dr B S Munje, the President of All India Hindu Mahasabha, supporting a joint electorate with the Hindus in lieu of the reservation of seats for Dalits in proportion to their population. When the Communal Award, making provision of separate electorate for the Dalits, was declared in August 1932, Mahatma Gandhi went on a fast unto death. He argued that it would create a permanent breach in the Hindu society and would do more harm to the Dalits than the caste Hindus. With the intervention of a number of Indian leaders, Ambedkar was persuaded to sign the Poona Pact, which favoured the joint electorate and made provisions for reservation of seats for the Dalits. Subsequently, Mahatma Gandhi set up the Harijan Sevak Sangh and launched his biggest campaign against the evil of untouchability. He devised a number of measures to ameliorate their conditions. He travelled extensively throughout the country to mobilise men and material for the Harijan cause. The Indian National Congress soon set up, for the first time, its own Dalit organisation, namely, the All Indian Depressed Classes League in March 1935 with Jagjivan Ram as its President. Ambedkar tried to widen the net for the toiling masses and the poor, transcending castelines by setting up the Labour Party in 1936. But during the 1937 elections, except in Bombay, it failed to cross the rubicon. The Congress Party, on the other hand, had an impressive performance by winning 73 out of 151 reserved seats. Ambedkar resented the Congress leadership and reverted to his old politics, when in July 1942, he set up a new Dalit organisation, called the All India Scheduled Caste Federation in Nagpur, which even M C Rajah joined. He did not support the Quit India Movement and in fact, in 1942 he had joined the Viceroy's Executive Council as a labour member. Through the Scheduled Caste Federation, Ambedkar tried to project his ideas that Dalits were distinct and separate from the Hindus. But the federation failed to become a mass movement. During the 1946 elections, the Federation was wiped out as it could win only 2 of the 151 reserved seats. On the other hand, the Congress Party made a spectacular show in the same election. And the Cabinet Mission accepted the Congress Party's claim of rightfully representing the Dalits. Ambedkar did try to launch an agitation but soon it petered out. However, the Congress soon pacified him by offering him the chairmanship of the Drafting Committee of the Constituent Assembly, the task he performed with great initiative and brilliance.

We find that like other deprived groups, backward classes and the Dalits had their problems with the mainstream national movement, led by the Congress Party. They looked upon it as being dominated by the upper castes. They tried to raise their problems and pressed the national movement to concede and integrate some of their demands in the national agenda. In the process, they moved closer to the British establishment: the Justice Party and the Ambedkar-led Scheduled Caste Federation were two cases in point. But their leaders were aware of the fact that if they moved too close to the British, they would be totally isolated from the mainstream of the national movement. But they were also wary of extending unconditional support to the national movement as, in that case, they could not have raised some of the basic issues for the betterment of their groups. And they could even have lost their voice and identity. They had to do a tight-rope walk without appearing to tilt too much on either side.

However, with all their limitations, by organising the poor and the socially disadvantaged groups and by raising a voice on their behalf, they did make an impact on the national movement which, in its turn, empathised with them and ultimately integrated some of their demands in the national agenda. The non-Brahmin and Dalit movements did make a significant contribution in radicalising the national movement.

It would not be unfair to the leaders of these movements also, to record that in their balancing acts between the pulls of the national movement and the British imperialism, they also at times played a divisive role in the national movement. In fact, they did give a handle to the British rulers to pinpoint the divided and fractured nature of the Indian National Movement. If at times they appeared as willing partners in the British game of 'divide and rule', they could not have helped it.

> *My ambition is to represent and identify myself with, as far as possible the lowest strata of the 'untouchables', namely, the invisible and the 'unapproachable' whom I have always before my mind's eye wherever I go, for they have indeed drunk deep from the poisoned cup.*
>
> MAHATMA GANDHI

31 Princely India and the Freedom Movement

And what, I asked, is your plan for the princes?
'We shall wipe them out' explained one with conviction.

KATHERINE MAYO

In the process of occupation by the British, the Indian subcontinent came to be divided into two parts: British India and Princely India. British India covered that part of India which came to be directly controlled and governed, initially by the East India Company and subsequently by the Crown. Princely India, on the other hand, was ruled by the native princes, though it also remained under the control of the paramount power of the British. Indeed, the relationship between each Princely State and the British was governed by a particular treaty and/or an agreement between the two. However, the overall system was characterised by the Indian state being under the British Paramountcy. In plain language, it meant that a princely state, though enjoying internal autonomy, was under overall control of the British so far as its external relation was concerned. As the system developed in the course of time, the British obligations in respect of a Princely State evolved around extending protection from external aggression and internal disorder and settling the cases of disputed succession. The Princely States in turn, were bound, not to establish any relation with any other external power and also to extend military help, if required by the British.

It is interesting to note that it was not always the British inability to take over a particular state which made it to be left alone. In fact, it was the overall British colonial interests which governed their policy in this regard. Thus, some of the Princely States which the British could have easily taken over, were left untouched; because they either did not have enough arable land to yield substantial revenue through crops or were located in a remote corner or in a hostile terrain.

It also needs to be underlined that the British relationship with the states did not remain static, rather it kept on evolving in the course of history. In the early days of the East India Company, British agents were appointed at the courts of different Indian states to look after the British commercial interests. During 1764–98, viz., from the days of the Battle of Buxar to the coming of Lord Wellesley – the roles of the British Residents posted in the states like Awadh, Bengal and Hyderabad, were limited. In the second phase, i.e. from 1798–1840, the relationship changed and the British Residents started playing a more active and dominant role in the affairs of the states. From 1840–57 there was yet another paradigm shift in the British policy towards the Indian states; using the Doctrine of Lapse, a crude attempt was made to annex new territories, which led to a takeover of a number of states like Jhansi, Nagpur, Satara and some of the states of Punjab. In the post-1857 rebellion period, the British realised that their hyperactive interventionist policy had significantly contributed to the 1857 rebellion. When the Crown took over India from the East India Company, a firm commitment was made to 'respect right, dignity and honour of the Princely India'. In practical terms, the policy change was reflected in the British acceptance of the adopted heirs in respect of a number of Indian states. But the British always kept the sword of Damocles, i.e. the issue of 'gross misrule' hanging over the heads of the non-pliant Princely States. The Gaikwad of Baroda was deposed in 1875 on that very ground of gross misrule. Similarly, in 1902 the Nizam of Hyderabad was forced by Lord Curzon to sign a fresh treaty which was more favourable to the British. During this period the British hardly faced any real challenge or threat from Princely India.

Princely India was also of enormous importance from the viewpoint of Indian nationalism. It constituted 562 states, covering two-fifth of the Indian territory and comprising roughly 25 per cent of the Indian populace. In terms of size of the territory and the number of people involved, it was too significant to be ignored by the Indian nationalists. Yet, it is surprising that the early nationalists did not involve themselves in the affairs of the Princely States. Perhaps they did not want to open a new front till they had consolidated their position in respect of the British India. One can rightly surmise that the struggle for civil and political liberty of India could not but make some impact on the people living within the territory of Princely India. More so when there was so much cultural, historical and linguistic unity among the people of the two halves. Besides, there were no travel restrictions and, hence, a lot of interaction was always taking place among the people of both the halves. There was a gradual rise in political consciousness of the people of Princely India, igniting in them a desire for better governance and a more libertarian system.

It was at the Nagpur session in 1920, that the Indian National Congress passed a resolution calling upon the Indian Princes to grant responsible government in their respective states. The Congress, while welcoming the people from Princely India as its members, made it clear that they could not start political work in their respective states in the name of the Congress. However, they had the freedom to start political work either in their own individual capacity or on behalf of some local organisation. Earlier, some of the fugitive revolutionaries, who had sought clandestine shelter in some of the states, had already created a wave of political consciousness among the people of some of the states: even some of the Indian Princes did not remain unaffected. For example, the Prince of Nabha, a state in Punjab, had risked his position while extending support to the Akalis in 1920s, when they were struggling to get control of the Gurudwaras. In spite of the Indian National Congress being quite cautious in 1920 in respect of Princely India, the Khilafat Non-Cooperation Movements were too people-centric to leave the people of the States unaffected. During and in the wake of the Non-Cooperation Movement, a number of local organisations called Praja Mandals came into being in the states like Baroda, Jamnagar and Indore. The process got further consolidated when, in 1927, the All India States People's Conference was founded in Bombay as its headquarters. Balwant Rai Mehta, Maniklal Kothari and G R Abhyankar were the prime movers behind this new organisation.

It is also interesting to note that the princes were not caught totally unaware. During the First World War the princes had contributed their mite to the British war effort by their generous financial contribution as well as by extending their help to the British drive for the army recruitment in their respective states. At the end of the War, the princes wanted the British to ensure: (a) non-interference from the political department and (b) taking up of some concrete measures to insulate their states from the ongoing political stir in British India. They also demanded a greater opportunity for being consulted by the British. Under the Act of 1919, a chamber of princes comprising 120 members was provided for as a consultative body between the Raj and the Princes. Despite some initial teething troubles, the chamber of the princes was inaugurated in February 1921. This was virtually a landmark in the Raj–Princes relationship, as it provided a new forum for wider consultation, backed by the collective wisdom of the princes. Thus, the British and the Princes joined hands to build up a counterveiling force to the Congress. Besides, an attempt was being made to insulate Princely India from the spillover of the ongoing political stir in British India in the course of the Khilafat–Non-Cooperation Movement. But the political currents arising out of Khilafat–Non-Cooperation Movement were too strong to be tamed and dammed so easily. Not only did Praja Mandals emerge in a number of states, but the entire process was in fact consolidated when in 1927, the All India States People's Conference was founded as a culminating point for the Praja Mandal movement. Even before the formation of the All India States People's Conference in 1927, the impact of the Non-Cooperation Movement was visible through the people's movement in Bijonia and Sirohi in Rajsthan, which had emerged against the oppressive jagirdari system. These movements had drawn their inspiration from Gandhiji's life and work.

In any case, the formation of All India States People's Conference (AISPC) marked a decisive phase in the life of popular struggle going on in Princely India. The conference demanded political reforms, viz., responsible ministries and independent judiciary, along with social and economic reforms. It strongly pleaded for the acceptance of the principle of popular representation in Princely India. This conference was the first to demand an Indian federation comprising British India and Princely India, which underlined the essential unity of the people of India and their united nationhood. Not only that, it also pleaded for the creation of larger states by amalgamating smaller states, so as to make them politically and economically viable. Considering the circumstances and the constraints under which AISPC had to work, these were radical demands, which certainly raised the levels of political hopes and aspirations among the people of the states. Subsequently, the AISPC became the main vehicle for carrying on the political struggle on behalf of the people of the states as well as a forum for uniting with the wider national movement being carried out in British India. The formation of AISPC also impacted the outlook of the Congress in respect of the problems confronting the people of Princely States.

Soon, the Congress took the stand that the people of the States alone had a right to decide about their future. The Princes, for obvious reasons, reacted violently to the demands of the AISPC. But soon they found themselves in a tight corner on account of a number of political developments. In the first place, the Indian National Congress in 1923 passed a resolution, asking the princes to introduce a responsible government in their respective states. Second, the Nehru Report prepared by Motilal Nehru on behalf of the All Parties' Conference had pleaded for an all India federation comprising both Princely and British India. Third, what was more agonising for the princes was the report of the Indian State's Committee chaired by Sir Harcourt Butler. The Committee, in its report submitted in 1929, had made it clear that the Raj could suggest constitutional change in a Princely State if demanded by the people of that state. In a way, this was an acceptance of the basic principle that in the governance of a state, the people should have a say; though the Butler Committee also tried to assure the princes that paramountcy could not be transferred even to an elected government of British India without their consent. On the top of all these developments came the Civil Disobedience Movement with its wide mass base, which must have been an un-nerving experience for the Princes. What was more disturbing for the princes was the fact that some of the leaders of AISPC participated in the Civil Disobedience Movement and in the process, cemented the close linkage with the Congress. Besides, AISPC demanded its right to be represented at the First Round Table Conference which, of course, was not accepted by the government. Not only that, AISPC presented a memorandum to the Congress demanding an All India federation which would grant all fundamental rights to the people of the states as enunciated in the Karachi Congress.

All these developments made the princes see the writings on the walls: the voice of the people of the states could not be gagged forever. They started seeing the idea of the All India federation as a last chance for their redemption. In their perception, the federation would provide them with an opportunity for greater autonomy from the Raj and at the same time, they would be able to preserve their internal autonomy from the Congress interference to a great extent. This approach of the princes was evident when they ultimately agreed upon the idea of the federation, which resulted in the 'Delhi Pact' in March 1932. This pact was subsequently endorsed by the Chamber of Princes in April 1932. But while endorsing the idea of federation, they insisted on their own rights, viz., rights arising out of earlier treaties which were to be respected. As such, they demanded that the federal subject should be decided only on the basis of a mutual agreement. They also wanted their ultimate right to secede from the federation to be accepted. This part of the princes' demand was neither acceptable to the nationalist leaders nor to the Raj. Thus they, subsequently, developed a lukewarm attitude to the idea of the federation.

The Act of 1935 provided for an all India federation, comprising both British and Princely India. According to the Act, the state's representative in the Federal Legislature, constituting one-third of its strength, would be the nominees of the princes: they were not to be directly elected by the people. This was neither acceptable to the Congress nor to the AISPC. The election of 1937 and subsequent formation of the popular governments by the Congress further strengthened the demand for popular representation in Princely India. It emboldened the AISPC, which could now agitate for its demands with greater legitimacy. The years 1938-9 marked a new and decisive phase in Praja Mandal's struggle. States like Jaipur, Kashmir, Rajkot, Patiala, Hyderabad and Mysore became the main centres of Praja Mandal's movement. Moreover, the Congress also took a more radical line in respect of the people's movement in Princely India under the pressure from the left-wingers in the Congress. In Haripura Congress (1938), it passed a resolution extending support to the Praja Mandal movement, though it refused to extend organisational support. In 1939, Jawaharlal Nehru took over the presidentship of the AISPC, and the Tripuri Congress in March 1939 upgraded its level of support to the Praja Mandal movement by proposing a joint action. This was followed by Praja Mandal movements supported by the Congress in a number of states.

Some of the states engulfed by the Praja Mandal movement were Hyderabad, Rajkot, Travancore, Mysore and a host of others. In Rajkot, Gandhiji went on a fast unto death to force the ruler to keep his commitments, but he subsequently withdrew it on the ground that it violated his basic principle of non-violence. In Travancore, the movement was against the autocratic behaviour of the Dewan as well as for the introduction of a responsible government therein. In a number of Princely States in Orissa the movement was launched against unjust forest laws and the system of *begar* (forced labour). In Mysore, the movement, which was for the introduction of a responsible government, resulted in police firing, in which a number of people lost their lives. In Hyderabad, the imposition of Urdu and the religious discriminations were the main issues for the movement. The Praja Mandal movement covered the bulk of the Princely States and brought the people of these states into the mainstream of the national movement.

Despite all these developments, there was no let up in the British attempt to prop up the Princes as a countervailing force to the ever-rising militancy of the Congress. In September 1939, the Congress refused to support the British unilateral decision to drag India into the War and demanded a serious discussion on the independence of India. The British retaliated by including an assurance to the Princes in their August offer in 1940, that the British intended to stand by their obligations under the treaties with the princes. This was an encouragement to the Princes to stand against the demand of the Congress for integration of states in the Indian union. This pro-Princes British policy became more pronounced in the proposals made by the Cripps-Mission in 1942, which gave freedom to them either to join the proposed Indian union or retain their separate existence. The Princes, being more wary of the idea of the federation, toyed with the idea of sovereign independent states of their own or at least independent status for the larger states. They even toyed with the idea of continuance of the paramountcy even after independence. But all these exercises remained at the ideational level and no concrete plan came out of it. The Quit India Movement virtually obliterated the distinction between Princely and British India as all Indians were urged upon to participate in the movement with a sacred mantra of 'do or die'. The people responded with great enthusiasm including the people from the Princely States.

When the war ended and serious negotiations were initiated on the issues of independence and unity of the country, the All India States People's Conference backed up by the Congress once again reiterated their demand for integration of the states in the Indian Union. The British, through the Cabinet Mission Plan, in May 1946, did propose an Indian union comprising the states as well as British India. The union was supposed to look after three major subjects of foreign affairs, defence and communications. The princes were given their share in the process of the constitution making, as well. The plan allocated 93 out of the total 385 seats to Princely India for the Constituent Assembly. However, as against the demands of the AISPC and the Congress that States representatives should be directly elected by the people, the mission left the issue to be decided by the consultation among the parties involved. Thus, it was left unsettled whether the states representatives would be elected by the people or nominated by the Princes. Subsequently, the Cabinet Mission Plan came to naught as the Muslim League rejected it, after Jawaharlal Nehru's controversial statement on the role of the Constituent Assembly. The states wanted to have a free choice on the issue of the accession to the Indian union and that of joining the Constituent Assembly. That the AISPC had the support of the Congress and that of the interim government was made the evident when Jawaharlal Nehru presided over the meeting of AISPC during 1946–47. Subsequently, the Constituent Assembly set up a States Committee with Nehru as the chairman to negotiate with the Princes for persuading them to join the Constituent Assembly. Ultimately, the issue was settled in a joint meeting with the negotiating committee with the Prince's chamber in March 1947. Then the Mountbatten plan gave the states the option of joining either of the two proposed union of India and Pakistan or to retain their independent status. Some of the states like Jodhpur, Bhopal, Travancore and Hyderabad toyed with the idea of retaining their independent status even against the wishes of their own people. But ultimately, they had to yield to the popular pressure as well as the astute and strong policy of Home Minister, Sardar Patel, ably assisted by his secretary V P Menon. They were made to sign the Instrument of Accession with the Indian union. In this process, Lord Mountbatten, the last Viceroy of India, also lent a helping hand by impressing upon the states to join the Indian union. Thus, by 15 August, except three recalcitrant states of Junagarh, Hyderabad and Kashmir, all other states had been integrated in the Indian union.

In retrospect, it can be fairly concluded that the integration of the Indian states in the Indian Union was one of the most outstanding achievements of the Indian leaders. In a way, it lessened the suffering of the Indian people inflicted by the partition of the country in 1947. It halted the process of balkanisation of India which could have inflicted a mortal blow to the people of India. It goes to the credit of Sardar Patel, who adopted both persuading and pressuring methods to make this feat possible.

> *If the Congress organisation were to have involved itself directly in the struggle underway in the various states (Princely), it might as well have abandoned its struggle for independence from the British Government.*
>
> J B Kripalani

PART IV

Armed Rebellion and the Indian National Movement

The revolutionaries sowed the seed of the Indian Revolution. The revolutionaries sowed the seed and left it to Gandhiji to look after the harvest. The spark was ignited – the spark that was to kindle the fire of the Indian Revolution. The fulfilment of the seed underground, its death-hungering effort, manifested itself in the seedling of the Indian Revolution that the world saw in the Non-Cooperation Movement of Gandhiji in the wake of the great commotion of feeling caused by the First World War.

BHUPENDRA KUMAR DUTTA

In the name of God, in the name of bygone generations who have welded the Indian people into one nation and in the name of dead heroes who have bequeathed to us a tradition of heroism and self-sacrifice, we call upon the Indian people to rally round one banner and to strike for India's freedom. We call upon them to launch the final struggle against the British and all their Allies in India and to prosecute that struggle with valour and perseverance and with full faith in final victory, until the enemy is expelled from India's soil and the Indian people are free once again.

SUBHAS CHANDRA BOSE

32 Armed Revolutionary Movement and the Indian Freedom Struggle

Devoted valiant we fear not
To shed our own or others blood.
In pride we hold our heads high
And bend them to mother's feet alone.

UNKNOWN BENGALI REVOLUTIONARY

These young men willingly forsook all that was dear and near to them, to carry on a lifelong struggle for their goal. Fear of death did not deter them, obstacles and difficulties couldn't deflect them from their goal. Deserted by friends and relatives, ignored if not derided by their countrymen, hunted by spies, fleeing from one shelter to another, these young men carried on heroic but hopeless struggle from day to day, from month to month, from year to year. They chose the life of hardship, and privation and consecrated their lives to the service of their country.

R C MAJUMDAR

In the preceding chapters we have already discussed the role of the Moderates and the Extremists in our struggle for independence. Apart from these two groups, there was a third group in the pre-Gandhian era, which was totally committed to the idea of freeing the country from the British hands by using violent means, including individual killings of anti-Indian British officials and their henchmen. They believed that the British had enslaved India by the sword and, therefore, it is by the sword alone that they would be driven out of the country. In brief, they believed in the cult of violence as an article of their faith and were more than willing to make the supreme sacrifice in the cause of our motherland. They have been described variously in history: the British called them terrorists, some called them militant nationalists, still others called them revolutionaries and yet others called them revolutionary terrorists. We have preferred to call them violent revolutionaries. The British branded them 'terrorists' in a pejorative sense and calling them revolutionary terrorists, even by some nationalist historians does not elevate their moral status in any substantial measure. We have preferred to call them armed/violent revolutionary as calling them revolutionary alone does not fully connote their faith as there could also be a non-violent revolutionary like Gandhi. Hence, in the present context we have preferred to characterise them as armed/violent revolutionaries.

Reasons for the Emergence of Violent Revolutionary Groups

A number of factors were responsible for the emergence and growth of the organised armed revolutionary groups in the first decade of the twentieth century. In the first place, by the turn of the century, there was a general disillusionment among our people with the policy of political mendicancy of the Moderates. But by 1908, the Indian National Movement suffered a major setback: the Congress stood divided: the Moderates reverted to their politics of mendicancy and prayerful petitioning, and the Swadeshi Movement petered out. The situation was no better on the Extremist front either. Some of the leaders were hunted out: Tilak was sent to Mandalay Jail in Burma with a sentence of six-year imprisonment, Lala Lajpat Rai left for USA for a long stay and Aurobindo was behind bars. Bipin Chandra Pal took retirement from active politics for the time being. There was a general atmosphere of despair on the political front of the country. As it happens in such a situation of despair, the youth has its ways to see light at the end of the dark tunnel. The atmosphere was ripe for the emergence of the revolutionary groups to fill up the vacant space in the political map of the country.

The second reason for the emergence of the violent revolutionary groups was the extreme repressive measures taken by the colonial administration. That partially contributed to the decline of the Swadeshi Movement. The British not only banned the shouting of the *Bande Mataram* slogan, which had proved to be the most effective and emotive battle cry for arousing the long-slumbering masses. They unleashed equally other stringent repressive measures like expelling students from their educational institutions, disqualifying all participants of the movement from government services, banning public meetings and arrests and convictions of leaders. A feeling started brewing in the hearts of the youth that a more drastic violent action was needed to drive out the British from India.

There was yet another way the Extremist politics contributed to the emergence of the violent revolutionary groups. It is true that the Extremists did not believe in the cult of bomb but they did not have firm commitment in the principle of non-violence either. For instance, Tilak defended the violent revolutionaries – be it the Chapekar brothers or Bengal revolutionaries. And on both occasions, Tilak defied the British and willingly suffered imprisonment. Aurobindo, of course, had no abhorrence for violent means and through his writings, he became the main source of inspiration for violent revolutionaries. Their new concept of religious nationalism created a rare fervour among the youth to make sacrifices. The imagery of one's mother being in bondage and her children's sacred duty to free her, caught the imagination of the youth of the country. The atmosphere was thus charged with a clarion call of 'dare, do and die' regardless of the consequences. So, the question of success or failure of the movement, strength or weakness of the British Rule became meaningless and irrelevant for them. The only thing that mattered was the spirit of supreme sacrifice. Martyrdom became a popular watchword. As Aurobindo wrote:

> Round whose mother's neck clanks the chain
> will he too stop to think
> if he is strong or weak . . .

Shivaji, Rana Pratap, Guru Govind Singh, Banda Bahadur and others like them came to inspire the young revolutionaries. Rabindranath Tagore had captured the popular mood in his poem on Sikh martyr Banda Bahadur when he wrote:

> the day has dawned at last,
> when millions hands have cast off fear
> . . . And minds have snapped all chains

A third source of the violent revolutionary movement could be traced in the earlier history of the violent movements. Perhaps, apart from other minor armed rebellions by different groups, the main source of inspiration came from the 1857 rebellion, when an attempt was made to throw out the Company Raj through armed rebellion. The rebellion failed but the culture of armed resistance persisted. For example in 1877, Wasudeo Balwant Phadke in Maharashtra had raised a band of armed followers with a long-term aim to throw out the British from the country. He was captured and was deported to Aden where he died subsequently. But revolutionary fire persisted in Maharashtra and was rekindled by the Chapekar brothers – Damodar and Balkrishna. In 1898 they killed a British official Colonel Rand, whom they identified as the person responsible for atrocities against the plague victims of Poona. Subsequently, they were hanged and Tilak suffered his first imprisonment while indirectly defending their violent act. All these factors perhaps contributed to the emergence of the third stream, viz., the violent revolutionary movement in the cause of our national struggle.

Primarily, the violent revolutionary movement was active in three major areas, viz., Bengal, Maharashtra and Punjab and, therefore, our study would focus on the revolutionary activities of these areas.

Bengal: In Bengal, Bankim Chandra Chattopadhyaya and his famous novel *Anandmath* and his hymn to the motherland enshrined in his song *Bande Mataram* (Hail the Mother) inspired a generation of revolutionaries who were more than willing to make the supreme sacrifice on the altar of the motherland. As R C Majumdar observes:

> The militant nationalism of Bengal was founded upon the twin rocks of the ardent patriotic call of Swami Vivekananda based on the philosophical teachings of Vedantá and Gita, and the religious devotion to motherland preached by Bankim Chandra Chattopadhyaya through his novel *Anandmath*.

It was in 1902 that a number of localised revolutionary groups emerged in places like Midnapore and Calcutta. However, there was no drastic or spectacular action on the part of any revolutionary group till 1905, when the partition of Bengal gave a new spurt to these groups. The Midnapore group was headed by J N Basu, whereas in Calcutta, the Anushilan Samiti was headed by Jatindranath Banerjee. Jatindranath Banerjee was one of the earliest revolutionaries of Bengal. He was inspired by Aurobindo and at his behest, joined the Baroda army under a disguised name. But his real identity was soon discovered. Consequently, he left Baroda and joined 'Anushilan' in 1902. Subsequently he had his differences with Barindra Kumar Ghosh and became a sanyasi known as 'Niralamba'. But he continued to work for the revolution and inspired some of the Ghadarites as well as Bhagat Singh. Because of his exceptional physical prowess, he was known as 'Bagha Jatin'. He died as a sanyasi in 1930. Subsequently, the Dacca Anushilan Samiti was set up in 1906 under the leadership of Pulin Behari Das. Pramathanath Mitra, a barrister in the Calcutta High Court was another founder of the Anushilan Samiti and played a crucial role in forging a united organisation of revolutionaries in the subsequent years. They were joined by Barindra Kumar Ghosh, younger brother of Aurobindo, in 1903. The idea behind the Anushilan Samiti was to organise and establish small centres involving the youth in different towns with an idea to take them ultimately to the villages. They were to be trained in all activities as a prelude to revolutionary actions. This idea caught the imagination of many young people and a large number of such centres soon came up. What came as handy to the group was the work of Sarda Ghosal, who was a pioneer in physical training programmes in Bengal. Initially, these groups were not committed to the cult of the bomb. It was the partition of Bengal and Swadeshi Movement and subsequent stringent repressive measures by the government that turned them towards the cult of violence. An attempt was made to interlink and unite all the revolutionary groups, and to that end, All Bengal conference of revolutionaries was held in December 1906. In 1907, Barindra Kumar Ghosh, along with Bhupendra Nath Dutta constituted their own inner group inside the Calcutta Anushilan Samiti.

Another milestone in revolutionary politics was reached when in 1906, a new Bengali weekly called *Yugantar* was launched with a view to propagate revolutionary ideas among the youth of Bengal. Aurobindo Ghosh was associated with the paper from the very beginning. *Yugantar* had a brief span of life but undoubtedly it was the most influential paper of revolutionary thoughts and action. Soon Aurobindo Ghosh became the actual editor of *Bande Mataram*, started by Bipin Chandra Pal, the Extremist leader. It also lasted from 1907 to 1908 as a daily paper. It played a crucial role in changing the pattern of political thought in India, freeing it from the impact of British liberal politics. It set complete and absolute independence as the goal of the country.

Barindra Kumar Ghosh was greatly influenced by Aurobindo's pamphlet 'Bhawani Mandir' based on the pattern of *Anandmath*. Barindra was back to Calcutta in 1906 by the time the Swadeshi

Movement was on against the partition of Bengal. By that time Aurobindo also moved to Calcutta and had become a leading light of the nationalist leader. He started pleading for the freedom of the country through revolutionary means. In 1907, Barindra along with his associates formed his own revolutionary group and started a centre in Maniktola – a suburb of Calcutta – which came to be known as Garden House. The chief aim of the centre was to train the youth in revolutionary ideology as well as in action programmes including bomb making and physical training, etc. They wanted to eliminate unpopular officials. The first attempt was made on 6 December 1907, to blow up the train in which the Governor of Bengal was traveling at Narayan Garh in the district of Midnapore. It failed. The next attempt was made on the life of the Mayor of Chandernagore who had earlier stopped a Swadeshi meeting on 11 April 1907. It also failed. But the most dramatic incident took place on 30 April 1908 when a bomb was thrown on the carriage of Mr Kingsford, district judge of Muzaffarpur in Bihar, who had earlier earned the displeasure of the Maniktola

Khudiram Bose

group by his harsh treatment to Swadeshi agitators as the chief Judicial Magistrate of Calcutta. However, Mr Kingsford remained unhurt and two ladies Mrs and Ms Kennedy were killed. The two young boys who threw the bomb at Muzaffarpur were Khudiram Bose and Prafulla Chaki. Khudiram Bose was barely eighteen years old and was subsequently hanged on 11 August 1908 at Muzaffarpur. So resolute was Khudiram that he promised to be born soon with a sole purpose of continuing his fight against the British. He boldly walked up to the scaffold with his head erect and embraced the gallows with a smile on his face. His emotion and mindset has been captured in a popular song:

Bid me farewell, O Mother (India)
  Soon I would be back
Let all the people of Mother India watch me
  Embracing the gallows with a smile on my face.
Bid me farewell, O Mother,
  I would be back soon.

Prafulla Chaki killed himself when confronted by the police before he could be arrested at Mokkama Ghat, Bihar.

Prafulla Chaki

In May 1908, the entire Maniktola group including Barindra and Aurobindo were arrested and along with their 36 associates, were tried for waging war against the King, in what came to be known as the Alipore conspiracy case. In the course of the trial, one of the accused, Narendra Nath Gossain, who had turned police approver in the case was murdered in the compound of the Alipore jail by Kanailal Dutta and Satyendra Nath Bose, on 31 August 1908. This was followed by the assassination of the investigating officer of the case – Ashutosh Biswas on 10 February 1909. In November 1907, an attempt was made on the life of Andrew Fraser, Lieutant Governor of Bengal in Calcutta. However, he escaped. Not only that, between 1908 and 1916, a number of police officials and police informers were killed and a number of political dacoities were committed to meet the financial needs of the movements.

After the Maniktola group trial and their imprisonment, the revolutionary movement did not come to an end. Several attempts at Swadeshi dacoities were made and bombs were thrown at several places. Anushilan Samities continued to be active. Calcutta Anushilan Samiti was headed by Jatindranath Mukherjee and Jadugopal Mukherjee. Another revolutionary who played a crucial role in the cause of Indian independence was Jatindranath Mukherjee. He was also a product of the swadeshi movement and a close follower of Aurobindo Ghosh. He was in close contact with the Indian revolutionaries at Berlin to import German arms through them. In the process, he along with his close comrades, was killed by the police in Balasore, Orissa in September 1915. The movement continued till the end of the First World War.

Maharashtra: Another area of revolutionary activities was Maharashtra, where V D Savarkar had organised Abhinav Bharat which had branches in Maharashtra, Berar and Central Provinces. In 1904, Savarkar went to England but continued to send arms and other materials to help the movement. Abhinav Bharat tried to organise meetings for the celebration of Ganpati Puja and Shivaji festivals. Savarkar translated the life of Mazzini, which sold 2,000 copies. Abhinav Bharat members were trained in martial exercises. A member of Abhinav Bharat, P N Bapat was sent to Paris to learn the art of bomb making from Russian revolutionaries. A copy of a bomb making book was secured and translated from Russian to English. An attempt was made to manufacture bombs and the Kolhapur bomb case was launched, which resulted in imprisonment of many revolutionaries. Some minor thefts were committed to support the activists at Nasik where the Karve group was active. Bomb manufacturing groups were set up at Aundh, Basai, Poona, Kolhapur and other places. Then came the Nasik conspiracy case. The Karve Group planned to eliminate Jackson, the District Magistrate of Nasik – as he had acquitted Williams, who had killed a farmer. On 21 December 1909, Anant Lakshman Kanhere shot dead Jackson at his farewell party. His arrest led to the exposure of the entire group which led to the virtual end of the movement in Maharashtra. It was in connection with the Maharashtra revolutionary movement that V D Savarkar was brought back to India and sent to Andaman jail as a life prisoner.

Punjab: Punjab was another place where the revolutionary movement was active. The prominent leaders were Lala Lajpat Rai and Ajit Singh. The main issue agitating the minds of the people arose from frequent famines, heavy land revenue and irrigation charges. What gave a new boost to the movement was the protest against the partition of Bengal. Here again, secret arrangements were made for distribution of revolutionary literature. Ajit Singh and Sufi Amba Prasad were leading the movement from the front. People connected with Arya Samaj were also in the forefront of the revolutionary activities. What perhaps precipitated the matter was the Golden Jubilee celebration of the 1857 rebellion. *Punjabi*, a paper edited by Lala Lajpat Rai was prosecuted, which led to riots in Rawalpindi and even some Europeans in Lahore were assaulted. Soon both Ajit Singh and Lala Lajpat Rai were deported and released after six months. Lala Hardayal, who had returned to India in 1908, pleaded for passive resistance against the British. S M Chatterjee, Amir Chand of Delhi and Dinanəth came into contact with Rasbehari Bose of Dehradun, who subsequently proved to be a great revolutionary leader. He was responsible for bringing Awadh Bihari and Bal Mukand in the group. Rasbehari Bose became a link between the revolutionaries of Punjab, Bengal, UP and Delhi. The major action taken by the group was when a bomb was thrown on Lord Hardinge in Delhi, though he escaped unhurt. Subsequently, Amir Chand and others were hanged.

Madras: Bipin Chandra Pal visited and delivered a number of fiery speeches in Madras in May 1907. This was followed by widespread discussion on the issue of independence for the country particularly among the youth. Chidambaram Pillai and Subramania Shiva also delivered speeches on 9 March 1908 in Trinnevelly, coaxing people to boycott everything of foreign origin. Both of them were subsequently arrested on 12 March 1908, which was followed by riots on the next day. Subsequently, Vanchi Aiyer shot dead Mr Ashe, the district Magistrate of Trinnevelly on 17 June 1909, who had an anti-people image. Soon the Trinnevelly conspiracy case was launched and nine persons were convicted.

Other Areas: Some other areas like Rajasthan, UP and Bihar also became centres of revolutionary politics. Some of the prominent names were: Arjun Lal Sethi, Birhat Keshari Singh and Rao Gopal Singh. They were connected with the Delhi revolutionaries like Amir Chand. The major action was of the murder of Jodhpur Mahant in June 1912 to secure funds for revolutionary activities. Patna, Deoghar and Dumka in Bihar, and Allahabad in UP were the other centres of revolutionary politics. Sachirdra Sanyal was active in Banaras, Bankim Chandra Mitra was a student of Bihar National College. He was tried in the Banaras conspiracy case, along with a number of revolutionaries who were sentenced to various terms of imprisonment.

An assessment: What did the revolutionaries actually achieve? They could neither free the country nor could they create a mass movement. Many scholars are of the opinion that they suffered from a number of limitations. They did not have a central command; they were scattered and did not have a comprehensive plan to liberate the country. Some scholars also allege that these revolutionaries weakened the secular social fabric of the country on account of their Hindu religious fervour. Ultimately, they were isolated, hunted out and killed or suffered imprisonment. The government was able to control their activities and their work remains stray incidents of personal courage and indomitable will.

Some scholars of the Indian freedom struggle pinpoint major weaknesses of the revolutionaries, viz., lack of organisation and the failure to raise the common masses to that emotional pitch, wherein the people join the vanguard on a massive scale. Besides, they also failed to forge horizontal alliances with other people's organisations. There might be partial truth in all these observations. However, all these observations arise from an ideal view of the revolutionary movements. A revolution begins with a small band of people, who are willing to sacrifice all that they have, including their lives. Not all revolutionary groups, however, reach the ideal stage of mass revolutionary politics. But there is no denying the fact that such a group works as sappers and miners of the struggle and they clear the road where the masses can march ahead. And this is what these young revolutionaries did. They definitely took the freedom struggle to a higher plane by setting the goal of complete and total independence. Second, they created and added a religious fervour to our national struggle, which inspired the next generation of freedom fighters. They set a high standard of sacrifice, which any nation can take pride in. No man can make a supreme sacrifice unless he identifies himself with the cause which appears higher than everything else. They totally dedicated their lives to the freedom of the country.

However, that does not mean they failed or their major sacrifice was a futile exercise. They created a fear among the British officials, who had to think twice before taking harsh measures. Besides, by involving extreme suffering, they exposed the cruel and ruthless nature of the British rule making it unpopular among the people. Third, their death-defying and daring acts forced the British to make constitutional concessions to the people. These revolutionaries will always be remembered for taking India as their mother, for whose freedom they would make any sacrifice and undergo any suffering. And for a grateful nation, people like Khudiram Bose and Prafulla Chaki, soon became popular heros. Lastly, more than any other group, they popularised the concept of total independence. They lived and died for the freedom of Mother India. It would be unfair to judge them on the basis of the actual result of their actions. Their acts of sacrifice would continue to inspire the people for generations to come.

If none will come at your call,
Walk alone
If they cower mutely facing the wall
Open thy mind and speak out alone
If no one holds a lamp for you
If in this stormy night, in the rain and dark
All shut their doors,
Let your breast be riven by thunder fire,
yet walk alone.

RABINDRANATH TAGORE

33 The Ghadar Party and its Role in the Indian Freedom Struggle

Neither rich nor able, a poor son like myself can offer nothing but his blood on the altar of mother. May I be reborn of the same mother and may I re-die in the same sacred cause, till my mission is done and she stands free for the good of humanity and in the glory of God.

MADAN LAL DHINGRA

The Ghadar Party played a crucial role in our freedom struggle during the First World War period. It was founded in the United States of America by some of the Indian immigrants who had migrated there in the search of better opportunities, but were disappointed with the kind of treatment they received there. Besides, they were greatly touched by the daring acts of the Indian revolutionaries. But before we discuss the formation and the subsequent role of the Ghadar Party, let us delineate the historical backdrop which led to its emergence.

As we have noted earlier, India was in the grip of a revolutionary movement, which assumed a big form in the wake of the movement against the partition of Bengal during 1905–08. But soon in the face of unprecedented repressive measures, a feeling grew, at least in some sections of the Indian revolutionaries, that foreign land might provide a better haven for the revolutionary work. Besides, an idea also dawned in their minds that foreign help for the Indian revolutionary movement could be procured in terms of money, men, materials and arms. Perhaps, the first major initiative for furthering the cause of the Indian independence in foreign lands was taken by Shyamji Krishna Varma (1857–1930). He was born in Mondvi Kutch in Gujarat and got his education in Bhuj. Subsequently, he shifted to Mumbai and came into contact with Swami Dayanand, the founder of the Arya Samaj and was greatly influenced by his ardent nationalism. He went to Oxford University and was called to the Bar in 1884 and returned to India in 1885. He soon came into contact with Tilak and even supported him in his struggle against the Consent Bill of 1891, which sought to raise the marriageable age of Hindu girls. When Tilak was imprisoned in the wake of Col. Rand's murder in 1897, Varma decided to shift to England to carry on the mission of Indian independence from there. He instituted scholarships and fellowships for visiting Indian scholars.

Subsequently, he started a journal called *Indian Sociologist.* Not being content with these intellectual efforts, he founded the 'Indian Home Rule Society'. He pleaded for 'Passive Resistance' as a weapon to get rid of the British rule from India. But more was yet to come. He set up 'India House' in England to house visiting scholars from India. Soon, it became the hub of revolutionary activities and its programme to celebrate the Indian rebellion of 1857 became an annual affair. When Lala Lajpat Rai was deported, Varma moved to Paris and India House was virtually taken over by V D Savarkar, who hailed from Nasik in Maharashtra. He became the prime mover of the Indian revolution in England and inspired Madan Lal Dhingra, who shot dead Curzon Willie in July 1909. Soon, Savarkar himself was extradited from England to face trial as an accused in the Nasik Conspiracy case. He tried to escape to France from the ship by which he was being brought to India, but he failed. In the Nasik conspiracy case, Savarkar was awarded an imprisonment of fifty years and was deported to the Andaman jail, where he spent many years. Meanwhile, the other Indian revolutionaries started working for the Indian Revolution from the European continent. Birendranath Chattopadhyaya was active in Germany. Madam Cama was working in Germany, she had started *Bande Mataram*, a paper committed to the independence of India. A number of Indian revolutionaries were active in various parts of Europe, working for the cause of the Indian Independence.

The land of the United States of America, though not untouched, had not become the hub of the Indian revolutionaries as yet. However, what provided a congenial ground for starting a major revolutionary initiative in USA, among the Indian immigrants, was the fact that a large number of Sikh peasants had migrated to USA in the area around the West Coast. Some of them, by the dint of their hard work had been successful and had even made good money. Even then, they were being subjected to racial discrimination and faced insulting behaviour at the hands of the local Americans. They were also reminded that they hailed from India, which was a slave country. All this inflicted a deep sense of humiliation among them. All this created a psychological environment among the Indian immigrants, who sought to do something spectacular for their motherland to get rid of their soul-wrenching sense of humiliation.

Against the backdrop of this ignominy, the Ghadar Party was established in 1913 on the West Coast of America. There are some controversies regarding the events leading to the actual formation of the Ghadar Party and also about who was its real founder. But one thing is indeed clear that the formation of the Ghadar Party in 1913 did not come as a bolt from the blue; there was a background to it. In fact, in the wake of the movement against partition of Bengal, which came to be called 'Swadeshi Movement', the Indians living in USA were also stirred by the call of Swadeshi. Perhaps Taraknath was the first Indian immigrant who organised a group in USA called 'Indian Independence League in 1907. He also brought out a pamphlet called 'Free Hindustan' and distributed revolutionary material among the Sikh immigrants and also shipped some of the material to India. In 1910, Kanshi Ram took over the leadership of the group and was subsequently joined by Lala Hardayal in 1913. It is this group which was responsible for the formation of the Ghadar Party in 1913. There is another account of the formation of the Ghadar Party which gives credit for it to Sohan Singh Bhakna – a Punjab immigrant to USA. According to this account, on 1 November 1913, a meeting was held in San Francisco, leading to the formation of 'Hindi Association of America', which brought out a paper called *Ghadar*. And that was the genesis of the Ghadar Party. Anyway, the Ghadar Party started its career with Sohan Singh Bhakna as the president and Lala Hardayal as secretary. It was perhaps, to express its affiliation and solidarity with the Indian revolutionary movement, that the headquarters of the Ghadar Party located in San Fransisco came to be known as 'Yugantar Ashram' The general aim of the party was to overthrow the British rule from Indian soil through armed rebellion. A word is called for, about Lala Hardayal who played a crucial role in Ghadar Movement. Born and educated in Delhi, he went to London on a scholarship but soon became an associate of Shyamji Krishna Varma. He came back to India and soon sailed for USA, arriving there in 1911. For a while he taught at Stanford University but was soon dismissed. He later joined 'Hindi Association of America' and through it got associated with the Ghadar Party. Subsequently, he became the secretary of the Ghadar Party.

The organisational structure of the party was quite democratic: the president and secretary were to be assisted by a central committee representing various local and state committees. The central committee were to meet once in three months though the president was authorised to call an emergency meeting if he felt the need. The main work of the central committee was to educate its members about the Indian situation. The educational work was to be carried out by publishing books, journals, pamphlets, etc. Its journal called *Ghadar* started being published from 1 November 1913. The first issue of its mission set the tone when it unequivocally declared, 'Today there begins . . . a war against the British Raj'. The paper also tried to expose the misdeeds of the British Government. Besides, it tried to inculcate a feeling of national unity and national respect among the Indian immigrants. The paper also tried to impress upon the Indians that relentless battle will have to be fought against the British using all conceivable means including sabotage. In an attempt to reach out to every section of the Indian immigrants, Ghadar was being printed in Hindi, Urdu, English and Gurumukhi. What gave a godsent opportunity to the Ghadarites to intensify their work, was the new immigration policy which was quite restrictive. This was opposed by the immigrants and Lala Hardayal left USA in 1914 to join Madam Cama in Switzerland and took over the editorship of her paper called *Bande Mataram*. However, this did not weaken the pace of the work in USA. The work in USA was carried on with Bhagwan Singh as president and Barkatullah as vice-president.

It was around that time that the First World War broke out. This was looked upon by the Indian revolutionaries as the godsend opportunity to work for the demise and dissolution of the British rule in India. Indian revolutionaries working in Europe tried to seek German help to intensity its fight against the British in India. Germany also had a vested interest in seeking Indian support to weaken the British hold over India. Germans thought of spreading discontent among the Indian soldiers fighting on behalf of the British and also tried to persuade the Indian Muslims not to lend any support to the British, as she was fighting against Turkey, the home of their Caliph. Birendranath Chattopadhyaya and Abinash Chandra Bhattacharya were active on the front of seeking German support. On 3 September 1914, a committee called, 'German Union of Friendly India', was set-up in

Berlin with some of the Indians as its members. By September 1915, the Berlin Committee was reconstituted and its membership became totally Indian. Champak Raman Pillai was another member of the Berlin Committee. Earlier, he was active in Zurich in Switzerland and had set up the 'International Pro-India Committee' and even published a paper called *Pro-India.* Lala Hardayal was another leading light of the Berlin Committee. The Berlin Committee tried to establish contact with all Indian revolutionaries working in India and abroad. The main aim was to work for general uprising in India with the help of foreign arms and materials. Hemant Lal Gupta went to Japan from USA to procure arms for the Indian revolutionaries, but failed to achieve much. Nearer home, Raja Mahendra Pratap and Barkatullah tried to seek German help while working in Afghanistan and even set up a 'provisional' Government of India with Raja as its head.

Earlier, some of the Indian revolutionaries working in USA had approached the German ambassador posted there to seek his support. However, Ram Chandra who was the leader of the Ghadar Party, did not agree with the proposal and hence the initiative failed. But through the efforts of the Berlin Committee, Ram Chandra, the leader of the Ghadar Party, was prevailed upon to send arms and men to India to help the Indian revolutionaries fighting against the British. Some of these men were sent to India through Shanghai in China. A group of 60 men with an iron will to fight for the Independence of India were sent through a ship called 'Korea', which sailed from San Francisco on 29 August 1914. When it reached Canton (China), it was joined by many more Indians. On 8 October 1914, it sailed for India with 1,500 men. However on reaching Calcutta they were arrested.

Germany, under the leadership of Zimmerman was in touch with Ram Chandra, the leader of the Ghadar Party. However, there was bickering in the Ghadar Party which led to the expulsion of some of its members by Ram Chandra, the leader of the party. But for the Ghadar Party, the worst was still to come. In March 1917, C K Chakrabarti, who was associated with the Berlin Committee, was arrested in New York and he spilled the beans by giving out all the details of the underground work of the Ghadar Party. In April 1917, Ram Chandra and others were arrested and put on trial. They were charged with inciting revolt in India, in collaboration with the Germans. In the course of the trial, Ram Chandra was shot dead, by another accused Ram Singh, who, in turn, was killed by the Marshal. Finally, the judgement was delivered, resulting in the award of imprisonment to a number of accused. Thus, ended a glorious chapter of the Ghadar Party. Another initiative taken by the Ghadar Party was to induce and send a large number of Indians with high motivation, to work for the revolution in India. Apart from the S S Korea incident, a large number of Indians were able to reach India. They were an inspired lot. Instructions were given to them to work for the revolution in India. Their assignment was also to induce the Indian army to revolt against the British.

A booklet. the 'Ghadar Gunj' (the echo of mutiny) was printed and freely distributed among the aspiring revolutionaries. It contained detailed instructions as to how to work for the Indian revolution. These aspiring revolutionaries were instructed to organise secret societies, to raise funds even by committing political dacoity, to work for raising the popular discontent against the British, and to cut off lines of communications and troops – movement including organising the derailment of trains. One of the important local contact persons was Rasbehari Bose, who was the main co-ordinator of all revolutionary activities in north India. He was also in contact with the leaders of Dacca Anushilan Samiti. Banaras was the main centre of revolutionary activities, wherein the moving figure was Sachindra Nath Sanyal. Rasbehari Bose coordinated with Sanyal in these revolutionary activities. They were successful in establishing contact with a large number of people who had been sent by the Ghadar Party to work for the Indian revolution. To that end, they concentrated on the main work of bringing about a general uprising among the members of the Indian armed forces. They successfully contacted the Indian soldiers located in different cantonments like Danapur, Meerut, Jallandhar, Ambala, Ferozpur, and Rawalpindi, etc. The Bengal revolutionaries were also taken into confidence and a joint attempt was made for bringing about such a popular uprising, with a view to end the British rule over India. The day 21 February 1915, was fixed as the D-Day for the armed uprisings. Fearing that the police had got a scent of it, it was decided to pre-date it on 19 February 1915. But the plan did not come through. Pingle, one of the 'conspirators', was arrested around Meerut cantonment and the Lahore conspiracy case was launched, which led to the hanging and imprisonment of a large number of revolutionaries. This bold initiative on the part of the Indian revolutionaries came to naught. This was followed by a number of conspiracy cases, including Banaras conspiracy case in which a large number of revolutionaries were either hanged or awarded long-term imprisonment. Earlier, Delhi conspiracy case had led to the hanging of the four accused. Amir Chand, Avadh Behari, Bal Mukand and Basant Kumar Biswas.

Komagatamaru Incident

In the history of the Ghadar Party and its revolutionary activities there is a special significance of S S Komagatamaru – a ship which brought a large number of the Ghadar activists from abroad to India. The moving spirit behind this initiative was Baba Gurdit Singh, a Sikh who had migrated to Singapore in the first decade of the twentieth century. In the beginning of 1914, he chartered a ship carrying a large number of people from Singapore to Canada. The genesis of this new initiative lay in the fact that there was a change in the Canadian immigration law in 1914. According to the new law, any citizen of any Asian country was to be allowed to visit Canada only if he had sailed directly from his motherland to Canada. Since there was no direct ship from India to Canada, Baba Gurdit Singh thought of hiring a ship from Singapore to Canada. On 4 April 1914, the ship sailed from Hong Kong. Some of the Ghadar Party activists were there and some Ghadar literature was also put on the ship. On 23 May 1914, Komagatamaru reached Vancouver with 351 Sikhs and 21 Punjabi Mohammedans on board. The Canadian authorities did not allow them to land on Canadian

The Komagatamaru encircled by Canadian Police boats off Vancouver with Gurdit Singh (inset, top left) who had chartered the ship, and the passengers (inset, bottom right) on the deck of the ship

soil. Despite protracted negotiations, the Canadian authorities persisted in their refusal. Hence, it started its return journey on 23 July 1914 and arrived at Hugli on 27 September 1914. The government had arranged a special train to take all of them to Punjab directly, with an aim to put restrictions on their free movements. But the Sikhs refused to board the train and expressed their desire to march to Calcutta. A riot broke out in which many Sikhs were killed. Altogether only 60 passengers boarded and the rest were either killed or arrested or escaped. Baba Gurdit Singh along with 28 associates escaped. Many looked at this incident as a replica of the Jallianwala Bagh massacre.

These were some of the bold initiatives which the Ghadar activists took in the cause of our independence. For reasons beyond their control, they could not succeed in their objective of freeing India from the clutches of the British rule, despite their willingness to sacrifice everything they had for it. Their critics may go on judging them on the counts of worldly wisdom and practical feasibility. Their bold acts of sacrifice and self-invited sufferings might be dubbed as sheer acts of bravado and futile sacrifice. Some others even might pin them down on the more doctrinaire issue of violence and non-violence, particularly killings of individual British officials and their henchmen. Some critics might even go to the extent of saying that they made the British regime more brutal and repressive, resulting in untold sufferings to the Indian people. For instance, it was in the face of the revolutionary challenge that a new law, the Indian Criminal Law Amendment Act of 1913 was passed. The New Act made 'conspiracy' an independent criminal offence and also widened its scope. All this might be nothing but a cold-blooded rational analysis with the help of our hindsight. In the wake of the partition of Bengal, when the full and mighty fangs of the British 'steel-frame' was in the ascendent, these young people thought of freeing the country with whatever means they had. The issue of success or failure was meaningless to them. All that mattered was to join the battle of Swaraj and sacrifice all that they had on the altar of their motherland. As Barindra Kumar Ghosh, one of the accused in Maniktola conspiracy case put: 'we did not expect to liberate our country by killing a few Englishmen. We wanted to show to our people how to dare and die'.

In the Greek fable, a song is sung for Titan who was chained and imprisoned. This song could be sung in the honour of our revolutionaries of all hues including the Ghadarites. It says:

To suffer woes which hope thinks infinite
To defy power, which seems omnipotent
To hope till hope creates
From its own wreck, the thing it contemplates
Neither to change, nor falter nor repent,
This is alone life, joy, empire and victory.

This is as true of our revolutionary titans of freedom struggle as it was true of the Titan in the Greek fable.

Come all who shall mind no danger
Death, oppression, accident or thunder
Who, looking steadfast on Mother's face
Long, broken to bits, to die.

34 The Revolutionary Movement 1925–1934

Onwards, my comrades, onwards never fall back. The day of bondage is disappearing and the dawn of freedom is ushered in . . . Be up and doing.

SURYA SEN

In the mid-1920s, a new wave of a revolutionary movement emerged, which soon developed as a major stream. In several important ways, this new phase differed from its earlier cousin which had created a stir in the first two decades of the twentieth century. First, the new movement was predominantly secular, shedding all its past religious tinge. In fact, Marxism became its main source of inspiration, which was also reflected in its new slogan of *Inquilab Zindabad* replacing the earlier battle cry of *Bande Mataram*. Along with the liberation of the country from foreign rule, ending of exploitation of man by man also became the main objective of the new movement. Second, there also occurred a paradigm shift in respect of the strategy and tactics of the movement: the new emphasis shifted from individual killings to mass liberation in terms of long-term strategic goals, though individual killings were not totally abandoned for tactical reasons. Third, the new movement paid a lot of attention to its organisational and ideological aspects. Fourth, even in terms of leadership pattern, the new movement was better structured; Bhagat Singh in the north and Surya Sen in the east emerged as the main ideologues of new the revolutionary movement. But before we go into the details of the new movement, it would be expedient for us to delineate its historical background.

A number of new forces and factors impinged upon the emergence of the new revolutionary movement. In the first place, the political environment created by the Khilafat and Non-Cooperation Movements preceded by the Rowlatt Satyagraha and Jallianwala Bagh massacre had created a groundswell of anger and resentment against the British. On the top of it, Gandhij's promise of 'Swaraj within one year' had created high hopes in the country. A number of young people, including a large number of ex-revolutionaries, particularly from Bengal, had joined the Gandhian movement with a lot of high expectations and enthusiasm. Viewed in this light, the withdrawal of the Non-Cooperation Movement in the wake of the Chauri-Chaura incident was a real anti-climax. With hopes belied, but full of grit, determination and enthusiasm, a number of young activists started searching for a new path. Now, they were, more than ever, convinced that there was no alternative to a violent path. The fact of the Russian revolution getting consolidated even in the face of Western hostility had further inspired them to take to the path of armed rebellion, which is why Marxism became a new source of inspiration for these revolutionaries. Besides, the emergence of a new working class and peasant organisations which had emerged in the face of deteriorating economic conditions also created a new hope for a revolutionary movement, providing these revolutionaries with a major social support base. How much the withdrawal of the Non-Cooperation Movement had affected the young political activists could be gauged by the fact that some of the prominent leaders of the new revolutionary movement like Surya Sen, Jatin Das, Bhagat Singh, Chandra Shekhar Azad and Jogesh Chandra Chatterjee were the old non-cooperators.

The genesis of the new revolutionary movement could be traced in the formation of the Hindustan Republican Association (HRA) in October 1924, in Kanpur. The moving spirit behind the new organisation were Sachindra Nath Sanyal, Ram Prasad Bismil, Jogesh Chandra Chatterjee and a number of other young people. The Hindustan Republican Association was basically committed to the objective of throwing out the British from Indian soil and the establishment of an Indian Republic based on adult franchise. But one of the difficult problems faced by these young revolutionaries was to acquire funds for recruitment and training of the cadre as well as for purchasing arms and ammunition. To them, the only course easily feasible was laying their hands on the government funds and treasury. As they were desperately looking for the funds for their revolutionary activities, they decided to strike soon. Thus, on the night of 9 August 1925, 10 members of the HRA looted government cash by holding up a train at Kakori Railway station near Lucknow. This prompted the government to launch the famous Kakori conspiracy case, in which Ram Prasad Bismil, Roshan Singh and two others were hanged, four of them were sent to the Andamans as lifers and the rest were awarded long-term imprisonment. This created a great stir in the country and these revolutionaries earned the admiration of even those who had differed from their methods of work. The HRA soon started getting replenished by new cadres and a band of new leaders like Bhagat Singh, Chandra Shekhar Azad, Shiv Verma, Vijay Kumar Sinha, Rajguru, Batukeshwar Datta and a host of others came to the fold. Soon they not only re-organised it but also changed its name to Hindustan Socialist Republican Association/Army in September 1928, in a meeting held in Delhi. The change of name of the organisation marked its new position with socialism as its main ideology. Chandra Shekhar Azad became the chief organisation leader and Bhagat Singh its chief ideologue. It was to act as a secretive and underground organisation. In terms of its action plan, the emphasis shifted from individual killings to armed rebellion. But the attack on Lala Lajpat Rai, a highly respected national leader, while he was leading a procession against the Simon Commission at Lahore on 30 October 1928 and his subsequent death in November 1928, forced them to revert to individual killings. On the 17 December 1928 Saunders, the police officer responsible for the attack on Lala Lajpat Rai, was shot dead by Bhagat Singh, Rajguru and Chandra Shekhar Azad. They escaped and none of them could be hauled up for a while.

Not fully contented with the murder of Saunders, HSRA decided to take more dramatic action which could widely catch the imagination of the Indian people and at the same time deliver a stern warning to the British rulers to desist from further oppressive measures. What came as a great provocation to the leaders of HSRA was the British Government's determined initiative to tighten its noose around the neck of the Indian people: It planned to press two Legislative Bills, 'Public Safety Bill' and 'Trade Dispute Bill', which were nothing but direct assaults on the liberty and rights of the Indian people. HSRA decided to protest against these Bills and consequently Bhagat Singh and Batukeshwar Datta threw a bomb in the Central Assembly on 8 April 1929. They also threw pamphlets in the Assembly, explaining the idea behind the bomb-throwing exercise. They made it clear that their intention was not to kill anybody as the nature of bomb itself revealed. In fact, the basic idea was to put the issue of the ending of the colonial rule on the national agenda. This also became obvious as none of them tried to escape after throwing the bomb in the Assembly. They wanted to get arrested to expose the ugly face of the British imperialism before the eyes of our people. Soon the government found some clues to haul them up in the Lahore conspiracy case along with a number of other comrades. Bhagat Singh, Rajguru and Sukhdev becarne the main accused of the Lahore conspiracy case. They demanded better treatment for the political prisoners and a number of them went on hunger strike to mark their protest against the inhuman treatment meted out to them. Jatindra Nath Das died on the 64th day of his hunger strike in Borstall jail at Lahore on 13 September 1929. When his body was being taken to Calcutta, a large number of people thronged different stations to salute this brave son of India and his last journey was followed by thousands of people. The trial in the Assembly bomb case and the Lahore conspiracy case provided an opportunity for Bhagat Singh and his comrades to put up the case for the liberation of the country on the national level. Defending their stand in the Assembly bomb case, Bhagat Singh and Batukeshwar Datta said: 'We dropped the bomb on the floor of the Assembly chamber to register our protest on behalf of those who had no other means left for expression of their heart-rending agony. Our purpose was to make the deaf hear and give the heedless a timely warming'.

But despite their stout defence, both of them were awarded life imprisonment in the Assembly bomb case. But the Lahore conspiracy case, involving the murder of the police officer Saunders proved more deadly. In the course of their trial, these young revolutionaries led by Bhagat Singh succeeded in creating a political storm. Their courage, grit and determination and their enthusiasm and cheerfulness even in face of death, inspired thousands of countrymen, including even some of those who differed with their violent methods. In the Lahore conspiracy case, the judgement of the special tribunal came on 7 October 1930. Bhagat Singh, Rajguru and Sukhdev were given death sentences and some of their comrades like Vijay Kumar

Bhagat Singh

Sinha, Jaidev Kapur, Mahender Singh, and Shiva Verma were given life imprisonment. The government had set up a special tribunal for conducting the trial of Bhagat Singh and his comrades which was boycotted by them.

Bhagat Singh refused to file an appeal despite pressure from his friends, and family members. He was more than ever convinced that his martyrdom would touch the soul of India in its very depth. Subsequently, on 23 March 1931, Bhagat Singh, Rajguru and Sukhdev were hanged and their dead bodies were secretly cremated at Hussainwala. All of them became legendary figures and people looked at their acts of courage with awe, emotion and reverence. In the course of their trial and even after they were sentenced to death, they remained as an epitome of courage and defiance. Just two days before his hanging Bhagat Singh had written:

> If I mount the gallows smilingly and bravely then our destination will come nearer. Indian mothers will long for their children to become Bhagat Singh and the number of martyrs for the freedom will become so big that it will be impossible for all the monstrous strength of imperialism to stall the revolution.

They had also made it clear that their resort to violence was not merely for the sake of violence. It was a part of their larger strategy to bring about a revolution in the country. In a pamphlet called the 'Philosophy of Bomb', the Hindustan Socialist Republican Association had explained its stand in the following memorable words:

> The revolutionaries believe that the deliverance of their country will come through Revolution. The Revolution will not only express itself in the form of armed conflict between the foreign government and its supporters and the people, it will also usher in a new social order.

Explaining the nature of the new social order further, the pamphlet added:

> The revolution will ring the death knell of capitalism and class distinction and privileges. It will give birth to a new state, a new social order. Above all it will establish the dictatorship of proletariat and will forever finish social parasites from the seat of political power.

Not only that, they even defended violence:

> Terrorism instills fear in the hearts of the oppressors, it brings hopes of revenge and redemption to the oppressed masses. It gives courage and self-confidence to the wavering; it shatters the spell of supremacy of the ruling classes and raises the status of the subject race in the eyes of the world, because it is the most convincing proof of the nation's hunger for freedom.

Bihar has its own share in the revolutionary movement. Jogendra Shukla, Kishori Prasanna Singh, Basawan Singh, Suraj Narain Singh and Baikuntha Shukla of Jalalpur were prominent revolutionaries from Bihar. Baikuntha Shukla, an ardent follower of Bhagat Singh, who had killed a renegade revolutionary turned police accomplice and approver, was hanged in Gaya jail on 14 May 1934.

However, after the execution of Bhagat Singh and his comrades, HSRA was in disarray with most of its other leaders behind bars. Chandra Shekhar Azad, who had earlier vowed never to get arrested, was killed by the police on 27 February 1931, in Alfred park, Allahabad. The Hindustan Socialist Republic Association/Army virtually came to an end by 1931 after playing a glorious role in our freedom struggle.

Finally, whether or not one agrees with their basic formulations regarding violence, the new social order and their new socialist ideology and even their incessant hankering for martyrdom, one could not but be highly impressed by their sincerity, courage and determination. In fact, one has to bow one's head before these young revolutionaries out of the respect and veneration they commanded. They contributed a great deal in the spread of national consciousness, and creation of a deep desire among our people for their own liberty and freedom. They have to be judged only by the courage of convictions: they walked on the path they chose, holding their heads erect, with a lot of confidence and convictions. Whenever the country's freedom will be in peril, people like Bhagat Singh and his comrades will become the main source of inspiration for the youth of the country.

Revolutionary Movement in the Eastern India

During the same period, Bengal was another area where the revolutionary movement revived and played a sustained role in the freedom struggle. It is relevant to recall that when a general amnesty was granted in the wake of the Act of 1919, a number of revolutionaries from Bengal were released and they joined the Non-Cooperation Movement at the call of the Congress leader C R Das. Surya Sen, who became a prominent revolutionary leader was one of them. However, the withdrawal of the Non-Cooperation Movement by Gandhiji led to a bitter frustration overtaking the youth of Bengal, Gopinath Saha attempted to kill the most hated Police Commissioner Charles Targert in January 1924. Despite popular protests Saha was sent to the gallows. Meanwhile, some arms, ammunition and a bomb factory was discovered by the police which led to the arrest of a number of political activists, including Subhas Chandra Bose, under a draconian law. Some other stray revolutionaries continued to be active in some parts of Bengal. One of them was Pramod Chaudhary, a detenue in Alipore jail and an active member of the Hindustan Republican Association, who fatally wounded a Bengal police officer in the course of his visit to the Alipore jail.

Subsequently, the most prominent revolutionary group known as Chittagong group emerged under the leadership of Surya Sen. By 1930, Surya Sen had succeeded in building up a band of dedicated revolutionaries under his leadership. Surya Sen and his group were firmly of the opinion that it was only through armed insurrection that the country could free itself from the foreign yoke. Surya Sen's group also was not in favour of the individual killing except when it became absolutely necessary. The Chittagong group believed that a demonstrative armed insurrection around Chittagong would inspire the Indian youth to plan and execute a similar rebellion in other parts of the country, forcing the British to flee out of the country.

Some of the prominent comrades of Surya Sen were Anant Singh, Ganesh Ghosh and Lokenath Paul. They were planning an armed insurrection around Chittagong for some time. Their preparation was marked by meticulous care and military precision. The day, 18 April 1930 was set out as the D-day. The main plan was to destroy telecommunications as well as railway communications so that Chittagong was cut off from the rest of the country, which would prevent the British from rushing with massive reinforcement to suppress the insurrectionists of Chittagong. Two groups of revolutionaries were assigned the task of cutting telecommunications and the railway communications at Dhum and Feni railways stations, located 80 and 60 miles from Chittagong. Inside Chittagong, the plan was to takeover the police armoury as well as the auxiliary police armoury and carry out an attack on the European club visited by high British officials. On 18 April 1930, the revolutionaries, under the leadership of Surya Sen, really struck in a well-planned move. Telecommunications and railway communication were cut off and the two groups of revolutionaries in Chittagaong succeeded in taking over the police armoury and auxiliary police armoury. However, being a Good Friday, the European club was virtually empty; hence their plan to capture British officials could not be executed. But in the course of the attack, some police officials also got killed.

Such a daring act on the part of the revolutionaries created panic among the British population, who fled in a ship anchored in the port. An Independent Revolutionary Government was set up under the leadership of Surya Sen, who appealed to his countrymen to extend all kinds of help to the revolutionary government. Soon the revolutionaries realised that they needed a safer base to operate and sustain their revolutionary movement. As such, they moved to a nearby hill known as Jalalabad Hill. By 22 April 1930, the revolutionary group well dug in Jalalabad Hill, was surrounded by British forces and in the ensuing battle both sides suffered causalities. Soon a realisation dawned upon Surya Sen and his comrades that with the new superior British forces a direct fight was not possible. Hence, they decided to move out of the hill and to go into hiding in the surrounding villages, so that they could continue the struggle using guerrilla techniques. Meanwhile, Ram Krishna Biswas, a young revolutionary who had killed a police officer was hanged in May 1931. Another hostile police officer was killed by Haripad Bhattacharya on 31 August 1931. In 1931, two young girls, Santi Ghose and Suniti Choudhury shot dead a British official in Comilla. Stray revolutionary activities continued in some parts of Bengal.

Meanwhile, police succeeded in locating the hiding place of Surya Sen and his comrades. In June 1932, they raided the place. Though Surya Sen succeeded in escaping, some of his comrades lost their lives. One of the followers of Surya Sen was Preetilata Waddedar, who successfully led an attack on the European Club on 24 September 1932 and committed suicide while making it possible for her comrades to escape. Finally, on 16 February 1932, Surya Sen was captured after being betrayed by a local landlord. This was followed by the surrender of Kalpana Datta on 18 May 1932. The final judgement of the Chittagong Armoury raid case came on 14 August 1933, in which Surya Sen along with Tarakeswar Dastidar were awarded a death sentence and Kalpana Datta was given life imprisonment. Finally, Surya Sen and Dastidar were hanged on 12 January 1934 which virtually marked the end of the rebellion.

Surya Sen

Some stray revolutionary incidents continued in the area for some time. For instance, in December 1935, a young revolutionary, Rohini Barua killed a police officer and he was subsequently hanged. Another daring attack by the Chittagong revolutionary group was on Paltan ground when a cricket match was on. Out of the group of four revolutionaries, Himmansu Chakravarty and Nitya Ranjan Sen were killed by police and the other two, Krishna Chandra and Haren Battacharya were hanged on 5 June 1934. Thus, by 1935, Surya Sen group had been wiped out and terrorist movement virtually came to an end.

In retrospect, it seems that primarily it was their daring style of functioning coupled with extreme government repression, violating all norms of civilised behaviour, which ultimately led to the decline of the revolutionary movement of this phase. The martyrdom of Chandra Shekhar Azad, followed by the martyrdom of Surya Sen, was the high watermark of the revolutionary movement of that period. The other revolutionaries were awarded life imprisonment and sent to the Andamans and those who were left behind were put behind bars. In the face of such a display of ruthless and inhuman repression by the government, sheer grit, determination and few dare devil acts of these young revolutionaries were hardly a match for the former's ruthless acts. Not that these young revolutionaries were not aware of the problem. In fact, many of them had already visualised their martyrdom as a price to be paid to become a living source of inspiration for the youth of the country.

The critics might continue to point out their lack of organisation, and their failure to mobilise and carry the masses along with them.

They might even say that by the acts of open defiance and bravery, these young people made it easier for the government to lay their hands on them. They may add that some of these young revolutionaries even appeared to be in a hurry to seek martyrdom. All these observations might contain some grains of truth. But there is no doubt that these limitations do not diminish their seminal contributions to the cause of Indian freedom. First, they made a tremendous impact on the minds and hearts of the youth, enthusing them to fight relentlessly for the freedom of the country. Second, they underlined the essential unity of our people and thus blazed a new trail on the front of secularism. Their contribution to promoting the secular fabric of India appears more spectacular as it was during that period when various communal groups had started eating into the vitals of India. Third, the lasting contribution of these revolutionaries was to demand and popularise the idea of Purna Swaraj. They were the first to raise and popularise it by making supreme sacrifices. Fourth, they also made some contribution towards linking the fight of independence with the fight for socialism and tried to put the sufferings of the poor and the downtrodden on the national agenda. Fifth, it should not be forgotten that every time the morale of the people became low and national movement was on wane, these young revolutionaries enthused their countrymen with their unprecedented acts of sacrifice and sufferings. In brief, the revolutionary movement between 1925–35 did make its own abiding contributions, both to the struggle for nationalism and socialism.

> *Revolution is an inalienable right of mankind. Freedom is an imperishable birthright of all. For these ideals, for this faith, we shall welcome any suffering to which we may be condemned. At the altar of this revolution we have brought our youth as an incense, for no sacrifice is too great for so magnificent a cause. We are content, we await the advent of Revolution. Long Live Revolution.*
>
> BHAGAT SINGH and his comrades on the Lahore Conspiracy Case

35 The Indian National Army and India's Struggle for Independence

Comrades! My soldiers! Let your battle-cry be 'To Delhi, to Delhi'. How many of us will individually survive this war of freedom, I don't know. But I do know this, that we shall ultimately win and our task will not end until our surviving heroes join the victory parade on another graveyard of the British Empire – the Lal Kila of Ancient Delhi.

SUBHAS CHANDRA BOSE

Subhas Chandra Bose was one of the leading lights and the stormy petrel of the Indian national movement. In his life time, he became a folk-hero creating an eternal niche for himself in the people's memory. Crossing all the barriers of caste, creed, language, religion, region and sex, his memory even now evokes a lot of emotion, passion and respect, verging on the point of veneration. Before we come to discuss his role in the freedom struggle through the Indian National Army, a few words about the highlights of his earlier life is called for.

Coming from an upper middle class family of Cuttack, he was educated in England and even successfully competed in the ICS examination. Coming back to India on the eve of the non-cooperation movement, he plunged into the national movement under the leadership of C R Das. He soon became a prominent leader, taking a bold and militant stand on various issues confronting the country. He was arrested in 1924 when the revolutionary movement started getting revived. After the death of C R Das in 1925, he virtually emerged as one of the tallest political leaders of Bengal. But soon he turned his attention to politics at the national level and along with Jawaharlal Nehru, emerged as a prominent left-winger in the Congress. He joined hands with Jawaharlal Nehru and they jointly took up the cause of Purna Swaraj (as against the Congress leadership's demand of dominion status for India). Together, they succeeded in getting a resolution passed, by the Madras Congress in 1927, which committed itself to the idea of Purna Swaraj. This led the Lahore Congress in 1929, under the presidentship of Jawaharlal Nehru to make a categorical demand for Purna Swaraj. But as Congress left-wingers, there was a fundamental difference of outlook between Nehru and Bose. Nehru, despite his ideological differences with Gandhiji, was always at the best of terms with him on a personal level. Bose, perhaps, carried his ideological differences with Gandhiji to the personal level. But his deep sense of patriotism and his commitment to the cause of freedom of the country always remained unchallenged. His popularity led him to be elected as the Congress President at the Haripura Congress in 1937. Despite his indifferent health, he insisted and got elected as the Congress President at the Tripuri Congress in 1938, by defeating Gandhiji's own nominee P Sitaramayya, which was taken by Gandhiji as his own defeat. As the sky was getting overcast with the Second World War, Bose became firmly of the opinion that the best policy of the Indian nationalists would be to give total opposition to the British during the war and forge an open alliance with the Axis powers. But the Congress leadership was still in a dilemma: to oppose or not to oppose the British at the critical juncture. After the Tripuri Congress, he failed to constitute his own Working Committee and his differences with the Congress leadership reached such a level that he was subsequently expelled from the Congress, prompting him to form his own Party, the Forward Bloc. The British Government was aware of Bose's line of thought and arrested him on 2 July 1940. Soon he had to be released on account of his failing health and was put under house arrest in his own home in Calcutta. But on 16 January 1941, he escaped from his house by dodging the police and reached Berlin on 28 March 1941 via Afghanistan and Moscow.

In Berlin he met Hitler and his associates, and was given an opportunity to deliver anti-British speeches from the Berlin Radio. He even succeeded in raising an Indian legion in January 1942, from among the Indian prisoners of war captured by the German Army. But Bose wanted the German government to make a categorical announcement for Indian independence, which the latter was not willing to do. Consequently, Bose did not see much of an independent role for himself from the German territory, which prompted him to look for an alternative.

Meanwhile, the Japanese had jumped in the war fray and were making spectacular success in the South-East Asian war front. When the Japanese captured Singapore on 15 February 1942, Bose visualised a better role for himself in the cause of Indian Independence, in the South-East Asian region. There was another reason for Bose's new plan to change his arena of operation to East Asia. The Indian Independence League, an organisation committed to the cause of Indian freedom, had been active in that region under the leadership of an old revolutionary war horse, Rasbehari Bose. In March 1942, a conference under the auspices of the League was called in Tokyo to discuss the war and the Indian situation. It was from this meeting that the idea of the Indian National Army emerged. Besides, it was also decided at the conference that to discuss all related issues, a bigger conference would be held at Bangkok in June 1942. The Bangkok conference was also attended by some of the representatives of the Indian soldiers taken as war prisoners by the Japanese. One of them was Captain Mohan Singh, who had been a war prisoner after the fall of Malaya in December 1941. He was entrusted by the Japanese with the task of raising an Indian brigade to fight against the British for independence of India. It was also decided by the Bangkok conference to extend an invitation to Subhas Chandra Bose to take up the leadership of the Indian National Army. Mohan Singh succeeded in enlisting the support of 20,000 prisoner soldiers out of 40,000 (being the total number of the Indian prisoners of war). It was on the 1 September 1942 that the Indian National Army was formally inaugurated under the leadership of Captain Mohan Singh. However, on the issue of the independent role for the Indian army, Mohan Singh fell out with the Japanese and was even arrested for a while.

Subhas Chandra Bose and Rasbehari Bose

Meanwhile, Subhas Bose reached Tokyo on 13 June 1943, sailing secretly through German and Japanese submarines.

Immediately he met General Hideki Tojo, the then the prime minister of Japan and got an assurance from him on the issue of Indian independence, which he had failed to get from Hitler in Germany. He appealed to all people of Indian origin living in the South-East Asian region, to extend every possible help in the cause of India's freedom. He reached Singapore on 2 July 1943 and received a tumultuous welcome. On 4 July 1943 he took over the presidentship of the Indian Independence League from Rashbehari Bose and, in the presence of thousands of his admirers, he made a solemn declaration to form a provisional government soon and also to lead the Indian National Army to fight for Indian freedom. This was followed by his declaration on the formation of *Azad Hind Fauz* on 5 July 1943 and he gave a clarion call of *Chalo Delhi* (on to Delhi). Subsequently, on 25 August 1943, he formally assumed the direct command of the Indian National Army. On 21 October 1943, the provisional government of India was announced in the presence of a large number of Indians with himself as the head of the Government and the commander-in-chief of the Army. A C Chatterjee was to be the in-charge of Finance; S A Aiyar as the in-charge of publicity and propaganda and Laxmi Swaminathan as the in-charge of womens affairs.

Subhas Chandra Bose called upon the Indian people to rally around, under the banner of the provisional government to prosecute the war of Indian independence with valour and dedication. This provisional government was soon recognised by a number of countries including Germany, Italy, Crotia, Burma, Thailand, Philippines and Manchuria. Subsequently, on 6 November 1943, the Japanese handed over the islands of Andaman and Nicobar to the provisional government of India, and Subhas Chandra Bose set his feet on the soil of India, renaming them as *Shahid* and *Swaraj Islands*. Initially, the Japanese commanders cold shouldered the Indian proposal to allow the Indian National Army to spearhead the war of Indian liberation. But on persistent demands, they agreed to the Indian proposal. A Guerrilla Regiment called Subhas Brigade was set up in September 1943, which reached Rangoon in January 1944. Meanwhile, after taking over the direct command of the INA, Subhas Bose concentrated on the twin-task of its expansion and reorganisation. He developed a detailed plan for recruitment and training. There were different training centres for male and female recruits. The training period for the recruits lasted for six months, after which they were absorbed in the INA. Women recruits came forward in a big way and there was a separate regiment for them called Rani Jhansi Brigade. The two other brigades were called Gandhi Brigade and Nehru Brigade. Shah Nawaj Khan was appointed as the chief of the Subhas Brigade whereas Laxmi Swaminathan was the chief of the Rani Jhansi Brigade. Subhas Chandra Bose insisted that the INA formations would remain under the Indian command and would be given an independent area of operations, to which the Japanese Commanders ultimately agreed.

The INA Campaign

As stated earlier, the Indian National Army had been set up to work for Indian liberation through armed struggle. A number of brigades named after the national leaders, viz., Gandhi, Nehru and Azad had been set up. Subhas Brigade headed for the Indian frontiers from Rangoon on 3 February 1944 – splitting into two – one heading to Kaladan valley in Arakan and the other towards Chin Hill via Mandala and Kalewa. On the way to Kaladan valley, they defeated the British formations and in May 1944 they entered inside the Indian Territory near Mowdock post – fifty miles east of Cox's Bazar. This was a historic occasion for the soldiers of INA, who had finally set their feet on the Indian soil and they celebrated the occasion with a lot of gusto and enthusiasm. And when the Japanese contingent decided to withdraw, the soldiers of INA continued to hold on to their position till September 1944. The other INA formation had left Rangoon on 4-5 February 1944, and soon reached Kalewa via Mandalay. The soldiers of INA once again displayed their mettle by capturing the British stronghold at Klang and a large contingent marched towards Kohima and arrived there in May 1944 and captured the adjoining area, fighting shoulder to shoulder with the Japanese forces against the British. The Indian tricolour was hoisted in and around Kohima. But they could not hold on to it as they, along with the Japanese, had to withdraw from this front. This marked the end of the Kohima campaign. On the Imphal front, there were initial successes in which the INA men displayed rare bravery and valour. But towards the middle of June 1944 it became difficult for the INA men to hold on to their positions in the face of severe British counter-attack and heavy monsoon, which led to the disruption of supply lines. That forced them to retreat to Kalewa. But the siege of Imphal did not succeed as the Japanese position had weakened on account of the involvement in the Pacific front and by June, the Imphal campaign had ended in a failure. The failure could be attributed to a large number of factors including bad monsoon, tough and treacherous topography of the fighting zone and gradual Japanese withdrawal of their war machines to the Pacific region.

Soon by the winter of 1944-5 the British launched their counter-offensive in a big way. By May 1945, the Japanese position became precarious and both the Japanese army and the contingent of INA had to withdraw from the Indian front. By May 1945, Rangoon was captured by the British force. After the Americans in August 1945 threw two atom bombs on Hiroshima and Nagasaki, the Japanese immediately surrendered. Subhas Chandra Bose was allegedly killed in an air-crash on 18 August 1945, though it is still being debated whether he really died on that date. Anyway, thus ended the brilliant political career of one of the bravest sons India ever produced.

Trial of the Soldiers of INA

A number of INA officers led by G S Dhillon, Prem Sehgal and Shah Nawaj Khan, belonging to the three communities Sikh, Hindu and Muslim, were put on trial in the Red Fort. This created a big stir in the politics of the country. The demand for the release of INA prisoners was universal as in every small or big town of India there were demonstrations demanding their unconditional release. The Congress Party made a big issue out of it even though its leaders had differed with Subhas Chandra Bose so far as his methods were concerned. Both Jawaharlal Nehru and Jinnah joined the team of defence lawyers with Bhulabhai Desai in defending the INA prisoners.

In fact, when the Congress leaders were released in June 1945, the main issue which they found handy for popular mobilisation was the trial of the brave and patriotic soldiers of the INA. There was a groundswell of sympathy, admiration and even adoration for them. The Indian National Congress passed a resolution in September 1945 in their support. Soon an INA relief committee was set up for fund mobilisation. The people liberally contributed to this fund. An INA week was observed from 5 to 11 November and large number of meetings were held all over the country in which every political party participated, including the Muslim League.

All these mobilisation attempts soon bore fruit. Though all the three prisoners, viz., Dhillon, Sehgal and Khan were awarded the death sentence, in view of unprecedented support for them, they were given pardon by the Governor-General using his special powers. And the Congress also got its political dividends by winning the 1945-46 election hands down.

It is true that the Indian National Army, despite its valour and dedication, failed to achieve its basic objective of freeing the country from the British yoke. There were many reasons for it including lack of resources, limited number of soldiers, lack of proper training and its dependence on Japanese support. Despite apparent failure, it made a singular contribution in the cause of the Indian independence. The tale of their bravery and sacrifices caught the imagination of the people all over the world. Second, the sacrifice of INA men struck a sympathetic chord in the hearts of even those Indian soldiers who were fighting on the British side. After the British were able to recapture Rangoon, the British-Indian soldiers warmly fraternised with the defeated soldiers of INA. Such a bonhomie raised a question mark against the continued loyalty of the Indian soldiers to the British rule. It soon affected the Indian army and revolt of the Royal Navymen was partly attributed to the resentment among the Indian armed forces against the INA trial. Perhaps the fear of a wider revolt by the Indian armed forces also contributed to the hastening of the end of the British rule. Third, the INA experiment demonstrated beyond doubt not only the unquestioned leadership qualities of Subhas Chandra Bose but also his pristine patriotism. Whether dealing with Hitler or Tojo he always kept the cause of the Indian independence in the forefront and refused to compromise on the issue of an independent line for the Indian people. There is no surprise that till today in millions of Indian homes, he is treated as one of the bravest sons of India. Fourth, INA experiment underlined the fact of the composite nature of our culture and the fact of Hindu–Muslim unity. This was remarkable as it was during that period that the Muslim League led by Jinnah was playing its nefarious game of Hindu–Muslim disunity. INA played a glorious role in promoting the secular character of our freedom struggle.

Royal Indian Navy Revellion

INA trial had evoked a strong protest in the Indian army. This was proved when a number of men in uniform, not only contributed to the fund being raised for supporting the INA men, but they also attended in uniform the reception being extended to the released INA prisoners. On the INA issue, a popular explosion took place on 21-22 November 1945, when in Calcutta a large procession was taken out, consisting of students as well as people, led by different political groups, including that of the CPI. A number of students were killed in this agitation which further spread in the subsequent days as it was joined by the working class and taximen. As a result of this hue and cry, the government conceded on 1 December 1945, that only those INA men who were accused of murder and such heinous crimes would be brought to justice. This was followed by a remission of sentences for the first batch of INA undertrials. Soon this was followed by the gradual withdrawal of Indian soldiers from Indo-China and Indonesia, which was one the major demands of the people. But that was not the end of the matter. When Abdul Rashid of the INA was sentenced to seven-years rigorous imprisonment, Calcutta once again exploded in February 1946. Once again firing took place in which a number of people were killed.

It was in this background that the uprisings in the Royal India Navy (RIN) should be viewed. On 18 February 1946 the Ratings of the Signal school in Bombay went on a hunger strike on the issue of pay, food and racial discrimination. The immediate provocation for the hunger strike was the derogatory racial remarks by their commanders, which was taken as a national insult. Soon they were joined by their comrades of the naval establishment. They took control of the ships and with mounted guns, they were willing to open fire. The Rating set up the Naval Central Strike Committee headed by M S Khan, which not only demanded better pay, food and end of racial discriminates, but also the release of INA prisoners and withdrawal of the Indian soldiers from the South-East Asian country. By 22 February, the strike virtually engulfed all the naval bases of the country involving 78 ships, 20 shore establishments and 20,000 Ratings. They were joined by the working class of Bombay, which struck work and joined demonstrations in their favour. The army was called in and in the army firings a number of people were killed. An attempt was made to pacify them and it was primarily through the efforts of Sardar Patel that they were persuaded to surrender on 23 February 1946.

It is true that the RIN revolt had a short span of life. But it clearly demonstrated that the British could no longer take the loyalty of the Indian soldiers for granted. Besides, a stern message also went home to them that in future the people and the army might join hands to throw them out from the Indian soil. All this, perhaps, hastened the process of the British decision to end their occupation of India at their earliest.

I am sure that Subhas will go down in history as one of our great and distinguished patriots and freedom-fighters.

J B KRIPALANI

Part V

Towards Independence and Partition

Musalmans are not a minority as it is commonly known and understood. . . . Musalmans are a nation according to any definition of nation, and they must have their homelands, their territory and their state.

Mohammad Ali Jinnah

I am a Musalman and am proud of that fact. . . . I am proud of being an Indian. I am part of the indivisible unity that is Indian nationalities. I am indispensable to this noble edifice and without me this splendid structure of India is incomplete. . . . I can never surrender this claim.

Abul Kalam Azad

Through a long night of waiting, a night full of fateful portents and silent prayers for the dawn of freedom, of haunting spectres of hunger and death, our sentinels kept watch, the lights were burning bright, till at last, the dawn is breaking and we greet it with utmost enthusiasm.

S Radhakrishnan

Part V

Towards Independence and Partition

36 The Cripps Mission

Thus this proposal (the Cripps's) was not mere acceptance of Pakistan or a particular partition, bad as that would have been, but something much worse opening the door to the possibility of an infinite number of partitions. It was a continuing menace to the freedom of India and a barrier to the fulfilment of the very promise that had been made.

JAWAHARLAL NEHRU

On several counts, the Cripps Mission marked an important milestone on the road to a negotiated constitutional settlement between the British Government and the people of India. For the first time, the British Government clearly accepted the principle of self-determination for the people of India as it conceded their right to frame their own constitution, which was a long-standing demand of the Indian national movement. Besides, it was the first major attempt of the Congress leadership to enter into a detailed negotiation with the British on their own: on all other earlier occasions, it was Mahatma Gandhi who had negotiated with the British. Moreover, the Cripps proposals for the first time clearly conceded the right of the British provinces and the Indian states to opt out of the Indian union and thus opening a wide road towards the vivisection of India.

For all these reasons, the Cripps proposal deserves detailed scrutiny and evaluation. But before doing that, let us delineate some of the factors and forces that prompted the Indian leadership and the British Government to engage in a serious discussion even when the Second World War was still raging. In fact, it was the deteriorating war situation particularly on the eastern frontier of India which forced both parties to engage in serious dialogue. The Japanese invasion of India appeared imminent as the allied defences had collapsed in the whole of South-East Asia. Thus, it was clear even to a diehard imperialist like Premier Churchill that the support of the Indian people and their leadership were needed by the British to successfully meet the challenge of the Japanese menace. What perhaps encouraged the British Government to take a new initiative was the fact that the Indian leadership also appeared inclined to give serious consideration to any fresh proposal from the British as they were doubly concerned about the defence of India. This had been made clear as the Congress leadership had refused to go along with Gandhiji on his proposal to a non-violent resistance to war so much so that he was relieved of his leadership after the withdrawal of the individual satyagraha movement in December 1941. It was therefore clear that the Congress leadership had no moral compunction in extending its support to the British war efforts if its demand for freedom was conceded by the British.

Moreover, there were other compelling reasons for the British to break the deadlock after the rejection of the 'August offer' in 1940 by the Indian leadership. During early 1942, Chiang-Kai-Shek, along with his wife visited India and extended moral support to the cause of the Indian independence. His visit made a very favourable impression on the world public opinion as China itself was a victim of Japanese aggression. What perhaps gave an added help was the interest shown by President Roosevelt in Indian affairs, prompting even Churchill to take some initiatives to seek the support of the Indian leadership. Roosevelt had even contradicted Churchill's statement that the Atlantic Charter was not applicable to the Indian situation. Not only that, a section of the British Cabinet led by the Labourites also favoured some fresh initiative on the part of the British to break off the Indian deadlock. Presumably, all this influenced the British Government to set up the Cripps Mission in March 1942.

Cripps and Gandhiji

Once the decision was taken, the obvious choice fell on Sir Stafford Cripps, a member of the British War Cabinet. He was a well known socialist leader having the reputation of bringing Russia on the side of the allies. Besides, he had earlier visited India and discussed the Indian situation with a number of Indian leaders. Additionally, he was on friendly terms with Jawaharlal Nehru. On all these counts he was supposedly the right choice for holding negotiations with the Indian leadership. He reached India on 22 March 1942 and stayed till 11 April 1942, engaging himself in serious discussions with the Indian leadership.

The Cripps Proposal

Cripps carried a draft proposal which subsequently come to be known as the Cripps Mission plan. The major components of Cripps' proposal were as follows:

1. The preamble of the draft proposal clearly mentioned that the basic objective of the British Government was to usher India to a state of self-governance. To that end, the government contemplated the creation of a new Indian Union, having dominion status and thus, being 'associated with the United Kingdom and other Dominions by a common allegiance to the Crown but equal to them in every respect'.
2. Two types of proposals were made for giving a concrete shape to the above objective: long-term and short-term. As a long-term measure, a promise was held that after the cessation of the war, an elected constitution-making body would be set up to frame a new constitution for India.
3. An electoral college would be set up for the election of the above body. As a first step immediately after the war, the election for the provincial assemblies would be held. All elected members of the provincial assemblies would constitute one segment of such an electoral college. The other segment would be provided by the representatives from the Indian states to be nominated by the Indian princes. Indian states would send these representatives in the same proportion to their total population as in the case of representatives of British India. State's representatives would have the same powers as those from British India.

4. The total number of the constitution-making body would be one-tenth of the number of the electoral college. The election would be held on the basis of proportional representation.
5. This Constituent Assembly would frame the new constitution for India. On its part, the British Government committed itself to accept and implement the new constitution subject to two conditions:

   (i) A province at any stage would be free to reject the new constitution and opt out of the Union and could retain its existing constitutional position. However, it would be also open to future accession to the Union on its own discretion. Besides, such non-acceding provinces could frame their own constitution, which, in the eye of His Majority's Government, would have the same status as the Indian Union.

   (ii) Indian states were given freedom to join or not to join the proposed union. In their case, the proposal made it clear that a new treaty arrangement would have to be re-negotiated in the light of the new situation. This would apply to both acceding and non-acceding states.

The second part of the draft proposal dealt with the interim phase. It was made absolutely clear that until the new constitution comes into being, His Majesty's government must bear the responsibility for and retain the control and direction of the Defence of India as a part of their World War effort. But it was also provided that the government of India would bear the responsibility for mobilising the military, moral and material resources of India with the cooperation of the people of India. It was further envisaged that the Indians would immediately become members of the Viceroy's Executive Council, primarily with a view to prop up war efforts. The leaders of the principal sections of the Indian people were invited for immediate and effective participation in commonwealth as well as in the United Nations. Thus, they were exhorted to give their active and constructive help in the discharge of a task, which was vital and essential for the future freedom of India.

It was clear that whereas the long-term goal was more clear and specific; the short-term arrangements were left deliberately vague and inconclusive. A number of political groups like the Hindu Mahasabha, the leaders of the depressed classes, the Akalis, Anglo-Indians, and the Indian Christians rejected the proposal for their own reasons. But the two dominant political organisations which really mattered, viz., the Indian National Congress and the Indian Muslim league, entered into a sustained dialogue with Cripps. The Muslim League was basically happy that the core idea of Pakistan (freedom to opt out of the Union) had been conceded by the Cripps proposal. Nevertheless, it did protest that the Muslim nation's right to self-determination had not been clearly and unequivocally conceded by the proposed arrangement. However, Jinnah waited for the final acceptance/rejection of the proposal by the Congress before giving his own decision.

Negotiations with the Congress

The Congress Party was unhappy with the Cripps proposal. Mahatma Gandhi, after he came to know of the details of the proposal, asked Cripps to go back to his country by the first available plane. He even nodded his agreement when someone commented that the proposal was like 'a post-dated-cheque drawn on a crashing bank'. However, he left it to the Congress leadership to negotiate and come to their own conclusions. Jawaharlal Nehru was profoundly depressed by the contents, nature and implications of the proposal. Nevertheless, the Congress entered into serious negotiations with Cripps on the interim arrangement to be made, even though it rejected its long-term arrangements. The Congress had serious objections to the long-term part of the proposal primarily on three counts:

(i) instead of Purna Swaraj only dominion status had been conceded;
(ii) both the British provinces and the Indian states had been granted the right to opt out of the union, which would result in the dismemberment of the country; and
(iii) the Indian princes had been given the right to nominate/appoint their representatives to the Constituent Assembly instead of the people being given the right to elect them directly.

However, the threat to the Japanese menace was too near to be ignored and the Congress leadership was interested in the optimal mobilisation of the people in defence of India. Hence, despite their reservation on the proposals, they willingly negotiated with Cripps on the nature and extent of immediate transfer of power to the people of India. Maulana Azad, the Congress President and Jawaharlal Nehru were the main negotiators on behalf of the Congress. They tried to impress upon Cripps that some kind of a national government would have to be set up, if the wholehearted support of the people of India were to be sought and achieved. The main hitch was on the power of the Executive Council vis-à-vis the Governor-General. The Congress pleaded for a kind of a cabinet government with the Governor-General acting as the constitutional head. In the initial stages of negotiations, Cripps did give the impression that he was willing to accept the Congress position on this score. But in the final stage, it became clear that all that he was willing to offer was that the Executive Council would be reconstituted with Indian members drawn from all major political groups. However, he was not willing to accept any curtailment of powers of the Governor-General. The second moot point was the status and power of the Defence member of the Executive Council. Initially, the Congress favoured an Indian working as a full-fledged Defence Minister, so that the optimal mobilisation for war could be achieved. However, the Congress was willing to accept the operational freedom of the commander-in-chief of the armed forces and even the ultimate responsibility of the War Cabinet. Initially, Cripps was willing to give only some minor role to the Indian defence member of the Executive Council. However, at one stage of negotiations, a compromise formula seemed to be in sight, with a helping hand from Colonel Louis Johnson, a personal representative of President Roosevelt. But ultimately, Cripps backed out at the behest of the British cabinet. In some British quarters, Cripps was accused of exceeding his brief as he had been handed over a draft proposal which he was to abide by. From the Indian point of view, that was immaterial; the real issue was that negotiations broke down and he virtually left in a huff on 11 April 1942. Thus, the entire exercise came to naught. The Muslim League was waiting for the final response of the Congress and once the Congress rejected the proposal, the League followed suit on the ground that its demand for Pakistan had not been explicitly conceded.

In retrospect, it seems that the Cripps proposal was an improvement on the August offer of 1940, as it openly conceded India's right to self-determination. But the proposal suffered from several incongruities. In the first place, conceding the right of the British Province/Provinces and the Indian states to opt out of the Union was nothing but opening a Pandora's box for the balkanisation of India. It would have meant not just one partition but several partitions. Second, the Cripps Mission gave a big boost to the Muslim League as it found in the proposal, a virtual endorsement of its idea of Pakistan. Thus, the Cripps Mission, even in its failure, cleared the road for the creation of Pakistan. Third, the British stand on the interim arrangement was even worse. In the course of negotiations, it became clear that the British Government never wanted to give any substantial power to the people of India. The exigencies of the war were being used as a pretext to deny substantial political concessions to the Indian people, while it tried to extract maximum concessions from the Indian leadership. It seems that it was more of a window dressing on the part of the British to meet the pressure of the world public opinion, rather than a genuine attempt to transfer substantial power to the people of India. This is also proved by the fact that when President Roosevelt tried to impress upon Churchill to make another attempt at negotiated settlement, he avoided it by saying that Cripps had already left India. Perhaps, the only positive impact of the Cripps Mission was that the British people of all political hues got committed to the idea of freedom for India, which none of them could retrace subsequently. It also cleared the road to Pakistan in yet another way. In the wake of the Cripps Mission the Congress Working Committee got committed to the idea that the people of any 'territorial unit' would not be compelled to remain in the Indian Union against their 'declared and established will'. Thus, it set the ball of independence with partition rolling which reached its final destination in 1947. But the immediate impact of the failure of the Cripps Mission was that it left the Indian people more determined to persevere on the path of struggle. It therefore, provided a historical backdrop to the Quit India Movement.

> *It is a thousand pities that the British Government should have sent a proposal for resolving the political deadlock, which, on the face of it, was too ridiculous to find acceptance anywhere. And it was a misfortune that the bearer should have been Sir Stafford Cripps, an acclaimed radical among the radicals and a friend of India.*
>
> MAHATMA GANDHI

37 The Cabinet Mission Plan

However, in the years to come,
if you are still living, never say never.
What is certain is not certain
Things will not stay as they are . . . and,
Never becomes Before the day is out

BERTOLT BRECHT

The Cabinet Mission Plan in 1946 was the last attempt towards a negotiated-settlement for Indian independence, while keeping its unity intact. The three major parties involved, the British, the Indian National Congress and the Muslim League did enter into serious negotiations, and at one stage success seemed to be within reach. However, the failure of the Plan virtually sealed the fate of united India, making the partition of the country as certain as independence, if not more. What did it really attempt to offer? What were its long-term major implications for independence as well as for the unity of the country? Which of the three contestants should be held responsible for its ultimate failure? These are some of the issues that have been the subject of heated debate among the historians. But before we go into all these issues, let us trace out its historical background.

In the background of the Cabinet Mission was the momentous victory of the Labour Party in England in July 1945, under the leadership of Clement Attlee. What was more, it was for the first time in British history that the Labour Party had won with an absolute majority and, as such, it had the mandate and confidence to take bold and major policy decisions. The Labour's victory had special implications for the Indian national movement. It was already committed to the cause of Indian independence and some of its leaders had close personal relations with the Congress leaders, particularly with Jawaharlal

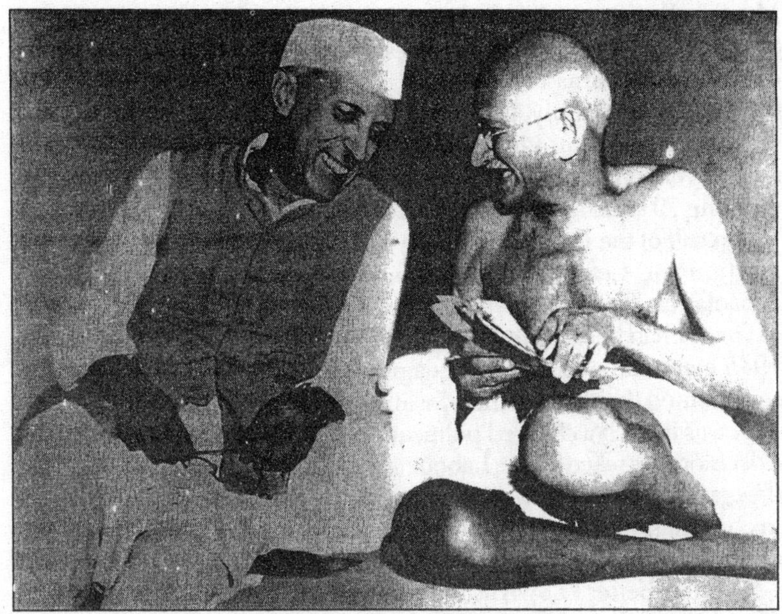

Nehru and Gandhiji

Nehru. In brief, the Labour victory was a good augury for the cause of Indian independence.

On the Indian front, things were not that sanguine. Immediately after his release in early 1944, Gandhiji's negotiation with Jinnah in September 1944 had turned out to be abortive and even the Simla Conference from 25 June to 14 July 1945, had failed to yield any concrete result, primarily due to Jinnah's insistence that the Muslim League should be taken as the sole representative of the Muslim masses. Thus, it was becoming gradually clear that nothing less than Pakistan was acceptable to the Muslim League and to its leader, Jinnah. All his feigned attempts at negotiations were nothing but a part of his tactical line: Pakistan, being his only real and ultimate goal. Notwithstanding this somber Indian scenario, on 21 August 1945 the Viceroy made an announcement that election to both central and provincial assemblies would be held during the winter of 1945. These elections were overdue as no elections had taken place since 1937, due to the war and other contingencies. It needs to be emphasised that these elections under the Act of 1935 had to be held on the basis of limited franchise and separate electorate for the Muslims. So far, in electoral terms the

Muslim League had failed to establish its position as the main spokesperson for the Muslim masses. But the election during the winter of 1945–46 came as a big morale booster for the Muslim League. In the Central Assembly, the Muslim League captured all the Muslim seats, and in the provincial assemblies it got 446 out 495 Muslim seats. Even in Punjab, it had tremendously improved its position by winning 79 seats as against the Unionist Party getting only 10 seats. The result of the Punjab Assembly was more dramatic as in the 1937 election the League had acquired only one seat. It was a poor consolation for the advocates of Indian unity that the League march of victory had been halted in NWFP. Thus, the real significance of the 1945 elections was that the League boldly started claiming that it represented the voice of the Muslim masses in India.

It was in such a charged political atmosphere that in January 1946, a decision was taken by the Labour government to send a parliamentary delegation to India, to work out a negotiated constitutional settlement in consultation with all major Indian political groups. This delegation comprising Sir Stafford Cripps, A V Alexander and Lord Pethic-Lawrence, better known as the Cabinet Mission, arrived in India in March 1946. Primarily the Mission had a two-fold task: (a) to work out an agreed method of framing a new constitution for India; and (b) to reconstitute a new Executive Council representing the main Indian political groups, viz., the Congress and the Muslim League. The Cabinet Mission was aware that it could not have a cakewalk as the battle lines between the Congress and the Muslim League had already been drawn. The Congress was committed to the idea of a united and independent India, whereas the Muslim League insisted on Pakistan, comprising six provinces of Sindh, Punjab, Baluchistan, NWFP, Bengal and Assam. So, the challenge before the Mission was to find a political package that could be acceptable to all concerned parties. The members of the Mission held intensive discussion with all concerned, viz., leaders of the Congress, the League, Sikhs, the Scheduled castes and a host of other groups. But these prolonged discussions did not yield an all-agreed plan. Hence, on 16 May 1946 the Mission, on its own, presented a plan for discussion, which had the following salient points.

(i) The union government would primarily deal with foreign affairs, defence and communications with a power to raise finances for the same.
(ii) Two groups of provinces comprising primarily Hindu and Muslim majority areas, would deal with such remaining subjects

as the provinces in the respective groups would like to deal with in common.

(iii) The provincial governments would be free to deal with all other subjects and would also have all the residuary powers.

(iv) The Indian states would take their appropriate place in the stated structure on the terms to be negotiated with them.

With these points of discussion, the Mission approached both the Congress and the League for further negotiations. Once again these negotiations bore no result. Hence, the Mission put forward a revised plan on its own, obviously taking into account the different viewpoints expressed in the course of the negotiations. The Mission, while putting forward its own plan rejected the idea of Pakistan, as being impractical and unjust. At the same time it also rejected the Congress scheme for a federation but with a proviso that provinces, if they so wished, could cede more subjects to the central government. The Mission rejected the Congress scheme on the ground that such a proviso would create constitutional anomalies and disadvantages. The revised plan of the Mission had the following major points:

(i) The union government with a federal set-up comprising both British India and Princely India would be concerned with three major subjects, viz., foreign affairs, defence and communications. It would, however, have the power to raise finances for the same.

(ii) All other powers including residual powers would be with the provinces.

(iii) The Indian states would retain all subjects and powers not ceded to the central government.

(iv) The provinces would have freedom to form groups and each group could determine the provincial subjects to be taken in common. Each group could have its own executive and legislature.

(v) The plan provided that the Legislative Assembly of a province, by a majority vote could demand a reconsideration of its constitution after a gap of every ten years.

(vi) As per the Cabinet Mission, each province was to be allotted seats in the Assembly on the basis of its population. The formula was to allot one seat for every one million people. The seats thus allotted to each province could be further divided among the main communities of the province in proportion to their population in the province. It further provided that the number of representatives allotted to each community would be elected by members of the Legislature Assembly belonging to that community. Further, the Mission recognised only three major communities: General, Muslims and Sikhs for the purposes of the composition of the Constituent Assembly. The method of election was to be proportional representation with a single transferable vote. The total number of the Constituent Assembly would be 389, out of which 292 members would be from British India, 93 from the States and 4 from the Chief Commissioner's provinces. The total number of seats allotted to the general category, Muslims and Sikhs would be 210, 78 and 4, respectively. The total numbers of seats allotted to the states would be 93, which would also be based on their total population being governed by the same principle of one representative for one million population. The Constituent Assembly thus constituted would meet in Delhi and elect the chairman and other office-bearers. It would have an advisory committee to determine the rights of the citizens and safeguards for the minority.

(vii) The existing provincial Legislative Assemblies were to be grouped in three sections: Section A comprising six Hindu majority provinces of Madras, Bombay, United Provinces, Bihar, Central Provinces and Orissa; Section B were to consist of Muslim majority provinces of Sindh, Punjab, Baluchistan and NWFP; and Section C of Bengal and Assam.

(viii) After settling the initial business of the Constituent Assembly, the provincial representatives of the Constituent Assembly would divide themselves into three sections, namely, A, B and C as provided above. Afterwards, they would settle provincial constitutions for the provinces in the group and would further decide whether any group constitution was needed and, if so, with what provincial subjects the group should deal with.

(ix) It was further made clear that the provinces would have no right to opt out of the group once the new constitutional arrangements have come into operation. Such a decision could be taken only after the first general election under the new constitution.

(x) The provinces could ask for the reconsideration of the schemes only after ten years and not earlier.

Once the Cabinet Mission formulated and concretised its plan, the ball went to the court of two major political players of India: the Congress and the League. Initially, none of the political groups were very enthusiastic about the plan as it fell short of everyone's expectations. It had ruled out the idea of an independent Pakistan as demanded by the League. Nor did it accept the Congress demand of immediate independence and the kind of federation that it had been demanding. The Sikhs were also sceptical about the plan as the bulk of the Sikh population were to remain in the Muslim majority of the B group provinces.

However, unlike the Cripps Mission plan, the new plan did not totally disappoint the Congress and the League. For the Muslim League there was a silver lining as all the six provinces, which the League wanted Pakistan to comprise, were put in Groups B and C which, in any case, would remain under the dominance of the League. Thus, as against six provinces under the Congress dominance, the League got six provinces almost bringing a kind of parity with the former. There was an added attraction for the League: from the long-term point of view, the basis and foundation for the emergence of fully independent and sovereign Pakistan was now within the realm of distinct possibilities. The fact that any province or group of provinces could opt out of the union after ten years was virtually a tantalising idea for the League. Waiting for ten years would not be much of a problem as the idea of Pakistan could be actualised without much of struggle and sacrifice like any deferred payment with a heavy interest. Hence, it was a welcome idea for the League. Perhaps that was the reason why the League accepted the plan on 6 June 1946 even without waiting for the Congress move. The idea of a weak centre was also attractive to the League as with six provinces of Groups B and C it would not find it difficult to dominate the centre. Thus from a short-term perspective the plan had ensured the Muslim interest and from a long-term perspective it had a built-in mechanism to ensure the emergence of Pakistan as conceived by the League. And which is why the League accepted the plan on 6 June 1946.

The Congress also initially found itself in a fix: it did not like the idea of grouping of provinces, more so because of its compulsory nature. The idea of NWFP and Assam compulsorily being put in Group B and Group C, respectively was anathema to it. It tried to wriggle out of the situation by putting its own interpretation on the grouping of the provinces – that it would be optional and not compulsory, which was rejected by the Mission. But the plan had its own attractions for the Congress as well: it was known that in the ensuing election to the Constituent Assembly, the Congress would enjoy absolute majority. And this forecast was proved right when, in the election to the Constituent Assembly held in July 1946, out of 296 seats allotted to the provinces, the Congress won 212 seats, while the Muslim League had to be satisfied with only 73 seats. Perhaps that was the reason why, despite some initial hesitation, the Congress also accepted the plan on 25 June 1946, which was ratified by AICC in its meeting, held during 6-7 July 1946. The Cabinet Mission left India for England on 29 June 1946, after having obtained the consent of two major groups.

Barely two weeks after the acceptance by the two major groups, a statement by Jawaharlal Nehru on 10 July 1946 about the Congress interpretation of the plan threw a spanner in its scheme of implementation. In that statement Nehru, who had taken over as the President of the Congress, made it clear that the Congress was simply committed to participate in the Constituent Assembly, which would have unfettered power to take all decisions. Besides, he also visualised the possibility of an end to the compulsory groupings of the provinces. Nehru's statement raised a hue and cry on the part of the League, which ultimately led to its rejection of the plan on 29–30 July 1946. The League was apprehensive about the whole scheme of the Constituent Assembly in view of the overwhelming majority of the Congress. While rejecting the Cabinet Mission Plan, the League gave a call for 16 August 1946, being observed as the Direct Action Day with a clearly stated objective of achieving Pakistan. The League's direct action was directed against the Hindus and not against the Government. The League instigated riots in Calcutta on 16 August as the League's government was in Bengal, which resulted in massive killings. Soon the League-inspired riots spread to the other parts of the country, which entirely vitiated its secular atmosphere. The situation further worsened when the League joined the interim government on 25 October 1946. For all practical purposes, the long-term component of the Cabinet Mission Plan was shelved for good.

The Formation of the Interim Government

The short-term objective of the Cabinet Mission Plan was the installation of an interim government, comprising all major Indian political groups. This part of the plan was also faced with intractable difficulties. The pace for the formation of the Interim Government was slow, the roadblocks were heavy and the path was tortuous. In June 1946, the Viceroy made an abortive bid for the installation of an Interim Government. But he failed in his attempt as Jinnah insisted on the League's parity with the Congress as well as its exclusive right to nominate all Muslim members – an idea which was not acceptable to the Congress.

However, on 6 August, Nehru was invited to join the interim government. This offer was accepted by the Working Committee on 8 August 1946. On 12 August 1946, the Viceroy invited Nehru to form the interim government. Nehru offered 5 seats to Jinnah which was rejected by the latter. On 24 August 1946, the Viceroy declared that an interim government comprising 12 members (6 Hindus, 3 Muslim and 3 from other minorities) would soon be installed. It was also announced that two more Muslim members would be subsequently added, taking its total strength to 14. On 2 September 1946, an interim government was installed under the leadership of Nehru. An attempt was made to persuade the League to join the Interim government, which resulted in the League joining it on 13 October 1946. But the League joined the interim government virtually on its own terms: it had neither withdrawn its resolution of 29–30 July 1946, rejecting the long-term component of the Mission plan, nor was it willing to join the Constituent Assembly. In fact, with the League's joining the interim

Members of the Interim Government after the Muslim League joined, October 1946. *From left, front:* Baldev Singh, John Matthai, C. Rajagopalachari, Jawaharlal Nehru, Liaquat Ali Khan, Vallabhbhai Patel, I I Chundrigar, Asaf Ali, C H Bhabha. *Rear:* Jagjivan Ram, Ghazanfar Ali Khan, Rajendra Prasad, Abdur Rab Nishtar.

government, the situation took a turn for the worse, so far as the issue of governance was concerned. In fact, the League's intention in joining the interim government was not genuine, as it wanted to wreck the government from within. Thus, the hopes that the League would be a sincere partner in the government and it would also soon join the Constituent Assembly were soon belied. With Liaqat Ali Khan in control of the Finance portfolio, all kinds of obstacles were put in the smooth functioning of the government. The interim government became a divided house, which greatly affected its smooth and effective functioning. The Muslim League boycotted the Constituent Assembly when it ultimately met on 9 December 1946. An attempt was made to work out a compromise formula but nothing much came out of it. Thus, after passing a resolution on its objective, it adjourned till 20 January 1947, in the hope that the Muslim League members might join it by that time. Meanwhile, the Congress raised the demand that either the League members should join the Constituent Assembly or leave the interim government. The League would neither leave the interim government nor would join the Constituent Assembly.

When the Constituent Assembly reassembled on 20 January 1947, the Muslim member continued to boycott it. Soon the League denounced the composition of the Constituent Assembly, which made the Congress demand the League's resignation from the government. But the Viceroy hardly took any concrete steps to seek the resignation of the League members from the Interim government or to make them join the Constituent Assembly. The stalemate continued on both the fronts and events started moving fast. On 20 February 1947, Premier Attlee declared that the British would be leaving India by June 1948. Lord Mountbatten came to India in March 1947 as the Viceroy with a clear mandate to hasten the process of the British withdrawal from India. By March 1947 the Cabinet Mission Plan, in its original form, was virtually dead. And new ideas for a constitutional settlement and the British withdrawal started being explored, leading to what came to be known as the Mountbatten Plan. The last attempt to keep India as a united country ended in a fiasco.

One of the major questions still being debated among the students of modern Indian history is why did the Cabinet Mission Plan collapse, even after being initially accepted by the two major contestants, viz., the Congress and the League? In view of the narration and analysis of the historical facts as delineated above, it is difficult to totally absolve any of the three major parties in the tortuous negotiations: the British, the Congress and the League. All the three had their own perspective on the issues involved and tried to have the best of the bargain. The British were out to ensure their future relations with both the Indian parties, which were needed to retain their future interests in the region, once they have got out of it. We do not find a major departure from the old British policy of throwing their weight in favour of the League at critical moments of history. In this regard, three glaring instances come to our mind. In the process of the formation of the interim government, they went out of the way to assure the Muslim League that they would have the sole authority to nominate all Muslim members. Two, when the Muslim League insisted on the continued boycott of the Constituent Assembly, the British Government, instead of reining it, went out of the way to make it clear that it could not impose a constitution, which was based on the non-participation of a large segment of the Indian populace. Third, the British played a crucial role in persuading them to join the interim government, and did not insist on their joining the Constituent Assembly. Nor did they insist on the withdrawal of the League's resolution of 29–30 July, which had rejected the Cabinet Mission Plan. Not only that, when the League declared the observance of 16 August as the Direct Action Day, which resulted in mass killings in Calcutta, the British did not use the Indian army to quell the communal riots, which was started by the supporters of the League. This was nothing short of abdication of authority in the face of mass frenzy. Not only that, when the League tried to put all kinds of roadblocks in the way of the smooth and effective functioning of the Interim government, the British Government hardly took any step in this regard: it remained a mute spectator to the political stalemate created by the League.

The Muslim League found in the Cabinet Mission Plan a rare opportunity to actualise its demand for Pakistan without much struggle and sacrifice. The League's leaders thought that they could walk out of the Union after ten years with all the six provinces of Groups B and C and form a sovereign and independent Pakistan, which is why making a departure from their earlier policy of waiting for the Congress response, they appeared to be in a mad hurry to accept the Cabinet Mission Plan even though it had rejected the idea of Pakistan. Their insistence on the compulsory groupings of the provinces was also a part of their well-thought-out strategy.

Once it became clear that the Constituent Assembly, in which the Congress had the overwhelming majority, would virtually remain unfettered and would be free to take its own decisions, they got scared as their game was up. Thus, the 10 July statement of the Congress President Jawaharlal Nehru, provided them with a pretext to get out of their previous commitment.

The Congress saw in the plan an opportunity for the people of India to frame their own constitution, which was its long-standing demand. It could feel a distinct possibility of India emerging as a free, independent and sovereign state, if the plan was to be implemented in its own perspective. Hence, it visualised a sovereign Constituent Assembly and optional groupings of the provinces. These were needed as working propositions to thwart the League's idea of Pakistan. It is clear that all three parties were working at the cross purposes. The 10 July statement of Jawaharlal Nehru, insisting on the unfettered nature of the Constituent Assembly and optional grouping of the provinces, could be viewed in this context. The League was, in fact, scared of being dominated in the Constituent Assembly, which might spoil its game for Pakistan. The League feared that its initial dream of walking away with all the six provinces after ten years could not be actualised in view of its weak position in the Constituent Assembly. In retrospect, it seems that they could have found some other excuse to wriggle out of a difficult situation even in the absence of Nehru's statement.

What gave a mortal blow to the long-term part of the Cabinet Mission Plan was the great Hindu-Muslim divide on the ground which had taken an ominous shape after the Direct Action Day declaration of the League and subsequent mass killings. All these led to the sad end of a grand plan to keep India united while making it a free and independent country.

> *There are several occasions when the Congress members of the Interim Government could have resigned. However, the Congress leaders in the Government were disinclined to part with the shadow of power they had achieved. It could have meant going to wilderness and passing some more years in jail. Their zeal for this was at the low ebb.*
>
> J B Kripalani

38 The Mountbatten Plan and the Partition of India

Unbiased at least he was when he arrived on his mission,
Having never set eyes on this land he was called to partition
Between two peoples fanatically at odds,
With their different diets and incompatible gods.
'Time,' they had briefed him in London, 'is short. It's too late
For mutual reconciliation or rational debate:
The only solution now lies in separation.
The Viceroy thinks, as you will see from his letter,
That the less you are seen in his company the better,
So we've arranged to provide you with other accommodation.
We can give you four judges, two Moslem and two Hindu,
To consult with, but the final decision must rest with you.'
Shut up in a lonely mansion, with police night and day
Patrolling the gardens to keep assassins away,
He got down to work, to the task of settling the fate
Of millions. The maps at his disposal were out of date
And the Census Returns almost certainly incorrect,
But there was no time to check them, no time to inspect
Contested areas. The weather was frightfully hot,
And a bout of dysentery kept him constantly on the trot,
But in seven weeks it was done, the frontiers decided,
A continent for better or worse divided.
The next day he sailed for England, where he quickly forgot
The case, as a good lawyer must. Return he would not,
Afraid, as he told his Club, that he might get shot.

W H Auden

In the preceding chapter we have seen that all attempts to work out the Cabinet Mission Plan in its entirety had come to a naught by the first quarter of the year 1947. With the Muslim League's continued boycott of the Constituent Assembly and the obstructionist policy of its representatives in the interim government, the die was cast for the non-implementation of the Cabinet Mission Plan in its entirety. On the top of it, Viceroy Wavell and Premier Attlee had different perspectives on the Indian situation. Wavell favoured the continued effort to pursue the Cabinet Mission Plan, which in Premier Attlee's view was no longer a workable and feasible proposition. Earlier in December 1946, an attempt was made to break the impasse in a meeting at London, called on the initiative of the Secretary of State, in which Nehru, Jinnah and a host of other Indian leaders participated. However, this meeting failed to find a solution for the vexed problems, as both the Congress and the League stuck to their respective positions. The country was moving towards a civil war situation. The communal riots that had started with the Direct Action Day on 16 August 1946, refused to subside and large parts of the country both in the east and the north-west were engulfed in a whirlwind of large scale communal violence. Even the Congress leaders were at their wit's end, not knowing how to get out of the impasse. Gandhiji was the only exception who, working as a one-man non-violent army, was trying his level best to extinguish the fire of the communal violence engulfing different parts of the country including Noakhali and Bihar. The Muslim League launched a civil disobedience campaign against the Unionist Party government headed by Khizr Hyat Khan and brought it down on 3 March 1947. Thus, the country was sliding down towards partition. It was not only the Muslim League alone which was fighting for partitioning India, even the Sikhs from Punjab and Hindus from Bengal were now clamouring for the partition of their respective provinces. Even a section of the Congress leadership was veering around to the view that partition of Punjab and Bengal was the only practical, even though unpleasant, solution. What gave a momentum to the slide down towards partition was Premier Attlee's declaration in the British Parliament on 20 February that the British would move out of India by June 1948. Wavell who had favoured the continuation of the British rule for a few years more was replaced by Lord Mountbatten who took over as the Viceroy and the Governor-General in March 1947. He had been given a clear mandate to arrange for the transfer of power to the Indian hands as soon as possible.

Lord Mountbatten took over the office of the Viceroy on 24 March 1947. He plunged into a serious discussion with all Indian leaders including the Princes. Based on his discussion with Indian leaders, as well as his own perception, he soon came to the conclusion that partition was the only practicable and feasible solution. There is enough evidence to state that Lord Mountbatten had initially proposed that Punjab and Bengal would be partitioned by simple majority and the Indian states would be free to take their own decisions. This plan was code-named as 'the plan Balkan' as it could have led to the balkanisation of India. But in view of Nehru's strong opposition to the plan, it was abandoned at an initial stage. An alternative plan, in which V P Menon had a hand, was prepared which came to be known as the Mountbatten Plan. This Plan was announced on 3 June 1947 and had the following components:

(i) The Constituent Assembly would go ahead with the task of framing the Constitution. The dissident group of the Muslim league would have its own Constituent Assembly.
(ii) The provinces of Punjab and Bengal would be partitioned on the basis of majority of population at the district level. The mechanism for this would be that in both these provinces, the members of the Legislative Assembly would meet in two parts: representatives from the Muslim majority district as one bloc and representatives from the rest would constitute the second bloc. If either of them were to decide in favour of partition by a simple majority these provinces would be partitioned.
(iii) In the NWFP, the people would exercise their choice of joining one or the other Constituent Assembly through referendum. The same mechanism would also apply to the people of Sylhet, a district in Assam.
(iv) There would be fresh elections in parts of Punjab, Bengal and Sylhet in Assam for choosing the representative for the Constituent Assembly.
(v) There would be a negotiated settlement between the successor government and the British Government about the matters arising out of the transfer of power.
(vi) The British paramountcy over the Indian states would come to an end with the transfer of power and these states would have the freedom to join either of the two unions or to remain independent.
(vii) In Sindh, the Legislative Assembly would decide whether the constitution should be framed by the existing Constituent Assembly or a separate one.

(viii) If any of the Punjab groups favours partition, Baluchistan would follow suit.

This was followed by Lord Mountbatten's declaration on 4 June that the transfer of power would take place by 15 August 1947. Admittedly, by June 1947 the partition of India was virtually a *fait-accompli*, as two major groups, the Congress and the Muslim League had already, informally, agreed to the ideas contained in the plan. How Lord Mountbatten succeeded in persuading the two major players to accept his plan could be anybody's guess. His line of arguments was incisive and clear-cut. To the Congress leaders he impressed upon the fact that with partition they could have a strong centre and the bulk of Indian territory including the Princely India. Besides, such an acceptance would lead to the immediate independence of India – a prospect which was very close to the heart of the Congressmen. The alternative was chaos, anarchy and communal killings, taking India to the brink of civil war. Mountbatten sternly told Jinnah and the Muslim

Lord Mountbatten, Mahatma and Lady Mountbatten

League that their dream of Pakistan comprising the six provinces was against the very principle of self-determination they were fighting for. How could the Hindu majority districts of Punjab and Bengal join the proposed state of Pakistan? They could not be denied their own right to self-determination. Perhaps apart from the pressuring and persuasive skill of Lord Mountbatten, the internal condition in the country and non-availability of an alternative also made both the Congress and the League to accept the Mountbatten plan after overcoming their initial hesitation and resistance. This informal acceptance was soon followed by the formal acceptance of the partition plan both by the Congress and the League. The Congress Working Committee endorsed the plan on 3 June 1947. This was followed by an AICC meeting during 14–15 June 1947, which endorsed the plan with some opposition, particularly coming from the members of the Congress Socialist Party. As a consolation, the AICC, while accepting the partition plan, expressed the hope that ultimately, the doctrine of two nations would be discarded by all. Nehru, Patel and Pant strongly pleaded for the acceptance of the plan. Gandhiji, despite his personal reservation, lent a helping hand in the passage of the resolution. This was soon followed by the acceptance of the plan by the Muslim league though it expressed its unhappiness on the partition of Bengal and Punjab.

There were some problems with the Mountbatten plan even after being accepted by the Congress and the League. In the North-West Frontier Province, the existing Assembly had a Congress majority and had voted in favour of joining the existing Constituent Assembly. But under the Mountbatten plan, a referendum was forced on the Pathans of Frontier Province despite the protestation of their leaders like Khan Abdul Ghaffar Khan (Frontier Gandhi). They were not given a choice to opt for their independent state which led to a boycott of the referendum by the Congress in the Frontier province. Thus it went to Pakistan, causing a great injustice to the brave Pathans who had stood by the Indian national movement through thick and thin. The Congress did not make it a breaking point while accepting the Mountbatten plan, which prompted Frontier Gandhi to complain that they had been thrown to the 'wolves'. In Bengal too, there was a move for a united sovereign Bengal. In May 1947, even some of the prominent Muslim leaders like Abul Hasheem and Suhrawardy toyed with the ideal of independent Bengal which, at one stage, had even the tacit support of Sarat Bose. Ultimately, on 20 June 1947, the Bengal Assembly decided for the partition of Bengal. This was soon followed by the decision of the Punjab Assembly on 23 June 1947 for the partition of Punjab followed by Sindh and Baluchistan. People of NWFP and the district of Sylhet opted for Pakistan. Thus the territory of the proposed dominions of India and Pakistan virtually got defined even before the passage of the Indian Independence Act of 1947.

Thus the decks were cleared for the passage of the Indian Independence Act, 1947 by the British Parliament in July which came into force on 18 July 1947, after getting the assent of the Crown. The major provisions of this Act, which was basically an endorsement of the Mountbatten plan, were as follows:

(i) The Act provided for the creation of two independent dominions – India and Pakistan from 15 August 1947.
(ii) The territory of Pakistan was to comprise Sindh, NWFP, West Punjab, East Bengal, Baluchistan and the Muslim majority district of Sylhet. And the rest of the Indian provinces including eastern Punjab and West Bengal were to remain with India.
(iii) The Constituent Assembly of each dominion would frame its own constitution and would have the right to withdraw from the British Commonwealth. It would also have the authority to make ordinary law in respect of its own territory which would have all legal sanctity.
(iv) The King of Great Britain would cease to be the Emperor of India from 15 August 1947. The office of the Secretary of State for India was to be abolished and the Secretary of the Commonwealth Relations Department was to deal with affairs relating to India and Pakistan.
(v) Both the dominions were to have separate Governor-Generals but if they so desired, they could have a common Governor-General. The Governor-General was authorised to take all necessary measures for the effective implementation of provisions of the Act and division of assets between the two countries. He was also authorised to make changes in the provisions of the Act of 1935 to facilitate its smooth functioning.
(vi) British paramountcy over Indian states would cease and they would be free to join either of the two dominions or remain independent.

This was followed by setting up of a Boundary Commission under the leadership of Radcliffe, to draw a boundary between West Punjab and East Punjab, and West Bengal and East Bengal. A Partition Council was also immediately set up with Lord Mountbatten as the chairman with equal number of members from both the Congress and the League. The Partition Council worked through various steering committees. An Arbitration Tribunal was also set up to iron out all differences between the two dominions. Meanwhile, the Constituent Assembly for India including Muslim League members from the non-Pakistan area started working in its all earnestness.

The real thorny problem arose on account of the ending of the British Paramountacy over the Indian States. Some of them tried to retain their independent status. But the bold and sagacious leadership of Sardar Patel, ably assisted by a host of officials led by V P Menon, brought about the integration of states in the Indian union. Thus except Junagarh, Hyderabad, and Kashmir, all other states had signed the Instrument of Accession and the Standstill Agreement by 15 August 1947. This was the greatest silent revolution which brought back most of the areas to the Indian Union.

On 15 August 1947, two dominions of India and Pakistan came into being. The Constituent Assembly of India met on 14 August 1947 and as the midnight approached Jawaharlal Nehru delivered his famous speech on India's 'tryst with destiny'. Lord Mountbatten was appointed

Declaration of India's independence on the midnight of 14-15 August 1947

as the first Governor-General of India and a new cabinet headed by Jawaharlal Nehru was sworn in by him. Similarly, on the same, i.e. 15 August, came into being, the Dominion of Pakistan with Jinnah as the Governor-General and Liaquat Ali Khan as the Prime Minister. It was a special day for Jinnah who had singlehandedly succeeded in carving out a Muslim State by getting India partitioned. For the People of India it was a red-letter day as independence had been achieved after a long and bitter struggle with lots of sacrifice and sufferings of our people. By an irony of fate, the man (Mahatma Gandhi) who had spearheaded the movement for independence of India, was not present to participate in these celebrations. He was far away, fighting almost singlehandedly, the entire army of marauders maddened by communal frenzy. The single incident was enough to establish his status of sainthood – putting him far above the motley crowd of politicians and even statesmen.

A question that has been raised and subjected to protracted debate is: why was there such a mad hurry on the part of Lord Mountbatten, in the second quarter of 1947, to effect the transfer of power to the Indian hands, irrespective of its cost and consequences? A related question is how could he find willing partners among the Indian leaders for his scheme of things? This question becomes more relevant as one of the arguments in his favour was the inconceivable consequences of non-partitioning India. But the horrendous nature of the cost of the partition of India could be gauged by the following facts: In the process of partition 10,000,000 people were driven out of their homes, almost 1,000,000 people killed and 75,000 women including young girls were either raped, murdered for forcibly converted to another religion. Critics argue that in no case non-partitioning India would have involved greater costs. And for this Lord Mountbatten as the prime-mover must take his lion's share of the blame. As one of the critics put it: 'It need not have happened. It would not have happened, had independence not been rushed through, at such a desperate rate with a little more patience all the troubles might have been avoided' (Mosley). But in sharp contrast to it, Lord Mountbatten and his supporters have patted themselves on their backs for carrying out such a swift operation in such a short period almost with military precision. Their main argument in favour of their contention is the critical situation prevailing in India during the early part of the year 1947. Some of these critical conditions were: a virtual stalemate, nay a deadlock in the interim government leading to its total dysfunction, ever-deteriorating communal situation leading to mass killings; and unwillingness of the Muslim League to accept less than an independent and sovereign Pakistan. The only viable alternative was a tough military handling of the situation, for which the British did not have the material and human resources: not even a strong will to act to tame the rot.

In retrospect, it seems that in the post-War situation the British found themselves unequal to the urgent task of restoring law and order in India. In fact, as revealed by the Wavell's 'Breakdown plan', the British were virtually on the point of abdicating their moral responsibility for maintenance of law and order. Perhaps, they found it more honourable to replace their old policy of 'divide and rule' by a new policy of 'Divide and Quit' In any case, it was a better face-saving measure than the total abdication of their responsibility. But what helped Lord Mountbatten was his ability to find the leaders of the Congress and the Muslim League as a willing partner which greatly facilitated his 'Operation Quit'. In any case, it also helped Britain to have good relations with the two proposed countries of the Indian subcontinent. What made the plan of partition more attractive to the British eyes was that the horrendous cost of partition was to be entirely borne by the people of India and not even shared by the British people. Thus, it was the best of the bargain for the British in the given situation. But what made the Indian leaders of all hues as willing partners for Mountbatten and his plan? Lure of political power, a sense of utter helplessness in the face of a challenging situation or the charm of Lord Mountbatten and his consort, Lady Mountbatten! Here your guess is as good as mine.

> *I shall perhaps not be alive to witness it (the partition), but should the evil I apprehend overtake India and her independence be imperiled, let posterity know what agony this old soul went through thinking of it. Let it not be said that Gandhiji was a party to India's vivisection. But everybody today is impatient for independence. Therefore, there is no other help.*
>
> MAHATMA GANDHI

39 Muslim Separatism and the Indian Freedom Movement

A Historical Survey

Musalmans are a nation according to any definition of the nation, and they must have their homeland, their territory and their state.

MOHAMMAD ALI JINNAH

Thousand years of our joint life has moulded us into a common nationality. The cast has been moulded and destiny has set her on it. Whether we like it or not, we have become an Indian nation, united and indivisible. No fantasy or artificial scheming to separate and divide can break this unity.

ABUL KALAM AZAD

The suppression of the 1857 rebellion and the subsequent takeover of the Indian administration by the Crown was of momentous importance to the Indian Muslims in several ways. In the first place, it left the Indian Muslims, particularly its elite section, with little hope to ever regain their lost political power in the country. Second, in the wake of the 1857 rebellion, a realisation had also dawned on the British that association of the Indians in the political and administrative set-up would have to be initiated to bridge the hiatus between the colonial administration and the people. That led to the enactment of the Indian Councils Act of 1861. As this was the first step towards the democratisation of Indian polity, it had a message for the Muslim community. The Muslim leaders clearly understood that henceforward, in any political game, the size of the community would matter most. And in the numbers game, the Hindus had a distinct advantage. Even if such a realisation was on the sub-conscious level, it was bound to affect the mindset of the Muslim community in the long run. Third, this was the period when the Hindu community was being stirred by a number of socio-religious reform movements, viz., Brahmo Samaj, Prarthana Samaj, Arya Samaj, Mahajan Sabha and a host of other organisations. These movements were being led by men of substance like Keshav Chandra Sen, Swami Dayanand, Justice M G Ranade and others. All of them had high standing in the Indian community. All these leaders, though critical of certain aspects of the Hindu society, were highly appreciative of its past. Besides, these leaders were also raising issues which were of secular concern and were pinpointing certain maladies afflicting the Hindu society.

There was some kind of a new awareness, a new resurgence and even a new renaissance in the Hindu society. Thus, it was evident that the Hindu community was on the move, and the weight of the numbers being on its side, it was quite likely that they would emerge as the dominant force. Naturally, the Muslims were getting apprehensive about the whole thing. What might have added to the quantum of their apprehension was the fact that a number of secular organisations like the Indian Association were also creating a nascent political stir among the newly emerging Indian elite. It was this process which ultimately culminated in the formation of the Indian National Congress in 1885.

Another aspect of the Indian political scene of those days was that there existed a certain kind of distrust and hostility between the British and the Muslim as the latter looked upon the former as being primarily responsible for its loss of power. What had added to the sense of hostility was the Wahhabi Movement which had started in Arabia towards the end of the eighteenth century and subsequently reached India through Saiyyid Ahmed Brelvi and had created an anti-British feeling among the Indian Muslims. The participation of the Muslims in the 1857 rebellion, under the leadership of Bahadur Shah Zafar had further widened the hiatus between the Muslims and the British. The rising renaissance in the Hindu community and the British hostility to the Muslim community started a process of a new thinking among the Muslim community. In 1855, in Bengal the first Muslim organisation that came into being was Anjuman-i-Islam. It was primarily committed to protect the interest of the community and also to instill a sense of loyalty in them towards the British rulers. This was followed by the Mohammedan Literary Society founded in 1863 by Abdul Latif Khan, who pleaded for the spread of English education among the Muslims within the framework of Islamic education. Later on, the process was joined by Amir Ali who set up the Central National Mohammedan Association during 1877-8 and stood for total westernisation of Muslim education. Perhaps this was in response to the data presented by the 1872 census, which had brought out the educational backwardness of the Muslim community, particularly in Bengal.

The Muslim elite in UP was suffering from an acute sense of relative deprivation as this region had been the seat of Muslim power and hence the sense of loss of power was deeper among the elites of the region. The man who struggled hard to grasp the depth and dimension of the Muslim predicament was Sir Syed Ahmad Khan, who, having served in the Indian administration since 1837, was well aware of the condition of the Muslims. Besides, he had become greatly impressed by the British liberal education system during his visit to England in 1869. He retired in 1876 and set up the Mohammedan Anglo-Oriental College at Aligarh. He was convinced that the Muslims, as a community that had ruled India for many years, as such, deserved to enjoy special power and position. But for that they had to acquire new skills. Besides, they would have to be well versed in English education. Initially, Sir Syed Ahmad Khan was fired by the nationalist feelings and he even went to the extent of describing Hindus and Muslims as the two eyes of Mother India. But once the Congress was formed and it started raising issues which made it a suspect in the eyes of the British, Sir Syed Ahmad moved closer to the British and even called upon the Muslims not to join the Congress. Perhaps Theodore Beck, the principal of the Aligarh College, had some hand in bringing the British and Sir Ahmad closer and also in affecting his thinking from a nationalist to a communalist. What created a hiatus between the Indian National Congress and Sir Syed Ahmad Khan was their fundamental difference about the concept of nationalism: whereas the Congress stood for a concept of nationhood based on universal citizenship, Sir Syed believed in the Indian nationhood as the federation of Quams (community). He further believed that the Muslims as an ex-ruling class, though in minority in terms of number, must have greater share in political power. He favoured an Anglo–Muslim united front against the Congress.

In 1887, Sir Ahmad set up the Muslim Educational Conference which started holding its annual meeting in different parts of the country. When there was a growing hiatus between the Congress and the British after 1888, a new organisation, the Anglo Oriental Defence Association was set up in 1893, with active support of the British, primarily to counter the growing popularity of the Congress. In this way, there was some kind of convergence of interest between the Muslims and the British, though another section of Muslims continued to work through the Congress. The British policy of divide and rule, by propping up the Muslims against the Congress, was fine-tuned by Lord Curzon, who carried it out with a rare brazenness by partitioning Bengal in 1905. In parenthesis, it is quite interesting to note that though Sir Syed Ahmad Khan worked for the protection of the rights of the Muslims, he never allowed ulemas (the Muslim theologians) to dominate his movement. Meanwhile, the Hindu–Muslim relationship had been soured by the government's decision to allow Devanagari script along with Persian script to be used as the court language in April 1900. However, after the death of Sir Syed Ahmad Khan in 1898, the Aligarh College came to be dominated by the new leadership of Muhammad Ali and Shaukat Ali. They, deviating from the path shown by Sir Syed Ahmad Khan, sought the support of the ulemas to further their cause and were willing to move away from the British. Maulana Abdul Bari became a moving spirit behind the new line of thinking. But the old leaders like Mohsin-ul-Mulk did not like the growing hiatus between the Muslims and the British and he started working to that end through the Mohammedan Educational Conference. Meanwhile, the partition of Bengal led to a big anti-partition movement, which came to be known as the 'Swadeshi Movement'. The Swadeshi Movement further widened the gulf between the Hindus and Muslims as the creation of a new province of East Bengal was supposed to favour the Muslims, which the Swadeshi Movement sought to annul.

Meanwhile, in 1906 another major political development had taken place: Lord Minto had set up a committee to examine further constitutional reforms for India. This was followed by Morley's statement that some concrete steps were going to be taken to introduce the representative government in India. The resignation of the Governor of Bengal, who was a pro-Muslim, in 1906, further alarmed one section of the Muslim community. Subsequently, on 1 October 1906, a Muslim delegation led by Aga Khan met Lord Minto at Simla and demanded separate electorate for the Muslims. Whether or not the delegation headed by Aga Khan was part of a 'command performance' might be controversial. What is, however, noteworthy is that subsequently the basic demand of the delegation for a separate electorate was accepted and integrated in the Act of 1909, which came to be known as Morley–Minto Reforms. A permanent wall was created between the Hindus and Muslims, who were to vote separately for the candidates of their own respective communities.

Meanwhile, a feeling was growing among the Muslim intelligentsia that the Muslim community also needed a political organisation like the Congress to protect and to promote their interests. In fact, as early as 1901, Sir Muhammad Shafi had advocated the formation of the Indian Muslim League, but it did not take any concrete shape. On 30 December 1906, the Muslim League was founded in Dacca during the meeting of the Mohammedan Educational Conference. The major objectives of the League were: (i) to protect the political rights and interests of the Muslims; (ii) to preach loyalty to the Raj; and (iii) to promote communal amity. The partition of Bengal was undone in 1911, which did create a feeling of resentment among the Muslims against the British. Lord Hardinge, the new Viceroy, believed in the policy of conciliation and not confrontation. Meanwhile, a major shift took place in the policy of the All India Muslim League. During its Lucknow Session in 1913, the Muslim League passed a resolution, which made a radical departure from its earlier pro-British policy and laid down its new objective as 'attainment of self-government by promoting national unity, by fostering public spirit among the people of India and by co-operating with other communities.' In the same year, Jinnah joined the League and it was widely believed that it was at his initiative and insistence that the new objectives were incorporated in the League's constitution. This was followed by the declaration of the First World War, Anglo-Russian entente and the British hostile policy towards Turkey during the Turkey-Italian War and the Balkan wars. All this created bad-blood between the British and the Indian Muslims. Besides, among the Muslim community, a new leadership of Muhammad Ali, Shaukat Ali, Maulana Abul Kalam Azad and Jinnah had emerged, who favoured giving up the League's old policy of servility to the British. They favoured a policy of working for the freedom of the country.

The League's resolution at the Lucknow session in 1913 was welcomed by the Congress, which pledged to take joint and concerted action on all the questions of national good. Jinnah came on the forefront of the League's leadership and pleaded for national unity and self-government. This led to the signing of the Lucknow Pact in 1916, which accepted a separate electorate for the Muslims. Jinnah and Bal Gangadhar Tilak were the main architects of the Pact. The

Congress accepted the principle of a separate electorate, weightage for the Muslims and a virtual veto right for them on the issues affecting them. This was done in good faith and in the hope that a Hindu–Muslim united front would emerge, which would force the British to grant self-government to India after the War. But the fact was that while the Hindu–Muslim amity turned out to be shortlived, the system of a separate electorate became a permanent feature of all constitutional developments till it reached its logical conclusion in the partition of the country. The principle of separate electorate was accepted by the Act of 1919 under the plea that the Congress and the League had accepted it under the Lucknow Pact. The Hindu–Muslim amity was further cemented by their joint support to the Khilafat and Non-Cooperation Movement. Congress under the leadership of Mahatma Gandhi played a crucial role in the entire process.

But the Hindu–Muslim bonhomie turned out to be shortlived. Soon communal riots started occurring in the country after the withdrawal of the Non-Cooperation Movement, which was a big shock to the Muslim community. For them non-violence was not an article of faith. Hence, they could not understand the rationale behind Gandhiji's action. Second, in the course of the mobilisation of Muslim masses, a large number of ulemas had been fielded which released a lot of communal viruses among the Muslim communities, making them more conscious of their religious identity rather than national identity. Hindu organisations like Hindu Mahasabha and Arya Samaj started talking of *Sudhi* and *Sanghatan* as against Muslims insistence on *Tanzeem* and *Tabligh*, All this released a lot of communal virus in the body politic of India.

The Congress, under Mahatma Gandhi's leadership, tried to contain the situation by calling an All Parties' Conference and holding several meetings to sort out the Hindu-Muslim problems. One positive outcome of all these efforts was that at least one section of the Muslim League led by Jinnah was willing to accept a system of joint electorate. Jinnah called a conference of Muslim leaders in March 1927. In this conference, a proposal of acceptance of a joint electorate was mooted, which was not acceptable to one section of the Muslim leadership led by Sir Muhammed Shafi, and thus a split took place in the League. The Jinnah-led League joined hands with the Congress in boycotting the Simon Commission whereas the Shafi group welcomed it. Meanwhile, as decided by the All Parties' Conference, the Nehru Report under the leadership of Motilal Nehru opted for a joint electoral system.

Jinnah and Mahatma

At the All Parties' Conference held in Calcutta in 1928, Jinnah made a conditional offer to accept the joint electorate, provided the following four conditions were accepted by the conference. These conditions were: (i) one-third seats to be reserved for the Muslims in the Central Assembly; (ii) in Punjab and Bengal reservation of seats for Muslims in proportion to their population; (iii) recognition of three new provinces of Sindh, Baluchistan and NWFP; and (iv) the central government to be federal but all residual powers were to be with the provinces. Jinnah's amendments to the Nehru Report failed to get support and for him it was the end of the road as a secular nationalist. Subsequently, he reached a compromise with the Shafi group and in September 1929, in the special session of the League, Jinnah submitted his famous 14 points, which were nothing but an elaboration of his four point demands presented at the All Parties' Conference in Calcutta in 1928. The new points were: reversal to separate electorate for the Muslims; reservation for Muslims in services and self-governing bodies and no change in the constitution by the Central Legislature without the consent of the provinces.

The demands enumerated in the 14 points became the rock-bottom of the Muslim demands, and when Gandhiji tried his level best to find an amicable solution during the Second Round Table Conference in 1932, no agreement could be reached on account of the Muslims insistence on acceptance of all their demands. It was the Communal Award which ultimately accepted all the demands put forward by the League. Earlier, it was Dr Muhammad Iqbal who first mooted the idea of a separate homeland for the Muslims and as its concomitant a Muslim state by consolidating the people of the north-west. However, he failed to make it clear whether or not it would be a fully sovereign state. Besides, the Muslim majority states in the north-east were also not mentioned. A more specific idea was subsequently put forward by Rahmat Ali, a Cambridge student during the Round Table Conference. He called it the state of Pakistan. But nobody took him seriously.

Another attempt was made for the resolution of the communal problems in July 1932. To that end a unity conference was held in Allahabad on the initiative of a number of leaders like Dr Syed Mahmood, Maulana Shaukat Ali, Abul Kalam Azad, Pandit Madan Mohan Malaviya. Some agreement on joint electorate with 32 per cent seat reservation for Muslims was agreed upon. But the British Government spoiled the game by declaring the Communal Award. Consequently, the Muslim leadership lost interest in the agreement reached at the unity conference as they had got more than that under the Communal Award. The Congress also did not take a clear-cut stand on the Communal Award as it 'neither accepted nor rejected' it.

Another landmark in the Hindu–Muslim relationship was reached in the wake of the election for the Central Assembly in 1934. It is relevant to note that the 1934 election had brought back Jinnah once again to the mainstream of the Indian politics. As a member of the Central Assembly, Jinnah opened negotiations with Rajendra Prasad with a view to getting the Congress endorsement for the gains made by the Muslims under the Communal Award. Jinnah was aware that other regional Muslim leaders were more interested in full provincial autonomy and the creation of new Muslim provinces. They would not mind the continuation of the British rule for an indefinite period, as the transfer of power at the central level posed a serious threat of Hindu domination. But for Jinnah, provincial autonomy alone was not of much consequence, as he did not have even a toehold in any of the Muslim majority provinces. Hence, he preferred negotiations with Rajendra Prasad as he was still interested in the power at the central level. The negotiations dragged on, in which Madan Mohan Malaviya, Bhulabhai Desai, Sardar Patel and some of the Sikh leaders from Punjab and Hindu leaders from Bengal also played a role from the ring side. Jinnah offered a bet of joint electorate in lieu of differential franchise for the Muslims, which would give them a big share in the national power. Meanwhile, Jinnah, in a clever move had got the Central Assembly to endorse the Communal Award by securing the official support. Besides, he also succeeded in blocking the federal scheme with the support of Bhulabhai who was the leader of the Congress Party in the Central Assembly. So he lost interest in carrying on with further negotiations. Perhaps, interests of the Sikhs of Punjab and the Hindus of Bengal could not be reconciled with Jinnah's proposal of differential franchise for the Muslims. Ultimately, nothing much came out of the negotiations.

The election of 1937 was fought by the League but not on virulent communal lines. The League was mauled up in the election except in UP and Bombay. When it wanted a coalition with the Congress, in these two provinces, it was rejected by the Congress, which infuriated Jinnah and led him to go in for virulent Muslim communal politics. So it was only after 1937 that Jinnah took to a rabid communal line and started mobilising the Muslim masses by appealing to their religious sentiments. War further strengthened Jinnah and his League as the British extended support to him to counter the growing militancy of the Congress.

It was for the first time in March 1940 in Lahore that the Muslim League passed a resolution propounding the two-nation theory and demanded a separate homeland for the Muslims.

The Cripps Mission accepted the basic principle of the League that the Provinces would have a right to secede. But ultimately the Cripps

Mahatma and C Rajagopalachari

Plan was rejected both by the Congress and the League. Subsequently, an attempt was made by C Rajagopalachari, who presented a plan which came to be known as C R formula. It had the following features:

(i) The Muslim League is committed to the idea of independence of India and would join the interim government.
(ii) After the War, contiguous districts in the north-west and eastern India, with Muslim majority would be demarcated by a Commission and a plebiscite would be held of all people on adult franchise basis to decide the issues of separation from India.
(iii) If plebiscite goes in favour of separation, this would be implemented and the border areas would have choice to join either of the two states.
(iv) In the event of separation, Defence, Communication and Commerce would be kept under common control.

When Gandhiji was released from jail on 6 May 1944, he approached Jinnah to find a solution to the communal problems. But Jinnah insisted on the idea of Pakistan comprising the six provinces of Punjab, Bengal, Assam, Sindh, Baluchistan and North-West Frontier Province.

Desai–Liaquat Pact

After the failure of the Gandhi–Jinnah talks in September 1944, another attempt was made by Bhulabhai Desai, the leader of the Congress in the Central Assembly and Liaquat Ali Khan, a prominent leader of the Muslim League to find a way out of the Hindu–Muslim impasse. There is a raging controversy about the genesis of the Desai–Liaquat Pact. Whether talks leading to the Pact were initiated on the behest of the Viceroy, Gandhiji or by Bhulabhai on his own initiative is not conclusively settled even today. A detailed discussion about this controversy is not very germane to our study. Hence, let us look at the specific terms of the Pact which were signed by Desai and Liaquat Ali on 11 January 1945. The main provisions of the Pact were as follows:

(i) The Congress and the League would join hands to form the interim government.
(ii) Such a government would comprise equal number of persons nominated by both the Parties but all nominees need not be members of the Central legislatures.
(iii) Besides, there would be also representatives of the minorities particularly from the Sikhs and the Scheduled Castes. And the Commander-in-Chief would also be one of the members of the proposed government.
(iv) The interim government would function under the provisions of the 1935 Act. However, in case of any proposal the Interim Government fails to receive the support of the Legislative Assembly, it would not seek to get it enforced under the reserved power of the Governor General.
(v) As a prelude to the formation of the Government, the Viceroy would be impressed upon to extend invitations to the Congress and the League. And as a sequel to that, Desai and Jinnah separately or jointly would express their willingness to form the government on the basis of the above formula.
(vi) If and when such a government would be formed, its first task would be to release the members of the Congress Working Committee.
(vii) Subsequently, an attempt would be made to restore the provincial autonomy by getting section 93 of the Act of 1935 withdrawn.

There is a serious controversy whether Bhulabhai, even if he kept in touch with Gandhiji, exceeded his brief or whether Liaquat Ali took Jinnah into confidence or not. M C Setalvad, in his biography of Bhulabhai Desai has defended him on the basis of a number of documentary evidences. On the other hand, J B Kripalani, a member of the Congress Working Committee asserts that Bhulabhai took this initiative at the behest of the Viceroy. And Gandhiji was not aware of all the details of the negotiations and the consequent Pact. In any case, the Congress Working Committee took strong objection to the entire plan on the ground of the parity of the Congress and the League in the Government. Besides, they also objected to the fact that such a government would have to function under the Act of 1935, and, therefore, it would not be a free government. In any case, Bhulabhai fell from grace of the Congress and was not given a nomination in the elections for the Central Assembly held in 1946.

The Wavell plan of 14 June 1945 sought to reconstitute the Executive Council so as to give caste Hindus and Muslims a parity. The Simla conference failed as Jinnah wanted the Muslim League to be recognised as the sole representative organisation of the Muslims. The Cabinet Mission Plan was the last attempt to keep India united with some kind of loose federation. But the plan collapsed. The Mountbatten Plan followed by the Indian Independence Act (1947) gave the final acceptance to the partition.

On the basis of this survey, some general remarks on the issues of Muslim separatism is called for. One, the Muslim leadership suffered from the ex-ruler complex and were never willing to accept Indian nationhood based on territorial representation and individual citizenship. They wanted a federation of communities. Even when they accepted the Cabinet Mission Plan they thought that it would, ultimately, lead to the creation of Pakistan. Two, it was neither their alienation nor competitive communalism which led to the emergence and growth of their separatist feelings. It would also be interesting to note that some scholars have called it Muslim alienation, while some other scholars have traced the history of Hindu and Muslim communalism. Still others have called it purely Muslim communalism. In our view there are problems with each school. The idea of Muslim alienation presumes that some other group was responsible for their alienation and they had genuine grievances, which prompted them to develop a feeling of alienation. Hence, it presumes that the responsibility for the Muslim separatism must be laid at the door of the Hindu communalism. In course of our survey, we do not find any conclusive evidence for such an inference. The Muslim communalists never attacked the Hindu communal organisation including the RSS and the Hindu Mahasabha as the chief villain of the piece. Their main target of attack was the Indian National Congress. Whatever may be its other limitations, the

Tragedy of Partition

Congress could not be accused of being a communal party. In the course of our survey, we have seen that the Muslim League not only accused the Congress of being a Hindu communal organisation, but also wanted it to confess to that effect. This was the basis on which Jinnah wanted parity with the Congress, when the issue of reconstitution of the Executive Council came up during the 1940s. So the inference that the Muslim League was reacting to Hindu communalism, does not appear to hold good.

In fact, our survey establishes beyond any reasonable doubt that when the cart of democracy started moving in the country and the process of democratisation of Indian polity was initiated, the Muslim leadership could see that the number would count and that certainly would put the Hindu community in an advantageous position. To counter that, every Muslim from Sir Syed Ahmad to Jinnah rejected the idea of Indian nationhood based on individual citizenship. They wanted India to be accepted as a confederation of communities. After all, the Lucknow Pact in which Jinnah had a big hand was based on the acceptance of a separate electorate for Muslims, which had been already granted by the Act of 1909. Jinnah, even in the heyday of his nationalist phase never rejected the system of separate electorate for the Muslims. Jinnah's acceptance of a joint electorate under the Nehru Report (1928) was also conditional, based on the acceptance of the four-point plan which was nothing but the Muslim demand for a separate electorate in disguise. And once his four-point plan was rejected during the Calcutta conference, he went back to the united Muslim League and presented a 14-point programme.

Not only that, he rejected Gandhiji's attempt to find an amicable solution for communal problems during the Second Round Table Conference. Again during 1937–40, Jinnah reacted to the Congress rejection of coalition politics. Subsequently, the Jinnah-led Muslim League indulged in communal tantrums including raising the slogan of 'Islam in danger'. Ultimately the League propounded the two-nation theory at the Lahore conference in 1940. Then onward, Jinnah rejected all proposals from the Congress for an amicable solution including the C R formula. Even during the Gandhi–Jinnah talks, he insisted that nothing less than Pakistan comprising the six provinces, was acceptable to him. Our survey makes certain things quite clear:

(i) Muslim leaders were quite conscious of their status of being ex-rulers of the country;
(ii) they wanted more than their share in political power;
(iii) they wanted to grab as much territory as possible hence their insistence on the six provinces.

The roots to the Muslim separatism lay in their psyche more than in their actual condition, and it is that which eventually resulted in the partition of the country. And that psyche was based on the feeling of being an ex-ruling class and belonging to a superior race with superior ideology (Islam). The plank of their politics was to generate communal consciousness among the Muslim masses to regain political power. That could have been satisfied only with a separate homeland for them or regaining their old dominant position which in any case was ruled out in our democratic age.

Come, let us lift suspicion's thick curtains once again
Unite once more the sundered, wipe clean division.

MUHAMMAD IQBAL

40 The Partition of India
An Overview

This stained light, this night bitten dawn.
This is not the dawn we yearned for
This is not the dawn for which we set out
Hoping that in the sky's wilderness
We would reach the final destination of the stars.

FAIZ AHMED FAIZ

The partition of India in 1947 was not only a momentous but also the most horrendous event in the long and chequered history of India. It brought in its trail massive and unprecedented sufferings for the Indian people: half a million killed, ten million people uprooted from their hearths and homes, and the worst of all, thousands of children and women maimed, killed and raped. The trauma of partition continues to visit and haunt millions of homes even today.

It is, therefore, not surprising that the theme of the partition has attracted a large number of scholarly works and a fierce debate around it is still on. Initially two questions were raised: What were the factors and forces that led to the partition of the country? Who among the leaders involved could be primarily held responsible for it? In the wake of partition, there was a widespread feeling among the Indian people that Jinnah was primarily responsible for the vivisection of India. Thus, the Muslim League led by Jinnah, backed by the British duplicity, was taken as the chief villain of piece for the partition of the country. The Congress party, along with the Indian people were taken as the victims rather than the prosecutors of the partition of India.

The first dent to this simple assumption was made by the publication of Maulana Azad's book, *India Wins Freedom* during 1950s. Even with the omission of 30 pages (which were incorporated in the new edition of the book published in the 1980s, as willed by Maulana), it threw enough hints that the Congress leaders, particularly Jawaharlal Nehru and Patel could not be totally absolved of their responsibility for the partition of the country. Azad's formulation was simple and straightforward: on two crucial occasions Jawaharlal Nehru, through his actions and utterances, alienated the Muslim League leaders, particularly Jinnah, from the mainstream of the national movement, making them go the whole hog towards partition of the country. The first instance which Maulana referred to was the rejection of the offer for a coalition government made by the League both in respect of Bombay and UP, immediately after the 1937 elections. Jawaharlal Nehru, according to Azad, spurned Jinnah's offer, which led to a state of desperation on the part of the League, forcing it to go in for rabid communalism. The entire behaviour of Jinnah after the rejection of his overtures to the Congress changed overnight as he went the whole hog to take to a no-holds barred communal line. The second incident referred to by Azad was the 10 and 20 July 1946 statements by Jawaharlal Nehru regarding the implications of the Cabinet Mission Plan (which had been earlier accepted by both the Congress and the League) in which he referred to the unfettered nature of the Constituent Assembly and optional, and not compulsory, grouping of the provinces. According to Azad these utterances of Nehru, despite subsequent attempts by the Congress Working Committee, to retrieve the situation, prompted the Muslim League to reject the Cabinet Mission Plan during 29–30 July 1946 meetings. Thus, the last attempt to keep India united was dashed to the ground, primarily on account of indiscretion on the part of Nehru, who was also holding the office of the Congress president during those days. Maulana also asserted that at least during 1946–7, Sardar Patel also became a pall-bearer of the carriage of partition.

In popular perception of our people, the British colonial rule was held as the second villain of the piece. For it always followed the policy of 'divide and rule' and thus played one community against the other. Not only that, it followed a deliberate policy of promoting the Muslim communalism, starting from the end of the nineteenth century when the tide of Indian nationalism prompted by the militant nationalists started surging ahead. The partition of Bengal in 1905 and the formation of the Indian Muslim League in 1906 were no accidental events of history, rather they were the outcome of a British policy of promoting Muslim communalism. Not satisfied with that, the British were the first to inject the virus of communalism in the body-politic of India by providing for a separate communal representation for the

Muslims under the Act of 1909. That was retained under the Act of 1919 which ultimately culminated in the Communal Award of 1932. Subsequently, during the Second World War, in the course of its confrontation with the Congress, the British propped-up the Muslim League as a counterveiling force to the Congress. Soon the League-led ministry took over Sindh, Bengal and NWFP within a very short period in 1943. In all these change of guards the British were hand in glove with the League. The Cripps Mission proposal for conceding the right of provinces to secede away from the Indian Union, was for all practical purposes, nothing but the endorsement of the two-nation theory enunciated by the Muslim League in 1940 at its Lahore Conference. This was followed by the British assurance to the Muslim League that no constitutional arrangement in India would be imposed which was unacceptable to the Muslim masses. What was more, it was during this period that the Muslim League, with the open support of the British, succeeded in consolidating its position in some of the Muslim majority provinces, which it had failed to achieve during the 1937 election. Thus, in Assam, the League succeeded in installing a ministry in August 1942 led by Sir Saadullah Khan. This was followed by the dismissal of Alla Baksh Khan as the Sindh Premier as he had extended support to the Congress. This made Jinnah more obdurate and recalcitrant as persistent pursuit of the idea of Pakistan had started paying larger and larger political dividends.

Though the Cabinet Mission Plan had apparently rejected the idea of Pakistan as 'impracticable', by providing compulsory groupings of provinces and their option to walk out of the union after 10 years, if they so desired (it) in reality, it promoted a scheme for deferred partition. For the Muslim League, nurturing the plant of Pakistan for ten years was not much of a price as ultimately it was going to have it free of cost. The Mountbatten Plan formalised and finalised the partition of the country in 1947. Thus, from 1939–40 to 1946–47, the British not only propped-up the Muslim League but ultimately led them to the garden path. For instance, when Jinnah launched 'Direct Action Day' on 16 August 1946, hell was let loose in Calcutta with the open connivance of the Muslim League government, which had even declared a public holiday to facilitate the marauders for their mass killing campaigns. The entire 'steel framework' of the British bureaucracy did nothing in the face of such a direct defiance and massacre. This was nothing but the total abdication of the Rajdharma, which the British had often boasted of in the past. Thus, in 1947 when the

British decided to quit, much water had flown under the bridges of the Jamuna and Thames making the partition inevitable. Ultimately, Lord Mountbatten in 1947, was entrusted with the task of running the knife into the body-politic of India, vivisecting her into two parts – India and Pakistan. In brief, all the three parties involved in the process of partition have been blamed by different scholars making each of them a prime-mover.

The critics have not even spared Mahatma Gandhi from bearing the blame for the partition of India. In fact, the critics do not hesitate to lay major blame at the door of Mahatma Gandhi for the partition of the country. He is accused of promoting Muslim fundamentalism by giving it a sanctity and respectability, which it never deserved and which ultimately led to the partition of the country. The critics feel that it all began with the Lucknow Pact, in which the Congress accepted the principle of separate electorate for Muslims in lieu of their support to the national movement. This was the handiwork of Jinnah and Tilak. The critics do concede that Gandhiji, though present at the Lucknow Congress, did not have much say in the process of making the Pact. But he did accept it as he was not opposed to it in principle. Thus, he had lent his tacit support for the Lucknow Pact.

But this was not the end of the matter. The worst was still to come. Gandhiji was the most prominent leader during the Khilafat–Non-Cooperation Movement. In fact, the entire movement was based on a set of ideas including Gandhiji's firm faith in Hindu–Muslim unity. As such, in terms of Hindu–Muslim unity, the Khilafat Non-Cooperation Movement was a culminating point of the process which had started at Lucknow. Gandhiji not only teamed up with the Ali brothers who were community leaders, but even supported the Khilafat which was basically a religious movement though wearing a political garb. Gandhiji's open alliance with the Ali brothers gave a much-needed respectability to the Muslim communalism. Gandhiji, in an attempt to seek and receive the Muslim support for the national movement, extended his open support to their communal demands, which was too much of a price to be paid by a national leader. Soon the Muslim communal politics showed its true colour and communal riots erupted in the country during 1923–24. This process of emergence of strong currents of Muslim communalism could not be stemmed despite serious attempts by Gandhiji along with Motilal Nehru, C R Das and a host of other Indian leaders during the remaining part of the 1920s. Towards the end of the decade, Jinnah came out with his 14 points when his demands for one-third representation in the Central Assembly was not accepted by the All Parties Conference in Calcutta in 1928. The attempt by Motilal Nehru for a joint electorate system, ultimately, turned out to be abortive. During all these years, Gandhiji was the tallest of the Indian leaders and hence he could not escape taking the lion's share of the blame for the nation's monumental failure on the communal amity front.

This failure became more pronounced with the announcement of the Communal Award in 1932. Gandhiji risked his life by going on a fast unto death on the issue of the depressed classes being ostracised from the Hindu-fold, which even forced Ambedkar to sign the Poona Pact, conceding the basic demand of Mahatma Gandhi. But he quietly accepted the system of separate electorate for the Muslims, which was also incorporated in the Act of 1935 and continued till the last elections before partition. And what was more, the Congress participated in all these elections without making much fuss about it. By the early 1940s, Gandhiji conceded the point that if the people of a particular territorial area wished not to be part of India, they could not be forced to remain in the union. Perhaps that is why he did not vehemently oppose the C R Formula, which virtually conceded the Muslim League's demand for Pakistan. Not only that, even during his talks with Jinnah, he virtually conceded the idea of Pakistan on a territorial basis, and was only opposed to the concept of two nations on the basis of religion. Subsequently, the Congress led by Nehru and Patel conceded the idea of partition in 1947. Gandhiji did not oppose the Congress leadership when they accepted the partition of the country, despite his personal reservation. In any case, he never resorted to his fast unto death on the issue of the partition of the country. Hence, as argued by his critics, he cannot be totally absolved of his share of responsibility for the partition of the country.

Diametrically opposite was the views of the Muslim communalists led by Jinnah on the secular credentials of the Mahatma. They characterised Gandhiji as an out and out Hindu communalist. They even misinterpreted his concepts like Ramdhun and Ram Rajya as nothing but a symbol of Hindu communalism. They completely ignored the fact and Gandhiji was not a believer of Dasarathi Ram. Ram for him was nothing but Nirakar God and Ram Rajya was a symbol of just, good and equitable rule. In a word, his secular credentials was suspect both in the eyes of the Hindu and the Muslim communalists. In fact, they negate each other rather than negating Gandhiji's pristine secular records.

So far, we have been discussing the viewpoints of the critics of all prominent leaders and their organisations involved in the process of the partition. But there is no dearth of defenders either. Let us start with a prominent defender of Nehru's, for his role in the process of partition. B R Nanda, a leading historian, in his paper on 'Jawaharlal Nehru and the partition of India', seeks to defend Nehru's position on both crucial occasions, which Maulana mentioned in his *India Wins Freedom*. Nanda advances a number of arguments and even many facts in defence of Nehru for his refusal to enter into a coalition with the Muslim League in UP and Bombay in the aftermath of 1937 elections. Some of Nanda's arguments are recapitulated here:

(i) The decision not to go in for a coalition with the Muslim League was a collective decision of the entire UP provincial leadership of the Congress including G B Pant, Rafi Ahmed Kidwai and P D Tandon all of whom were prominent leaders of the Congress Party.
(ii) The entire Congress leadership was convinced that the Muslim League, with its social base among landlords, if made a partner in the government, would distort the Congress programme of land reforms to which the entire Congress Party was committed. And which is why the Congress insisted on the acceptance of the policy programme of the Congress by the Muslim League as a pre-condition for taking it as a partner.
(iii) The case of Bombay was slightly different. There the Congress was willing to concede to Jinnah's demand for inclusion of two members in the Bombay cabinet. But this idea was ultimately given up as there was genuine fear in the minds of the Bombay Congressmen that Jinnah would impose his dictatorship through his ministers in the coalition cabinet.

In sum, the idea of the coalition cabinet was abandoned in the favour of cohesion of the cabinet.

Similarly, Nanda defends Nehru's statement in July 1946 on the implications of the acceptance of the Cabinet Mission Plan. Nanda concedes that in July 1946, Nehru did make a statement to the effect that the Congress would not be bound by a single thing except that we had decided to go to the Constituent Assembly and that the provincial grouping might turn out to be optional rather than compulsory. Nanda tries to contextualise these two statements to bring out their real import.

He reminds the critics that Nehru's statement regarding the Constituent Assembly was in response to his socialists critics like Achyut Patwardhan and Aruna Asaf Ali who had characterised the Constituent Assembly as being a 'sham'. Nanda further argues that in the same statement Nehru had conceded that there would be only two limitations on the powers of the Constituent Assembly – limitations arising out of the Indo–British Treaty and also from issues related to minorities. Hence, Nehru never talked about a totally unfettered Constituent Assembly: as alleged by the League and accepted by Maulana on its face value. Similarly, Nanda defends Nehru's statement on the optional and compulsory groupings of provinces on the ground that Nehru was talking in terms of the actual situation, as both the NWFP and Assam were against compulsory groupings. Nanda further argues that the Muslim League Council meeting had been called much before Nehru made his statements. In fact, the meeting was called to protest and formulate its position on the British failure to invite the Muslim League to form the interim government even after the plan had been accepted by it. So Nehru's statement was made a mere pretext by the League to revise its position on the Cabinet Mission Plan. Even without Nehru's statement the League could have found some other pretext for its rejection of the Cabinet Mission Plan. Even though Nanda's arguments are a little over-stretched and look like an attempt to defend an icon, nevertheless, there is some substance in his basic premise that the League's new position on the Cabinet Mission Plan must have some other considerations apart from Nehru's statements.

Similarly Jinnah, the man who almost singlehandedly divided India finds a defender in Ayesha Jalal, a Pakistani historian, who virtually relishes being a 'Devil's Advocate'. But let us first look at her basic formulation and her arguments. Jalal's basic formulation is that Jinnah could not be held responsible for the partition of India. And she has a number of arguments in support of her basic contention. First, Jalal argues that Jinnah never wanted partition of the country. What he really sought was a confederation of federating units with maximum provincial autonomy. Moving on the same line of argument, she avers that Jinnah was only underlining the fact that Muslims should not be taken as simply constituting a minority in India rather they should be treated as a nation on their own. Therefore, Muslims should enjoy equal rights with Hindus in the decision-making process of the Indian subcontinent. Unfortunately, the Indian National Congress, she argues, was not at all willing to accept this basic contention of Jinnah. In support of her novel formulation that Jinnah never wanted partition, she scans and re-examines the oft-quoted League's Lahore resolution in 1940 propounding the two-nation theory. She further asserts that there was no mention of Pakistan in the Lahore resolution. By proposing the two-nation theory with the assertion that Muslims constitute a separate nation, all that Jinnah sought was to be at par with Hindus in the decision-making process of the country. In her view, the Lahore resolution underlining the Muslim right of self-determination, was an attempt to achieve a kind of confederation between Muslim and non-Muslim provinces on the basis of parity.

In Jalal's view the real purport of the two-nation theory was to make it a bargaining counter to achieve parity with Hindus in every respect and was never meant to be an irreducible minimum bargain itself. She also cites the fact that the Muslim League rejected the Cripps Mission even though it had conceded the right of the provinces to secede from the Union. On the other hand, the Muslim League had accepted the Cabinet Mission Plan even though it had rejected the idea of Pakistan. In Jalal's view, the Cabinet Mission Plan provided Jinnah with an opportunity to work out a confederation as it provided for the compulsory groupings of the Muslim majority provinces while retaining the overall unity of the country. But Nehru's statements in July 1946 made it clear to Jinnah that there could be no possibility of ever achieving parity between the Muslims and Hindus in the decision-making process of the country. Thus, Jinnah and the Muslim League had no option except to go the whole hog on the issue of the partition of the country. Jalal concludes that the blame for the partition of India should be laid at the door of the Congress and that of the British and not at the door of the Muslim League. This is the sum and substance of the basic formulation as well as the supporting evidence produced by Ayesha Jalal.

However, Jalal's thesis does not hold good if subjected to closer and critical examination. The logic behind her thesis appears to be a little overstretched and even based on twisting of facts and events. She seems to go all out to prove her thesis even by ignoring the substantive part of the argument. For instance, she attaches too much importance to 'Pakistan' not being mentioned in the League's Lahore resolution of 1940. Here she stresses on the letter rather than the spirit of the resolution. A closer examination of the said resolution makes it absolutely clear that the League insisted on the Muslims constituting a separate nation, and their right to self-determination, which obviously included the right to form a sovereign independent state. If this was not the demand for Pakistan, then what it was, one may ask Jalal. In fact, Jinnah consistently refused to define and even present the full contours of Pakistan. His keeping the idea of Pakistan as vague and undefined as was part of his strategy to mobilise the Muslims in the Hindu majority provinces. Hence, non-mentioning 'Pakistan' in the Lahore resolution could be a part of his larger strategy for mass mobilisation of the Muslims in the Hindu majority provinces.

Perhaps Jinnah was not even sure of getting support from the Muslim majority provinces, which is why the non-mentioning of Pakistan in the Lahore resolution does not lead to the kind of inference that Jalal would like us to believe. So far as Jalal's argument that Jinnah rejected the Cripps Mission (which had granted the provinces the right to secede), whereas he accepted the Cabinet Mission (which had rejected the idea of Pakistan) is concerned, one could very well argue that the Cabinet Mission Plan gave the same right at the end of the ten years. Besides, by insisting upon the compulsory groupings of the provinces, Jinnah could have walked away with all the six provinces after a decade, which was his life's ambition. Besides, under the plan, there was a possibility of power-sharing in the interim government virtually on equal footing with the Congress, which, even according to Jalal, was one of the dreams of Jinnah. Jalal forgets that in a democratic country the principle of parity in respect of Muslims could not be applied as they constituted only about 25 per cent of the population of India. That would have been the total negation of the basic principle of democracy. Thus, Jalal's argument, that the absence of explicit mention of Pakistan in the Lahore resolution could be interpreted as a bargaining counter rather than a demand for Pakistan, is far from being convincing.

After the election of 1937, which established the electoral predominance of the Congress in most of the provinces and the poor performance of the League in the Muslim majority provinces, Jinnah got desperate and started building up a separate mansion of Muslim nationhood brick by brick. He spurned all attempts by the Congress leadership to come to a negotiating table. Even when Gandhiji went out of his way to hold talks with Jinnah, he hardly entered into a serious dialogue except reiterating his demand for Pakistan. In fact, he never seriously and sincerely responded to the Congress offer for negotiation, not to talk of taking any initiative for having a frank and direct talk with the Congress leadership. He always clung to the British apron-strings, particularly after 1939, when the process of the final confrontation between the Congress and the British started. In fact,

Jinnah was so possessed by his ambition to carve out a separate independent Muslim state that he even did not care much about the fate of 35 million Muslims who were left behind in India. Till 1940, when the Lahore resolution was passed, none of the Muslim majority provinces including Sindh was under the League's fiefdom. By enunciating the basic principle of self-determination for the Muslims based on separate nationhood, he was trying to sell his ideas to the

Gandhi, aged 77, Noakhali, November 1946

people of the Muslim majority area who, till then, were not at all enamoured of the idea of Pakistan. If he was cautious enough not to mention 'Pakistan' in the Lahore resolution, it might have been a part of his tactical line and does not speak for his intention not to have Pakistan. Thus, Jinnah cannot absolve himself from taking the lion's share of the blame for partitioning India, which created more problems than it actually solved, even of the Muslims of India.

A lot has been written about Mahatma Gandhi's agonies and mental torture which he went through on the eve of partition. Since his days of the South African struggle, Hindu–Muslim unity was one of the basic articles of his faith. For Gandhiji, this was not a tactical line for just putting up a united national fight against the British. It was the core of his belief system as it was based on his basic faith of *Sarva Dharma Sambhava.* Thus, his support to the Khilafat Movement and subsequent attempt to forge Hindu–Muslim unity, his support to Rajagopalachari's Pakistan thesis and his talks with Jinnah should be viewed as a part of his basic belief in the Hindu–Muslim unity and not an encouragement to the Muslim communal politics. During the worst period of communal carnage during 1946–47 he made serious efforts to contain the virus of communalism. His efforts in Calcutta, Noakhali, Bihar and his subsequent fast unto death in Delhi was a living demonstration of his firm faith and resolve for communal harmony. It is not for nothing that Lord Mountbatten described his efforts as 'one man' boundary force.

The basic question that has been raised was that despite his declaration to the effect that India would be divided on his dead body why did he accept partition both in the Working Committee of Congress held on 3 June and subsequent AICC meeting. Several explanations have been offered for this. In the first place, both in the Working Committee as well as in the AICC, he left nobody in doubt that personally he was opposed to partition. But why did he not take a firm stand by supporting the socialist leaders like Jayaprakash Narayan, Rammanohar Lohia and Kamaladevi Chattopadhyaya, who were totally opposed to the idea of partition. Not only that, he went even to the extent of persuading them not to oppose the resolution on partition which made them abstain in the final head count. Several explanations have been offered in this regard as well. One, that he did not want to oppose Nehru, Patel and other Congress leaders, whom he had built up as leaders and who, in their turn, had given their best years to the cause of national struggle under his leadership. Second, as a leader who had his fingers on the pulse of the people he knew very well, that communal madness had overtaken them and they were not inclined to listen to and act upon his sane advice at least for the time being. He thought the communal frenzy would die soon, then he would be able to work out a new plan for people's unity and communal harmony. That is why he was thinking of going to Pakistan, not on an Indian passport but as a man for whom the boundary between India and Pakistan did not exist. Thus he never accepted partition as a matter of permanence but only as a temporary affair. His unhappiness on the partition could be illustrated by the fact that he never participated in the celebration on 15 August as a day of independence. His agony, his suffering during 1946–47 and finally his martyrdom on 30 January 1948 proved beyond any doubt his prophetic vision that India would be divided only on his dead body. And lo and behold! India was really divided on his body as he was assassinated on the issues related to partition.

What about the role of the British in general and Lord Mountbatten in particular? The fact of the British consistent policy of 'divide and rule' is too well known to be taken up for analysis here. But this policy of 'divide and rule', was replaced by a policy of 'divide and quit' during the last phase of the British rule in India. When, during the Second World War, a final breach took place between the British and the Congress, the British openly propped up the League as a counterveiling force to the Congress and even handed over the governments of Bengal, Sindh, NFWP and Assam during 1942–43, which greatly raised the League's stock in the Muslim majority provinces, which it had earlier failed to secure. In fact, the lack of support in the Muslim majority area had been the Achilles' heel for the League – a problem which was solved during the War by the open collusion between the British and the League giving some legitimacy to the League's claim of being the sole representative of the Muslim masses. Besides, the British also unequivocally made a declaration that no constitutional arrangement in India would be made, overriding the interests of the Muslim masses – which contributed greatly to the recalcitrant attitude of Jinnah not accepting anything less than Pakistan. Even the Cabinet Mission Plan, at most, gave a moratorium of ten years on the issue of Pakistan. But the worst was yet to come. Lord Mountbatten took over his office of the Viceroy towards the end of March 1947, and within five months, succeeded in running a knife in the body of India, cutting her in two pieces. He advanced the date of British withdrawal from June 1948 to 15 August 1947. By the end of May 1947, he virtually forced the Congress to accept his plan of the partition of India or face total anarchy and chaos and a virtual civil war situation in the country. His own self-defence had been that in the prevailing circumstances the solution provided by him, was the best, which is why both the Congress and the League ultimately accepted it. This plan ensured a good relationship between the British and two successor states of India and Pakistan proposed under it. Besides, it would also usher in a new era in the life of the people whose representatives would have a much sought-after opportunity of framing their own constitution.

Moreover, they would also gear up their own administrative machinery to effectively tackle the problem confronting their people. In retrospect, it seems that the British were more concerned with their future interest in the region rather than the problems faced by the people. They had lost the will and capacity to tackle the problems which the Indian subcontinent faced on the eve of independence and they found themselves unequal to the task. That alone explains the mad hurry displayed by Lord Mountbatten and he indeed cannot escape the responsibility for the mayhem, which occurred in the wake of partition.

But the fact remains that everybody including the League, the Congress and even Mahatma Gandhi accepted the partition plan enunciated by Lord Mountbatten and hence everybody had his share of responsibility for it. Perhaps all other involved parties except Gandhiji had their own consolation prizes. The League got Pakistan and the Congress, an opportunity to build up a strong central government with the bulk of the Indian territory, including Princely India. The British succeeded in wriggling out of a difficult situation and also in ensuring better future relations with both dominions. Perhaps Gandhiji alone was the total loser and made the supreme sacrifice in the process. Whether there was a better alternative could be anybody's guess.

However, the number of people drawn, both from the world of politics and academia have raised question marks against the inevitability of the partition of India. They lay the blame at the doors of the Indian leaders who failed to join hands to frustrate the British policy of 'divide and rule' being turned into that of 'divide and quit'. Maulana Azad, one of the prominent Congress leaders, strongly believed that it was not the people of India but the leadership that led her up the garden path. In his memoirs, *India Wins Freedom* he writes:

> The people of India did not accept partition. In fact, their heart and soul rebelled against the very idea. I have said that the Muslim League enjoyed the support of many Indians, but there was a

> large section of the community which has always opposed the League. They were naturally cut by the decision to divide the country. As for the Hindus and the Sikhs, they were to a man opposed to partition.
>
> *India Wins Freedom*, p. 224

Rammanohar Lohia, the socialist leader, in his book *Guilty Men of India's Partition* also believed that it was the lust for political power among the ageing leadership of the Congress which prompted them to accept the partition in 1947. Mushirul Hasan, a leading academician, in the book *India's Partition: Processes, Strategy and Mobilisation* edited by him, shared similar feelings of deep anguish when he writes: 'Never before in the South Asian history did so few divide so many so needlessly' (p. 43) H M Seervai, in his book *Constitutional Law of India* who has made a detailed study on the 'Partition of India: Legend and Reality' also argues that the partition could have been avoided if the Congress leadership could have accepted Maulana Azad's proposal for giving to the Indian Muslims the power sharing parity both in respect of legislature as well as in the executive of the country. Ayesha Jalal's *The Sole Spokesman: Jinnah, the Muslim League and Demand for Pakistan* also harps on the same theme of Hindu–Muslim parity in power-sharing being the real intention of Jinnah and the demand for partition being just a bargaining-counter. In her view, it was only when the parity proposal was rejected by the Congressmen that partition became inevitable.

In response to all these submissions and formulations, one's instantaneous response is to just quote a poet:

> For all sad words of tongue or pen;
> The saddest are these: 'It might have been'.

But on second thoughts one is also reminded of the Churchillian warning: 'It is wrong not to lay the lessons of the past before the future'. It is, therefore, incumbent on us to closely examine the underlying ideas behind these anguished hearts. For, one need not doubt the genuineness of the feelings of remorse compelling so many brave hearts to pick up the gauntlet. But that does not prevent us from saying that all of them are crying over spilt milk. But they have failed to detect and analyse the acids that spoiled the garden party. All these scholars forget that the nitty-gritty of the Muslim League's demands was based on its leader's self-image as well as that of the community being larger than life. A bird's eye view of the Muslim League's ever-insatiable demands would prove that it was not possible to meet them. Sir Syed Ahmad Khan was the first to assert with a raised voice that Muslims, being the ex-ruling class, had to be treated as a privileged class despite their numerical weakness vis-à-vis the Hindus. Then the Muslim League demanded separate electorates, which was accepted by the British under the 1909 Act. It further emboldened them when the same was endorsed by the Lucknow Congress in 1916 as a quid-pro-quo for Muslim support to the national movement. The Khilafat and Non-Cooperation Movements were the apogee of the Hindu–Muslim bonhomie. But the slide-down began so soon after the withdrawal of the Non-Cooperation Movement. When the Nehru Report tried to work out a scheme of joint electorate, Jinnah demanded reservation of one-third seats in the Central Legislature as well as reservation of seats for Muslims both in the Punjab and Bengal Legislatures. Having failed there, he soon upgraded his demands through his oft-quoted 14 points from the forum of the united Muslim League. Despite being beaten in the 1937 elections, he demanded power-sharing with the Congress in the form of the coalition government. Then came the Lahore resolution of the League in 1940, propounding the two-nation theory and demanding a distinct homeland for the Muslims. When the transfer of power from the British hands to the Indian hands became a distinct possibility, then the parity formula of power-sharing was taken out of the League's political bag. The Muslim League led by Jinnah started demanding half of the national cake in the form of parity formula of power-sharing or deferred partition, which both the Cripps Mission and the Cabinet Mission Plan actually implied. All this was nothing but an attempt to get a large share in the national cake despite the law of numerical weightage going against them. To make up their numerical weakness, the Muslim League started talking in terms of parity with the caste Hindus with a view to justify their demand for parity. It is evident that the acceptance of the League's demand for parity in power-sharing or deferred partition might have temporarily solved the problem, but in the long run, it might have proved more disastrous for the country. In fact, such an acceptance might have led, not only to the fragmentation of the body-politic of the country but also to that of its civil society. All those who have any doubt about the real intention of Jinnah should read his presidential address delivered at the Lahore conference of the League in 1940. The following two small quotes from that speech clearly reveal the real intention of Jinnah:

> Muslim India cannot accept any Constitution which must necessarily result in a Hindu majority government. Hindus and Muslims brought together under a democratic system forced upon the minority can only mean Hindu Raj. Democracy of this kind . . . would mean the complete destruction of what is most precious in Islam.

If any one is still left with any doubt about the real intention of Jinnah, sample this from the same speech.

'Musalmans are a nation according to any definition of the nation, and they must have their homeland, their territory and their state'.

One simply shudders to think that if Jinnah had his way, under what kind of political system we might have been living today! But that is not to deny the continuing trauma of the after-effects of partition even today. Thousands of families are divided and are living on both sides of the border, living away from their loved ones. Besides, since the day of their inception, India and Pakistan are not on the best of the terms: they have fought four wars including the recent one at Kargil.

Moreover, cross-border terrorism is reaching an alarming stage posing an ever present threat to the life and liberty of the Indian people. However, there is a growing feeling among the people of both the countries that the time has come to forget the past acrimonies and bury the hatchets. If in the coming days, this feeling gathers momentum; both these countries can start a journey towards the final destination of amity and understanding. If they find the road of amity smooth, they can even think of the 'unthinkable': they can go in for a confederation with a minimum common agenda – a dream which was very close to the heart of Rammanohar Lohia – the stormy-petrel of Indian politics.

If ever the people of India and Pakistan decide to find a common destiny for themselves, they can take great inspiration from the experience of the American people who moved from the confederation to the federation emerging as the mightiest power on the earth. Further, the people of the Indian subcontinent could greatly benefit from 'objectives-resolution' moved by Jawaharlal Nehru in the Constituent Assembly on 13 December 1946, which inter alia reads as follows:

1. This Constituent Assembly declares its firm and solemn resolve to proclaim India as a Independent Sovereign Republic and to draw up for her future governance, a Constitution;

2. WHEREIN the territories that now comprise British India, the territories that now form the Indian States, and such other parts of India as are outside British India and the States as well as such other territories as are willing to be constituted into the Independent Sovereign India, shall be a Union of them, all; and
3. WHEREIN the said territories, whether with their present boundaries or with such others as may be determined by the Constituent Assembly and thereafter according to the Law of the Constitution, *shall possess and retain the status of autonomous units, together with residuary powers, and exercise all powers and functions, of government and administration, save and except such powers and functions as are vested in or assigned to the Union,* or as are inherent or implied in the Union or resulting there from; . . . .

This resolution talks of 'autonomous units with residuary power' and hence could be used as a basis for raising a confederation. It is also interesting to note that the Constituent Assembly never repealed this resolution: it simply moved on the frame a federal constitution with a strong centre in the wake of the independence of the country. Equally interesting is the fact to be recalled that while accepting the resolution on the partition of India, the All India Congress Committee also reminded the people that the old map of united India, which had inspired many people to make the supreme sacrifice would continue to inspire the people of the Indian subcontinent.

Thus, the time has come for the people of the Indian subcontinent to bury the hatchet and take a fresh initiative towards a new road of amity and understanding. If that happens, nothing can prevent them from emerging as a great power as was expected by the objectives-resolution: 'this ancient land could attain its rightful and honoured place in the world and could make seminal contributions to 'world peace' and 'welfare of mankind'.

Even Jawaharlal Nehru, who had played a crucial role in the partition of the country subsequently observed:

> I know that we have been to blame in many matters. . . . Partition came and we accepted it because we thought that perhaps that way, however painful it was, we might have some peace. . . . Perhaps we acted wrongly. It is difficult to judge now. And yet,

> the consequences of that partition have been so terrible that one is inclined to think that anything else would have been preferable. . . . Ultimately, I have no doubt that India and Pakistan will come close together . . . some kind of federal link. . . . There is no other way to peace. The alternative is . . . war.
>
> Wolpert, *Shameful Flight*, p. 192

It is interesting to note that once Jinnah succeeded in carving out Pakistan by vivisecting India, he himself repudiated his 'two nation theory'. This is evident from his statement in the Pakistan Constituent Assembly on 11 August 1947, in which he inter alia stated:

> We should begin to work . . . and in the course of time, all these angularities of the majority and minorities, the Hindu community and the Muslim community will vanish . . . you are free to go to your temples, you are free to go to your mosques or to any other places of worship in this State of Pakistan. You may belong to any religion or caste or creed – that has nothing to do with the business of the State.

Admittedly, this was nothing but the total repudiation of his oft repeated 'two nation theory'. Only Gandhiji remained consistent in his 'India of his dream', which he had enunciated as follows: 'I shall work for an India in which the poorest shall feel that it is their country, an India in which there shall be no high class and low class of people; an India in which all communities shall live in perfect harmony. Women will enjoy the same rights as men. We shall be at peace with all the rest of the world. This is the India of my dreams.'

There is no denying the fact that on this road of amity, there are many roadblocks. This is not a call for undoing the partition, but a call for undoing the heartaches and hangover of the partition. In a different context, the poet saw a flickering ray of hope beyond the never-ending dark tunnel when he wrote:

When these paths are erased by the dust
Hundreds of new ways will appear
Hold firmly to your heart
Hundreds of arrows will break in it.

FAIZ AHMED FAIZ

Appendices

I Historiography of Colonialism and Nationalism in India

An Overview

In the historiography of modern Indian history, in general and that of colonialism and nationalism in particular, India has been a subject of major contestations and controversies among historians. In the last thirty years or so, a number of new approaches to the study of colonialism and nationalism have been developed, primarily based on distinct ideological frameworks. Many scholars have started their studies with a discussion on these approaches. In our view, it would be much easier for our students to grasp the entire gamut of the issues involved in the debate once we have completed our survey of colonial rule as well as the national movement, along with their dialectical inter-connections and inter-actions. Hence, the decision to place it at the end of our study.

Taking a synoptic view of the entire debate on the historiography of colonialism and nationalism in India, one can easily conclude that there have been three major issues involved in it. One, what was the inter-connection between the British colonial rule and the emergence and growth of Indian nationalism? In other words, whether Indian nationalists were only responding to the British initiatives or they formulated and concretised the interest of the entire nation on their own and launched a national movement to actualise it. Second, whether the national movement sought to serve the interests of the dominant classes or those of the entire nation? Third, apart from the elite-led national movement, whether there existed, a subterranean national movement with its occasional eruptions and rebellions, which could be described as the real nationalism of the masses. With this brief introduction, we turn to the discussion on the main submissions and contentions of the major schools, viz., the imperialist; the nationalist; the Marxist, the subalterns and semi-Marxist nationalists.

The Imperialist School

This school of thought is as old as the British rule in India itself. Initially, it was built-up by the protagonists of the British rule in India, including a number of Viceroys and British administrators. They underlined the providential and benevolent nature of the colonial rule and rubbished all talks of colonial exploitation resulting in the immense sufferings of the Indian people. Subsequently, its liberal academic variant was developed by Reginald Coupland and Percival Spear who argued that the British proved their bonafides of benevolence by ultimately handing over the reign of power to the Indians. However, today there are no takers for this line of thinking. Hence, it has gone barren. But there is a band of neo-traditionalists connected with the Cambridge school, led by Anil Seal, J A Callaghar, Judith Brown and others who had picked up the old gauntlet of contestation. Their main formulation is that India was not even a 'nation-in-making' what to talk of a real nation. In their view, India was nothing more than conglomerations of castes, communities and religious and linguistic groups, which, in fact, provided the social bases for varied political organisations. In their view, the Indian people could never develop a common national identity: they continued to be governed more by their primordial loyalties. Thus, the organic growth of Indian nationalism was ruled out. They further aver that the national movement was nothing more than a cover or forum for these diverse competing groups, particularly their elite sections, to pursue their group or personal interests. If people were mobilised, it was for the promotion of group interest and not for national commonweal. Some of these scholars even went to the extent of saying that these competing elite groups were even vying with each other for the British favour to promote their group interests. They further argue that the people were mobilised on the basis of patron–client relationship and even the national leaders like Gandhiji, Nehru and Patel played the role of national brokers. They also argue that whatever mobilisation of the people took place, it was triggered by the British initiatives in the field of western education and legislative institutions. Some of these scholars have done field studies on regional and local politics to support their contention that it was not the national commonweal but the regional group-interests that was the motive force behind mass mobilisation.

It is not surprising that such a blatant neo-colonialist approach has attracted severe criticism at the hands of Indian scholars. Tapan Raychaudhuri sarcastically commented that such a neo-colonialist's view, of the Indian National Movement reduced it to 'animal polities'. More harsh and stinging was the comment of noted historian S Gopal who wrote: 'the School has taken not only mind but also decency, character, integrity, and selfless commitment out of the Indian National Movement'. One can only say that this is a most cynical and Machiavellian view of politics, which totally rules out any space for higher human values in polities except naked pursuit of power politics. For shorn of all its verbiage and mass of collected data, all that the school is trying to emphasise is that it was not the exploitative nature of British colonial rule, resulting in the mass pauperisation of people and in the process, raising it to the level of the enemy symbol, which triggered the nationalist feelings, but the mutual jealousies of competing elite groups for the picking of the crumbs fallen from the British master's table. Such a cynical view of politics does not leave any space for the role of ideology, high ideas and ideals which have moved man since time immemorial. Thus, cynicism behind such a banal view of polities is only matched by its ahistoricity.

The Nationalist School

Totally opposed to the views of the imperialist school were those of the nationalist school. It not only emerged out of the national movement but even had a hand in its emergence as well. In any case, it strengthened and enriched the various streams of national movement. Among its early protagonists were: Surendranath Banerjea, Lokmanya Tilak, Bipin Chandra Pal, Lala Lajpat Rai, Swami Dayanand, Swami Vivekanand, Aurobindo and a host of others. Subsequently, it was enriched by the academic contributions of R C Majumdar, Tarachand, Bisheshwar Prasad, B R Nanda, B N Pandey and others scholars and academicians. Their main formulations are as follows:

(i) They underlined the exploitative character of the British colonial structure. They were firmly of the opinion that in the course of their rule, the British tried to transform India into a captive market for the British industrial goods as well as a reliable supplier of raw materials for the British industries. They further asserted that the British not only destroyed the traditional base of Indian agriculture and handicrafts, but also thwarted its industrial development by subordinating Indian economy to the British economy.

(ii) They also believed that it was the pride of India, its cultural and intellectual heritage which has sown the seeds of Indian nationalism. Subsequently, the ideals of nationalism and human liberty also contributed to the growth of Indian nationalism. Some of them even asserted that India, as a cultural and national entity always existed, while others took it as a nation-in-making.

(iii) They firmly believed that the Indian national movement represented the collective will as well as the commonweal of our people, and in no case it was a class movement. As a people's movement it went on encompassing all sections of the Indian society and their interests, particularly after the advent of Gandhiji on the national scene. They also believed that the Indian National Congress was a representative of all sections of the Indian people. Marxist scholars have criticised the nationalist school on the ground that they ignored the class-cleavages present in the Indian society and concentrated more on elite-led movements.

The Marxist School

The Marxist school has primarily relied on the writings and commentaries of Karl Marx, on the nature and role of the British colonial rule in India. Initially, this school of thought was promoted by R P Dutt, S A Dange, P C Joshi, and a host of other Marxist intellectuals. Along with the writings of Karl Marx, R P Dutt's *India Today* and A R Desai's *Social Background of Indian Nationalism* became the bible of this school in analysing the nature and structure of the British colonial rule as well as those of the Indian nationalism. Their main formulations were as follows:

(i) Borrowing the basic ideological framework from Karl Marx and Lenin, they have subjected the British colonial policy to a critical analysis. They discussed three phases of the British colonial policy, viz., mercantile, industrial and finance capital and submitted that in all three phases different policies were pursued to promote the interests of the British bourgeois classes.

(ii) They agreed with the nationalist school that the British rule has resulted in the mass poverty of our people by destroying the traditional base of the Indian agriculture and handicraft industries. But following Karl Marx, they made a distinction between the destructive and positive role of the British rule. They were in unison with the nationalists so far as the destructive side of the British rule was concerned. However, they also underlined the fact that it had a positive side as it brought about a structural transformation of the Indian society, taking it up from feudal mode to the capitalist mode of production, even though an 'imperfect and distorted' one. Thus, it gave a mortal blow to the feudal hierarchies and created a new basis for the emergence of the new classes in the Indian society. It also created a new state structure with its concomitant bureaucratic and administrative set-up. Not only that, it also introduced modern means of transport and communication along with a system of modern education. They agreed with the nationalists that all this was being done to promote the British interests. But they were of the opinion that whatever might be the British motive, the structural transformation of the Indian society heralded a new progressive era in India.

(iii) The school conceded that this structural transformation led to a primary contradiction between the interests of the Indian people and those of the British colonial rule. And the roots of the emergence of Indian nationalism lay in this primary contradiction between the two.

(iv) The school was divided and confused about the nature and role of the Indian national movement in general and that of Mahatma Gandhi in particular. This confusion arose primarily because of their being deeply rooted in the theory of class and class-struggle as a tool of social analysis. Besides, they had to take into accounts the conclusions drawn by the international communist movement about the class-character of the Indian National Movement. Most of the times, they were confused

> about the identification of their main class enemy. Thus they could not decide whether their priority was to oppose international bourgeois-led British imperialism or the national bourgeois-led Indian struggle. Hence, they went on taking contradictory stands on different stages of the Indian struggle. Their opposition to the Quit India Movement is a case in point.

The basic methodological difficulty of the Marxist school is rooted in its lack of independence from the international communist movement. Its insistence on the universality of class-centric approach to the study of historiography is faulty in the sense that it neglects the social matrix, historical moorings and cultural conditioning of a society. Their basic approach to the study of colonialism and nationalism, and rational movement in India is methodologically determinist and reductionist in nature.

The Subaltern School

The Subaltern school is the latest school to join the rank of Indian historiography. Its chief ideologue is Ranajit Guha who had been primarily inspired by the ideas of an Italian leader, Gramsci. Subsequently, a number of other scholars have joined the group and have brought out a number of volumes on subaltern studies. For them the only correct and intellectually fruitful approach to study modern Indian history is the subaltern approach. In plain language, the school stands for the study of modern Indian history from the viewpoint of subordinate masses, mostly comprising poor peasants, tribals, women, untouchables and a host of other dispossessed sections of the Indian society. They are firmly of the opinion that Indian society is divided into two distinct groups: the elite and subaltern and there exists a primary contradiction between their interests. They point out that the study of the Indian history has been dominated by the elitist's historiography. They further believe that there was no real conflict between the Indian elite and the British elite which ruled India. In fact, they were on the same side of the battle lines drawn between the people and the elite. They argue that the national movement led by the Indian National Congress was nothing but a cover under which the real battle for power was being fought among the elites. They further contend that it is the subaltern groups that became the worst victims of the British rule. Hence, the real national movement was one in which the subaltern groups were involved. It is the subalterns who really fought against the British by launching rebellions in different parts and different occasions. And it is these political and social eruptions and rebellions that need to be studied and explored.

On close scrutiny, however, several infirmities appear in the basic formulations of this school. In the first place, they take into consideration a sectional and even a sectarian approach which wants to turn a part into a whole. Second, and ironically enough, there is some common ground between the imperialist school and the subaltern school as both look at the Indian elite as the chief villain of the piece.

Semi-Marxist Nationalist School

Bipan Chandra and his co-scholars have tried to reconcile the basic formulations of the nationalist school with those of the Marxist school. Hence, it can be characterised as semi-Marxist nationalist school. Their basic formulations could be summed up as follows:

(i) There was a primary contradiction between interests of the British colonial rule and those of the Indian people, and it is this which led to the emergence of the Indian National Movement.
(ii) They do concede that there are secondary contradictions among different sections of the Indian society but it never overshadowed the primary contradiction between the Indian people as a whole and the British colonial rule.
(iii) The Indian national movement was never a single class movement, rather it always remained a multi-class movement. Hence, it can be really characterised as the people's movement.
(iv) The national movement, in the process of its growth, greatly contributed to the emergence of India as a nation but it never tried to obliterate all other narrower identities of the people.
(v) The Indian intelligentsia did play a leading role in the national movement but it tried to reconcile the conflicting interests of the different sections of the Indian society.
(vi) The transfer of power in 1947 was not a compromise but it was the culmination of the 'war of position' in which the national movement was involved for many years.

In the light of our study and on the basis of this brief survey of different approaches to the historiography of colonialism and nationalism in India, only one conclusion becomes inescapable: most of these approaches, even at their best, are nothing more than sectional or at least segmented in their nature. One cannot grasp the entire gamut of the issues involved by using any one of them singularly. They might even remind us of the six blind men and the elephant they tried to visualise. Hence, the best ways to deal with the complex phenomena of colonialism and nationalism is to have a multi-pronged approach. And this is what we have tried to do in the course of our present study.

II Colonialism and Theories of Imperialism

Colonialism and imperialism as terms of political discourse are quite often used interchangeably. It is true that they cover a lot of common grounds, yet there are subtle differences between the two. In this section our attempt is to discuss these two terms with a view to present their clear and concise meanings. Besides, we would also be discussing different theories of imperialism.

Let us first look at a few definitions of colonialism. The *Soviet Encyclopaedia* describes it as 'military and economic enslavement of any dependent country, accompanied by bestial exploitation and extermination of indigenous population'. According to Palmer and Perkins 'colonialism is the resultant complex of political and economic controls imposed by advanced capitalist countries over their dependencies in backward parts of the world'. The Oxford dictionary defines colony as 'a country or area under the full and partial control of another country typically a distant one and occupied by settlers from that county'. It defines colonialism as 'the policy or practice of acquiring full or partial control over another country, occupying it with settlers and exploiting it economically'. The literal meaning of the terms, colony and colonialism' is quite plain. Thus, when a group of people settle down in a foreign land with a view to take advantage of its resources, that land is called a 'colony' and the entire enterprise is called colonialism.

But in modern parlance, colonialism has come to be associated and identified with the occupation of the countries of Asia and Africa by European capitalist countries. In the process, colonialism has assumed three different forms. In its first form, a particular country physically takes hold of a distant and alien land and overwhelms and subjugates the native people both in the terms of number, resources and territory. In the process, the native people are either exterminated or pushed to the backyard reservations. European occupation of land masses of North America, Australia and New Zealand are a case in point. The second type is when a small group of alien people occupy a foreign land by permanently settling there and getting hold of their wealth and resources and taking the natives as slaves. The 'white settlers' occupation of South Africa and their rule over the native people, with their policy of Apartheid is an illustrative case. In both these types of colonialism, these alien settlers gradually lose or at least loosen their ties with their old motherland. In the third type of colonialism, there is a political domination of a foreign land by a metropolitan country. Here the political control by alien power, with all its concomitant institutional set-up, ensures economic exploitation of the colony and the flow of resources to the metropolis. The British occupation of India and its subsequent colonial rule falls in this category.

Imperialism is a much wider term than colonialism. Basically, it implies socio-economic-cultural control of an alien country by a foreign power. Traditionally, imperialism implied an extension of rule of a nation over another nation. Roman imperialism of old times is an illustrative case. In our times, imperialism basically refers to imperialism of the European countries, which became a dominant system during the last quarter of the nineteenth century and continued till the first part of the twentieth century. According to Eckert, imperialism 'is a type of politics, characterised by the striving for the extension of political, economic and intellectual power of a nation, of people and its culture over areas which lie outside its political boundaries'. The Oxford dictionary defines imperialism as 'policy of extending a country's power and influences through colonisation, use of military force or other means'. It defines an empire as 'an extensive group of states or countries under a single supreme authority'. Such an imperialist relationship could be established and maintained through various means: military domination, colonisation, direct conquest, trade, aid or even diplomacy. In plain language, it denotes a relationship between two countries marked by domination, dependency and exploitation. In such a relationship, domination covers the entire spectrum of the other country's national life – social, political, economic and cultural.

In the post-war period, there was a subtle paradigm shift in meaning and implication of the term, imperialism. Earlier, in the definition of imperialism the emphasis was on its aspect of physical conquest, viz., the Roman Empire and Ottoman Empire. But in the Post-War period the emphasis shifted to a more subtle form of exploitation and domination – trade, economic aid and diplomacy became its major tools, though military and physical power did remain at the back of them. The American occupation of Iraq has once again demonstrated the military aspect of imperialism. Thus, in the Post-War period a new term like neo-imperialism or new-colonialism started being used to underline its subtle forms marked by domination, dependency and exploitation.

As we have seen earlier, more often than not, colonialism and imperialism have been used interchangeably. Yet at least some difference, at least in terms of nuances, could be underlined between these two terms.

(i) In a formal sense, colonialism came to an end once the process of decolonisation was completed in the post-war period. But imperialism continue to survive and, in fact, is spreading its tentacles in the different parts of the world.
(ii) Imperialism is a much wider concept as compared to colonialism. It denotes a relationship of domination and dependency in various overt and covert forms. Colonialism has been one of its tools and symbolises its particular form at a particular stage.
(iii) Colonialism denotes the entire process of the colonial domination from trade to direct political rule. But imperialism according to the Marxist scholars, denotes only the phase of monopoly capitalism.
(iv) Colonialism was marked by its directness and visibility, the features of imperialism are much more subtle and indirect.

In fact, colonialism created the ground through its various institutional frameworks on which the edifice of imperialism could flourish. And which is why imperialism is still flourishing and its challenge is much more serious than that of colonialism.

Theories of Imperialism

A number of scholars have analysed and dissected the nature and structure of imperialism and on the basis of their studies, have enunciated different theories. Here, an attempt is being made to make a quintessential presentation of the views of three theories, namely, Hobson, Rosa Luxemburg and Lenin.

Hobson, a British labour party intellectual, in his book *Imperialism* (1902), conceded that an imperialist expansion is inherent in the very nature and structure of capitalism but it is not inevitable. His formulations, along with argumentations behind them are summed up here:

(i) Capitalism creates many layers of uneven income groups as the bulk of the earnings are pocketed by a small group of the capitalists.
(ii) The wages of the working class are deliberately kept at low level, resulting in the limited nature of their purchasing power and their 'low consumption' level and that leads to a glut of industrial products in a capitalist country. Hence, there arises a need for colonies as captive markets.
(iii) But the volume of profits and savings of the capitalist class results in 'over-accumulation' of capital.
(iv) This 'over-accumulation' of capital, coupled with 'under-consumption' on the part of the general masses, prompts the capitalist class to look for colonies for the investment of their accumulated capital wherein it could have better profitability.
(v) This leads to a competitive hunger among the capitalist countries for acquisition of colonies which, more often than not, produces conflict among them.

In brief, in Hobson's theory of imperialism, 'over-accumulation of capital' and 'under-consumption of goods are inherent in the very nature and structure of capitalism. But Hobson was optimistic that this problem of lopsided development of capitalism could be tackled through corrective measures. Hence, he did not reject the capitalist system of production per se. He suggested that this distortion could be taken care of by enforcing a better and more equitable system of income distribution. His critics point out that Hobson could not see imperialism as a natural progeny of capitalism and not just a distortion which has crept in the system.

Rosa Luxemburg's Theory of Imperialism

Rosa Luxemburg, a Polish-born German socialist, also propounded her own theory of imperialism in her book *Accumulation of Capital*, which was published in 1913. In this connection, her basic formulation is that capitalism can expand and flourish only so long as it has non-capitalist colonial markets. In her view, the completion of the process of acquisition of new non-capitalist countries and their gradual conversion to capitalist system of production is bound to seal the fate of capitalism. Thus, she looks at imperialism as a desperate attempt to prolong the life of capitalism. But she is convinced that ultimately, capitalism would reach the end of the road and would meet its nemesis. But she does not visualise its end as being so smooth. In fact, in its final phase, capitalism is bound to bring many a catastrophe.

She was firmly of the opinion that militarism is an integral part of capitalism, as it is used as a means to subjugate the colonies. She further avers that militarism and competition for acquisition of colonies lead to war among the capitalist countries.

But the bulk of the cost of militarism and war are met by indirect taxes. Hence, imperialism is baneful not only for the people of colonies but also for the working class of the metropolitan countries, as they also bear these costs. However, she was fully convinced that capitalism, along with its progeny, i.e. imperialism would ultimately meet their nemesis.

Rosa Luxemburg's theory of imperialism was a product of her times as it tried to explain the gathering storms of the First World War. But subsequent historical development, both in the capitalist world and socialist world, could not be explained in terms of her theory of imperialism. The demise of capitalism is nowhere in sight. On the contrary, it is going from strength to strength and in the process, turning even the socialist-roaders to capitalist-roaders.

Lenin's Theory of Imperialism

Before we take up Lenin's theory of imperialism, it is relevant to refer to another work *The Finance Capital* (1910) by Rodolf Hilferding. He was a German social democrat and an intellectual in his own right. He made a penetrating analysis of the last phase of capitalism, that he called finance capitalism. His main thesis was that during the phase of finance capitalism, banks and other big financial institutions working in close collaboration with monopolist industrial houses take it on the road to monopoly and finance capitalism. Lenin drew heavily from his work when he wrote a pamphlet 'Imperialism: The Highest Stage of Capitalism' (1916); there were both practical and theoretical considerations that prompted Lenin to come out with his work during the war itself. His practical objective was to dissuade the people of Russia, particularly the Russian working class, from supporting the war. The primary theoretical consideration was to understand and explain the nature of imperialism and its symbiotic relationship with capitalism. Besides, he also wanted to explain that the genesis of the First World War lay in the competitiveness of the capitalist countries to divide the world in their respective spheres of influence.

The major formulations of Lenin in respect of imperialism could be summed up as follows:

(i) He looked at imperialism as a 'direct continuation of the fundamental properties of capitalism'.
(ii) According to him, imperialism appears during a particular phase of capitalism when it had reached the stage of monopoly capitalism. It is during this stage of capitalism that export of capital becomes much more profitable than the export of ordinary goods.
(iii) Lenin saw a direct relationship between the monopolistic capitalism resulting in imperialism and militarisation of its economy. He looked at the First World War as an imperialist war, being fought among the capitalist countries for the control of colonies. Hence, he called upon the international working class to not to lend any support to it.
(iv) Lenin also explained the fact why it was inherent in the very nature of capitalism, to reach the stage of monopoly capitalism. According to him, initially capitalism is fed on with limited capital of individual entrepreneurs and partnership firms. But soon a stage is reached when a big capital is required on account of new technological inventions and innovations. Thus large enterprises became the need of the hour. On account of cut-throat competition small enterprises are eliminated and only bigger enterprises survive. All these developments lead to what Lenin calls, monopoly capitalism.

Lenin summed up the entire process by enumerating five features of imperialism:

(i) Monopolies develop on account of concentration of capital and production in a few hands. In every industry a small number of concerns achieve the dominating position, which is further strengthened by their mutual interlocking arrangements leading to joint monopoly.

(ii) Banking capital coupled with industrial capital leads to the emergence of financial oligarchy.
(iii) The export of capital supersedes the export of commodities as the former becomes more profitable than the latter.
(iv) Emergence of monopolies at the international level, which try to divide the world among themselves.
(v) In the process, the territorial division of the world among the capitalist powers is completed.

Despite these distinguishing features, imperialism, as Lenin asserts, does not symbolise a new mode of production, rather it is the highest stage of capitalism itself.

Lenin's theory of imperialism has been criticised on the following counts:

(i) Lenin's theory of imperialism is based on the limited experiences and evidence from a small number of capitalist countries. And there too, some of his generalisations are based only on a very limited amount of empirical evidence. A number of scholars have raised question marks against his theoretical generalisation, as there is paucity of historical evidence to support and substantiate them. For example, there is little evidence to support Lenin's major theoretical formulations that it was the decay and technological retardation which necessitated export of capital in place of export of commodities.
(ii) The attempt to explain all the actions of colonial powers in terms of need of industrial capitalist economy virtually amounts to economic determinism, which has already become an outdated concept.
(iii) There is a historical evidence to prove the fact that colonial and imperialist expansion preceded the monopoly stage of capitalism. British colonial expansion in India is a case in point which counters one of the major formulations of Lenin that imperialism comes only when capitalism has reached its monopoly stage.
(iv) Lenin's basic formulation that imperialism is the child of capitalism has been refuted by subsequent historical developments. The erstwhile Soviet Union and the People's Republic of China also have their own exploitative relationship

with East European countries and the people of Tibet, respectively. And what is more, even these two communist states went through a brief war which goes against Lenin's theory that war is the result of the competition among the capitalist countries alone. Besides, both these states now have taken to capitalist road.

Nevertheless, the credit goes to Lenin for pointing out the economic and political abuse of the western European industrial states in respect of their colonies in Asia and Africa. Second, the debate on imperialism did not die with Lenin. The debate on imperialism and its new facets in the form of neo-colonialism and neo-imperialism is still on. It has not subsided even with completion of the process of decolonisation in the post-War period. Scholars of new Left and the world-systems have further given their own perspective on the debate on imperialism. Even the collapse of the Soviet Union and the People's Republic of China and their subsequent march towards a capitalist set-up has not ended the debate on imperialism. It is still on even in today's environment of liberalisation and globalisation. The persistence of this debate in itself is a great tribute to Lenin.

III Chronology of Major Events from AD 1600 to 1947

1600	Royal Charter for the English East India Company
1612	First English factory at Surat in western India
1613	Mughal Emperor Jahangir grants trading rights to the English company
1639	Foundation of Fort St. George in Madras
1651	English factory at Hugli in eastern India
1698	The English obtain zamindari (landowning) rights in Kolikata, Sutanuti and Gobindapur in eastern India
1707	Death of Aurangzeb
1717	Mughal Emperor Farruksiyar grants duty-free trading rights to the English company
1745-49	First Anglo-French War
1751-54	Second Anglo-French War
1756-63	Seven Years' War in Europe Third Anglo-French War in India resulting in the elimination of French competition.
1756	Nawab of Bengal captures Calcutta from the English, leading to confrontation between the two
1757	Battle of Plassey
1761	Third Battle of Panipat
1764	Battle of Buxar
1765	Grant of *Diwani* (revenue collecting rights) for Bengal, Bihar and Orissa to the English company
1767-69	First Anglo-Mysore War
1773	The Regulating Act
1775-82	First Anglo-Maratha War and Treaty of Salbai by which the British Government acquired control of Salsette
1780-84	Second Anglo-Mysore War
1784	The Pitt's India Act

1790-92	Third Anglo-Mysore War
1793	The Permanent Settlement of land revenue in Bengal
1799	Fourth Anglo-Mysore War
1802	Peshwa Baji Rao II seeks British protection and accepts a subsidiary alliance by the Treaty of Bassein
1803-05	Second Anglo-Maratha War resulting in defeat of the Maratha chieftains forcing them to accept subsidiary force
1817-18	Third Anglo-Maratha War resulting in the abolition of the office of Peshwa and annexation of his territory by the English
1829	Prohibition of *sati* (self-immolation by widows)
1833	Renewal of the Company's Charter Abolition of the Company's monopoly trading rights
1835	Lord Macaulay's Minute on Indian Education
1845-46	First Anglo-Sikh War
1848-49	Second Anglo-Sikh War and Annexation of Punjab
1853	Railways opened from Bombay to Thana
1856	Annexation of Awadh
1857-58	Mutiny and the Revolt: India's First War of Independence
1858	Establishment of Crown rule in British India
1861	Indian Councils Act
1883	The Ilbert bill controversy
1885	Foundation of the Indian National Congress
1892	Indian Council's Act of 1892
1905	Partition of Bengal and Swadeshi Movement
1906	Foundation of the All India Muslim League
1908	Tilak's trial and six years' imprisonment
1909	Morley-Minto Reforms
1911	Partition of Bengal annulled
1912	Imperial capital moves from Calcutta to Delhi
1914	The First World War begins
1916	Lucknow Pact between Indian National Congress and the Muslim League, the formation of the Home Rule League by Tilak and Annie Besant
1917	Russian Revolution, Champaran Satyagraha of Mahatma Gandhi
1919	Montagu-Chelmsford Reforms; Massacre of Jallianwala Bagh
1920-21	Gandhiji takes over leadership of the Indian National Congress; Khilafat and Non-Cooperation Movements under the leadership of Mahatma Gandhi

1922	Non-Cooperation Movement withdrawn after Chauri-Chaura violence; Gandhiji's trial and imprisonment
1923	The formation of the Swaraj Party: its candidates enter the Legislative Councils
1925	First Conference of the Communist Party of India held at Kanpur
1928	Visit of the Simon (Indian Statutory) Commission All Parties conference held in Calcutta; Motilal Nehru Report on the future constitution of India presented; rejection of Jinnah's amendments to the Nehru Report
1929	Lahore Congress and the resolution on Purna Swaraj
1930	Civil Disobedience Movement under Gandhiji's leadership
1931	Gandhi–Irwin Pact The Karachi Congress and its Resolutions on the Fundamental Rights
1932	Second phase of the Civil Disobedience Movement, The Communal Award and the Poona Pact
1934	Civil Disobedience Movement called off, The Formation of the Congress Socialist Party
1935	Government of India Act
1937	Inauguration of provincial autonomy Elections under the new Act Congress ministries in eight provinces
1939	The Second World War begins, resignation of the Congress Ministries
1940	The Muslim League Pakistan resolution; Lord Linglithgow's August offer of dominion status
1942	Cripps Mission ends in a failure Quit India Movement
1943	Mahatma Gandhi's Fast in Aga Khan Palace, Formation of the Azad Hind Fauz (INA) by Subhas Chandra Bose
1944	Gandhi–Jinnah talks
1946	Cabinet Mission to India, Interim Government, The Muslim League' Direct Action
1947	Mountbatten Plan and Indian Independence Act of 1947; Partition of India and the creation of Pakistan as an Independent State; India attains Freedom on 15 August 1947

Select Bibliography

General

Chandra, Bipan, *India's Struggle for Independence*, New Delhi, 1987.

Desai, A R, *Social Background of Indian Nationalism*, Bombay, 2005 (Reprint).

Dutt, R P, *India Today*, Bombay, 1940.

Majumdar, R C, *History of the Freedom Movement in India*, vols 1–3, Calcutta, 1963.

Nanda, B R, *Mahatma Gandhi: A Biography*, London, 1958.

Nehru, Jawaharlal, *The Discovery of India*, New Delhi, 1981.

Pandey, B N (ed), *A Centenary History of the Indian National Congress*, vols 1–3, New Delhi, 1885.

Ram, M S (ed), *Freedom of India: In the Words of Its Architects*, Chennai, 2003.

Sitaramayya, P, *History of the Indian National Congress*, vols 1-2, Bombay, 1946.

Spear, Percival, *The Oxford History of Modern India*, 1740–1947, Oxford, 1965.

Sarkar, Sumit, *Modern India 1885–1947*, Delhi, 1999.

Tara Chand, *History of the Freedom Movement in India*, vols 1-4, Delhi, 1961.

Part I: British Challenge and Indian Response

Basu, Aparna, *Essays in the History of Indian Education*, Delhi, 1982.

Bhagwan, Vishnoo, *Constitutional History of India and National Movement*, Lucknow 1974.

Chandra , Bipan, *Colonialism and Nationalism in Modern India*, New Delhi, 1979.

——, *The Rise and Growth of Economic Nationalism in India*, New Delhi, 1966.

Desai, T B, *Economic History of India under the British 1757–1947*, Bombay, 1972.

Desika, C, *Readings in the Constitutional History of India*, Delhi, 1983.

Dirks, Nicholas B, *The Scandal of Empire*, Delhi 2006.

Dutt, R C, *Economic History of India in the Victorian Age*, Delhi, 1960 (Reprint).

Heimsath, C H, *Indian Nationalism and Hindu Social Reform*, Princeton, 1964.

Majumdar, R C, *British Paramountcy and Indian Renaissance*, Bombay, 1966.

Mishra, B B, *Administrative History of India, 1834–1947*, Bombay, 1970.

——, *Indian Middle Class, Their Growth in Modern Times*, New Delhi, 1978.

Naoroji, Dadabhai, *Poverty and Un-British Rule in India*, (Reprint) Delhi, 1984.

Philips, C H, *The East India Company, 1784–1834*, Bombay, 1961.

Raychaudhuri, Tapan and Habib, Irfan, *The Cambridge Economic History of India*, vol 1, 1982.

Sen, S N, *Eighteen Fifty-Seven*, Delhi, 1957.

Singh, V B, *Economic History of India 1857–1957*, Delhi, 1965.

Stokes, Eric, *Peasants and the Raj*, Cambridge, 1978.

Thompson, E and Garrat, G T, *Rise and Fulfilment of the British Rule in India* (Reprint), Allahabad, 1976.

Part II: The Mainstream of the Indian National Movement

Argov, Daniel, *Moderates and Extremists in the Indian National Movement*, Bombay, 1967.

Bose, Subhas Chandra, *The Indian Struggle 1920–42*, Bombay, 1972.

Das, Durga, *India from Curzon to Nehru and After*, London, 1969.

Ghosh, Shankar, *From the Renaissance to Militant Nationalism in India*, Calcutta, 1969.

Hutchins, F G, *India's Revolution: Gandhi and the Quit India Movement*, Harvard, 1973.

Kripalani, J B, *Gandhi: His Life and Thought*, New Delhi, 1975.

Low, D A (ed), *The Congress and the Raj*, London, 1977.

Majumdar, B B, *Militant Nationalism of India*, Calcutta, 1966.

Malhotra, C L, *From Civil Disobedience to Quit India*, Chandigarh, 1979.

Masani, Minoo, *Bliss was It in that Dawn*, New Delhi, 1977.

Mathur, J B, *Quit India Movement*, Delhi, 1979.

Mehrotra, S R, *The Emergence of the Indian National Congress*, Delhi, 1971.

Minault, Gail, *The Khilafat Movement, Religious Symbolism and Political Mobilisation in India*, Delhi, 1999.

Moin, S, *From Khilafat to Partition*, Delhi, 1980.

Namboodiripad, E M S, *History of Indian Freedom Struggle*, Trivandram, 1986.

Narayan, Jayaprakash, *To All Fighters for Freedom*, Lahore, 1946.

Nehru, Jawaharlal, *An Autobiography*, Delhi, 1982.

Prasad, Amba, *Indian Revolt, 1942*, Delhi, 1958.

Prasad, Bisheshwar, *Changing Modes of Indian Nationalism*, New Delhi, 1966.

Pyarelal, *Mahatma Gandhi. The Last Phase, Ahmedabad*, vols I and II, Ahmedabad, 1956.

Seal, Anil, *The Emergence of Indian Nationalism, Competition and Collaboration in later Nineteenth Century*, Cambridge, 1968.

Tendulkar, D G, *Mahatma, Life of Mohandas Karamchand Gandhi*, vol. 1–10, New Delhi.

Tripathi, Amales, *The Extremist Challenge, India between 1890 and 1910*, Calcutta, 1967.

Wolpert, Stanley A, *Tilak and Gokhale: Revolution and Reform in the Making of Modern India*, Delhi, 1991.

Part III: The Minor Streams of the Indian National Movement

AITUC Fifty Years, Documents, New Delhi, 1973.

Chaudhury, A K, *Socialist Movement in India (The C-S P; 1934–47)* Calcutta, 1980.

Desai, A R, *Peasant Struggles in India*, Bombay, 1979.

Dev, Narendra Acharya, *Socialism and the National Revolution*, Bombay, 1946.

Dhanagare, D N, *Peasant Movements in India, 1920–1950*, Delhi, 1991.

Ghosh, Shankar, *Socialism and Communism in India*, Calcutta, 1971.

Hauser, Walter, *The Bihar Provincial Kisan Sabha, 1929–42*.

Kaye Cecil, *The Communism in India*, Calcutta, 1971.

Keer, D, *Dr Ambedkar, Life and Mission*, Bombay, 1954.

Kuber, W N, *Dr Ambedkar, A Critical Study*, New Delhi, 1973.

Lakhanpal, D L, *History of the Congress Socialist Party*, Lahore, 1946.

Leela Kasturi, and Majumdar, Vina, *Women and Indian Nationalism*, Delhi, 1999.

Menon, V P, *Story of Integration of States*, Bombay, 1956.

Nanda, B R (ed), *Essays in Modern Indian History*, Delhi.

Narayan, J P, *Why Socialism*, Bombay, 1936.

———, *Towards Struggle*, Bombay, 1946.

Natrajan, L, *Peasant Uprisings in India*, Bombay, 1953.

Phadnis, Urmila, *Towards the Integration of Indian States, 1919–47*, Bombay, 1968.

Raichoudhury, Satyabrata, *Leftist Movement in India, 1917–1947*, Calcutta, 1947.

Ranga, N G, *Fight for Freedom, Autobiography*, Delhi, 1968.

Rasul, M N, *A History of the All India Kisan Sabha*, Calcutta, 1974.

Roy, Subodh, *Communism in India, 1925–34*, Delhi, 1972.

Saraswati, Sahjanand, *Mera Jeevan Sangharsh* (Hindi), Delhi, 1985.

Sen, Sukomal, *Working Class of India: History of Emergence and Movements, 1930–1970,* Calcutta, 1977.

Sen, Sunil, *Peasant Movements in India: Mid Nineteenth Century to the Twentieth Century,* Delhi, 1982.

Shankar, Girja, *Socialist Trends in Indian National Movements,* Meerut, 1987.

Sharma, G K, *Labour Movements in India,* Delhi, 1963.

Singh, K S, *Birsa Munda and His Movement 1874–1901,* Calcutta, 1983.

Sinha, L P, *The Left Wing in India,* Muzaffarpur, 1965.

Stokes, Eric, *The Peasant and the Raj,* Cambridge, 1978.

Verma, A C, *Indian Tribes Through the Ages,* New Delhi, 1990.

Part IV: Armed Rebellion and the Indian National Movement

Banerjee, S, *The R.I.N. Strike,* New Delhi, 1981.

Bose, A C, *Indian Revolutionaries Abroad, 1905–22,* Patna, 1971.

Chaturvedi, Banarasidas (ed), *Ram Prasad Bismil, Autobiography* (in Hindi).

Ghosh, K K, *The Indian National Army,* Meerut, 1969.

Josh, Sohan Singh, *Hindustan Ghadar Party: Brief History,* Delhi, 1977.

———, *Baba Sohan Singh Bhakna, Life of the Founder of the Ghadar Party,* Delhi, 1970.

Mukherjee Uma and Haridas, *India's Fight for Freedom or the Swadeshi Movement, 1905–1906,* Calcutta, 1958.

Puri, Harish K, *Ghadar Movement,* Amritsar, 1983.

Ray, Nitish Ranjan (ed), *Challenge – A Saga of India's Struggle of Freedom,* New Delhi, 1984.

Singh, R, *Netaji Speaks to the Nation,* Delhi, 1946.

Thakur, Gopal, *Bhagat Singh: The Man and His Ideas,* New Delhi, 1952.

Vaishampayan, Vishwanath, *Amar Shahid: Chandra Shekhar Azad* (in Hindi), Banaras, 1976.

Verma, Shiv (ed), *Selected Writings of Shahid Bhagat Singh,* New Delhi. 1986.

Part V: Towards Independence and Partition

Ambedkar, B R, *Pakistan or Partition of India,* Bombay, 1945.

Azad, Abul Kalam, *India Wins Freedom,* Bombay, 1959.

Aziz, K K, *The Making of Pakistan; A Study in Nationalism,* New Delhi, 1988.

Chandra, Bipan, *Communalism in Modern India,* New Delhi, 1987.

Choudhry, K, *Pathway to Pakistan,* Lahore, 1961.

Collins, L and Lapierre, D, *Freedom at Midnight*, New York, 1975.

——, *Mountbatten and the Partition of India*, Sahibabad, 1983.

Coupland, R, *The Constitutional Problem of India*, Oxford, 1943.

Edwardes, M, *The Last Years of British India*, London, 1963.

——, *Escape from Empire, the Attlee Government and the Indian Problem*, New York, 1983.

Gandhi, M K, *Communal Unity*, Ahmedabad, 1949.

Gupta, A K (ed), *Myth and Reality: Struggle for Freedom in India, 1945–47*, Delhi, 1987.

Gandhi, Rajmohan, *Mohandas: A True Story of a Man, His People and an Empire*, Delhi, 2006.

Haq, Mushirul, *Muslim Politics in Modern India, 1857–1947*, Meerut, 1970.

Hasan, Mushirul, *India's Partition: Processes, Strategy and Mobilization*, Delhi, 1993.

Jalal, Ayesha, *The Sole Spokesman: Jinnah, the Muslim League, and Demand for Pakistan*, Cambridge, 1985.

Jha, D C, *Mahatma Gandhi, the Congress and the Partition of India*, Delhi 1995.

Kaura, Uma, *Muslims and Indian Nationalism: Emergence of the Demand for India's Partition, 1928–40*, New Delhi, 1977.

Kripalani, J B, *My Times: An Autobiography*, Delhi, 2004.

Lohia, Rammanohar, *Guilty Men of India's Partition*, Allahabad, 1960.

Limaye, Madhu, *Indian National Movement: Its Ideological and Socio-Economic Dimensions*, Delhi, 1989.

Mahatma Gandhi Correspondence with the Government, 1944–47, Ahmedabad, 1959.

Mehta, Asoka and Patwardhan, A, *The Communal Triangle in India*, Allahabad, 1942.

Menon, V P, *The Transfer of Power in India*, Bombay, 1957.

Mansergh, N, *Transfer of Power Documents* (12 volumes), London, 1970–83.

Moon, P (ed), *Wavell: The Viceroy's Journal*, London, 1973.

Moore R J, Churchill, *Cripps and India (1939–1945)*, New York, 1979.

Munshi, K M, *Pilgrimage to Freedom (1902–1950)*, Bombay, 1967.

Mosley, Leonard, *The Last Days of the British Raj*, London, 1961.

Philips, C H and Wainwright, M D (eds), *The Partition of India: Policies and Perspectives, 1935–1947*, London, 1970.

Prasad, Bimal, *Gandhi, Nehru and J P, Studies in Leadership*, Delhi, 1985.

Prasad, Rajendra, *India Divided*, Bombay, 1947.

Pyarelal, *Mahatma Gandhi – The Last Phase*, vol 2, Ahmedabad, 1958.

Singh, Anita Inder, *The Origins of the Partition of India, 1936–1947*, Delhi, 1987.

Singh, Bhim Sen, *The Cripps Mission*, New Delhi, 1979.

Stanley, Wolpert, *Jinnah of Pakistan*, New York, 1984.
Wolpert, Stanley, *Shameful Flight*, New York, 2006.
Zakaria, Rafiq, *The Man Who Divided India*, Bombay, 2004.
----, *Gandhi and the Break-up of India*, Bombay, 1999.

Referred Works for Appendix-I

Broomfield, J H, *Elite Conflict in a Plural Society Twentieth Century Bengal*, Los Angeles, 1968.
Chandra, Bipan, *India's Struggle for Independence*, Delhi, 1989.
Desai, A R, *Social Background to Indian Nationalism*, Bombay, 1973.
Dutt, R P, *India Today*, Calcutta, 1970.
Guha, Ranajit, *Subaltern Studies*, vol. 1, Delhi, 1982.
Nanda, B R, *Essays in Modern India*, Delhi, 1980.
Pannikar, K M, *A Survey of Indian History*, Delhi, 1957.
Raychaudhuri, Tapan, 'Indian nationalism as animal politics', *Historical Journal*, 22(3), 1979.
Rottermund, D, *The Phases of Indian Nationalism*, Bombay, 1970.
Sarkar, Sumit, *Modern Indian History, 1885–1947*, Delhi, 1999.
Seal, Anil, *Emergence of Indian Nationalism*, Cambridge, 1968.
Valentine Chirol, *Indian Unrest*, London, 1910.

Referred Works for Appendix-II

Hobson, J A, *Imperialism: A Study*, London, 1930.
Lenin, V I, *Imperialism, the Highest Stage of Capitalism*, Moscow, 1966.
Luxemburg, R, *Accumulation of Capital*, New York, 1951.
Marx and Engels, *On Colonialism*, Moscow, 1968.
Schumpeter, J A, *Imperialism and Social Classes*, New York, 1951.
Sweezy, Paul M, *Modern Capitalism and Other Essays*, New York, 1972.
Szymansky, Albert, *The Logic of Imperialism*, New York, 1981.

Index